IN THE GARDEN

OF THE

RIGHTEOUS

———————————

IN THE
GARDEN
OF THE
RIGHTEOUS

THE HEROES WHO RISKED THEIR LIVES
TO SAVE JEWS DURING THE HOLOCAUST

RICHARD
HUROWITZ

HARPER

An Imprint of HarperCollinsPublishers

Cover, photo credits:
First row, from left to right:
Center: Courtesy Sousa Mendes Foundation; *right:* Courtesy Yad Vashem
Second row, from left to right:
Left: Courtesy Swarthmore College Peace Collection; *center:* Courtesy AF Fotografie / Alamy Stock Photo; *right:* Courtesy Yad Vashem
Third row, from left to right:
Left: Courtesy United States Holocaust Memorial Museum; *center:* Courtesy Sousa Mendes Foundation; *right:* Courtesy United States Holocaust Memorial Museum
Fourth row, from left to right: Center and right: Courtesy Eric Saul/Visas for Life
Fifth row, from left to right: Left: Courtesy Sousa Mendes Foundation; *second from left:* Sueddeutsche Zeitung Photo/Alamy Stock Photo; *center:* Courtesy Eric Saul/Visas for Life; *right:* Courtesy Robert Kim Bingham

FIRST EDITION

Library of Congress Cataloging-in-Publication Data has been applied for.

ISBN 978-0-06-303723-6

23 24 25 26 27 LBC 5 4 3 2 1

For Asher, Sasha, and Sharon

The daughter of Pharaoh came down to bathe in the Nile, while her maidens walked along the Nile. She spied the basket among the reeds and sent her slave girl to fetch it. When she opened it, she saw that it was a child, a boy crying. She took pity on it and said, "This must be a Hebrew child."

—EXODUS 2:5–6

The righteous shall flourish like the palm tree: he shall grow like a cedar in Lebanon.

—PSALMS 92:12

Contents

Introduction

THE UNITED STATES HOLOCAUST MEMORIAL MUSEUM HAD RECENTLY OPENED ITS doors on the National Mall when my parents took our family to Washington to see it. Most of my relatives had arrived in America in the nineteenth century from Austria, and the last to immigrate was my grandfather, who had fled the Russian pogroms when Theodore Roosevelt was president. The Holocaust always seemed something distant to me. I remember vividly knowing survivors as a child—the friend's nanny who spoke in a thick German accent, and the owner of a local grocery store whose numbered tattoo terrified me. But other than the required reading of Elie Wiesel's *Night* in school, I did not spend much time thinking about the Holocaust as a child.

Visiting the Holocaust Museum is a completely enervating experience. The darkness of the Shoah, quite intentionally, envelops you as you shuffle through the exhibit showing the enormity of the Nazis' crimes. The boxcars into which the doomed were crammed, the striped pajamas in which they endured unimaginable cruelties, and the haunting images of the now destroyed world of the European Jews are suffocating. Particularly disturbing to me was the enormous pile of shoes that had belonged to concentration camp victims. Many of them were in small sizes, the property of some of the one and a half million children who perished.

At the end of the exhibition, a small gallery was devoted to a handful of those very few who had tried to save the hunted from the Nazis.

On the wall there was a photograph of a young man in profile, not much older than I was then, smiling, a small pipe jauntily stuck in his mouth. He was Alexander Schmorell, a twenty-five-year-old medical student at the University of Munich and a member of the White Rose, a group of young German idealists who had dared to speak out against the Nazis. Their mesmerizing story was like a flicker of light penetrating just slightly the oppressive gloom of the Shoah, and it restored to me a faith in humanity. It has inspired me to this day, and ultimately inspired the writing of this book.

The White Rose's founder and driving force was Hans Scholl, another medical student, who was joined in his effort by his younger sister Sophie. The siblings grew up in Ulm, a city on the Danube outside Munich where Albert Einstein was also born. Their home was both tolerant and religious. "What I want most of all is that you live in uprighteousness and freedom of spirit, no matter how difficult that proves to be," their father had told them.

Like many his age, Hans joined the Hitler Youth. But he had doubts almost immediately. He was horrified by the Nuremberg rallies and recoiled at rules that forbade him from singing certain songs, from flying a special flag designed by his troop, or from reading his favorite author, Stefan Zweig, who was Jewish. For her part, Sophie could not understand why her Jewish best friend could not join the Bund Deutscher Mädel (League of German Girls) despite her blond Aryan looks, while she, with dark hair, was welcomed.

Hans Scholl was a free thinker, dynamic and magnetic. With the outbreak of war, he was drafted and posted as a medic in France. When he returned to Germany, he enrolled in medical school at the University of Munich. He read widely—Plato, Socrates, Saint Augustine, and Blaise Pascal—and decorated his dorm room with modernist French art. He soon attracted a circle of like-minded students: Christoph Probst, Willi Graf, and Schmorell, the son of Russian immigrants. They found an intellectual mentor in Kurt Huber, a professor of philosophy and religion and ardent believer in liberal democracy.

In the summer of 1942 Hans was inspired by the sermons of Clemens August Graf von Galen, the anti-Nazi bishop of Münster. "Finally, a man has the courage to speak out," he mused to his siblings. He began to distribute typewritten leaflets denouncing the regime. They were signed by a group whose name he took from a Mexican novel: "The White Rose." Their language was incandescent. "Every honest German today is ashamed of his government," Hans wrote. It had committed "crimes that indefinitely outdistance every human measure." Those who stood by were complicit—"Guilty! Guilty! Guilty!" All citizens should resist the Nazi state and its war efforts, including through sabotage, boycotts, and protests.

The White Rose also became among the first to publicize the Holocaust. In the group's second leaflet, Schmorell reported the news that three hundred thousand Jews had been murdered "in the most bestial way. Here we see the most frightful crime against human dignity, a crime that is unparalleled in the whole of history. For Jews, too, are human beings." They pulled no punches even when it came to the führer: "Every word that comes from Hitler's mouth is a lie," they declared. "His mouth is the foul-smelling maw of Hell, and his might is at bottom accursed." Sprinkled with erudite references to Aristotle, Ecclesiastes, Goethe, Lao Tzu, Friedrich Schiller, and others, the leaflets concluded with a plea to circulate them. "We will not be silent," concluded the fourth. "We are your bad conscience. The White Rose will not leave you in peace."

The leaflets appeared in mailboxes and phone booths throughout Munich between late June and mid-July 1942 and spread to sympathetic students in Frankfurt, Hamburg, Berlin, and Vienna. Then Hans, Schmorrel, and Graf were suddenly, on a day's notice, shipped east to the Russian front. On the way Hans saw a young Jewish girl in a labor brigade by the side of the road. Running from his train, he handed her a chocolate bar and a daisy for her hair. When he stopped in Warsaw, he was horrified by the ghetto. "There are half-starved children whimpering for bread," he wrote home. "A sense of doom is all around." Then while the young men were in Russia, the Scholls' father was arrested and imprisoned for several months by the Nazis when an employee reported an anti-Hitler comment he had made.

At the front, the boys witnessed the defeat at Stalingrad and the first cracks in German invincibility. "We will have to let the truth ring out as clearly and audibly as possible in the German night," Huber told his protégés when they returned home. The White Rose released two more leaflets warning that with the loss at Stalingrad, German defeat was inevitable. In a paean to freedom, they asked their countrymen, "Are we forever to be a nation that is hated and rejected by all mankind?" The pamphlets again circulated throughout Germany. One night green and black graffiti appeared in Munich declaring "Freedom!" and "Hitler Mass Murderer!"

On February 18, 1943, Hans and Sophie were placing neat stacks of leaflets in corridors at the university before the bell rang to let out classes. As they left, Sophie realized she had extra copies in the red suitcase they carried and headed to the top of the marble stairs, which overlooked an atrium three floors below. She hurled the remaining leaflets in the air and watched as they drifted down the stairwell. The maintenance man, Jakob Schmid, was also watching. An ardent Nazi, he immediately locked the doors and notified the authorities. The siblings were hauled to the Wittelsbacher Palace, the infamous headquarters of the Gestapo. Soon after, Probst, whose wife had had a third child weeks before, was also arrested. The three were interrogated for several days but refused to implicate others.

Hitler's chosen high court judge, Roland Freisler, was flown in from Berlin to preside in his ominous red robes over their trial five days later. The proceedings were a travesty and the result a foregone conclusion. All three were quickly found guilty of high treason and sentenced to death. "There is a higher court before which we all must stand," the Scholls' father shouted in the courtroom. They were executed by guillotine hours later. Before Hans placed his head upon the block, his final words echoed through the prison: "Long live freedom."

Within weeks the other core members of the White Rose were apprehended and executed, including Schmorell, who was betrayed to the Gestapo by a former girlfriend. Others were tried and imprisoned. Thomas Mann broadcast the case on the radio from exile in the United States. It was reported in the newspapers. British airplanes dropped copies of the last leaflet over Germany. But the hope that the group's members had of inspiring their fellow citizens was not fulfilled; their call was almost entirely ignored. "What we wrote and said is also believed by many others," Sophie had declared. "They just don't dare express themselves as we did." Sadly, this was not the case. The White Rose were beautiful souls in a time of nightmare, a breath of fresh air sweeping through the hellish landscape of the Holocaust. I took them with me when I left the museum.

―――

Many years later, I wrote an op-ed in the *New York Times* recounting the story of the White Rose on the seventy-fifth anniversary of the Scholls' execution. At a time when many were becoming concerned for the first time in years about the stability of our own democracy, it struck a chord. Readers drew a parallel to the activism of young people, particularly the students in Parkland, Florida, whose gun-control campaign was then in the headlines. By then I had written a few other stories about rescuers, and the response each time had been similar. I also invariably received emails from people—both strangers and those I knew—telling me that the subject of my article had saved their family. There are literally hundreds of thousands of people alive today because of the rescuers you will meet in this book; their acts of righteousness truly echo down through the ages.

Of course, we must acknowledge that rescue was very rare during the Holocaust. It remains both a celebration of what is best in us and, in its extreme scarcity, an indictment of the worst. When Yad Vashem, Israel's memorial to the Holocaust, was founded in 1953, one of its core missions was to recognize those who risked their lives to save Jews and so realize the injunction in the Book of Chronicles "to vindicate the righteous by rewarding them for their righteousness." The title Righteous Among the Nations—a reference to the belief that those of any faith in Israel who adhere to the seven basic laws of morality given to Noah are promised a place in the world to come—is bestowed at a special ceremony and often accompanied by the planting of a carob tree in a special garden in Jerusalem. The criteria are strict: rescuers must have risked their life, liberty, or career; they cannot be Jewish; there must be eyewitness testimony or unequivocal evidence of their actions; and they must not have received any monetary or other reward. As of 2021, over twenty-seven thousand people have been so honored.

While this may seem like a large number, it represents just half of one-hundredth of one percent of the European population during the Second World War, or about one person out of twenty thousand. The Yad Vashem criteria do, of course, exclude many rescuers, including some in this book. There are also those many who never came forward, who rescued anonymously, or who were otherwise forgotten. In the years following the war, many rescuers kept their stories to themselves, traumatized by their experiences or afraid of retribution from hostile neighbors or governments. There are those who tried to help and failed, their courageous and tragic efforts lost. Many of them were caught by the Nazis and killed. Then there are those who might have made a small gesture of food, or given shelter for a few minutes or a night, or even just kept a secret: they too contributed to a rescue. Yet even if we assume the actual number of rescuers is ten times greater than the Yad Vashem rolls of honor, we are left with less than half of one tenth of one percent of the population. The rescuers were, indeed, truly rarae aves, the rarest of birds.

The extraordinary stories of the rescuers are too little told and too little known. For many years people knew only of the Swedish diplomat Raoul Wallenberg and, after the film by Steven Spielberg, the German industrialist Oskar Schindler. But beyond these two archetypes, the rest are little more than footnotes to history at best. There are several reasons for this historical omission. Again, as we will see, many rescuers were reticent to tell their own stories or preferred to remain anonymous. In their own countries, many were shunned or even punished after the war. And while many who survived the Holocaust were determined to thank their saviors, there were others—particularly those who lived through concentration camps—who feared that a focus on the rescuers would distract from the crimes of the perpetrators and the suffering of the victims.

Yet the very existence of rescuers offers proof of the Holocaust to counter any who would deny it or diminish it. Every rescuer is a rebuke to them. "Why did the Polish farmer have to hide a Jew in the pigsty?" the historian Mordecai Paldiel observes. "Because someone wanted to kill that Jew." And they certainly demonstrate for us the kind of behavior we must foster to prevent anything like the Holocaust from happening again and to create a more beneficent society. By studying what motivated the rescuers, we can perhaps distill the values and manners we wish to cherish and to encourage.

It is also a historical injustice if the names of Heinrich Himmler and Hermann Goering remain more well-known than those of Wallenberg and Schindler. "Which code of ethics argues that evil be allowed to eclipse the good?" asked Harold Schulweis, one of the earliest advocates for honoring the Righteous. "Which perverse logic holds that we obliterate the memory of man's nobility so as to preserve the memory of his degeneracy?" We should value the kind over the pathological. We should value the courageous over the selfish. For, as Martin Luther King Jr. put it, "Darkness cannot drive out darkness, only light can do that."

"We must know these good people who helped Jews during the Holocaust," the Nobel laureate Elie Wiesel once wrote. "We must learn from them, and in gratitude and hope, we must remember them." The world owes the rescuers a debt of gratitude, a debt best repaid by recalling and celebrating their deeds. Not only those who are alive because of their actions, or those who would have been in peril had they lived in a different time and place, but all of us should thank them for showing that even in the darkest moment, the best part of humanity could survive and, in some discrete places, triumph. "In the darkness that engulfed Europe there were some shining lights," wrote Gideon Hausner, Attorney General of Israel and prosecutor at the Adolf Eichmann trial. "Their names are engraved in our memory forever, as we still [bear] in thankful memory the name of Cyrus of Persia, who enabled the exiles to return to the promised land." Gratitude is a fundamental Jewish value and indeed an important and all too rare humanist one, indispensable to building a just and kind society.

At the dedication ceremony for the Avenue of the Righteous at Yad Vashem in Jerusalem on May 1, 1962, the first eleven carob trees were planted in honor of eleven of the rescuers. "The Jewish people remember not only the villains, but also every small detail of the rescue attempts," Golda Meir declared in her remarks. Today, some sixty years later, the garden is verdant with foliage as hundreds more trees have been planted. The rescuers were like drops of love in an ocean of poison, Meir declared. They had not only saved Jews but had "saved hope and faith in the human spirit." We must honor those who stood up for the persecuted, often at the risk of their own lives, when so few did.

The great Holocaust scholar Yehuda Bauer has written, "The existence of rescuers on the margins provides a hope that these evils are not inevitable, that they can be fought." It is critical that children in particular not lose faith in humanity and that they learn that some people tried to help in an hour of need. "For the first fifty years after the Holocaust, survivors bore witness to evil, brutality, and bestiality," declared Abraham Foxman, the longtime director of the Anti-Defamation League and himself a hidden child saved by his Polish Catholic nanny. "Now is the time for us, for our generation, to bear witness to goodness. For each one of us is living proof that even in hell, even in that hell called the Holocaust, there was goodness, there was kindness, and there was love and compassion."

For those who are committed to remembering the Holocaust, and to making sure it never happens again, the most important task is to educate as many as we can. The stories of rescue provide an opportunity. The filmmaker Pierre Sauvage, born in occupied France, believes that the "stories of rescuers are really almost like a banister which you can hold on to while looking at the evil of this world." This is particularly true when talking to children about a highly traumatic moment in history. I hope that this book will be read by young people who have the power to shape our world, to help them see that we can all make a difference, and to show what happens if we do not.

We are fortunate that we do not need to know how we would have acted during the Nazi era, but the math says that very few of us would make the same choices the rescuers did. It is one thing, and a challenging one indeed, to simply inconvenience oneself by taking the time or offering the resources to help another in need. It is even more difficult to jeopardize your livelihood or well-being, let alone to risk your life or, even more extreme, the lives of your children. Most of us would not. But if people believe that they would have acted as the righteous did, that is a good thing. The stories of the righteous allow us at least to contemplate the enormity of man's cruelty by asking ourselves how we would hope to react when confronted with it. There is still much in our own lives far short of atrocities—bullying, pain, cruelty, desperation—that we can be inspired to combat or ameliorate with positive action, with empathy, and with kindness.

————

The ten stories I have selected in the following chapters are intended to offer a broad spectrum of backgrounds, professions, beliefs, nationalities, and geographies, but they are also, in the end, stories that particularly spoke to me. A volume like this necessarily requires choices, and I could have written an entire additional book—indeed several—about others as remarkable as those included here. I have not included Oskar Schindler or Raoul Wallenberg, whose name was for many years synonymous with the Righteous. Both have had their story widely told and have entered into the global consciousness. Nor have I included the diplomats who helped Wallenberg in Budapest in 1944 by issuing protective papers, among them the Swiss consul Carl Lutz, the operation's mastermind, who once dove into the Danube to save a woman shot by Fascists; Angel Sanz-Briz, the Spanish "Angel of Budapest" and his colleague, the Italian businessman Giorgio Perlasca; the Portuguese ambassador Carlos Sampaio Garrido and his chargé d'affaires Carlos de Liz-Texeira Branquinho; the papal nuncio Angelo Rotta; and Friedrich Born, the Swiss delegate to the International Committee of the Red Cross. As there are already several diplomatic stories in this book, I have also not included Dr. Feng-Shan Ho, the Chinese consul general in Vienna, or Sellahatin Ülkümen, the Turkish ambassador on the island of Rhodes, who both saved many Jews. Their names all deserve to be remembered forever and always.

Opportunity for rescue was often driven by circumstance and location. The selected stories largely deal with those on the ground. There are also many important stories of those in government who did their best to save Nazi victims through policy initiatives, mass programs, and political lobbying. Some senior American government officials made valiant efforts to help Jews, only to be shut down by the unfortunate and rampant anti-Semitism in the Roosevelt administration. Two weeks after Kristallnacht, for example, the legislature of the Virgin Islands voted unanimously to welcome Jewish refugees with support from the territory's governor, the Columbia University academic Lawrence W. Cramer, and US secretary of the interior Harold Ickes, who also tried to create a haven in Alaska, then not yet a state. More successfully, the first elected president of the Philippines, Manuel Quezon, and its last US high commissioner, former governor of Indiana Paul McNutt—a political rival sent halfway around the world by FDR—worked with a Jewish family that owned a local cigar factory to rescue over twelve hundred Jews from Europe. A more ambitious plan to bring as many as one million Jews to the island of Mindanao was proposed by Quezon but was sadly preempted by the Japanese invasion of the islands. And a small group of lawyers in the US Department of the Treasury successfully pressured FDR to establish the War Refugees Board late in the war, saving over one hundred thousand Jews from the death camps. The ultimate rescue, of course, was by the Allied soldiers who defeated the Axis and liberated the occupied nations, including the concentration camps. Particularly powerful, perhaps, are the stories of the liberation of a subcamp of Mauthausen by the segregated 761st Tank Battalion, known as the Black Panthers, and of Dachau by the 522nd Field Artillery Battalion, made up entirely of Japanese American soldiers, many of whose relatives were then being forcibly incarcerated by the Roosevelt administration.

After the notorious Evian Conference in July 1938, when most of the world largely turned its back on Jewish refugees, Britain was alone among the major powers in opening its doors to thousands of Jewish children in Germany, Austria, and Czechoslovakia under the legendary Kindertransport. Images of these children at the train station, alone without their parents, with identification tags around their necks, became iconic wartime symbols in England and later inspired the creator of Paddington Bear, himself a refugee. One of my favorite organizers was Nicholas Winton, a young banker who canceled his ski holidays in December 1938 to volunteer to oversee the evacuation of Jewish children from Prague, saving over six hundred. Some would famously be reunited with him decades later during a surprise broadcast on live television, a clip which has been viewed tens of millions of times in recent years. "We must carry his spirit from generation to generation," the Dalai Lama once said of Winton. "Then humanity's future will be brighter."

Those given a platform in the media or through their stature have unusual opportunities to make a difference. At a time when the world was largely silent, a few political leaders denounced the persecution, perhaps most prominently Winston Churchill. Franklin Roosevelt's predecessor, Herbert Hoover, was outspoken about the plight of the Jews, as was another internationalist Republican, New York governor Thomas Dewey, who in 1943 declared a day of mourning for the millions of Jews of Europe murdered by the Nazis. Other leaders, including the Czechoslovak president Edvard Benes, El Salvadorian president Salvador Casteneda Castro, and Swiss councilman Jean-Marie Musy, also spoke out strongly. Especially effective was Dimitar Peshev, the vice speaker of Bulgaria's parliament, who worked with the church leaders Stefan, Metropolitan of Sofia, and Kiril, Metropolitan of Plovdiv, to pressure King Boris III to halt the deportation of the Jews, allowing virtually the entire community to survive.

The Nazis hated royalty, many of whom also distinguished themselves by supporting their Jewish subjects. We will meet some of them in this book. Among the others of note were Elisabeth of Bavaria, Queen Mother of Belgium; King Gustav of Sweden; and Queen Mother Elena of Romania. Zog of Albania, who crowned himself Zog I, the only Muslim monarch in Europe, granted citizenship to several hundred Jewish refugees before himself fleeing his country in a high-stakes operation run by Ian Fleming. And Muhammed V, the young sultan of Morocco, protected his millennia-old Jewish population from Vichy France and its Nazi overlords. "There are no Jews in Morocco," he declared. "There are only Moroccan citizens."

There were also those, like the White Rose, who went to great lengths to publicize the Holocaust, itself an act of righteousness. It is what the philosopher Bernard-Henri Lévy has called "the will to see." We will meet the Polish diplomat Jan Karski, who risked his life to personally witness Nazi atrocities in Poland and reported what he saw to Anthony Eden and FDR to little effect. Even some in Hollywood tried to make a difference. At the behest of the activist Peter Bergson, Kurt Weill and Ben Hecht organized a traveling pageant of Hollywood stars in 1943 called *We Will Never Die* to protest the murder of then two million Jews: several Christian stars participated, including Frank Sinatra, Burgess Meredith, and Ralph Bellamy, adding their voices and helping gain attention.

As I wrote this book, I often imagined what it must have been like for a refugee, hunted, terrorized, with nowhere to turn, to come upon the kindly face of a rescuer, a friendly smile in a hellish landscape. We also must recognize the gift of dignity and of goodness, the small gestures made to acknowledge someone's humanity—a coffee, a hot bath, a smile, a kind word—which were almost always recalled years later by survivors as helping give them the strength to go on. They do not often on their own add up to a dramatic story, but they were crucial and certainly something that we can all do every day. Primo Levi wrote of an Italian laborer who brought him soup each night, "I believe that it was really due to Lorenzo that I am alive today; and not so much for his material aid, as for his having constantly reminded me by his presence, by his natural and plain manner of being good, that there still existed a just world outside our own, something and someone still pure and whole, not corrupt, not savage, extraneous to hatred and terror; something to define, a remote possibility of good, but for which it was worth surviving." Gustav Schröder, the captain of the MS *St. Louis*, is famous for desperately trying to find a safe place to disembark his nearly one thousand Jewish passengers during the infamous "voyage of the damned." Passengers remembered that as they unsuccessfully moved from port to port in Cuba, the United States, and Canada, the German captain ordered that his charges be treated with dignity as paying passengers and even permitted religious services to be held on board. His kindness was never forgotten.

There are, indeed, many other remarkable stories. There was Jan Żabiński, the director of the Warsaw Zoo, and his wife Antonina, who rescued hundreds of Jews by letting them use the empty cages of their abandoned park. And Roddie Edmonds, a Tennessee-born master sergeant in the US Army, who when captured by the Germans was ordered to identify his Jewish soldiers. He ordered all his men to appear and declared "We are all Jews here" to the commandant, daring the man to shoot him. The teacher Joop Westerweel in the Netherlands organized an escape network that saved as many of two hundred Jewish youth pioneers. Nearby, the German lawyer Hans Calmeyer used his position in the Dutch occupation authority to remove Jews from lists of non-Aryans, saving several thousand from deportation. And Father Bruno, the clerical name for the young priest Henri Reynders, hid some four hundred children from the Nazis in Belgium, while his countryman Joseph André rescued hundreds in Narmur. All their stories, too, are worth learning.

Finally, I also made the decision not to include any Jewish rescuers, although several make cameo appearances. They deserve their own volume.

———

It is said that the first of the Righteous Among the Nations was Pharaoh's daughter—known by tradition as Bitya*—who defied her father's edict against newborn Jewish boys to save the infant Moses. She did this publicly, in front of her retinue of maidens, at great danger of exposure. She steadfastly continued the operation with courage, agreeing to publicly adopt the child, whom she herself named Moses. And then with kindness she secretly arranged for the infant Moses to be cared for by his own mother, who served as the baby's nurse. "Pharaoh's daughter did not simply have a moment's compassion," Jonathan Sacks has written. "She will adopt him and bring him up as her own son. This is courage of a high order."

As it is told in Exodus, Pharaoh's daughter's act was motivated entirely by compassion and came at great risk to her own life. According to Jewish tradition, the princess was rewarded by God as one of nine people so righteous they were permitted to enter paradise while still living. The Talmud says, "Although Moses had many names, the only one by which he is known in the whole Torah is the one given to him by the daughter of Pharaoh. Even the Holy One, blessed be He, did not call him by any other name." In so doing, it is said that even God Himself paid tribute to the most legendary righteous rescuer of all for her kindness.

One of the most difficult questions asked in the years since the Second World War has been: Where was God during the Holocaust? Man's cruelty to man is, of course, as old as recorded history. But the Nazi crimes seemed to bring a new level of evil to our world, and to sharpen the intractable philosophical dilemma known as the problem of evil. Almost all great theologians and philosophers have attempted to reconcile the existence of evil with the existence of an all-powerful, loving God. At the heart of the matter is the issue of free will. If we

---

* Bitya's name is not given in Exodus, where she is referred to as "Pharaoh's daughter," but in 2 Chron. 4:18.

cannot choose evil, it is argued by some, we cannot choose good. (Or, as Boethius put it, "We cannot raise the question, 'How can there be evil if God exists?' without raising the second, 'How can there be good if He exists not?' ")

But for me, at least part of the answer to the question lies in the story of Pharaoh's daughter. When we consider the stories of those who selflessly saved others during perhaps the worst moment in history, we can perhaps see that God is in the actions of the Righteous. Their kindness and heroism are the divine spark that we all possess and which we must do our best to cultivate within ourselves and in our societies if we wish to build a better world. Right did prevail in the end. The acts of the rescuers were, as the writer Cynthia Ozick has put it, "goodness separated from desecration." Their impact cannot be measured by their number, but rather by the "metaphysical, and belongs to the sublime."

Now, let us turn to the stories.

I hope you will find them as profound as I do.

IN THE
GARDEN
OF THE
RIGHTEOUS

———————————

1

We Are All Refugees

WHEN PARIS FELL TO GERMANY IN JUNE 1940, THRONGS OF DESPERATE REFU-
gees, as many as five million, fled south through France to try to escape
the Nazis. The Swiss and Italian borders were sealed, and the German
army was pushing quickly into the north of France. The only way out
was south across the Pyrenees into neutral Spain, on to Portugal, and
beyond to freedom. A traffic jam of colossal proportions snaked its way
down the country as every type of vehicle crawled along, furniture and
belongings strapped to roofs, while the Luftwaffe buzzed overhead,
strafing the crowds with machine-gun fire. Hans Augusto Reyers-
bach and his wife, Margarete Waldstein, German Jews originally from
Hamburg, rode homemade bicycles, weaving through cars that were at
a virtual standstill. Hidden in what belongings they had been able to
throw in two suitcases in the rush to leave their home in Montmartre
were potentially lifesaving documents: their Brazilian passports, which
could provide a safe haven if they could somehow get across the Atlantic.

Hans had already led a peripatetic existence. He had grown up
well-to-do and served in the Great War, but in 1924, in the aftermath
of the hyperinflation that devastated Weimar Germany, he moved to
Rio de Janeiro in search of better prospects and landed a job selling
bathtubs in the Amazon. There the thirty-six-year-old Hans reconnected with Margarete, then twenty-nine, whom he had last seen as a
child in Hamburg sliding down a banister. The serendipity of meeting
an attractive, flame-haired Jewish girl from his hometown was almost

too good to be true. They also shared a creative passion. He was a talented amateur artist and had worked as a poster painter for the circus while in university. She had made her way to Rio by way of London, where she had worked as a photographer, after studying at the Bauhaus and showing her watercolors in Berlin. Together they started an advertising agency and changed their name to Rey, which was much easier for the locals to pronounce. Margarete and Hans, with his broad yellow hat to block the sun, took to strolling past the striped umbrellas of the Copacabana Beach as he learned his sixth language, Portuguese. Crucially, it was then that they became Brazilian citizens.

They were married in August 1935. On their honeymoon, they set sail for Europe and then decided to settle in Paris, the lure of an artistic life in the cafés of the City of Lights too great to resist. A publisher was taken with a cartoon of a giraffe by Hans, who quickly wrote and illustrated several children's books that were published in France and England. Endlessly inventive, Hans also created books of cut-out and folded animals, a method he patented. Then in 1939 Hans and Margarete collaborated on a children's book inspired by the two mischievous marmoset monkeys they had kept as pets in Rio. Hans drew the illustrations, and Margarete contributed to the story. *Raffy and the Nine Monkeys* was published by the prestigious French publishing house Éditions Gallimard, and the Reys had just received a contract for a spin-off, *The Adventures of Fifi*, about the youngest monkey of the nine, who was always getting in trouble. When the German invasion of France forced them to flee for their lives, this new manuscript fled with them. The publisher's advance had paid for the bicycles and other expenses of their escape.

The Reys left Paris on June 12, two days before the Germans entered the city and hoisted the swastika above the Eiffel Tower. The previous day, they had gone to a bicycle shop, only to find the only thing left was a tandem *vélo*. After a quick spin around the place Vendôme in front of the Ritz Hotel, Margarete declared the vehicle unrideable.

They brought it back to the store, where, for 1,600 francs, Hans bought enough spare parts to build two rudimentary bicycles with baskets for their belongings. Two million people had already fled the capital when, at five thirty the next morning, with rain pouring down on the stone streets, they began the journey on their ramshackle vehicles. For three days they pedaled south before finally boarding a train at the Orléans station for Biarritz. Eventually they reached the neighboring town of Bayonne in the South of France, near the Spanish border. Thousands of other refugees crowded the streets, desperate to get exit visas, which literally meant life or death. A week after they had fled Paris, after waiting four hours on the sidewalk in Bayonne, the Reys were successful, thanks entirely to the kindness of a local Portuguese consul. They made their way to Lisbon and on to Rio and eventually to New York. The next year the American company Houghton Mifflin published their new book. The title page listed Hans as H. A. Rey. The name of the protagonist had been changed by the publisher from Fifi to George.

Stories about the Reys' little monkey have sold more than seventy-five million copies in twenty-six languages around the world and inspired myriad movies, television shows, toys, and merchandise that have informed countless childhoods. Were it not, then, for the Portuguese consul who signed the Reys' visas, *Curious George* would have been another casualty of the Second World War.

The monkey's savior was Aristides de Sousa Mendes, and the Reys were two of the estimated thirty thousand people he rescued over several weeks in the summer of 1940. Defying explicit orders from his government, Sousa Mendes answered instead to his own conscience to help mobs of desperate people fleeing the Nazis and likely deportation to concentration camps or extermination. He possessed the power to issue visas to neutral Portugal by using passport stamps that, with his signature, allowed bearers out of France. During a frenzy of activity in the early summer of 1940, this little-known midlevel Portuguese diplomat quite possibly saved more people than any other individual during the Holocaust.

———

The world had been a very different place when Aristides de Sousa Mendes do Amaral e Abranches was born in Cabanas de Viriato, a village in northern Portugal, on July 19, 1885, the younger of identical twin boys by an hour. Belle Epoque Portugal was still an aristocratic nation, a stately and traditional society ruled by a king as it had been for centuries, and his parents were both scions of old noble families. His father was the son of a wealthy landowner and a direct descendent of a courtier to the Napoleonic-era king Joao VI. His mother's family, the Abranches, was even nobler, tracing their ancestry back to the knight Alvaro Vaz de Almada, who had been made an earl by the English after an exceptional victory at Avranches in Normandy.

The twins grew up with a younger brother in the family's large ancestral home in the province of Beira Alta with a magnificent view of the Serra da Estrela mountain range and servants in attendance. The boys were raised with a strong sense of noblesse oblige and given a devout Catholic education. Their father, José, was an appellate judge of impeccable reputation, and both Aristides and his twin brother, César, followed in his footsteps and pursued degrees in law, considered the most prestigious course of study at the time. They graduated in 1908 at age twenty-two from the University of Coimbra, one of the oldest in Europe.

Portugal is perched on the Atlantic, and since the days of Prince Henry the Navigator, when the small Iberian nation was among the world's most powerful, its native sons often traveled far on behalf of the nation. The golden age of exploration was long over, but Aristides and César followed this same restless path and entered the Foreign Service. César was the more serious student of foreign policy. Aristides was more of a fun-loving bon vivant, but well suited to the social side of his profession. He would be joined in his adventure by an attractive dark-haired girl, his cousin Angelina, one of four children of a wealthy landowner. They married in 1909. After a brief stint at the Portuguese Ministry of Foreign Affairs, he and his twin brother were both sent abroad the following year. With his new bride and infant son and namesake in tow, Sousa Mendes took up his first post as second-class consul in the English sugar colony of British Guiana on the northern coast of South America.

Very shortly after the couple left Lisbon, the Portuguese monarchy came suddenly to an end after eight hundred years. The twenty-year-old King Manuel II, who had ascended the throne two years earlier when his father and brother were assassinated, went into exile, and a new republic was declared. The age of Portuguese aristocracy too was over, and Sousa Mendes now worked for a new government somewhat wary of his class.

Nonetheless, the next two and a half decades would be for the young couple an exciting adventure. Sousa Mendes was a born diplomatic host, with a sparkling personality and wonderful sense of humor. Pictures show a tall young man cutting a dashing and authoritative figure, beaming in his brocaded Foreign Service uniform, sword at his side, medals across his chest. And Angelina too proved herself adept as a hostess.

In the summer of 1911 Sousa Mendes was promoted to consul and posted to Zanzibar in East Africa, a critical locale as a neighbor of the important Portuguese colony of Mozambique. He quickly endeared himself and his nation to his hosts. Sultan Khalifa bin Harub awarded him the Second-Class Medal of the Shining Star, the nation's highest honor for a foreigner, and presented him with ceremonial dress, complete with a scimitar and a silver-inlaid dagger. In the six years they lived in Africa, the Sousa Mendeses welcomed four more children. The youngest, Feliciano, had the sultan as his godfather.

From Africa, it was on to southern Brazil, where Sousa Mendes was appointed consul in the city of Curitiba in 1917. He was now in his early thirties, and some of the tendencies that would come to hinder his career began to come to the fore. Not bureaucratically astute enough to hide his strong monarchist loyalties, he was briefly suspended as hostile to the republican government before being quickly reinstated. He also showed a pattern of spending well beyond his means, a problem that accelerated with the needs of his rapidly growing family.

In 1921 Sousa Mendes was sent to San Francisco as consul general, a significant position: he was not only the most senior diplomat in a major metropolitan area but also oversaw others in smaller neighboring consulates. But it was also in California that his altruism first caused him trouble, when his support for poor Portuguese workers created friction with the wealthy expatriate business community. Throughout their lives, Sousa Mendes and his wife always showed a great concern for the needy. Whenever they were home at their estate in Portugal, they would distribute food, money, and clothing every Thursday, and also often prayed together for those who were poor or persecuted.

Sousa Mendes settled his family in Berkeley and commuted daily into the city. It was there that Angelina added two American sons to their brood. Then, after two years in California, the family was again on the move. They took the four-day rail journey cross-country to Boston, where they boarded a ship bound for Brazil for a brief second tour there in the southern city of Porto Alegre. Later they were posted for three years in Vigo, a small northwestern Galician city near the Portuguese border.

Aristides and Angelina had continued to visit Portugal regularly, but other than a brief stint back at the Foreign Ministry before the posting to Spain, they had been away for fourteen years. Their return to Europe allowed them to spend more time in Portugal, and especially at Quinta de Sao Cristovao, known as Casa do Passal, their estate in Cabanas de Viriato over which they flew the flags of the countries where their offspring—ultimately nine boys and five girls—had been born. Sousa Mendes was constantly expanding the three-story mansion in the hopes that one day it would be a place of reunion for his children. The French-and-Portuguese-style yellow home was topped by a gray slate mansard roof with red tiles, complete with a traditional rooster weathervane. One of the family's crests was emblazoned on the ceiling in an entryway dominated by a sweeping staircase and leading into some four dozen rooms. The grounds too were marvelous, with myriad trees, birds, and animals populating a veritable playground for the children.

In 1929 forty-three-year old Sousa Mendes was promoted to consul general in Antwerp. The family resettled into Louvain, the university town made world-famous when its medieval library was torched by invading Germans during the First World War. Sousa Mendes would remain there for the next decade and become the dean of the consular corps. The social whirl was tremendous, and the entire family was a part of it. It was in Antwerp that the last of the Sousa Mendeses' children arrived: a boy in 1931 and a girl in 1933, just a month after Adolf Hitler became chancellor of Germany.

The Sousa Mendeses believed in exposing their children to the widest possible experiences and education. The younger children were sent to local schools while the older ones enrolled in the university. Angelina personally saw to it that they learned proper Portuguese, instructing them herself. The arts suffused their lives, with piano, violin, and painting lessons, and plenty of opera, Sousa Mendes leading family concerts for friends from all over the world in his joyful tenor voice. Among those they entertained were the Nobel laureate playwright Maurice Maeterlinck, the deposed Spanish king Alfonso XIII, and Albert Einstein, who discussed relativity with one of Sousa Mendes's sons who was fascinated with mathematics. The children were often brought along to formal diplomatic dinners, including at the Quai d'Orsay in Paris, where Sousa Mendes's daughter Teresinha was made a flower girl to Queen Astrid of Belgium. Sousa Mendes even had a special vehicle built with eighteen seats—half car, half bus, cream-colored and nicknamed the Expresso dos Montes Herminios after the mountains in Beira Alta where he grew up—that could fit the whole clan after the logistics of moving the entire family by rail became as complicated as transporting an army. He often drove the family to picnics and outings, sometimes going as far afield as the Netherlands, Germany, France, Luxembourg, and even Denmark. And of course back to Portugal.

While the Sousa Mendes family was immersed in life in Belgium, back at home dramatic changes were underway. For years Portuguese politics had been in turmoil. Following the declaration of a republic in 1910, there had been an almost uninterrupted string of weak governments, economic disasters including rampant inflation, and a steady increase in disorder and violence. A military coup in 1926 brought to power a series of generals who were almost as incompetent as the republicans. A debt crisis soon brought Portugal to the brink of collapse.

Then a savior suddenly appeared. At the finance ministry, a brilliant economist named António de Oliveira Salazar rose to the occasion. Salazar had attended the same law school as the Sousa Mendes twins and worked his way up as an academic and bureaucrat of strong technical ability. With a firm hand, Salazar almost singlehandedly righted the Portuguese economy. In 1932, when he became prime minister of Portugal, he pushed through a new constitution giving him extraordinary powers. Shrewd, cynical, and ruthless, Salazar brought order to Portugal at the expense of civil liberties, centralizing power in the executive and restricting freedom of the press, freedom of assembly, and parliamentary powers. An authoritarian with strongly anti-Communist views, he was nonetheless an opponent of fascism and ruthlessly suppressed the Blue Shirts, a local far-right group with thirty thousand followers. But above all else, Salazar was against political parties, which he viewed as dangerous, and worked tirelessly to ensure that none, including his own, would dominate. He was at heart a technocrat whose team largely drew from academic and intellectual circles, and who wielded power in the background. A good friend was not taken in by appearances, however, noting that "behind that cold exterior, there is an inexhaustible ambition."

Salazar was impressed with the talented César de Sousa Mendes, whose star was in the ascendant, and appointed him as his first foreign minister. Aristides, by contrast, did not have a strong reputation as an executive; he continued to serve in more midlevel positions. Never good with managing money, his own or his government's, he also continued to spend more than he made and was supported by loans against his home and from his brother.

In Louvain, the shadow of tragedy visited the Sousa Mendeses in 1934, when their second son, Manuel, died suddenly shortly after graduating from university when one of his blood vessels ruptured at his own celebration. "This was a terrible blow to my father and mother and to us life was not the same anymore," one their children later recalled. A few months later, their youngest daughter, Raquel, died at one year old of an intestinal illness.

The family was devastated, and in 1936 they sought a change of surroundings, moving into Antwerp itself, where they lived on the avenue Rubens, near Sousa Mendes's office at the avenue de France. The move failed to raise their spirits, and in 1938 Sousa Mendes requested a transfer to China or Japan as chargé d'affaires, only to be denied by Salazar. Instead he received a new assignment: consul general at Bordeaux, the legendary port in the southwest of France.

International tensions were high when Sousa Mendes arrived on September 29, 1938. In ordinary times the posting would have been a plum job for someone as social as he was. Bordeaux traced its history back two and a half millennia, to a Celtic village brought under Roman control by Julius Caesar during the Gallic War. The Romans had introduced the vine to the temperate region near the Atlantic coast, and the rest was history. The historic district boasted some five thousand magnificent buildings, including monuments of Gothic architecture such as the medieval Saint-André Cathedral and the place des Quinconces, the largest square in France. The harbor was the subject of paintings by Édouard Manet, and so magnificent was the architecture that Baron Georges-Eugène Haussmann, its longtime prefect, used it as his model when he was charged by Napoleon III to level and rebuild the Paris we know today. "Take Versailles, add Antwerp, and you have Bordeaux," Victor Hugo remarked in awe.

The consulate at 14 Quai Louis-XVIII overlooked the river Garonne as it wound its way through the city. It offered an excellent view of the botanical gardens on the other bank and sat directly across from a large warehouse overlooking the port. A few blocks away was the Grand Theatre, where the great ballet master Marius Petipa staged some of his earliest work, and the place de la Bourse, designed by Louis XV's architect Ange-Jacques Gabriel himself. Sousa Mendes moved into a large apartment above the consulate. One of his older sons, Pedro Nuno, who was studying in Bordeaux, remembered the building as "palatial," with mirrors on the walls and decor in the style of Louis XVI. The chancellery occupied two magnificent rooms, the living room and dining room, which in ordinary times were more than enough to handle the business of the consulate and provide offices for the consul, his deputy, and their secretary.

Initially the family enjoyed the city, basking in the warm sun and visiting the local chateaux with an elderly local they befriended named Monsieur Redeuil who was obsessed with Portuguese culture. Sousa Mendes even led the local Bastille Day celebrations in white tie and tails. But after the German invasion of Poland in September 1939, he began to worry about the safety of his children. César had been sent as ambassador to Warsaw, and his reports of German atrocities on the front lines were alarming. As the Wehrmacht turned west, invading

Norway and Denmark in April, Sousa Mendes became even more disturbed.

Soon the effects could be felt in Bordeaux. In a gathering wave before the advancing army, refugees began streaming into France. Sousa Mendes's son John Paul, then nine, recalled the crowds forming outside the building: "The fear of Hitler seeped past the desks and into our home." Aristides and Angelina packed most of the children into the Expresso dos Montes Herminios and sent them back to Casa do Passal for safety. Only the two eldest there—José António, age twenty-seven, and Pedro Nuno, age twenty—remained with them. The consulate suddenly felt empty.

———

Back in Portugal, Salazar was directing a complex and Machiavellian scheme to keep his country out of the conflict. He was not an admirer of Adolf Hitler or Benito Mussolini and was also firmly opposed to the Soviet Union. Technically, he was bound to England by the Treaty of Windsor of 1386, the world's oldest diplomatic alliance, but he managed to avoid this entanglement as well. His closest ally was Francisco Franco, the dictator of neighboring Spain, whom he had backed in that nation's bloody and recently ended civil war, and to whom he served as informal foreign affairs adviser.

Salazar calculated that if the Spanish republican forces had won the Spanish Civil War, his staunch anticommunism would surely have motivated them to topple his own regime next door. On the other hand, he presumed that if Franco were to join the Axis in the rapidly expanding war, Portugal would likely be absorbed into a greater Iberia on the chessboard of Europe. Moreover, the First World War had resulted in well-remembered devastation wherever it went. Conflict of any kind, he consequently concluded, was an existential threat to his country.

Salazar's primary strategic objectives—overriding all else—were to keep Franco out of the Axis and to ensure that the Iberian peninsula both stayed neutral and was spared any fighting. A March 1939 treaty of friendship and nonaggression between the two nations—the Pacto Ibérico—was his diplomatic masterstroke. He reinforced it by supplying wheat and corn to Franco to feed the exhausted Spanish population and maintained diplomatic support for Spain on all fronts to prop up the regime.

The torrent of refugees fleeing the Nazis and the fighting on the eastern front suddenly became a risk to Salazar's general policy of neutrality, even as this very neutrality made Portugal a destination of choice for refugees. The pathway there was almost exclusively through Spain, but the war-racked Spaniards had no appetite to take in the swarms of poor and desperate people fleeing from German-occupied territory. Also, Franco had no desire to oppose the Nazis, his patrons in the Spanish Civil War, who were zealously determined to prevent Jews and political opponents from escaping.

Salazar consequently fell in line to prevent refugees from crossing the border from France into Spain and bringing political headaches with them. On November 11, 1939, the Portuguese Ministry of Foreign Affairs issued Circular 14 to all embassies and consulates. Noting "current unusual circumstances," it put in place new temporary procedures to "prevent abuses" of its consular procedures. Regular travelers in transit through Lisbon on the way to America would not be hindered. But several categories of people could not be issued visas without prior approval from the Foreign Ministry. "Aliens of undefined, contested or contentious nationality, stateless persons, Russians and holders of 'Nansen passports' "* were all precluded. So was anyone who could not provide "valid reasons" for coming to Portugal, anyone who was unlikely to be able to freely return to their home country, and anyone who

---

* Special papers given to stateless people deprived of their national passports.

did not seem to have adequate means to support themselves. The final category was stark: "Jews expelled from the countries of their nationality or from whence they came." Thus Circular 14 covered those very refugees for whom passage through Portugal was a matter of life and death.

The prior-approval requirement in Circular 14 was included to ensure that it would be almost impossible for those to whom it applied to be admitted into Portugal in the event of a true refugee crisis, as there would never be enough time to gain advance permission from Lisbon. In this way its drafters had created a powerful mechanism by which the government could block visas entirely or allow their issuance to become moot simply by delaying their response, or even refusing to answer. In the event of a flood of asylum seekers, control over who got into Portugal would stay firmly with the Foreign Ministry.

Sousa Mendes first experienced the challenges of Circular 14 when an Austrian Jewish professor from the University of Vienna, Arnold Wiznitzer, requested a visa in November. Twice, Sousa Mendes telegrammed the ministry for instructions. Twice he heard nothing back. Knowing that Wiznitzer would be interned and separated from his wife and son if he could not leave France, Sousa Mendes issued his visa anyway. "I considered that it was a duty of basic humanity to spare them such an ordeal," he wrote later. The fact that Wiznitzer was Jewish and stateless was not relevant to Sousa Mendes. "A university professor can in no way be regarded as undesirable," he declared, despite the fact that, as the ministry reminded him in a telegram sent in January, Circular 14 took a different view. He defended himself by saying, "Harmonizing these instructions with the extraordinary and sometimes imperative circumstances of each concrete case was the wish of this functionary who only wishes to do right."

A similar story played out the following February, when Eduardo de Neira Laporte, a Barcelonian professor fleeing Franco, requested a transit visa through Lisbon to Bolivia, which had offered him refuge.

Again, Sousa Mendes cabled home for instructions. Again, he received no response. On March 1 the panicked professor returned to the consulate, now in danger of missing his connection in Lisbon. Once again, without approval, Sousa Mendes issued the visa. When he finally received notice, ten days later, that the visa request had been denied, Neira Laporte was already in Lisbon, where he embarked for South America the next day.

In response, the secretary general of the Foreign Ministry, Luis Teixeira de Sampaio, one of Salazar's closest aides, sent a sharp reprimand to Sousa Mendes. "Any new fault or infraction in this regard will be considered disobedience," he warned, "and will entail disciplinary proceedings where it will have to be taken into account that you have repeatedly committed acts that merit warnings and reprimands." Sousa Mendes wrote to his brother, "The Portuguese Stalin decided to pounce on me like a wild beast. I hope that will be the end of the matter, but I can't rule out another attack. I've no problem with my conscience."

In mid-May 1940 the Nazi blitzkrieg began sweeping through Belgium, the Netherlands, Luxembourg, and the Ardennes Forest into France. Now, in Bordeaux as elsewhere, fear and confusion were everywhere. Tens of thousands descended on the city on trains, in cars, on bicycles, even on foot. Hotels, restaurants, and cafés were overwhelmed. Refugees slept in automobiles, on benches, even in the train station. Crowds began to form at the Portuguese consulate.

Once again Sousa Mendes cabled Lisbon for instructions. The response: enforce Circular 14. As the numbers seeking visas escalated everywhere, Salazar himself telegraphed the diplomatic corps: "Visas to clean people only with a ticket on a ship out of Lisbon. No visas to Russians or Czechs, and under any circumstances, no visas to Jews." The Policia de Vigilância e de Defesa do Estado (PVDE), Salazar's secret police, requested that all consulates "check thoroughly if those that request to emigrate are Jews in order to prevent people of that kind arriving in Portugal."

———

Germany had invaded France three times in seventy years. Each time, Bordeaux had become the French nation's temporary capital. On June 14 Paris fell, and the next day the motorcade carrying prime minister Paul Reynaud and the rest of the nation's leaders crossed the Pont de Pierre. The government was in its final stages. Winston Churchill had flown to Tours the day before to convince the French to stay in the fight, to no avail.

Marshal Philippe Pétain, Pierre Laval, and Maxime Weygand, the notorious French collaborators, would be in power by the weekend. They began negotiations for an armistice that would effectively hand France over to the Nazis, dividing the country into a directly occupied zone in the north and a "free" zone in the south, administered by a collaborationist government in the spa town of Vichy in the center of the country. Recently appointed minister of war Charles de Gaulle, who had checked into the Hotel Majestic just a stone's throw from Sousa Mendes's consulate, would flee two days later for London to found the Free French Forces and begin the long struggle to reclaim France from fascism.

Sousa Mendes had been sensitive to the plight of the Jews since his days in Antwerp. Now he became more and more tortured by what he saw. One day he drove along the Garonne and got out at the Great Synagogue of Bordeaux, located off the Pont de Pierre just west of the city's Gothic Basilique Saint-Michel. The synagogue had seating capacity for fifteen hundred congregants, making it the largest in France and one of the biggest in Europe. Now Jewish refugees crowded in the courtyard in front of its stately facade, beneath its cornice topped with the Ten Commandments. It was there, in the crowd, that Sousa Mendes met Chaim Kruger, a young red-haired Polish rabbi who had fled with his family from Belgium and joined the thousands of Jews camped in the square. With a long beard and black hat, Kruger looked much older than his thirty-five years. Like all the refugees, he was desperately hoping to get papers to reach safety. Sousa Mendes invited him to bring his wife and six children to the consulate, where he would endeavor to obtain visas for them. And he inquired of the rabbi where he would spend the night.

"Why, in the street, of course, like all the others," Kruger told him in fluent French.

Sousa Mendes offered to let them stay in his apartment, which was largely empty at this point. There the two men talked late into the night, and Sousa Mendes confided to Kruger that, while a devout Catholic, he was, like many Portuguese, a descendent of Jews who had been forced to convert during the Inquisition. For his part, Kruger told the story of his original flight from his native Poland to Belgium, where life for Jews had been good until the German invasion. Their lives were now once again in jeopardy.

"No Jew is safe as long as the Nazis are in control," Kruger told him. "If we should be trapped here, I don't know what would happen to us."

Over the course of a week, Sousa Mendes submitted requests for thirty visas for refugees, including the Kruger family. In most cases they were met with silence, freezing the effort. The request for the Krugers, however, was actually denied on June 13, the day Paris was declared an open city.

Despite the rejection, Sousa Mendes told the rabbi that he would do everything in his power to issue the visas for his family. Kruger was grateful but told him he could not accept visas just for himself and leave the others behind. "It's not just me that needs help," the rabbi told him, "but all my fellow Jews who are in danger of their lives."

The rabbi's words hit the consul like a thunderbolt. "All of a sudden my father seemed terribly weary, as though he had been struck down by a violent disease," recalled Pedro Nuno. "He just looked at us and went to bed." For three days Sousa Mendes was confined to his room, tossing and turning, agitated as if with a fever. He did not eat or sleep. He received his colleague, the ambassador to Belgium, lying down. "The situation here is terrible," he wrote to his brother-in-law, "and I am in bed with a severe nervous breakdown."

Sousa Mendes's nephew César, his twin brother's son and namesake, had been living in the nearby town of Saint-Jean-de-Luz, studying with the violin virtuoso Jacques Thibaud, but with the invasion spreading "panic and terror" everywhere, had decided to come help his uncle with the crisis. He arrived the next day and was immediately horrified by the scenes of the frightened people in Bordeaux. As he approached the consulate, he was swept up in a large crowd of refugees, which grew larger and larger as he approached the building.

"There were lots of old and sick people," he later wrote, "pregnant women who did not feel well, people who had seen, powerless to defend themselves, their relatives die on the highways killed by the machineguns firing from planes." All of them "wanted desperately to get visas to go to Portugal." Sousa Mendes's son Pedro Nuno tried to calm the refugees as he passed them, assuring them his father would help. "I am sure there will be no difference between what I saw and hell," he remarked.

Outside the consulate, uniformed French guards with bayonets tried to keep a semblance of order, but the consul's hospitality did not permit much of it. For several weeks the entire building, including the offices and living quarters, had been crammed with refugees sleeping on chairs, on the floor, anywhere space could be found. They were, Sousa Mendes later remarked, "shipwrecked."

Traumatized by their flight and exhausted from days of waiting, both inside and outside, the refugees looked terrible, Pedro Nuno remembered, "anguish etched on their faces." Bordeaux was undergoing a heat wave, but many did not eat or drink, afraid to leave the line for fear of losing their places, and occasionally altercations broke out. Even a tremendous thunderstorm on June 18 could not move them from their spots in line.

After three days, Sousa Mendes arose.

"My father got up, having apparently recovered his serenity," Pedro Nuno remembered. "He was full of punch. He washed, shaved and got dressed." As he strode out of his bedroom, a startled Angelina asked him where he was going. "Look, Gigi," he told her, "I heard a voice that told me to get up and give everyone visas. To all, with no exceptions. And that's what I have decided." He was, he told his family, compelled to act by a divine power greater than himself. "I cannot allow all of these people to die," César recalled his uncle saying.

I have it all in my hands now, to save the many thousands of persons who have come from everywhere in Europe in the hope of finding sanctuary in Portugal. They are all human beings, and their status in life, their religion or color, are altogether immaterial to me. Furthermore, the clauses of the constitution of my country relative to such cases as the present say that under no circumstances shall the religion or political belief of a foreigner bar him from seeking refuge in Portuguese territory. I am a Christian and, as such, believe that it is not for me to let these refugees perish. A large number of them are Jews.

Sousa Mendes then loudly addressed the refugees. "From now on, I am going to issue a visa to anyone who asks for it—regardless of whether or not he can pay." He paused for a moment and looked at Angelina. "I know that Mrs. de Sousa Mendes agrees with me," he said, "and I feel certain that my children will understand and not hold it against me if, by giving a visa to each and every refugee, I am discharged tomorrow from my duties for having acted contrary to orders which, in my estimate, are vile and unjust." It was a defining moment in his life. "I would rather stand with God against man," he declared to the crowd, "than with man against God."

And with that, he set to work.

Rabbi Kruger collected the passports of the Jews in the synagogue's square. They were stamped with visas, and Sousa Mendes signed them all. He then proceeded to sign every other passport put in front of him, with no questions asked about the bearer's religion, national origin, or ethnicity. Moving a low coffee table in front of a couch in his office, he set up a veritable assembly line. José António, Pedro Nuno, César, and Rabbi Kruger prepared the passports and visas for signature and shuttled up and down the stairs with bags filled with papers.

Sousa Mendes's deputy, thirty-two-year-old José Seabra, dutifully rubber-stamped the paperwork and kept a detailed ledger in beautiful handwriting of the papers issued, but he was not sanguine about the turn of events. A small bespectacled man, polite to a fault, Seabra was highly respectful of the consul but terrified of breaking the rules.

"For the sake of your wife and children, please stop!" he begged. "You're ruining your life and that of your family."

Other local consulates had slammed their doors. By one account, the American consulate informed applicants that a visa would take five years to process. "It is a fantastic commentary on the inhumanity of our times that for thousands and thousands of people a piece of paper with a stamp on it is the difference between life and death," the journalist Dorothy Thompson observed. News quickly spread of what Sousa Mendes was doing, and the consulate was soon filled to capacity. Without the help of the usual coterie of diplomatic servants, Angelina personally tended to many of the refugees. One of their sons played the piano to soothe those gathered. Sousa Mendes worked "around the clock," often until two or three in the morning, signing plain paper when the official diplomatic stationery ran out. His signature morphed from "Aristides de Sousa Mendes" to "Mendes" as his hand tired.

Seabra desperately tried to maintain order, begging applicants to come only during normal hours. Sousa Mendes would have none of it. "Come back when the dictator is not here!" he joked to them. Soon Seabra stopped keeping track of each document, writing instead, "Visas have been issued outside operating hours." Kruger recalled of Sousa

Mendes, "He did not eat, nor sleep until late at night. And during this short time he issued several thousand visas until the enemy approached Bordeaux and we were forced to flee to Spain."

"My attitude was motivated solely by feelings of altruism and generosity," Sousa Mendes later reflected, "of which the Portuguese, during the eight centuries of their history, have so often given eloquent proof." He did not accept payment for the visas, waiving even the standard registration fees. His son recalled one eight-year-old girl who ate supper with the consul and his family; her parents had been machine-gunned and she needed help escaping. The girl produced an envelope with a diamond tucked in it and tried to give it to Sousa Mendes.

"Quick," he told her, "hide that in your pocket."

The writer and Sorbonne professor Charles Oulmont, a very wealthy but wanted man who had criticized the Nazis in print, moved into the consulate for several nights, never removing his pajamas. While he was there, Bordeaux was bombed and hundreds were killed or wounded. Traumatized, Oulmont—who carried with him four potato sacks filled with solid gold—offered Sousa Mendes half of the fortune in return for visas. "My uncle turned the offer down," his nephew remembered, "but granted him the visas." Sousa Mendes was, Oulmont wrote later, "filled with pity and compassion."

Many other prominent leaders and intellectuals also found their way to Bordeaux in desperation. A French ambassador literally fell to his knees and begged for a visa. A well-known Flemish politician, Albert de Vleeschauwer, not only received one but was invited to stay as a guest at the consul's home in Portugal once he arrived there. The American actor Robert Montgomery, who had played opposite Greta Garbo and Norma Shearer and served as president of the Screen Actors Guild, found himself on the run after his stint as a volunteer ambulance driver in France had ended with the evacuation at Dunkirk a couple of weeks earlier. On June 18, Sousa Mendes got him out. The aristocratic Jewish bankers Édouard, Henri, and Maurice de

Rothschild all owed their lives to Sousa Mendes, as did the Surrealist artist Salvador Dalí and his wife, Gala. The interior designer Jean-Michel Frank, artistic collaborator of Alberto Giacometti, and Paul Rosenberg, the art dealer who represented Pablo Picasso, Henri Matisse, and Georges Braque in Paris, were also given visas. "There was something," Sousa Mendes later explained, "that could not be ignored: the fate that awaited all those people should they fall into the hands of the enemy."

Archduke Otto von Habsburg was a high-value target of the Nazis. Hitler had denounced the Habsburgs in *Mein Kampf*, confiscated all their property, and particularly hated Otto, who had once refused to meet with him. In exile in France, Otto had further infuriated the führer when he worked to try to offer material aid to Austrian refugees, including Jews, and to prepare a fallback evacuation plan for them in the case of invasion. Now he found himself on the run in Bordeaux. His aide Count Henry von Degenfeld went to the embassy and spoke to an exhausted Sousa Mendes. It was clear that once an armistice was reached, likely within days, the imperial family would be turned over to the Nazis. When the count returned at ten that evening after the consulate closed, Sousa Mendes signed the nineteen passports Degenfeld had brought to him. These included two for Otto's mother, the Empress Zita, who had narrowly missed being arrested by a special unit of German paratroopers specially sent for the purpose, and his grandmother, the Duchess of Parma. The archduke also requested several hundred visas for Austrian nationals trapped in France, many of them Jewish. These too were immediately forthcoming and given to anyone stating they had worked for the archduke.

Sousa Mendes worked for three days straight without really stopping. Around him, a bizarre atmosphere settled in on Bordeaux. Many aspects of normal life went on uninterrupted—courts remained open, schools were in session, and *The Adventures of Sherlock Holmes* played alongside a Laurel and Hardy movie in the cinemas—while tragedy was everywhere and refugees continued to pour in. On June 19 the Luft-waffe bombed Bordeaux, killing dozens of people.

Unbeknownst to Sousa Mendes, his actions had quickly been brought to the attention of his superiors back home. An Englishwoman had appeared a few days earlier at the consulate for a travel visa in the ordinary course. Asked to wait a few hours given the backlog of ref-ugees, she grew irritated and then finally exploded, declaring as she stormed out empty-handed her intention to file a complaint. In an act of supreme pettiness, she reported Sousa Mendes to the British em-bassy in Lisbon, which duly wrote to the Foreign Ministry on June 20, complaining that Sousa Mendes was operating outside of normal business hours and alleging—entirely untruthfully—that he was de-manding fees or charitable donations in return for visas. In addition to Sousa Mendes's earlier reprimand, other suspected "irregularities" had been uncovered (three Polish nationals were arrested in Portugal with visas bearing his signature), followed by rumors that he had ordered subordinates to issue visas without charge to anyone asking.

The report was too much for Salazar, and perhaps a convenient catalyst. He refused to abide insubordination any longer from a man he considered a spoiled aristocrat. Salazar instructed his ambassador to France, now relocated from Paris to Bordeaux, to investigate what pre-cisely was going on. Two bureaucrats from the Foreign Ministry also arrived in a shiny limousine to control Sousa Mendes and even take him back to Lisbon. "The Ministry is concerned for your safety," one of them told Sousa Mendes. But he refused their escort and continued his efforts.

Sousa Mendes moved farther south toward the border with Spain. As in Bordeaux, thousands of refugees had descended on Toulouse, Hendaye, and Bayonne, where the local consul bombarded Sousa Mendes, his supervisor, for instructions on how to deal with the cri-sis. Sousa Mendes told him to ignore Circular 14, but when he re-ceived word that this directive was not being followed in Bayonne, he concluded that the state of panic throughout southwest France, which mounted steadily as news of the French troops' retreat arrived, must have overwhelmed his colleagues and prevented them from following his instructions. So he personally went to assist when telephone lines ceased working.

Bayonne is a seaside town around two hundred kilometers south of Bordeaux, situated next to the Basque country in Spain, a short drive to San Sebastian and Bilbao, and right at the foot of the Pyrenees, which mark the border with the Iberian peninsula. Its Portuguese consulate sat on the third floor at the top of a rickety wooden staircase in a small, narrow building on 8 rue de Pilori. When Sousa Mendes arrived, some five thousand refugees surrounded the building, and twenty thousand more wound through the streets. The staff was forced to sneak in and out through the roof.

Sousa Mendes confronted the local consul, Faria Machado. "Why do you not help those poor refugees?" Sousa Mendes snapped. "How would you like to find yourself, your wife and children in the same circumstances?"

Machado objected that they were only following orders from their superiors in Lisbon.

"I am still consul at Bordeaux and, consequently, your superior," Sousa Mendes snapped. "I, therefore, order you to pass out as many visas as may be needed." He gathered the consulate's seals and rubber stamps and ensconced himself at the consul's desk. Machado refused to participate, but his vice consul, Manuel de Vieira Braga, enthusiastically helped issue hundreds of visas. Sousa Mendes also telephoned Émile Gissot, the honorary Portuguese consul in Toulouse, to ask for help. Like Vieira Braga, Gissot also rose to the occasion, directing refugees to the Dutch consulate, which provided visas for their Caribbean colony in Curaçao, which provided him an excuse to issue a transfer visa through Portugal.

For three days and two nights, Sousa Mendes signed papers in

Bayonne. He knew they were all in a race against time. An armistice was imminent, at which point the border would most likely be sealed and the last exit route closed. Passports were hurriedly brought up from the crowd outside by consulate functionaries, for fear that the staircase would collapse if too many people came inside. Eventually Sousa Mendes set up a table on the street. Witnesses also recalled seeing him, clad in a raincoat and a brown hat, signing visas in his hotel, and even in his car.

Spain may not have wanted refugees. But under the Pacto Ibérico it was obliged to recognize Portuguese visas, even without transit papers, and so Sousa Mendes improvised a highly unusual document that read, "The Portuguese government requests the Spanish government the courtesy of allowing the bearer to pass freely through Spain. He is a refugee from the European conflict en route to Portugal." Not only did the Spanish provide safe conduct to holders of these papers, they further insisted that their Portuguese allies take the refugees off their hands on the other side. The Spanish were thus deftly co-opted by Sousa Mendes, who turned these unique pieces of paper into tickets to freedom.

Machado soon panicked and wired Lisbon that he and his staff had been forced to violate Circular 14 on Sousa Mendes's orders. The Foreign Ministry sent an official, Armando Lopo Simeão, down from Lisbon. Simeão went directly to Bayonne to confer with the Portuguese ambassador to Spain, Pedro Teotónio Pereira, one of Salazar's closest confidants. Teotónio Pereira had reported to Salazar that Franco was complaining about the inundation of Spain with refugees bearing Portuguese visas, almost all of which bore Sousa Mendes's signature.

In an attempt to control the chaotic situation, Teotónio Pereira and Simeão issued even tighter restrictions on refugees. They declared explicitly that no visas would be issued to those with Nansen passports, most of them Jews, unless they could show a paid boat ticket leaving Europe, thereby excluding all but the most wealthy. Visas were limited to British, North and South American, Belgian (if they were famous), and French nationals, but only if they were *gente limpa*, an Inquisition-era Portuguese term that excluded Jews. Strict adherence to procedures was enforced to slow everything down intentionally. The purpose was clear. As Simeão wrote to Lisbon, "We wanted to keep out the mass of unworthy and socially undesirable people." The pro-Axis Teotónio Pereira was even more explicit: taking in "the scum of the democratic regimes fleeing before the German victory," he advised, looked bad to the Spanish. Simeão telegrammed his strong advice on June 23 that Sousa Mendes be quickly punished by the Foreign Ministry "to offload its responsibility entirely."

Meanwhile, Sousa Mendes had moved on to Hendaye, the small town right next to Spain, which was threatening to close its border as the Nazis were bearing down. He was there on June 23 when Salazar sent telegrams, one to Bayonne and one to Bordeaux, formally stripping him of most of his power, in particular his right to issue visas. From that point on, although he never received the cables, Sousa Mendes was in defiance of the dictator's explicit orders if he issued any visa at all.

Teotónio Pereira had also held a series of meetings with Spanish authorities at the border and in Madrid, distancing the Portuguese government from the actions of Sousa Mendes, who, he reported, was "out of his mind due to events." He instructed the Spanish authorities not to accept any visas issued by Sousa Mendes, and a sign was posted in Bayonne warning, "All visas issued in Bordeaux are illegal." The Associated Press reported that ten thousand people were trying to cross into Spain, but that certain Portuguese visas had been declared invalid.

When Sousa Mendes appeared in the square in Hendaye, he was instantly mobbed. He again wrote as many visas as he could, signing not only passports but also identity cards, and often merely scraps of paper or newspapers, documents that nonetheless with his signature could give the holder the legal right to enter Portugal. Though the border had by then been closed and his authority officially revoked (still unbeknownst to him), he instructed a group of refugees to follow him by car. He led them to a little-known crossing he often used to avoid traffic, where he guessed—correctly—that the Spanish guards, who had no telephone, had not yet received word from Madrid of either the border closure or any visa irregularities. Despite his disheveled appearance, Sousa Mendes maintained his aura of authority. "I'm the Portuguese consul. These people are with me," he informed the guards. "They all have regular visas, as you can check for yourselves, so would you be so kind as to let them through?" Permission was immediately granted, and Sousa Mendes escorted them over the border. By at least one account, this caravan encompassed one thousand souls. At another part of the border, he personally opened the frontier gate and ensured that his visas were honored.

Teotónio Pereira and Simeão caught up with Sousa Mendes at the crossing from Hendaye to Irun and demanded that he return to Bordeaux, driving him as far as Bayonne, where they left him for the night. But the moral stakes were clear to Sousa Mendes, who stayed at the border and continued to issue visas, knowing not only that he would be shut down at any moment but also that the Nazis were days away from arriving. "To refuse a visa to those poor people would be an effort greater than my strength," he told Simeão repeatedly.

On June 22 the French capitulated and the Vichy government signed an armistice. It came into effect on June 25, and the door slammed shut. The same day, a local newspaper in San Sebastian ran an item, presumably with information from the Foreign Ministry, that "the Consul of Portugal in Bayonne" had lost his mind. Teotónio Pereira later testified, "From all that I heard [him say], and from his generally unkempt appearance, my impression was of a disturbed man, not in his right mind." Other eyewitnesses begged to differ. Vieira Braga, the vice consul in Bayonne who had helped Sousa Mendes, observed the consul at peace with himself and quite "lucid and determined."

Sousa Mendes stayed near the border until June 26, when German troops arrived in Bayonne. He then returned to Bordeaux, where he finally received the telegram notifying him that he had been relieved of his post and summoned home. The next day Bordeaux was occupied by the Nazis, and the day after Hendaye was as well.

For several days Sousa Mendes issued Portuguese passports quietly to refugees who were now trapped. At least, he hoped, these precious documents would prevent deportation from France to concentration camps by offering the protection of the Portuguese government. A Viennese Jewish girl would later testify that these passports saved her and her father's lives during the occupation.

———

On July 8 Sousa Mendes returned to Portugal with his wife. Lisbon— the glimmering White City overlooking the Atlantic—was no longer the elegant port known for its melancholy folk music, fado. Its neutrality and the amorality of the regime had made it a hotbed of intrigue, home to more spies on all sides of the conflict than any other city in the world, and a decadent metropolis where stranded Europeans of all political persuasions spent their money on pleasures and gambled in the casinos. It was here that the Duke of Windsor took refuge by the sea and where spymaster Ian Fleming would find his inspiration for the character of James Bond. "By day Lisbon has a naive theatrical quality that enchants and captivates," wrote the author Erich Maria Remarque, who spent the war there, "but by night it is a fairy-tale city, descending over lighted terraces to the sea, like a woman in festive garments going down to meet her dark lover." There was now a cynicism, a realpolitik, and a darkness in the country Sousa Mendes had left behind. And Salazar was at the center of it all.

Soon after his homecoming, Sousa Mendes received the alarming news that Salazar had opened up disciplinary proceedings against him four days earlier. He wrote to request a meeting with the dictator to explain himself, seemingly unaware of how Salazar perceived him. His request was denied.

It quickly became apparent that Sousa Mendes had misjudged Salazar, whom he had assumed shared his Christian ethics. The inquiry went forward. Simeão testified that Sousa Mendes was fully aware of what he was doing and that the consul had responded to warnings "about the gravity of his attitude" by obstinately refusing to obey his instructions.

Sousa Mendes was at his home in Beira Alta with his children on August 2 when he received a copy of his indictment on disciplinary charges, which included testimony from Teotónio Pereira; from Agostinho Lourenço, the head of the PVDE; and from Simeão, who had reported with pride that other consuls on the ground had not given into the desperation of the "slime."

Even Sousa Mendes's friend Francisco de Calheiros e Menezes, the Portuguese ambassador to Brussels who had been an eyewitness in Bordeaux and Bayonne, conceded in testimony given in defense of the consul, who asked him to describe the scene, that it was never right for a diplomat to disobey orders and was at pains to declare that he himself did not issue any visas. The best he could offer was that in the panicked and heart-wrenching atmosphere, it was understandable that a weaker person might break down. "A functionary has no need to be human when it is a question of obeying orders, whatever they may be," he declared. A different man than Sousa Mendes, he said, "less impressionable or physically and morally stronger, might have withstood the torment and thus resisted the vehement and anguished pleas they heard." By contrast, Calheiros wrote, the kindly Sousa Mendes "allowed himself to be overcome . . . by the horror of the tragedy he was witnessing." The perverse moral universe of Salazar's regime, which valued obedience above all, was on full display. Sousa Mendes told his children that he had done what his conscience had impelled and had no regrets. But he asked them to have courage for what may lay ahead.

"My aim was first and foremost humanitarian," Sousa Mendes tried to explain in his response to the inquest. "I thought of the fate that would be in store for those people were they to fall into the hands of the enemy. Many of them were Jews who had already been hounded and who were trying to escape from the horror of further persecution." He also worried about women who would be at the mercy of German troops and about the many children "who had witnessed their parents' suffering." He had himself seen countless suicides and acts of desperation that compelled him to act. "Their suffering cannot be expressed in words: some had lost their wives, others had no news of their children, and others again had seen their loved ones die during German bombing raids," he explained. "All this could not fail to impress me vividly, I who am the head of a large family and know better than anyone what it means not to be able to protect one's family."

Sousa Mendes strongly disputed the accusation that his actions had caused damage to Portugal. What did it matter what the Germans, who were not even present, thought? Or the French, who had surrendered? He himself had been loudly applauded by hundreds of people as he crossed the square when he left Bayonne, with cheers for the nation and for Salazar as well. Many leading figures of Europe he had helped also thanked not only him, but Portugal and its leader.

Poignantly, he appended a statement from the writer Gisèle Quittner Allotini. "You are the best advertisement for Portugal and a credit to your country. All those who have known you praise your courage, your kind-heartedness and your gentlemanly spirit," she wrote. "If the Portuguese are like consul general Sousa Mendes," Allotini concluded, "they must be a people of knights and heroes."

"It may be that I made mistakes," Sousa Mendes said, "but if I did so it was not on purpose, for I have always acted according to my conscience. I was guided solely by a sense of duty, fully aware as I was of my responsibilities." He added, "My conscience considers the words [of the refugees] the most precious reward for what I did for them, I am particularly consoled now to see in the Portuguese newspapers that these foreigners are enjoying their stay and how grateful to and worthy of Portuguese hospitality they are. To my knowledge none of them so far has disturbed the public peace or in any way abused this hospitality."

The Foreign Ministry was unimpressed and unpersuaded. Its report concluded that Sousa Mendes's actions had "caused a situation that reflected very badly on Portugal in the eyes of the Spanish authorities and German occupying forces," and noted that he had been violating his instructions as far back as November. When his own views contradicted his orders, he "invariably placed his personal criterion before the Ministry's. I believe this is serious." The author of the report, Francisco de Paula Brito, the head of the department of economic affairs, however, did note the "extenuating circumstances" and recommended only between one and six months' suspension.

But it was Salazar's friend Pedro de Lemos, the Count de Tovar, acting as judge advocate, who issued the verdict. In his view, Sousa Mendes seemed not only not to regret his actions but to revel in them. "One cannot find any remorse or even intention to mend his ways," he declared. "The Defendant is unlikely to grasp that the acceptance of a post and of a salary by the State gives him the ineluctable duty strictly to obey any orders he receives." The count ordered his demotion below the rank of consul, deeming him not fit to run a consulate. His decision was affirmed by the disciplinary council.

As harsh as this was, it was not harsh enough for Salazar. Determined to punish the aristocrat who had dared defy him, he ordered Sousa Mendes withdrawn from active service for one year at half pay and then retired without a pension. Salazar personally sealed the personnel file. At age fifty-five, Sousa Mendes's career as a diplomat was over.

Sousa Mendes was stunned, but he held out hope that the government might come to its senses. He filed an immediate appeal, asking the president of the tribunal to reconsider on the grounds of "the powerful imperatives of human solidarity." He even telegrammed Salazar and begged him to consider his desperate financial situation in supporting his family, "one of the largest in Portugal." He was, he said, in "absolute need of funds." Would "His Excellency . . . be so good as to order as urgently as possible that the sums" he was entitled under his pension for his years of service be paid to him?

Salazar ignored the request. From his perspective, no money was due and no compassion merited. Sousa Mendes's final appeal was denied, the court affirming that "a civil servant is not competent to question orders which he must obey." Salazar himself would never again speak to Sousa Mendes, who now found himself jobless, shunned, and in dire financial straits. Former colleagues ignored him, pretending not to see him on the street. He was persona non grata at the ministry, now housed in the pink palace compound overlooking the city that had been the favorite of Amelia of Orléans, Portugal's last queen. At one point he spent the entire day there, waiting—and failing—to be seen. His friends now kept their distance. He even went to the local archbishop for help from the church. Instead of compassion, all he got was a suggestion to pray to Our Lady of Fatima, the patron saint of the nation.

Sousa Mendes was sanguine, putting on a brave face, although lines of worry and exhaustion were noticeable upon it. Rabbi Kruger ran into him in Lisbon shortly after his dismissal from the diplomatic service. They embraced, and Sousa Mendes told him he had no regrets. "If thousands of Jews are suffering because of one Christian [i.e., Hitler], surely one Christian may suffer for so many Jews," Sousa Mendes told him.

To its credit, the small Portuguese Jewish community of 850 did not forget Sousa Mendes. It provided him with a monthly stipend to the modest extent it could and helped pay his rent, and he and his children were invited to eat at the Jewish soup kitchen in Travessa do Noronha in Lisbon run by the Hebrew Immigrant Aid Society (HIAS). A teenager volunteering at the kitchen recalled a dignified, impeccably dressed man, in a dark suit and round black diplomat's hat, speaking perfect Portuguese with his wife and several children. "Impressed by his presence, I went up to him and told him that next to the dining-room for refugees there was another room, on the left, for the Portuguese," the boy remembered. "He looked at me with a strange smile and said in a very calm voice: 'You know, we are all refugees.'"

———

While Sousa Mendes suffered, Salazar was occupied with the monumental events of the Second World War. Churchill viewed Salazar as "intolerable," but the dictator managed to persuade the British that he was conniving with them to keep Franco out of the war, frustrating a major German objective. At the same time, he also convinced the Nazis that he was really on their side, prompting Joseph Goebbels to write in his diary that "as long as Salazar is in power in Portugal, nothing really hostile to us will be done." He traded wolframite, a critical ingredient for arms manufacture, to the Wehrmacht until late in the war, and took advantage of Nazi looting to quadruple Portugal's gold reserves. But in 1943, as the Allied victory he had begun to expect became increasingly certain, Salazar moved his official stance from strict neutrality to "cooperative neutrality" and allowed the Allies to use the Azores as bases for bombing runs. Accordingly, Sousa Mendes was optimistic that Salazar might come to his senses and revisit his case, seeing instead of defiance a profound humanitarianism. "Mr. Sousa Mendes never lost faith and hoped he [would] be forgiven for all the good deeds he did for us. But his government did not pardon him," Marguerite Rollin, a little girl he had rescued, recalled.

In May 1945, after Hitler committed suicide in his bunker as

Allied troops overran Berlin, Salazar ordered the flag lowered to half-staff and joined Franco and the Irish Taoiseach, Éamon de Valera, as the only heads of state offering condolences. A week later he celebrated the "victory" of the Allies. And then, on May 16, he declared in a speech to the national assembly, "As regards the refugees, we did our duty, though it is a pity we could not do more."

Sousa Mendes heard the words crackle over the radio from his home. Salazar now seemed to be taking credit for the very actions for which he remained ostracized. It was too much to take, even for the good-natured Sousa Mendes. He exploded in uncharacteristic rage.

He wrote again to the president of the national assembly, begging to know why he was being punished for acts that won "praise of the administration, both in Portugal and abroad." The government had opposed him and now was happy to take credit, an "evident and absurd injustice." Like Don Quixote tilting at windmills, he continued to argue that Circular 14 violated Article 8 of the Constitution, which guaranteed "the freedom and inviolability of beliefs by making it illegal for anyone to be persecuted because of those beliefs, or to be forced to reveal their religion." A civil servant, he declared, could not therefore "question anyone about their religion without contradicting the principles of the constitution," which would "imply the most odious religious persecution, especially at a time when the right of asylum that every civilized country has always recognized" during wartime was being ignored. There was no response.

"Papa always showed a high degree of optimism and he was sure that with victory the government would review his case," his son Luís Filipe, who served as his father's secretary, recalled. "He did not lose hope despite refusal upon refusal from Salazar." Sousa Mendes wrote to every member of the legislature, asserting that what he had done was "a reflection of the benevolence of the Portuguese people" and begging for reinstatement. Again, he received no response. A letter to Pope Pius XII asking for help was also met with silence.

Toward the end of the war, he had suffered a stroke that left his right arm paralyzed. As his health slowly continued to deteriorate, his financial situation grew even more precarious. While his law license was reinstated, he could not afford the yearly dues. His brother, César, tried to personally appeal to Salazar. He pressed the point that the dictator was himself constantly boasting of Portugal's efforts to save refugees, a national reputation that was allowing the nation to move firmly into the Western camp as the Cold War emerged and eventually to shelter under the American security umbrella as a founding member of NATO. The rhetorical question being asked in the capitals of the free world was: How horrible could the dictator be if he had helped so many during the war? "Your excellency no doubt remembers my brother Aristides facilitated the entry of the fugitives into Portugal," César wrote. "He did so, inspired exclusively by sentiments which so fully and so nobly characterize the Portuguese soul." Describing Sousa Mendes's poor health and depression, he pleaded for his brother: "I implore your Excellency not to let him die." Salazar did not reply.

A few months later, a wide-ranging political amnesty was declared as Salazar restored some civil liberties in an effort to improve his reputation among his Western allies. César tried again, requesting that Aristides be included. "Pardon me, Your Excellency, if I offend you in any way," he wrote to Salazar, "but I am a very devoted brother and it would be wrong of me not to employ all the methods at my disposal to save his honor and very probably his life."

Salazar was again unmoved.

Some historians have assumed that Salazar took a hard line with Sousa Mendes because of the importance of the Spanish border to his delicate strategy of neutrality. But it is hard not to suspect a personal vendetta. During the war, Salazar had, after all, allowed some other refugees into Lisbon and permitted the Hebrew Immigrant Aid Society to relocate its headquarters there from Paris after the German occupation. And in 1944 Carlos Sampaio Garrido, his ambassador in

Budapest, received Salazar's tacit consent to rescue an estimated one thousand Jews (albeit of Portuguese nationality) from deportation to the camps. But violating the chain of command for any reason was intolerable to Salazar: as one of Sousa Mendes's sons put it perceptively, his father "had disobeyed an order, a most unforgiveable sin."

Whatever Salazar's motivations, he destroyed the former consul. Sousa Mendes struggled to keep up appearances—he continued to wear his formal diplomatic attire, now threadbare, and to maintain his sense of humor among his family—but in time he found himself near ruin, crippled with debt, and forced to borrow over and over again against his home and assets. He sold whatever he could—silver, paintings, furniture—but at times he was short of basic necessities, even milk for breakfast. The family moved to a three-bedroom basement flat in Lisbon, which flooded whenever it rained. "We had a lot of misery," remembered his youngest son. "We ran out of things to sell."

When Sousa Mendes could no longer afford tuition for his younger children, he was forced to rely on support from the Jewish community to send them to school. But they often found themselves unfairly graded by their teachers and shunned by their friends. The older children failed to find employment as the family was ostracized, and were forced to move from Portugal. The American Jewish Joint Distribution Committee paid the expenses for several of them to emigrate, as did HIAS, and provided members of the family subsidies for years. Many of his children, for some time, would struggle with the consequences of his actions.

Both Angelina and Sousa Mendes declined in health. "Anxiety and despair filled their hearts while material conditions worsened year to year, from month to month," one of their sons recalled. "Very few were those in his professional circles and among his former friends and relatives who stretched out a supportive, compassionate hand." They had no money or insurance for medical care. In early 1948 Angelina suffered a massive stroke from which she never recovered. In

August she died of a cerebral hemorrhage, four days after her sixtieth birthday.

Sousa Mendes soldiered on, seeming to find some joy in his children and grandchildren. He could often be seen with a rosary, deep in prayer. "He seemed at peace with himself," his nephew wrote. But he also continued to appeal to anyone who he thought might listen—to the government, to members of the national assembly, to the diplomatic corps in Lisbon, to the head of the Catholic Church, and to those in Salazar's inner circle—all to no avail. At one point, he suggested that his brother César write the king of Belgium, hoping that he would "take an interest in someone who has rendered such real services to the Belgians, without receiving anything in return." After all, he had saved the nation's cabinet. But it too proved to be a dead end.

At the end of 1952, another stroke left his entire right side paralyzed. In its aftermath, he could walk only very slowly with the help of a stick; he could barely use a knife and fork or write. He sometimes fell out of bed at night. Two years later, on a trip to Lisbon, he suffered a third stroke, contracted pneumonia, and died at the Franciscan Hospital of the Tertiary Order on the Rua Serpa Pinto, a narrow street leading down to the water. Only a niece, Madelina, was with him. He was buried in Franciscan robes donated by the hospital. His death was barely noted outside an obituary in a local newspaper in the Belgian Congo, where one of his sons was living. Salazar sent César a two-word note: "My condolences."

Sousa Mendes never lost the conviction that he had acted justly. He told his son Pedro Nuno that he believed that he would be rewarded in the hereafter, that "he had never regretted his action saving thousands of refugees, and that he would do it all over again, should it be necessary."

"I disobeyed, but my disobedience does not dishonor me," he once told his lawyer. "I chose to defy an order that to me represented the persecution of true castaways who sought with all their strength to be saved from Hitler's wrath. Above the order, for me, was God's law, and that's the one I have always sought to adhere to without hesitation. The true lesson of Christianity is to love one's neighbor."

"To his last days, he remained true to himself, never regretting his altruistic deed," recalled his son Luís Filipe. "For me and I know, for each one of my brothers and sisters he was, and is, a hero, a person whose example I wish to follow throughout my life." His son Sebastian vowed to him, on their last visit: "I shall tell the whole world what you did in Bordeaux." Later he asked, one month after Sousa Mendes's passing, "Was he mad in showing so little instinct for self-preservation?" Sebastian's conclusion was clear. "The answer lies in all of us when we try to pass judgement on him. In any case I am proud of the fact that I was lucky enough to have such a man as my father."

Those Sousa Mendes rescued did not forget. In 1966 he was recognized as Righteous Among the Nations, and a grove of twenty trees was planted in his honor at the Forest of the Martyrs in Jerusalem. Six years later a medallion was issued to honor his actions and presented to one of his daughters. Several streets in Israel bear his name, and in 1987 he was also honored by the US Congress for his "extraordinary acts of mercy and justice during the Second World War." A European stamp in his honor bears the inscription: "His signature saved thousands."

"I believe that my father was without a doubt probably the greatest Portuguese hero in history because he saved thousands of people," his youngest son declared when Sousa Mendes received a posthumous honor. In 1988 the Portuguese government finally officially rehabilitated him, awarding him the title of ambassador by a unanimous vote of the national assembly. The entire body rose to its feet and gave a five-minute standing ovation.

During those chaotic days in mid-June 1940, Sousa Mendes issued some 1,575 official visas and many thousands more informally. Some accounts credit him with saving as many as thirty thousand people. His was, according to a leading scholar, "the largest rescue action by a single individual during the Holocaust."

One of those saved was, of course, Otto von Habsburg, who wrote years later to Sousa Mendes's grandson: "I wanted to say to you in writing how eternally grateful I am to your grandfather. He was a great gentleman, a man of admirable courage and integrity who served his principles to the detriment of his personal interests. At a time when many men were cowards, he was a true hero."

2

Life in the Circus

IRENE DANNER WAS AN EXQUISITE BEAUTY. HER MILKY-WHITE SKIN AND FLOW-
ing dark hair reminded some of the young girl in the film *Snow White*,
which had been released a few years earlier, just prior to the outbreak
of the Second World War. A trained ballet dancer and trick rider of
enormous agility, Irene belonged in the spotlight of the circus, like so
many of her ancestors. Instead she was now crouched with her family behind the bales of straw piled in the stables. The elephants stood
nearby, shuffling their tremendous blue-gray bodies and rustling the
hay underfoot. Irene could see their enormous ears and the shadows
they cast across the room. Her newborn, Peter, was causing the same
anxiety small children across Germany often did among those hiding
from the Nazis. One innocent cry could lead to discovery, arrest, and
deportation. Members of the Gestapo were at that very moment inspecting the circus where the family worked. Just as a flying circus elephant named Dumbo from another Walt Disney movie performed
feats of wonder, this herd performed an even greater miracle in real
life for their human colleagues by muffling sounds from the baby with
their casual trumpeting.

But while his elephants provided cover, the real hero of the day was
the twenty-eight-year-old proprietor of the circus, ringmaster Adolf
Althoff, who had courageously sheltered Irene and her relatives. The
circus is a family business, and its history is inextricably intertwined
with the stories of the great dynasties, stretching back sometimes

hundreds of years. Circus families like Adolf's and Irene's worked to-gether and often married into each other, sometimes across ethnic and religious lines. But it was the advent of Nazism and the war that had now brought two of these clans together.

Irene was a Lorch, a member of one of the great Jewish circus fam-ilies. The multicultural world of the circus enabled Jews to thrive. Itinerant by nature, circuses traveled all over the world. "Cosmopolitan in their lives and in their art, the artists are knit together by one tradi-tion, one technique, one terminology," wrote one historian of the time. "The world may be Balkanised, but its amusements are still as universal as the Church of the Middle Ages." As a visual art form that tran-scended language barriers, the circus became a global phenomenon in the nineteenth century, when international communications were still fairly rudimentary. Circus companies often took on an international flavor as performers from different countries worked together, with certain nationalities dominating particular disciplines.

Against this backdrop, Jewish circus families became as renowned as their Christian colleagues. The most well known were the Blumen-felds, who in 1811 were among the first to transform their magic act into a full-blown traveling circus with tents. They adopted many in-novations from America, where the traveling show, complete with sideshow attractions and wild animals, had been invented. Soon the Blumenfelds had several circuses. "Wherever variety or circus artists are at work," wrote a circus writer of the time, "one is sure to meet with Blumenfelds."

The Lorches were another Jewish dynasty, a family of acrobats with its own storied history. Irene was at least a fifth-generation mem-ber, a remarkable pedigree. The Lorches had started as "banquists," performers who dazzled crowds with tricks and acrobatics at the an-nual fairs universal across Germany. Irene's great-grandfather Hirsch Lorch, born in 1817, owned a show that traveled along the Rhine. But his son Louis's ambition was to be a champion equestrian, and in 1861, at the age of fourteen, he ran away from home and headed for Paris. Trained as a rider, Louis was entranced by the haute école shows put on by François Baucher, the honorary master of the stables for the emperor Napoleon III. These performances were the rage among Parisian high society and at the royal court, and in 1863 the most sensational social event of the season was the riding debut of James Fillis, the son of a London barrister. At a horse-mad time, Fillis's special style of holding a double bridle—the snaffle rein used to control speed and major movements over the index finger, the curb rein for flexing the horse's neck under the little finger—was a revolution. One day, as the beau monde crowded in to watch Fillis, Louis Lorch pushed forward among them to watch the spectacle. It was at this moment that a horse gave him a swift kick with its hoof, inflicting an injury that ended any hope for the sixteen-year-old of his own career in the equestrian ring.

With the benefit of hindsight, it was a lucky blow. The horse triggered the founding of the famous Lorch Circus itself and launched Louis Lorch on a stellar career as an impresario. At the time of his injury, Lorch had a total of one hundred francs and two dogs to his name. But he also had the profound love and loyalty of Jeanette Meyer, a talented rider who soon became his bride. "A circus man of the old school was able to do anything," one wag commented, "all the more so when he had two trained poodles and a pretty wife." Lorch traveled to the country fairs all over western Germany, performing for an audience of peasants. In addition to the two dogs, the show featured a clown, an acrobat, a high jumper, a strong man, a juggler, and a tightrope walker—all of them the multitalented Louis Lorch. At the end of each performance he passed a plate around and asked for tips, soon raising enough money to buy Jeanette a horse. Within five years he had saved enough to acquire his own tent, which had the critical benefit of allowing him to charge admission rather than relying on the generosity of those he entertained. After a decade the Lorch Circus had become one of the most important traveling shows in the south of

Germany and Switzerland, featuring at its height some one hundred horses.

The circus is not an easy business, and Lorch would have his ups and downs. A corrupt business manager and a streak of terrible weather conspired at one point to bring the circus to the brink of collapse. But Lorch had a secret weapon: his eldest son, Julius. For a number of years the boy had excelled brilliantly as a tightrope walker with his sister Rosa, an act that ended when the girl married Alphonse Althoff, a cousin of Adolf's, and emigrated to America. Left without a partner, Julius began to train three of his four younger brothers—Arthur, Eugene, and Rudi—as acrobats. He drilled into them proper jumping techniques and the critical gymnastic skill of walking on one's hands. In short order he had developed an acrobatic troupe.

But his real stroke of genius came one day when he saw a Chinese or Japanese performer (he could not recall which) do what were known as antipodean tricks. The artist would lie on his back and balance a barrel or some other object on his feet before throwing it in the air and then catching it again. As he recalled it years later, Julius asked himself, "Why should not one do the same thing with a little human object?" What better object than a little brother? Eugene became the first to master the technique. He would sit on his brother's feet while Julius lay on the ground on a cushion and began to tread him like a bicycle. Making his body as flexible and bouncy as possible, Eugene was eventually able to do a complete somersault and land back on Julius's feet. In no time, he could do a triple flip, and a star was born.

This kind of act was called an Icarian, and although Julius was not the first to imagine it, the Lorches perfected it. They were soon by far the most famous Icarian troupe in the world. They became so renowned that they were invited to perform as a star attraction in the center ring of Ringling Bros. and Barnum & Bailey Circus in the United States. From 1909 to 1912 the four brothers, their two sisters, Jeanette and Hedwig, Julius's son Egon, two acrobats, and two apprentices—eleven in all—entertained tens of thousands of delighted fans. In the winter, they performed to sellout crowds in New York.

The act created a sensation. The Lorch troupe would enter the ring dressed in the costume of Spanish bullfighters and begin jumping, tumbling, and flipping. Then three tossers took up position on three red velvet cushions and hurled the smaller members of the group in the air, passing them to each other and catching them as they fell. The highlight of the show was the Icarian flips. Julius—known as the King of Icarians—was able to throw his son in the air three times, and each time Egon would execute a double somersault. For the grand finale, they formed a human pyramid. Once they were in position, a dwarf who was part of the group scrambled up and stood on top of the highest acrobat. Trumpets would blow and cymbals crash as he pulled out the American flag, two ponies on either side of the group standing at attention. Then, as the entire group tumbled to earth, Julius would catch the dwarf, still holding the flag, and throw him into the air in a perfect Icarian twelve times. It was a showstopper.

Ringling Bros. posters featured the scene, emblazoned with the words "The Lorch Family, Europe's Greatest Acrobats" and the "Most Marvelous Feats Ever Seen." Across the bottom was another announcement: the Lorches had been "Engaged at the Highest Salary Ever Paid Any Single Attraction." They had become rich.

Their home base was a large estate Louis Lorch built in Darmstadt, a picturesque fourteenth-century town that boasted the Frankenstein Castle, Mary Shelley's alleged inspiration. All the members of the troupe, including the dwarf, had private apartments and gardens on the grounds. But the circus life is an itinerant one. After the Ringling Bros. engagement, they traveled to performances around the world.

But now they traveled in style. As a circus journalist recalled of the legendary mid-1920s tour of South America run by the Circus Sarrasani, the Lorch caravans were more luxurious than most homes. Julius's was like a five-star hotel, complete with a living room of carved oak furniture, glass vitrines filled with objets d'art, and blue leather armchairs. His sisters' quarters boasted an eiderdown quilt on which celebrities were asked to embroider their names. His brother Eugene gave full rein to his passion for photography, filling his caravan with cameras, gadgets, and hundreds of photographs he had taken on his travels. The Lorches themselves dressed in multicolored clothes with exotic accessories: watch chains from India made of human hair with lion's claws, tiepins in the shape of Egyptian scarabs, cuff links made of crocodile scales, and scores of rings.

The Lorch work ethic was legendary—they acted as performers, ushers, ticket takers, and laborers. Louis Lorch never lost his own zest for the circus, prowling the grounds with his walking stick. When he died in 1925 in the palm-tree-filled district of Palermo in Buenos Aires, he had spent the day inspecting the caravans and stables and then watching his sons perform, carefully observing the crowd's reaction. At age seventy-eight, he could look back proudly and see that he had created a dynasty. After his passing the troupe returned home on the steamship *Cap Polonio*, arriving at Hamburg dressed in mourning black. The children helped Jeanette down the gangway, supported by Julius and his son Egon. She clutched a leather case that contained an urn with her husband's ashes. Even in death, Louis Lorch would continue to travel with the circus wherever it went.

Julius Lorch was now the head of the family. In 1927, at the height of Lorch fame, he purchased, along with his brothers Arthur and Rudi, the Circus W. Althoff, which had been founded by another one of Adolf's cousins, Wilhelm, in the nineteenth century. They renamed it the Circus Lorch. The family was no longer just an act for hire but owners of their own circus, which traveled during the summer months in the south of Germany, and they continued to perform their lucrative Icarian routine for other companies in the winter.

The Lorches were respected, prosperous, and renowned. But Adolf Althoff, to whom Irene Danner had turned for help, was true circus royalty. His ancestors had been pioneers of the art form since it arose during the Renaissance, evolving out of the juggling acts of the Middle Ages. After the French Revolution, the family had received a commission directly from Napoleon to perform as tightrope walkers and equestrians. The Althoffs had a number of children, and ultimately there were twenty-eight different circuses bearing their name. The descendants branched into three main lines, and it was to the so-called Rheinische one that Adolf Althoff's father, Dominick, belonged. Dominick Althoff had founded his own show in 1905 and married a haute école equestrian, Adele Mark, with whom he would have eight children. Adolf was the second to last of these, born on the grounds of his parents' circus. It was 1913, the year before the outbreak of the First World War and a boom time for the circus. In Paris, at the Circus Medrano, the Swiss clown Grock was the highest-paid entertainer in Europe, and across the Continent, the circus was a sensation.

Adolf Althoff would prove a natural in the business. By the age of seventeen, he was working as his parents' publicity director and developing as a horse and elephant trainer. In 1936, at the age of twenty-six, he joined forces with one of his older sisters, Hélène, to form the Circus Geschwister Althoff, seeded by his father with the gift of eight ponies, four horses, and an elephant named Dicki. A stroke of genius came the next year—they trained a tiger to ride on horseback, an act that became a tremendous hit. In 1939 Hélène left to start her own circus, and Adolf renamed the company the Circus Adolf Althoff, which would be celebrated as "one of the most technically proficient circuses in the world and . . . one of Germany's most popular shows." Not even thirty, Althoff became a prominent ringmaster, employing some ninety artists and crew. The same year, he married a member of another well-known circus family, Maria von der Gathen, who like him was also an accomplished horse trainer. Five years older than Adolf, she joined him in running the circus.

———

In the years leading up to the war, Jews were persecuted everywhere in Germany. The circus was no exception, and the joyous glory days of just a decade earlier were soon at an end. The art form itself was something the Nazis prized, however; even during the darkest days of tyranny, the circus could offer citizens a respite from the horrors of everyday life. And despite its international reach, the Nazis did not view the circus as subversive, as they did modern art, literature, and theater. In fact minister of propaganda Joseph Goebbels saw the circus as an example of German excellence, sending several Aryan troupes on international propaganda tours.

Both Jewish owners and performers quickly became targets, though. The Lorches saw many of their workers flee and their audiences evaporate. Combined with the devastation of the Great Depression, it was too much: the Circus Lorch filed for bankruptcy. It was not the only casualty. Jewish circuses were systematically driven out of business over the next few years by the Nazis. The great Circus Blumenfeld also went bankrupt, and the Strassburgers were forced to sell their eponymous circus for a song to Paula Busch before fleeing the country. Jewish performers became virtually unemployable, and many were forced to find jobs working for gentile companies outside of Germany. In 1934 the Circus Sarrasani—where the Lorches had performed—was labeled a *Judenzirkus* for employing Jews and forced to return to South America. (It did, however, return at Goebbels's request to perform at the 1936 Berlin Olympics, where its owner's beautiful young wife served as an Aryan icon—before she was imprisoned for anti-Nazi activities.)

Many German circus owners capitalized on the opportunity created by this devastation. Circus luminaries such as Busch and Carl Krone joined the Nazi Party and received the patronage of the Third Reich, rewarded with years of boom. But Adolf Althoff would not do so, nor would any other member of his family. They had a reputation for integrity and openness, and regularly socialized with people of all backgrounds, including Jews. The Althoffs not only refused to capitalize on the tragedy of their Jewish circus brethren but chose to help them. The penalty for harboring Jews from the Nazis was summary execution or deportation to concentration camps. But, as Althoff would later remark, "in a circus you can do a lot and keep it a secret."

Adolf's older brother Franz and sister Carola were the first to do so. When their father retired in 1936, they had taken over his circus and used it to give safe harbor to Jews on the run. In their pantry wagon, they built a hidden double wall where they could hide those they were sheltering during the regular Nazi inspections of their premises. Adolf and Maria protected Gerda Blumenfeld, matriarch of the dynasty, and hired one of her sons, Alfred, as a director and press agent. With their help, Alfred was also able to support and hide his two brothers Willi and Fritz. But the three brothers eventually decided to flee Germany to France for safety. Sadly, their flight proved futile; after the occupation of France they were rounded up and sent to Auschwitz, where they were murdered.

In 1941 the Circus Adolf Althoff pulled into Darmstadt in southwestern Germany, the city where the Lorch family had its home. Soon after their arrival, eighteen-year-old Irene Danner came to the performance and knocked on the Althoffs' door. She was aware that Adolf and Maria knew her family. Indeed, it was Adolf's cousin who had married Rosa Lorch, Irene's great-aunt and Julius's erstwhile tightrope partner, whisking her off to America. Hoping that the circus bond would prove indelible, Irene confided in Adolf and Maria that she had been hounded from the circus because she was Jewish, that she had no job, and that her family feared for their lives.

Adolf Althoff, likely dressed in the white tie and tails he donned as ringmaster, listened intently as Irene told him of the Lorch family's recent catastrophic descent. She explained that her grandfather was Julius, and her mother Alice, the younger sister of Egon, the boy his father had so spectacularly thrown in the air in the Icarian show. Alice herself had had two daughters with her husband, Hans Danner, who was not Jewish. Irene was the elder, born just over the Belgian border in Liège in January 1923.

The family lived at the Lorch estate, and Irene grew up hearing the exciting stories of transatlantic travel on ocean steamers and of the thunderous applause of admiring crowds in South America. She had fond memories of her earliest childhood, years marked by fairy tales and friendship, needlework projects and joyous singing, and socializing with other members of her synagogue. Irene did well at school and, as might be expected from a member of her family, excelled as a gymnast. She was even decorated with a certificate by the Reichsjugendführer (Reich youth leader) Baldur von Schirach for her abilities.

But then the Nazis had ratcheted up their campaign against the Jews. After the devastating bankruptcy of the Lorch Circus, the Icarian troupe, including Hans and Alice, continued to perform. While their parents were on tour, Irene and her sister Gerda, four years younger, lived with their maternal grandmother Sessy while they attended school.

When Irene was ten, shortly after the Nazis took power, Darmstadt became the first town to force Jewish-owned shops to close for a government-mandated boycott. Nazi propaganda soon infected her school. Her teacher personally led her classmates in Nazi songs. The children would bellow, "Germany awaken, Judea perish!" and look at her. Other girls suddenly refused to play with Irene. She was no longer allowed into the Bund Deutscher Mädel and was kicked out of the evangelical church choir. Her classmates teased her. "They giggled and pointed their fingers at me," she remembered. "And they said: 'Jews stink.' I was ashamed to be a stinking Jew. In school I sucked peppermints. But it did not help." She was banned from physical education. One day the local forester appeared on her doorstep, determined to enforce a ban on Jews owning dogs. Irene's two puppies stood wagging their tails next to her grandmother. The man seized the dogs, shot them, and threw them in the garbage dump.

When she was thirteen and a half, Irene was expelled from school for being a Jew. She started to travel with her parents at the Circus Jakob Busch, where they now worked. Her father performed dangerous feats on the high wire, but as an Aryan he was not at risk from the Gestapo. Her Jewish mother, on the other hand, was afraid to go in the ring. At fifteen, Irene was forbidden by the Nazis to take ballet lessons. But she practiced handstands and leaps on the sidelines of the circus. A well-known Italian trick-riding troupe, the Carolis, spotted her one day and immediately hired her. For a brief time she performed in many large variety shows. But then, when she was sixteen, the Carolis received a letter from the Reichstheaterkammer (a subdivision of the Reich Chamber of Culture) in Berlin informing them that, as a Jew, Irene could no longer perform. She returned home to Darmstadt with her mother.

The same year Irene was banned, her uncle Egon was deported to Dachau, before a bribe secured his release and he fled to Italy. Then her grandfather, the great Julius, also went to Italy for an engagement. Never allowed to return to Germany, he would die in 1942 without ever again seeing his home or the family he had loved and led for decades. His brothers Rudi and Arthur—his partners as Icarians from the start—were similarly stranded in Belgium. After the German invasion, they were arrested and sent to the Saint-Cyprien camp in the south of France; from there, they were sent to Drancy and then to Auschwitz, where they both perished.

Everywhere across the Continent, the great Jewish circus families were being destroyed. Some hundred and fifty members of the Blumenfeld family alone were murdered in the Holocaust. The Hungarian clown Zoltán Hirsch, so famous throughout Europe that mail addressed simply to his stage name Zoli arrived at his home, died in the gas chambers. In a particularly chilling case, the seven Ovitz siblings of Romania—the largest family of dwarves ever recorded, who had once performed for King Carol II in Bucharest—were deported to Auschwitz, where they were tortured for an entire year by the sadistic Dr. Josef Mengele, the notorious "angel of death" who experimented on prisoners in the camp.

Irene pleaded for a job from Adolf Althoff, who did not hesitate and found her a place in the show. First she worked with Maria and another girl in an act with three elephants. Then she became part of the clown group "The Three Bentos." Hiring a Jew was illegal, but Althoff allowed Irene to work without papers and under a false name, thus literally hiding her from the Nazis in plain sight. The Althoff circus was very popular, and senior Nazis were often in attendance to watch the feats of aerial daring and the hijinks of the clowns. They had no idea, of course, that the latter included a young Jewess, but Irene's religion was a poorly kept secret among her coworkers. The tolerant culture of the circus would ultimately be tested to the extreme.

One of the performers who was there when Irene first knocked on the door of the Circus Adolf Althoff was the clown Peter Bento-Storms. Peter, also eighteen, had made his debut in his father Jose Bento's clown act at the age of four. The Bentos worked in Great Britain with the Great Carmo Circus in the 1920s and then joined the Circus Sarrasani in Germany, traveling with it to South America on the same journey Louis Lorch was on when he died in Argentina. Then father and son both joined Adolf Althoff in his circus.

Peter was an Auguste clown, the generally stupid and clumsy stock character clad in a garishly colored outfit several sizes too large. As the butt of other clowns' jokes or from his own incompetence, the Auguste was a proven crowd-pleaser, and Peter had an impeccable sense of comic timing. Before each performance, strict rules dictated that the Auguste clown apply white makeup around his eyes and mouth and a flesh-colored greasepaint on the rest of his skin, and he often wore the large red nose familiar to everyone. He would also paint his lower lip to give a sad appearance, exaggerate his eyebrows, and wear a colorful wig. But despite Peter's wacky appearance in the ring, he was deadly serious about Irene.

The Bento circus family was friendly with the Lorches, and Peter could relate to her childhood in the business. He listened sympathetically as she told him about the Nazi persecution she'd experienced, and he fully supported the Althoffs' decision to hire and shelter her. Soon Irene and Peter fell in love. Forbidden to marry under Nazi law, they nonetheless lived as husband and wife under the Althoffs' protection. During the war they would have two children, making Peter a potential target of the Nazis as well.

Maria took care of Irene throughout her pregnancies, making sure she had enough food and proper treatment. During the birth of their first child, named Peter, in December 1942, Irene required a caesarean section and was admitted to the city hospital, where she was promptly denounced as a Jewess by the mayor of Eschollbrücken to the senior attending physician, a member of the Nazi Party. The doctor saw to it that the operation was not properly carried out, resulting in severe complications, and refused Irene nursing care during her six-week stay. As a result, Irene almost died. When an air raid alarm sounded at the hospital, the staff left Irene by herself while they ran to safety in the shelter.

The Althoffs were horrified when they learned what had happened. Irene was pregnant a second time the following year, and became very sick due to the injuries she had sustained during her botched caesarean. This time the Althoffs brought her to a close friend of theirs, a Dr. Grobe, three hundred kilometers away at the hospital in Pößneck in Thuringia, who was willing to treat a Jewish patient despite the risks. When Grobe saw the mutilation from the previous caesarean, he was shocked. "What pig committed this crime?" he gasped. In February he successfully delivered the Storms' second son, Jano. "Without Dr. Grobe I would not have survived this birth," Irene later recalled. Before the end of the war, Adolf and Maria welcomed their own infant, Franz.

If their actions were ever discovered, their own baby too would be in peril. They were all in mortal danger for hiding Jews.

The situation became even more dangerous after the Jews of Darmstadt were deported in 1942 and 1943. Irene's grandmother Sessy, the wife of Julius Lorch, was now reduced to wearing a yellow Star of David. One day in March 1943, Irene was nursing her baby upstairs at Sessy's home. Her grandmother, Irene could still recall years later, shrieked "high and loud like an animal" as soldiers stormed up the stairs and broke open the door to the room where she was sitting. They arrested her grandmother and her great-uncle Eugene, the photography lover who had been the first to master the Icarian flip that launched the family to fame and fortune. "You and your bastard, you will be next," the Nazis barked at Irene on the way out. Sessy and Eugene were both sent to Auschwitz, where they were murdered. The great family house was confiscated, leaving the Danners homeless and desperate.

Irene again prevailed upon Adolf and Marie for help and the Althoffs immediately agreed to protect her mother and sixteen-year-old sister Gerda. "There was no question that we would let them stay," Althoff recalled. "I couldn't simply permit them to fall into the hands of the murderers. This would have made me a murderer." They were soon joined in hiding by Irene's father, Hans Danner, who had been fighting with the Wehrmacht in North Africa and Russia and was sent home from the front with orders to divorce his Jewish wife. Instead, he went underground. The number of family members now under the Althoffs' protection had grown to seven.

The Althoffs took responsibility for hiding them all from certain death. They all worked for the circus under assumed names and without proper papers. Adolf tried to make the situation as bearable as possible. "He was good to everybody," Irene remembered, "but especially to us." He housed the family in a trailer on the outskirts of the grounds, away from view, where they lived in very small quarters and generally stayed inside. Maria made sure the family was properly fed, sneaking them even such minor wartime luxuries as fresh fruit and coffee whenever possible.

The risk of being caught was constant, but it was particularly dangerous when the circus moved locations. It was then subjected to inspection by the Nazis, who wanted to make sure that the tent was structurally safe, that the living conditions were acceptable, and, most ominously, that the circus was not employing any "unwanted foreigners" or, worse, Jews. "The years in the circus, which through the war visited many different locations, were difficult for all of us," Peter Storms remembered. "The fear of denunciation and discovery by the Nazis travelled with us from location to location."

Althoff's contacts at various tour stops would provide advance notice of Gestapo inspections. A subtle knock on the door (sometimes a somewhat panicked banging) and a whisper to "go fishing" were the signal for Irene and her family to hide in their quarters or run into the forest. On occasion they would go on a picnic, pretending to be an ordinary family. Sometimes they would shelter in circus wagons on the edge of the grounds. When there was no time to escape, they hid behind bales of hay or the cables in the electricity cabin. Althoff, remembered Peter, "developed a great skill for circumventing the Nazi authorities. At every new location the circus was closely monitored. Several times, we all risked getting arrested or shot." The danger was extraordinary. "Without him and his wife," Storms declared, "we would not have survived."

One terrifying time, the family was caught in the Althoffs' parlor car and had to hide behind a tapestry and listen in frozen silence as Adolf entertained the Gestapo. He had become adept at dealing with them. As soon as the officers introduced themselves on an inspection, Althoff would turn on the charm. He had repeatedly refused to join the Nazi Party, and inspectors often wanted to know his political views and questioned why he was so friendly to them. "I kept telling them that I was a circus man," he said, "and that circus people live in the entire world and are of the entire world." The competitive landscape in Germany was crowded, so he had traveled all over and had learned over the years to adapt himself to his hosts abroad and to be on his best behavior. In communicating with the Nazis, he had to be particularly clever. "I could never really say no or yes. One had to improvise," he recalled.

The Nazis were impressed with the whole operation. "They admired our circus because it was so neat," said Althoff. He plied them with drinks, provided free tickets for their families, and entertained them with stories from his past. Anecdotes of his adventures in Russia, where he had performed with bears, never failed to captivate. If the inspections became too intrusive, Althoff deftly diverted them, telling the men he had to meet with their superiors and leaving them in the care of Maria. "By that time she had set the table in our wagon, and offered them coffee," Althoff recalled. "She never forgot the bottle of cognac. Our hospitality became famous."

With their actions, Irene recalled, the Althoffs were "saving our lives and exposing them[selves] to the greatest of dangers." If he were caught, Althoff could have been arrested and shot. "The situation could not be totally hidden from the large circus of artists and circus workers. He took upon himself the risk of denunciation," Irene recalled. Throughout Europe, this was often what led to capture and execution of both victim and rescuer, as ordinary citizens traded Jewish lives for small monetary rewards or acted out of bigotry or resentment. But no one betrayed the Althoffs.

"People in the circus knew my opinion," Althoff recalled. "And they knew I was the boss. They knew they would be fired if they talked about what I had done. There was no discussion." On only one occasion did an employee complain about the Jews in their midst. A tightrope walker and confirmed Nazi accosted Althoff, asking "Why are there Jews in this circus?" In response, Althoff assured him he would get rid of those hiding soon. Althoff then provoked an argument vicious enough to give him grounds to fire the man on the spot and kick him off of the premises. "Somehow I found a reason," he remembered. "I said, 'You are dismissed without notice. Get out of this place right now!'"

When the war ended in 1945, Irene and her family were at last able to come out in the open. She and Peter married and had three more children, and they returned to Eschollbrücken. Still traumatized by the experience, Irene avoided going into town to shop for fear of seeing the many faces of those who had participated in the persecution. The Storms, however, maintained a lasting friendship with the Althoffs, their wartime bond indelible. When their children grew up, Irene and Peter both worked in their circus, known as Clowni. Peter reprised his old role as Auguste, and Irene worked the cash register and told her grandchildren the fairy tales her own beloved grandmother had told her as a little girl, in the years before the Nazis stole her childhood.

The Althoffs too kept performing. When Adolf's circus experienced financial difficulties in the postwar period, he and Maria joined his sister Carola at the enormously successful Circus Williams, founded with her second husband, the legendary British performer Harry Williams, who tragically died performing a chariot race in London. After the Circus Williams acquired the prominent Circus Friederike Hagenbeck, the business became even more successful, eventually appearing in the Cecil B. DeMille epic *The Greatest Show on Earth* and serving as the second unit for the Ringling Bros. and Barnum & Bailey Circus. Althoff continued to perform and to train elephants and horses. He also taught the lion tamer Gunther Gebel-Williams, who took over his elephants and became the most famous circus performer of the last third of the twentieth century.

Althoff then revived his own circus for several years. Its wild animal acts were a hit, as were the Gaonas, renowned Mexican trapeze artists. The tiger-on-horseback routine from his first show even returned, an act that his son Franz would bring to America for Ringling Bros. In 1965, at age fifty-one, Althoff closed his show at its peak, but he would continue performing in other troupes on and off for another twenty years until he was slowed down by diabetes and heart trouble. At age seventy he even finished an act after suffering a tiger bite, calling for a quick bandage and going on with the show. Franz took over the business and eventually represented the Moscow State Circus under the name Circus Williams-Althoff. Adolf and Maria continued to advise and help their son, traveling part of the year with him. "Whoever once sniffs the ring air never can get away from it," Althoff declared. The now gray-haired Althoff adored being in the circus, even if the younger generation often did not live up to his standards. He could be seen picking up litter and paper scraps from the floor, grumbling beneath his small mustache, "Such would not have happened in my time."

Althoff died in his sleep at age eighty-five. He was eulogized for his amazing circus career. "His operation was regarded as a model circus because of its discipline and the beauty of its numbers," reported the German press breathlessly. But Althoff never sought thanks and certainly never sought publicity for his selflessness in saving the Danner family. Decades after her rescue, Irene Danner applied to recognize Maria and Adolf Althoff as Righteous Among the Nations. "It was only natural for the Althoffs to help us. They didn't want our gratitude," she wrote. "It would make us very happy to see them honored for their courageous and unselfish actions."

Adolf Althoff did not view himself as a hero. "What have I done that is so special?" he asked a German newspaper. "I have only done my duty and protected the human beings that were entrusted to us." When recognized years later for his deeds by Yad Vashem in Jerusalem, he stated simply, "We circus people see no difference between races or religions."

Others saw it differently. "Without their help," Irene Danner concluded, "my family would not have survived the Holocaust."

3

On the Glory of Athens

BRIGADEFÜHRER JÜRGEN STROOP WAS NOT USED TO INSUBORDINATION. THE notorious SS officer was so proud of crushing the Warsaw Ghetto uprising that he wrote a book-length report describing it in detail. Now in occupied Greece, where he had been sent to enforce the iron will of the Nazis, he found the local population difficult to keep in line. The metropolitan, Damaskinos, archbishop of Athens and thus head of the entire Greek Orthodox Church, was particularly frustrating. Stroop had once summoned Damaskinos and threatened to shoot him if he refused to meet his demands. Damaskinos calmly handed him a length of rope. "If you wish to hang me, as the Turks did Gregorios, here is the rope," he told the Nazi, recalling a famous incident in 1821. Stroop was stunned. "According to the traditions of the Greek Orthodox Church," Damaskinos quipped, "our prelates are hung and not shot. Please respect our traditions!"

In his early fifties and sporting the tangled but rectangular grayish beard standard for men in his profession, Damaskinos stood a towering six feet, four inches tall. Born Dimitrios Papandreou, the youngest of thirteen children, he was a figure of extreme determination and powerful charisma who had risen from peasant roots in Thessaly. A star student and athlete—gifted at the javelin like an ancient Olympian—he had briefly studied law before devoting himself to theology. He rose rapidly in the church and distinguished himself after the horrible Corinth earthquake in 1928: it was largely through his efforts, including raising funds in the United States, that the ancient city was rebuilt. Worldly and cosmopolitan, Damaskinos had traveled widely over the years. A *Time* cover story would describe him on a diplomatic mission to the United Kingdom: "Berobed in the black garb and silver chain of his churchly office, he cut a figure unique among modern statesmen. He impressed London hostesses by his great appetite for oriental pilaf (his aides cornered the dwindling London rice stocks), his fine Greek cigarets, the quantities of boiling Turkish coffee he consumed."

Damaskinos had recently reclaimed the leadership of the Greek Orthodox Church and was not afraid to disagree with authorities. His courage should not have surprised the Germans. He had first been elected as archbishop in 1938, but after he criticized the strongman Ioannis Metaxas he was exiled to the island of Salamis, site of the celebrated Greek naval victory over the Persians. There he made productive use of his time, teaching himself to play Gregorian chants on a harmonica with his pet goat and dog beside him. Not realizing with whom they were dealing, the Germans permitted his recall after the invasion, when his successor Chrysanthos refused to take an oath of loyalty to the new collaborationist prime minister, Georgios Tsolakoglou.

Damaskinos was a humanitarian and maintained close relations with leaders in the Jewish community. Jews had lived in Greece for over two thousand years. The Romaniote Jews traced their ancestry to at least the time of Alexander the Great, hundreds of years before the destruction of the Second Temple in Jerusalem. The oldest known reference to their presence is a mosaic outside Athens dating back to 300 BCE, and a synagogue can be found among the ruins of the agora at the foot of the Parthenon. Located largely in Athens, the Peloponnese, and on the various islands of the Aegean and Ionian seas, the Romaniotes, who numbered in the thousands, had been for centuries fully integrated into all aspects of the life of the nation; they gave their children Hellenic names and spoke a fluent, unaccented Greek. These were the Jews who lived around Damaskinos in the capital.

At the time of the Second World War, however, the Romaniote population was dwarfed by the much larger Sephardic community in the north. It was from there that a trickle of refugees was now arriving in Athens, bringing word of horrible crimes being committed against the Jews. The Sephardic Jews had first arrived in 1492 at the invitation of the Ottoman sultan Bayezid II following their expulsion from Spain, and were largely concentrated in the port city of Salonika in Macedonia. The second largest city in the country, Salonika had only joined Greece proper in 1912 after the Balkan Wars. It had been renamed Thessaloniki* in 1937, but the Ottoman stamp remained in the large white cylindrical tower that loomed over the metropolis on the waterfront.

For centuries, Jews had been a majority in Salonika. Stores and the post office closed on the Sabbath. Jews were present in all walks of life, not just as merchants, bankers, and businessmen but also as civil servants, manual laborers, sailors, and dockworkers. They dried tobacco and made bricks and owned cafés. The city captured the imagination of budding Zionist leaders. David Ben-Gurion lived there in 1911 and declared it "a Jewish labor city, the only one in the world." His rival, the right-wing intellectual Vladimir Jabotinsky, had visited two years earlier and called Salonika the "Jerusalem of Turkey" and "the most Jewish city in the world." Even French and English visitors called it the New Jerusalem and speculated that it might be the location of the messiah's arrival.

Unlike the Romaniotes, the Sephardic Jews of Salonika maintained their own distinctive culture. They largely spoke Ladino, the mix of Spanish and Hebrew that was the language of the Sephardic diaspora the way Yiddish was for the Ashkenazim. For centuries they

---

* For clarity, I have referred to the city as Salonika throughout this chapter.

had lived in peace with their neighbors, mostly Muslims, Vlachs, and Dönme, descendants of Jewish converts to Islam. Minarets towered over the city, and Jewish men wore fezzes. Even the Jewish and Muslim mystics worked together, singing Sufi and kabbalistic texts. Under the Ottoman system of hands-off governance, the Jewish community was largely left alone, and the metropolis was a self-governing entity, the third largest city in the empire. Salonika was such a model for coexistence that as its future was debated during the second decade of the twentieth century, its multiethnic population, who preferred Jewish rule to annexation by Greece or Bulgaria, strongly supported serious proposals put forth for creating a Jewish city-state.

It was not to be. By 1913 the Ottoman Empire was in its death throes, and at the end of the Balkan Wars Greece annexed Salonika. The Jewish community tried to remain neutral, and some began to learn Greek. When King George I came to visit, chief rabbi Jacob Meir welcomed him, as he had Sultan Mehmed V a few years earlier, pledging the allegiance of the Jewish community and offering a blessing to the sovereign. With the annexation, the Jewish population of Greece multiplied from fewer than ten thousand to almost ninety thousand. But the turning point was the collapse of the Ottoman Empire and the subsequent Greco-Turkish conflict. In 1923 the Treaty of Lausanne created the new nation-state of Turkey, and a massive compulsory population exchange took place. Five hundred thousand Muslims were expelled from Greece, and one and a half million Greek Orthodox Christians sent from Turkey. Jews were exempted, but in Salonika a hundred thousand Greeks replaced their Muslim neighbors. The Jews were now for the first time in the minority.

Aggressive Hellenization intensified: street names were changed to Greek, multilingual signs were replaced, and the new national flag flew everywhere. The goal was to eliminate all traces of Salonika's Ottoman, Muslim, and Jewish history. The difficult economic conditions and language barriers that faced the new settlers inflamed the anti-Semitic views many brought with them. In 1917 a terrible fire left seventy thousand homeless, including fifty thousand Jews, and thirty-two synagogues burned down. The Greek state refused to permit rebuilding, taking the opportunity to reshape the city along more modern lines.

In 1924 under Eleftherios Venizelos, a new Hellenic Republic was declared. Venizelos's stronghold was in the north, where antimonarchist sentiment was most fervent among the recent immigrants. He had little patience for the Salonikan Jews, with their alien culture, refusal to assimilate, and loyalty to the throne. In 1924 the city's legendary status as the "Shabatopolis"—closed on Shabbat—was ended with the passing of a Sunday closing law. Jewish laborers were banned from the port to create jobs for Greek Orthodox workers. The first pogrom ever in Salonika took place in 1931, in the Campbell neighborhood. During the regime of Venizelos's archrival, the strongman Ioannis Metaxas, the Jews were offered protection, which only further alienated the local Greek Orthodox. When the Germans arrived in early April 1941, many of the locals were only too happy to assist the invaders.

Almost from the moment they invaded Greece, the Nazis focused on the Jews in the zone they occupied directly (Bulgaria and Italy administered other parts of the country), an area that included Salonika. Three days after the invasion, the Nazis banned Jews from cafés and cinemas and confiscated their homes and charitable institutions such as the Baron Hirsch Hospital. Zvi Koretz, the chief rabbi of Salonika, was arrested for protesting the bombing of the Saint Sophia church and taken to Vienna. Thousands of books and manuscripts were looted and Torah scrolls burned. One survivor testified at Adolf Eichmann's trial how the scholars wept at the destruction of their libraries: "These books matter, above all," he said. Famine took hold in Greece, and was particularly bad in Salonika. In these terrible early months, most of the Jews who had foreign passports fled.

On July 11, 1942, all Jewish men between the ages of eighteen and forty-five were ordered to Eleftheria Square in the center of Salonika. Nine thousand men were subjected to brutal calisthenics in the scorching heat for seven hours as German soldiers and spectators jeered. Over three thousand were sent to hard labor. By October, word of desperate conditions in the camp arrived. Koretz, who had already been arrested twice, negotiated with Max Merten, the local German commander, to ransom the Jews at the cost of two and a half billion drachmas. When Merten changed the ransom to three and a half billion, the Jews were forced to hand over the five-century-old, eighty-six-acre Jewish cemetery in the heart of the city to Aristotle University, which had long coveted the land for expansion. On December 6, 1942, the cemetery was razed, its over 350,000 headstones smashed and buried in a ditch. For years after the war, students would still regularly find bone fragments on campus.

In early February 1943 two SS officers, Hauptsturmführer Dieter Wisliceny and his deputy Alois Brunner, an assistant to Eichmann, arrived in the city. Merten announced a curfew and ordered all Jews to wear the Star of David. "Salonika is filled with moving yellow stars which could be seen from a great distance," one survivor wrote. The entire Jewish community was segregated into ghettos, one in the Baron Hirsch neighborhood next to the railway station. Houses, offices, shops, and land were classified as Jewish; inventories of Jewish assets, including pet dogs, were required; and Jews were forbidden from joining any associations or organizations or engaging in any occupations. Soon they were even prohibited from commercial transactions. On March 6 the ghettos were sealed. Barbed wire surrounded the wooden walls, and five control towers and three gates were erected. Disease and crime ripped through the community. The local Greeks sold off all Jewish assets, with the proceeds placed in a special bank account. On March 10

Rabbi Koretz desperately offered the Germans half of all Jewish real estate in exchange for postponing rumored deportation to Poland. His offer was rejected.

On March 15, the first deportation train containing the 2,800 Jews trapped in the Baron Hirsch ghetto left for Auschwitz. Five days later they arrived in Poland, and all but six hundred were immediately put to death. The now vacant Baron Hirsch ghetto in Salonika became a holding pen where Jews were moved from other ghettos to await deportation. Four more trains left for Auschwitz during March. In early April the local metropolitan, Bishop Gennadios—counterpart and subordinate of Damaskinos in the capital—mediated a meeting at his office between Rabbi Koretz and Greek prime minister Ioannis Rallis to try to stop the deportations. The next day the rabbi was stripped of his office and arrested once again.

Another nine trainloads departed in April. In May four more followed, including Jews rounded up from surrounding communities. June saw 820 "privileged Jews" shipped to Auschwitz. In August the last two trainloads departed, carrying Rabbi Koretz and his family, over three hundred Jews with Spanish citizenship, and all the survivors of the forced labor camps. Koretz ended up in Bergen-Belsen and then in Theresienstadt, where he contracted typhus and died. By the end of the summer of 1943, almost no Jews remained in Salonika. The only ones left in the country were the several thousand who lived in Italian-occupied Greece, centering on Athens, and those who had managed to flee there.

In Athens, Damaskinos was shaken by what he heard was happening in Salonika and elsewhere to the Jews. By contrast, the capital was a hotbed of resistance. Within days of the occupation, the partisan Manolis Glezos had torn down the swastika flying over the Acropolis. Resistance groups of all political stripes immediately began to form. They would fight the Nazis from the hills, and even if they did not agree with each other, they would work together to save Jews and other refugees.

A number of prominent Athenian Jews soon approached Damaskinos and other leaders of civil society for help. The archbishop was sick in bed when they arrived, but was immediately moved to tears. "We all decided to protest in writing," recalled Thodoros Moridis, a well-known actor and head of the National Theatre of Greece. The great poet Angelos Sikelianos composed letters to the quisling prime minister Konstantinos Logothetopoulos and to German plenipotentiary Günther Altenburg, overseer of the Reich's puppet government in Greece. First to sign was Damaskinos. By going on record, he became the only head of a European church to formally condemn the Nazis for the Final Solution. He was joined by almost thirty heads of academic, cultural, commercial, and professional associations, from the University of Athens to the Greek pharmacists' association, bar association, chamber of commerce, and actors' guild. It was, in the view of its signers, "a protest by the totality of the citizens of Athens."

The letter to the prime minister declared that the Orthodox Church, the academy, and the Greek people were shocked and "deeply grieved" to hear that the first deportation trains had already departed, a violation of the terms of the armistice, which stated that all Greeks would be treated equally regardless of religion. It continued at length, describing the contribution of the Greek Jews to the nation: "For a long time, we have lived together in both slavery and freedom, and we have come to appreciate their feelings, their brotherly attitude, their economic activity and, most important, their indefectible patriotism. Evidence of this patriotism is the great number of victims sacrificed by the Greek Jewish community without regret and without hesitation on the altar of duty when our country was in peril." The letter concluded with an appeal to the judgment of history:

Let no one forget that all actions done during these difficult times, even those actions that lie beyond our will and power, will be assessed some day by the nation and will be subjected to historical investigation. In that time of judgment, the responsibility of the leaders will weigh heavily upon the conscience of the nation if today the leaders fail to protest boldly in the name of the nation against such unjust measures as the deportation of the Greek Jews, which are an insult to our national unity and honor.

In fact, both Logothetopoulos and his predecessor, Georgios Tsolakoglou, had tried to intervene for the Greek Jews, but to no avail. After Logothetopoulos was replaced with Rallis, the Damaskinos group sent a second letter directly to Altenburg again, pointing out that at the surrender of Salonika, the Germans had declared that they would "protect the lives, honour and property of the population," including the Jews. Indeed, they quoted a proclamation by Tsolakoglou that "no Jewish issues exist or will ever exist in Greece."

The letter was entirely ignored.

The almost total destruction of the Sephardic community in Salonika shocked Jews and non-Jews alike. The Salonikan Jews did not go quietly, however. Even at Auschwitz, they maintained their distinctive manner. In his memoir, Primo Levi recalled a group of "those admirable and terrible Jews of Salonika" who had managed to stay alive. "These few survivors from the Jewish colony of Salonika, with their two languages, Spanish and Greek, and their numerous activities, are the repositories of a concrete, mundane, conscious wisdom, in which the traditions of all the Mediterranean civilizations blend together." To Levi, "their aversion to gratuitous brutality, their amazing consciousness of the survival of at least a potential human dignity, made of the Greeks the most coherent national nucleus in the Lager, and in this respect, the most civilized." Not surprisingly, they would be part of the attempted uprising at Auschwitz on October 7, 1944. But in the end, almost all perished.

——

Things suddenly became mortally dangerous for the remaining Jews of Greece. On September 8, 1943, Italy capitulated to the Allies, and Jews under their occupation were immediately endangered as the Germans moved into the former Italian zone. As elsewhere, the Italians had refused to round up Jews, viewing the Nazi program as barbaric. "The Italians are extremely lax in their treatment of Jews," Joseph Goebbels complained in his diary. But now the Germans moved to implement the Final Solution. The Gestapo arrived in Athens within two weeks, and Wisliceny immediately summoned the chief rabbi of Athens, Eliyahu Barzilai, and demanded a complete census of all local and foreign Jews, a list of their assets, and the names of the ten richest Jewish residents in Athens be turned over within two hours.

Barzilai somehow managed to get the deadline extended over the weekend. He quickly convened the community council and communicated the German demands, then got in touch with his friend and counterpart Damaskinos for help. Damaskinos was convinced that there could be no accommodation with the Nazis that did not end in tragedy, and he strongly urged Barzilai to advise all Jews to immediately flee and seek protection with the partisans. The Nazi plans, he explained, were the murder and destruction of the Jews. Damaskinos offered to arrange for the rabbi to flee to Turkey on a British submarine. Unwilling to leave his wife and daughter, Barzilai declined.

Damaskinos now moved into action. He called his friend Panos Haldezos, the general director of the Athens municipality. "I have made my cross, have spoken with God, and decided to save as many Jewish souls as I can," he told him. "Even if I were to endanger myself, I will baptize the Jews, and you will issue Municipal documents, so that they obtain identity cards, as Christian Greeks." At the heart of this massive operation would be Angelos Evert, the police chief of Athens and scion of an aristocratic Hellenophile German family that had moved to Greece in the late nineteenth century. He had been appointed police commissioner in September 1941, shortly after the Nazi invasion. A clandestine supporter of the Resistance who maintained contact with the Greek government-in-exile in Cairo, Evert was willing to risk his life to help the Jews, many of whom lived in his jurisdiction.

Damaskinos and Evert went to work to provide papers to as many Jews as possible. The church issued hundreds of Greek Orthodox baptismal certificates. Evert oversaw the production of even more identity cards with false Greek names for those in hiding or fleeing for their lives. With such papers, the Jews were able to change houses, hide, and circulate throughout the city. Evert was joined by many colleagues in the police force, in particular Dimitrios Vranopoulos, police chief of the port of Piraeus, and Michail Glykas, the commander of the Athenian Sixth District, where many of the Athenian Jews lived. The number of papers issued by these men and their colleagues is estimated to be over twenty-seven thousand. Vranopoulos was particularly focused on keeping families together, and personally issued more than five thousand fake identification cards to Greek Jews.

Other officials provided papers to the extent they had the power to do so. Dimitrios Vlastaris, a director of the Service for Foreigners, gave papers to hundreds of Jews from Austria, Germany, Hungary, and Czechoslovakia; aid to Greeks from central Europe making their way by boat to Palestine, despite vociferous complaints from the German embassy; and hundreds of transit visas to German Jews so they could travel to the United States through the port of Piraeus. Reverend Irineos Typaldos of the Spanish embassy provided identification cards to descendants of Spanish Jews expelled from the country four hundred years earlier, papers that spared them from being deported to Auschwitz. The risks to all were enormous. Had anyone denounced them to the Gestapo, they would have been summarily executed.

———

Among the Jews in the capital, forty-eight-year-old Sam Elie Modiano, a former newspaper editor and publisher in Salonika and now director of Reuters in Greece, was near the top of the Gestapo's most wanted list. Modiano had fled from Salonika a few months earlier, having arranged for Italian identity cards from Giuseppe Castruccio, the local consul general, and given them to four hundred Jews whom he transported with him to Athens in an Italian military convoy, "to the great chagrin of the German authorities." With the help of Greek friends, he requisitioned two schools in Athens where he housed these "pseudo-Italians." The Germans were so livid that when they initially summoned Barzilai they specifically demanded to know the whereabouts of Modiano and his refugees.

Barzilai got a warning to Modiano through a member of the community council. Police chief Evert advised him to change where he was living and have the "pseudo-Italians" at the schools spread out into different neighborhoods of Athens. "I followed this advice," Modiano wrote, "and thanks to the help of Mr. Pierre Nuccio, consul-general of Italy in Athens, distributed to [the other refugees] amounts of money generously provided by Italians." Evert also provided identification cards to Modiano, his wife, Nella, and his sons, Elie and Mario, signing them himself and affixing the official embossed seal of the office of police. The papers allowed the family to survive in hiding in Athens. At least fifty other families were similarly rescued by Evert, who often distributed papers through the intermediation of trusted Christian friends. As Modiano later testified, Evert "provided counsel to Jews and cooperated with Damaskinos, on one occasion personally saving young Jewish girls who were assigned to Christian families until the end of the war. He risked his life and could have been betrayed at any time by employees or Gestapo spies, German or Greek."

Evert also told Modiano not to worry about Rabbi Barzilai. After he saw Damaskinos following his summons by the Nazis, the rabbi had immediately met again with the Jewish community council, destroyed all community records, and advised all Jews to take flight as he had been instructed. Sunday at dawn, a jeep pulled up in front of Barzilai's house and took the rabbi and his family to the mountainous areas of western Greece controlled by the Resistance. On Monday morning the rabbi did not show up for his meeting with the Gestapo. When the Nazis went to look for him at home and at the synagogue, he was gone. The intended message to his coreligionists was dramatic: get out, fast. And as the rabbi noted in his memoirs after the war, his escape was possible only because of Damaskinos and Evert. Without them, he and the other Jews would have been captured.

After he met with Barzilai, according to one Jewish leader who was present, Damaskinos immediately instructed his secretary Ioannis Georgakis (later director general of Olympic Airways) to give "the order that the priests should assist the Jews and that the convents be open to those who wished to hide there." At his direction, the Church of Greece denounced Hitler's plans and instructed its metropolitans to make this position clear in their sermons. Members of congregations were urged to hide Jews. One Athenian nun, Sister Hélène Capart, smuggled food to hidden Jewish families who could not obtain any of the heavily rationed supply. In Volos, the metropolitan Ioakeim worked with the mayor to smuggle Jews to the countryside, saving nearly three-quarters of the local population. Many of the clergy risked their lives to take action. It is estimated that 250 Jewish children were personally saved by Orthodox clerics. At least six hundred clergymen were arrested for helping Jews. In one instance, a priest was executed for his bravery.

Other members of the Greek community did their part as well. The partisans in the hills and the countryside protected those Jews who made it to their territory. Dr. Mano Karzis, for example, a prominent doctor and former vice president of the Chamber of Deputies, obtained fake identity papers, scarce food, and even official positions in hospitals for Jewish doctors and dentists and their families. When Jews were no longer able to circulate in Athens at the peak of the danger, he also used his car, as president of the medical association, to deliver medicine to Jews in hiding, risking his life.

And on the arrow-headed island of Zakynthos, twelve miles offshore in the Ionian Sea, the mayor Loukas Karrer and the metropolitan Chrysostomos—inspired by Damaskinos—resisted an order by the local German commander to turn over the names of the two hundred Jews who lived there.

"Here is the list of Jews you require," Chrysostomos had said when he handed over the document.

On the paper, he had written only two names: his own and the mayor's.

Under their leadership, the islanders hid their Jewish neighbors in their homes all over the hills and mountains. All of them survived. Its Jews would thereafter refer to Zakynthos as "the island of the just."

Athens and its environs were thus able to remain something of a refuge despite the Nazi presence. The Germans were simply unable to track the many Jews with fake ecclesiastical and municipal papers. When Stroop ordered the assembly of all Jews in October 1943, just two hundred showed up, despite dire warnings of punishment for not appearing. By March of the following year, the Nazis had only managed to track down fifteen hundred Jews. Sadly, some eighty boxcars of Athenian Jews were nonetheless eventually deported to Auschwitz, as well as Jews from Chalkis, Thessaly, and the Dodecanese. But in the end, two-thirds of the Jews of Athens would survive due to help from their neighbors.

Among the two thousand Jews who had fled Salonika was Haimaki Cohen, a wealthy banker who left on the eve of the occupation in 1941 for Athens with his wife, Rachel, and five children. Cohen had previously served several terms as a deputy in the Greek parliament and been a friend of the royal family for decades. He hosted King George I and his sons at his home in Trikala in Thessaly twice, and after Salonika formally joined Greece, the king offered Cohen a medal for his important services to the nation, which he declined out of modesty. The king told him that if he ever needed help, all he need do was ask. Cohen relocated with his family to Salonika after the First World War. Although King George was assassinated in 1913, Cohen frequently traveled to Athens over the years and often saw the royal family. These connections would prove far more crucial than he ever could have realized.

The Cohens had been secure in Athens until the Italian surrender in September 1943, when the situation became dire overnight. Haimaki had passed away in January and his son Alfred, a lawyer, had assumed leadership of the family. While he and his brothers Michel, Elie, and Jacques planned to escape to the mountains to join the partisans or across the Aegean to the free Greek forces fighting alongside the Allies in the Middle East, they first had to find refuge for their mother and their sister Tilde. Initially they found an ideal hiding place on the farm of three elderly women, the Cristakis, whose long-deceased father had known Haimaki years earlier. Well-educated Protestants originally from Crete, the sisters lived quietly on the outskirts of Athens along with one of their sons, a devoted servant, and an old gardener. Although they barely knew the Cohens and despite the Gestapo's declaration that they would execute anyone harboring Jews, the Cristakis agreed to hide not only the Cohen women but also the four boys.

Unfortunately, the sanctuary lasted only a few weeks. Purely by chance, one of Alfred's friends overheard a conversation in an obscure area of Athens. "As far as the Cohens are concerned, no need to worry," he heard someone say. "They are all very well hidden on the Cristaki farm." Their cover had been blown. That night Alfred could not sleep, racking his brain for some solution to their predicament. Then he remembered King George's promise. The royals were by then in exile, but two princesses had decided to stay in Athens, one of whom had been a guest in the Cohen home as a young woman and who was known as a humanitarian. Alfred determined to track down Princess Alice of Battenberg, the current king's sister-in-law.

When Princess Victoria Alice Elizabeth Julia Marie was born on February 25, 1885, in the Tapestry Room at Windsor Castle, her great-grandmother Queen Victoria insisted on being present. The infant, the Queen noted in her diary, was "very small, thin & dark. I held it for a few moments in my arms." Victoria would be a major part of the baby's life until she died when Alice was sixteen. Alice's father was the German prince Louis of Battenberg; her mother was Princess Victoria of Hesse-Darmstadt, whose father, the Grand Duke Ludwig IV, had made a spectacular match by marrying the daughter of Queen Victoria, thus propelling himself from lord of a small garrison town to a position as a highly prominent diplomat. Princess Alice's pedigree was extraordinary: one aunt was the Czarina Alexandra, and her cousins included Kaiser Wilhelm II, the kings of Norway and Denmark, and the queens of Spain and Romania.

When Princess Alice was a young child, her mother noticed that something was wrong with her pronunciation, and she was slow in learning to talk. Alice was diagnosed with deafness. Her mother was determined that she would overcome the infirmity, and by the age of eight, Alice could fluently read lips in multiple languages. Although she would not hear anything until, in 1922, she allegedly heard a cuckoo bird, by the time she was fourteen she had learned to speak adequately in English, German, and French. Although it greatly upset her younger brother, the future Lord Mountbatten, Victoria insisted no one give extra accommodations to Alice. The girl appeared to take it in stride.

In 1902 at the coronation of King Edward VII, the teenage Princess Alice met Prince Andrew of Greece and Denmark, the fourth son of George I, king of Greece, and his Russian wife Olga, a member of the Romanov dynasty. Alice and Andrew were married a year later in Darmstadt at one of the last great weddings of old Europe. She became Princess Andrew of Greece and Denmark, learned Greek, and moved to her husband's homeland, where he was in the army. Alice and Andrew had five children over the next eighteen years, four daughters and the youngest, born in 1921 on Corfu, a son, Philip, the future Duke of Edinburgh and husband of Queen Elizabeth II.

In 1908 Alice had a transformative experience when she traveled for a royal wedding to Russia. There she spent time with her aunt and godmother, Grand Duchess Elizabeth Feodorovna, whose husband, Grand Duke Sergei Alexandrovich, had been assassinated by a socialist three years earlier. The grand duchess had warned her husband—who espoused the extreme anti-Semitism of the Czarist court—that "God will punish us severely" when he expelled twenty thousand Jews from Moscow, and she believed there had been divine retribution. Deeply religious, Elizabeth went into profound mourning but also forgave her husband's assassin and unsuccessfully petitioned to have him pardoned. She devoted herself to the poor and the sick, selling off her jewels to found the Martha and Mary Convent for nurses, where she served as abbess. Alice was present for the laying of the foundation stone and would forever view her aunt as a model and inspiration. On her return to Greece, she threw herself into charity work.

The first two decades of the twentieth century were a catastrophic series of crises and tragedies for most of the royal households of Europe, culminating in the First World War. The Habsburgs' Austro-Hungarian Empire collapsed with the war, and the kaiser was forced to abdicate. The Russian Revolution of 1917 led to the fall of the czar. After the Bolsheviks seized power in November, the royal family were doomed. In July 1918 Alice's aunt Alexandra and her family were executed under orders of Lenin. The same night, Grand Duchess

Elizabeth and five other Romanovs were taken to an abandoned iron ore mine and thrown down a sixty-foot shaft, with hand grenades following after them. Lenin was quite pleased with Elizabeth's execution. "Virtue with the crown on it," he declared, "is a greater enemy to the world revolution than a hundred tyrant czars."

The war took its toll on Alice's parents as well. Louis was regularly criticized as a foreigner, although he was a naturalized British subject. He was unfairly passed over as First Sea Lord because of his German heritage in 1911, taking up the post of Second Sea Lord instead, and at the outbreak of the First World War, anti-German sentiment forced his resignation. He and Victoria instead lived out the rest of the war on the Isle of Wight.

In the run-up to the Great War, major fault lines had also developed in Greece, which would plague the nation for decades. Andrew's oldest brother, Constantine, ascended the throne after their father's assassination in 1913 and maintained a controversial policy of neutrality during the First World War. Following the political intervention of France and Great Britain, Constantine agreed to go into exile with the crown prince George in June 1917, leaving his second son, Alexander, as king of a reunified, pro-Allied government. Andrew followed Constantine to Switzerland, taking Alice and his family with him.

Three years later, Alexander was bitten by a monkey while walking on the palace grounds and died of an infection. The resulting groundswell of affection led to the restoration of King Constantine in a plebiscite with near-unanimous approval, and he returned from exile in December 1920 to once again take up his throne. Princess Alice and Prince Andrew returned as well, moving into Mon Repos, a villa on Corfu originally built for the British high commissioner. Andrew was reinstated in the army as a major general. At the disastrous Battle of Sakarya against Turkey in August 1921, he rightly refused to follow orders to attack from his commanding officer, Anastasios Papoulas. After the Greeks lost the war, a group of pro-Venizelist officers led a revolt against the government. In its wake, the king was again forced from his throne, abdicating in favor of his son George II.

Seeking scapegoats for the loss, the government arrested Andrew on Corfu and court-martialed him on charges of disobeying his orders at Sakarya. Along with several other senior officers and politicians, he was tried in the infamous "Trial of the Six," an extralegal tribunal established to lay blame for the war. He was initially given a death sentence, but it was subsequently commuted to banishment for life. Alice, Andrew, and their five children, including the infant Philip, were evacuated on a British cruiser to Brindisi, in the heel of Italy. The family lost their Greek nationality and traveled under their Danish citizenship. They made their way to a small house in Saint-Cloud outside Paris that was owned by Andrew's sister-in-law, who was also Napoleon's great-niece. In 1924 a Hellenic Republic was proclaimed, and King George too was forced into exile.

Alice once again focused on work for the sick and poor and opened a shop to benefit Greek refugees. She became more and more religious, and in October 1928 she converted to the Orthodox Church. Alice soon began to claim that she was receiving divine messages and could heal the sick. Then she suffered a complete nervous breakdown. Several of the leading psychiatrists in Europe diagnosed her with paranoid schizophrenia, and she was committed in 1930 to the famous sanatorium at Kreuzlingen, in Switzerland, where one of her fellow patients was the ballet dancer Vaslav Nijinsky. The director of the facility, Ludwig Binswanger, confirmed the diagnosis and consulted with Sigmund Freud, who recommended electroshock and X-ray treatment. Alice repeatedly insisted that she was sane and made several attempts to escape over the two years she was held against her will. Devastated by the experience, she severed ties with all her relatives except her mother and wandered the Continent.

During Alice's commitment, all four of her daughters had married German princes. Philip was sent to Britain to be educated and lived with Alice's mother at Kensington Palace. Andrew moved to the Riviera, where he took up with Andrée Lafayette. He and the rest of his family had not seen Alice since 1931.

On November 16, 1937, Alice's third daughter, Cecilie, died tragically in a Sabena plane crash, causing an unexpected family reunion at the funeral in Darmstadt. Alice restored contact with her family, in particular her son, Philip. In 1938 she moved back to Athens, renting a two-bedroom flat on the rue Coumbari, which she decorated with old-fashioned furniture and pictures of the Battenbergs. In mid-1939, having completed his course at the Royal Naval College, Philip moved to Athens to spend time with his mother and begin to know his countrymen.

Greece was now firmly under the control of Ioannis Metaxas, an aristocrat and military officer who had a long history of staunch loyalty to the monarchy. Metaxas banned anti-Semitic propaganda, his officials were outspoken in protecting Jewish rights, and there were Jews in his government. Metaxas even wrote the Jewish community in Athens to say that he was "moved deeply" by their support, which "gives me strength to carry on my task."

War was the foremost issue. In October 1940, after an accelerating campaign by Benito Mussolini against Greece, Italy invaded. The Italian forces were met with fierce resistance and ultimately repelled back into Albania. The Jewish community sent thirteen thousand soldiers to join the fight, and the first senior Greek officer killed was one of them, Colonel Mordechai Frizis. At the peak of Greek momentum, Metaxas suddenly died of a bacterial throat infection on January 29, 1941. In February Churchill dispatched British foreign secretary Anthony Eden to meet with the Greek government and offer troops to help them fight back. But when Bulgaria joined the Axis in March, German troops began to mass. After another disastrous offensive by the Italians, the Germans invaded Greece themselves on April 6.

On April 27 Athens fell to the Germans. On May 20 the bombardment of Crete, where the king and government had moved, began, and within the next two weeks, despite heroic resistance, the Wehrmacht took over the island, forcing the government to flee to Cairo. Determined not to be a puppet of the Nazis, George II then fled to England. There he oversaw the government-in-exile with his son, Crown Prince Constantine, and his new prime minister, Emmanouil Tsouderos.

The rest of the royal family went into exile in South Africa with the sole exception of Princess Alice and her sister-in-law Elena, a first cousin of the last czar, who wanted to stay because her husband was buried near Athens. Since the war had broken out, Alice had been in the awkward position of having two of her sons-in-law fighting for the Germans—Berthold, Margrave of Baden, who was injured with the Wehrmacht in France in 1940, and the Nazi SS officer Prince Christoph of Hesse—while her son was in the Royal Navy. Meanwhile Andrew, trapped in Vichy France, was completely severed from communication with either Alice or Philip.

Alice somehow got a stipend from the king and devoted herself to the Swedish and Swiss Red Cross, even flying to Sweden to visit her sister Louise, who was married to the crown prince, and bringing back medical supplies. Early in the occupation, food became extremely scarce. Mass starvation set in, killing up to a thousand people a day in Athens and Piraeus, many of them children. Alice moved into her brother-in-law Prince George's vacated three-story villa on the corner of Academia and Demokritou Streets in the center of Athens to be closer to her charity work. During the bitter winter, she lost over fifty pounds. Nonetheless, she organized one of the largest soup kitchens in Athens, serving dry bean and chickpea soup cooked in large cauldrons, garnished with parsley, onions, and olive oil. She reported to her brother that the kitchen was feeding seventeen thousand children six years old and younger. She also founded two orphanages, one for boys, one for girls.

———

It was not surprising, then, that Alfred Cohen thought that the princess would be sympathetic to his family's plight. But he needed to find an intermediary to convey the request for shelter. The Cohens approached an acquaintance from Athenian society, Madame Eliasco, who agreed to talk to Alice. Shortly thereafter, Alfred and his sister Tilde, who wore a veil to disguise herself, were walking on the sidewalk outside the villa where Alice lived. Suddenly a woman across the street crossed over to talk to the siblings. As it turned out, she was the wife of Themistoklis Sophoulis, an archaeologist from Samos and three-time prime minister of Greece. She too was eager to help and Tilde confided in her their desire to get in touch with the princess. At that very moment as it happened, the door to the palace opened, and another woman came down the stairs and introduced the Cohens to Madame Deligianni, her best friend, whom she said could make the necessary approach to Princess Alice.

Madame Deligianni soon came back with the news that Alice was happy to host Tilde and Rachel in her home.* The next day Alfred escorted his mother and sister to the back entrance to the palace. Alice gave them a two-bedroom apartment on the third floor, which had recently been the home of her husband's cousin Prince Peter, now out of the country. She told her staff that she was hosting her children's former Swiss nanny, who was now under threat from Hitler, and that she expected the servants to make the stay as comfortable as possible. Alice tried her best to guard their identities, Jacques Cohen noted, "and successfully covered the courageous part she was playing in these rescues."

With their mother and sister well hidden, the Cohen brothers

———

* It was a lucky meeting. In fact, when Madame Eliasco had recently asked Alice to hide the Cohens, the princess had demurred, considering the socialite too talkative to keep a secret. Alice had been trying to get in contact with the Cohens but did not know how to reach them.

now decided to make their escape. Michel took up an offer from a friend to hide in his apartment on the island of Spetses, which was not occupied by the Germans. The other three brothers—Alfred, Elie, and Jacques—were determined to make it to Cairo, where the Greek government-in-exile was headquartered. Their family friend Demosthenes Pouris arranged for false identity cards from Damoskinos's palace and served as intermediary with the Resistance, which each evening provided a different safe house for each brother. Pouris also had good relationships at the Ministry of Foreign Affairs and put the three boys in touch with members of the underground who were preparing a voyage to get several diplomats to Egypt. After significant challenges and great expenditure, the Cohens departed for the Attic coast opposite the large island of Euboea, which was to serve as their embarkation point as it had for the Greek armada under Agamemnon when it departed for Troy. When darkness fell, a guide took them across the canal to the island, and they traveled by foot and mule to Euboea's other side, where they were scheduled to meet the diplomatic boat to neutral Turkey and from there go on to Cairo.

Unfortunately, Communist partisans intercepted the Greek diplomats and forced them to return immediately to Athens. Those fleeing the Germans, like the Cohens, were left to their own devices on the island. After several days of wandering, the brothers reached the village of Tsakeous, where the British were providing partisans with supplies. Here Pouris helped them find passage on one of the small wooden boats departing for Turkey, paying for the tickets as they had no more money. The Cohens boarded one vessel filled with Jews from Athens who had been waiting on the coast or in a nearby cave. They were able to talk to the ship's British commander, who took them under his wing and dropped them off after twenty hours at an isolated village on the Turkish coast near Chesme.

After a night beneath the stars, the authorities transferred the brothers to Smyrna, where they were interned in a concentration camp.

The British consulate quickly liberated them and transferred them to a refugee camp in Aleppo, where they were given the choice of going to Palestine and forfeiting their Greek citizenship or of joining the Greek army in the Middle East, which they immediately opted to do. In the first days of December 1943 they were transferred to a camp on the outskirts of Cairo and made themselves available to the Greek government for service. Jacques was attached as an interpreter to the Ministry of Foreign Affairs. Alfred, the attorney, was appointed captain of military justice. Elie, who was an engineer, served in the Ministry of Reconstruction.

Meanwhile, however, things had not gone smoothly for Michel on Spetses. A few weeks after his arrival, a rumor went around that the apartment in which he had taken refuge was occupied by a British officer. Having decided that he could not take the risk of being taken for an enemy soldier, he made his way back to Athens. There he made contact with Demosthenes Pouris, who informed him that his brothers had made it to the army in Cairo, and that his mother and sister were living with Princess Alice. Michel wanted to escape to the Middle East as well, and attempted to find a way with the help of Jean Vamvakaris and his sister Frosso, children of one of the Cristakis, but ultimately passage could not be found.

Pouris, acting as the family's go-between, brought word that the princess's lady-in-waiting, Madame Simopoulou, had arranged for Michel to join his mother and sister on the third floor of the palace. In December they were reunited, and Michel was told he would have to avoid all contact with the outside world. The time in hiding felt endless; the only people allowed to visit the Cohens other than the princess were Madame Simopoulou, who oversaw their care, and Pouris, whom Michel described gratefully as "relentless in his devotion to the family."

The princess regularly visited her guests, and Michel noticed that she was "visibly happy to be able to provide hospitality to a persecuted Jewish family." She spent long afternoons drinking tea with Rachel, confided that she felt very close to Judaism, and continually asked questions about their beliefs. The danger was constant, despite the princess's stature; an Italian princess had been sent to a concentration camp for harboring Jews. Signs were everywhere in Athens warning of dire consequences for such actions, including summary execution.

Damaskinos's palace was across the street from the villa, and German guards were posted there. Because of her German heritage, the Nazis initially assumed that Alice was an ally. But when a general visited her, she refused to shake his hand. When he asked what he might do for her, she replied, "You can take your troops out of my country." Nonetheless, she was mostly left alone. Later, perhaps on a tip, the Gestapo grew suspicious and came to question her several times. She pretended not to understand them due to her deafness and a feigned dimness. "She thus saved [my family's] lives," Jacques Cohen recalled. Had she been caught, she would have likely been shot.

———

In October 1944 Athens was liberated, and the Cohens were able to come out of hiding. Their apartment had been occupied by the Germans, so Princess Alice allowed them to stay for several weeks while it was being refurbished. The last few months had been brutal, including for Alice. The future British prime minister Harold Macmillan visited her and noted that she was "living in humble, not to say somewhat squalid conditions." She wrote to Philip to say that in the last week before liberation, she had only bread and butter and had not eaten meat in months. At the end of 1944, talk of the royal family returning was beginning to circulate. But Alice was informed that her husband had died at the Hotel Métropole in Monte Carlo. Prince Philip traveled to get his father's effects, including a signet ring he would wear from then on.

By December the joy of liberation was quickly overshadowed by a full-blown civil war between Communists and a coalition of royalists, Metaxists, and republicans backed by British forces. Alice wandered the streets freely, and the British army was terrified that she would be hit by a stray bullet as she went to distribute food to children and soldiers. "They tell me that you don't hear the shot that kills you and in any case I am deaf. So, why worry about that?" she said.

On December 26 Churchill made a Boxing Day visit to Athens. Although he was determined to have George II restored to his throne as soon as possible, a May 1944 conference in Lebanon of the parties to the civil war called for a regency to be followed by a referendum on the future of the monarchy. On December 31 King George appointed as regent a hero of the war: Archbishop Damaskinos. After a chaotic year that saw several governments fall, Damaskinos briefly became prime minister. At the end of 1945 the king was finally restored to his throne, and reigned for two more years until his death.

Princess Alice stayed in Greece after the civil war and founded a nursing order of nuns, the Christian Sisterhood of Martha and Mary, modeled on her aunt Elizabeth's Martha and Mary Convent in Moscow, which had inspired her decades earlier. She funded the enterprise in part by selling her possessions and, while she never took formal vows, took to dressing in the gray habit of a nun.

Alice never talked about what she had done for the Cohens. She continued to visit them in the years following the war, often at their home, but would never accept their thanks. "We were very privileged," Michel Cohen said of Princess Alice. "Very few Jews survived in Greece. It took great courage to defy the Germans." His brother Jacques added, "She showed her courage and humanity, ignoring the menace of the Nazis, by giving help to those in peril [and] despising German occupation law."

At the end of the war, the Greek government-in-exile transferred to Cava de' Tirreni, near Salerno, and Jacques Cohen was attached to the Greek delegation for Italian affairs. After relations between the two countries had been reinstated, he joined the Greek embassy in Rome, the start of a diplomatic career that would eventually take him to the Greek delegation to NATO. In 1947 Princess Alice passed through Rome on her way to Philip's wedding to Princess Elizabeth, the heir to the British crown, and Jacques arranged to see her. "I expressed to her my sincerest thankfulness to which she answered in minimizing her courageous action."

The story only became known to Alice's family because Alfred Cohen shared it with his friend the antisubmarine expert Rear Admiral Clarence Howard-Johnston, who relayed it to Lord Mountbatten, Alice's youngest brother. After the Colonel's coup in 1967 drove the Greek royal family into permanent exile, Alice lived out her remaining two years at Buckingham Palace with her son and daughter-in-law. When she died in 1969 with virtually no possessions, she was buried at Windsor Palace. But her wishes were eventually honored when she was reinterred in 1988 in Jerusalem at the Church of Mary Magdalene on the Mount of Olives, next to her great-aunt Grand Duchess Elizabeth. The story of her heroism became more widely known after an effort by the Cohens to have a street named after her in Israel. She was recognized as a Righteous Among the Nations in 1993. Michel Cohen, who had moved to Paris, came to the ceremony, but was too moved to speak.

The fate of the Greek Jews was one of the most dire in Europe. Almost 90 percent were murdered by the Nazis. At the war's end, of the 79,000 Greek Jews, only around 5,000 remained. But nearly all who survived owed their lives to courageous action on the part of the church, the police, the partisans, and their ordinary neighbors. Without Damaskinos and those many who followed him, the result might have been complete annihilation of the Jews, a feat the Nazis were not able to accomplish even in Germany itself.

As was often the case, the Righteous did not believe they had done anything heroic, and they rarely spoke about their actions. So it was with Damaskinos and so it was with Princess Alice. As Prince Philip remarked at Yad Vashem, "In retrospect, this reticence may seem strange, but I suspect that it never occurred to [my mother] that her action was in any way special. She was a person with deep religious faith and she would have considered it to be a totally human action to help fellow human beings in distress."

4

Some Medals Are Pinned to Your Soul

IN 1938 GINO BARTALI WON THE TOUR DE FRANCE AND BECAME ONE OF THE most famous athletes in Europe. It should have been a triumph—not only for him, but for Benito Mussolini and his Fascist regime. Sports were incredibly important to Il Duce, who is said to have proclaimed his intention to turn Italy from a nation of mandolin players into one of warriors. The propaganda machine showed Mussolini himself as a great sportsman. He encouraged participation in athletics of all kinds and closely managed physical fitness for schoolchildren. To his delight, Italy had racked up victories on the international stage. The Italian team earned the second highest medal haul at the Los Angeles Olympics in 1932, and in 1933 boxer Primo Carnera became the heavyweight champion. Then in 1934 the Italy hosted and won the soccer World Cup. Now, in cycling-obsessed Italy, Mussolini desperately wanted victory at the Tour, the sport's most prestigious event. Italian fans flocked to France to cheer on their countryman Bartali as he stormed through the brutal climbs in the Alps and Pyrenees. On July 31 he crossed the finish line in the famed yellow jersey of the leader. In Paris "the ovations were not only directed at the triumphant one of the Tour de France," the *Gazetta dello Sport* proclaimed. "They were exalting the athletic and moral virtue of an exemplar of our race."

But unlike other Italian champions, Bartali did not dedicate his victory to Il Duce. Largely apolitical and a devout Catholic, he was instead loyal to the church. Bartali opposed fascist doctrine and did not want to present himself as an Aryan champion. "They always tried to show off what he did as proof of what fascism could do," one of his teammates noted. "But Bartali wouldn't cooperate." On Italian radio, Mussolini's secret police complained, he "mumbled" rather than offer praise to the government. On the French radio, he merely thanked his fans in France and at home. The next day, trailed by the press, Bartali went to mass at Notre-Dame-des-Victoires and laid his victory wreath at the feet of the Madonna.

The slight did not go unnoticed by Mussolini. A major French cycling magazine sent a reporter to cover what it assumed would be a rapturous homecoming. "Not a cat at the train station. No organized reception. Nothing. I don't understand," the journalist wrote. "An Italian wins the Tour de France, he wins a sensational international victory and his compatriots—who are Latins prone to delirious joy—don't react much at all? There's a problem." Mussolini canceled a special medal ceremony, and the head of the Italian Cycling Federation did not attend Bartali's victory lap at the velodrome in Turin. The Ufficio Stampa, the official press office, gave its instructions on August 9: "The newspapers should cover Bartali exclusively as a sportsman without any useless accounts of his life as a private citizen."

The public insult to Il Duce risked not just muted press coverage. "The party has started a campaign against me, accusing me of a lack of patriotism," Bartali wrote. "But I'm not the type to back down." The danger was real. The only other Italian to win the Tour de France, Ottavio Bottecchia, had spoken out against the regime more than a decade earlier. Shortly thereafter, in 1927, he was killed in a highly suspicious accident while on a training ride. Most believed he had been murdered by the Fascists. And if Bartali's postvictory behavior had not now put him in similar danger, then his clandestine work helping refugees a few years later certainly would.

———

Bartali was born on July 18, 1914, the son of a day laborer and his wife. A slight, blue-eyed boy with dark curly hair, he grew up in a two-room apartment without running water or electricity with two older sisters and a younger brother, Giulio. The main business of his hometown of Ponte a Ema, four miles southeast of Florence, was laundry, which the local women did and the men delivered back into the city. It was as picturesque as it was poor, surrounded by vineyards, rolling hills, and orchards. Bartali spent much of his time outdoors. He had a competitive streak from the beginning, and spent hours playing marbles, games often ending in brawls that the smaller Bartali inevitably lost.

Bartali was fascinated by the bicycle his father used to ride to the various jobs he managed to scrounge up. The boy would sneak onto it, teaching himself how to balance when he was still too small to reach the pedals from the seat. Unaware of the sleek racing bikes with curled handlebars capturing the Italian imagination, Bartali was entranced by even the rudimentary bikes he saw everywhere. "A lot of time was still to pass before I set eyes on a sports paper," he remembered, "and before I knew about the existence of a world in which you could go racing in a pair of black shorts and a colored jersey." But he desperately wanted his own bicycle.

As it happened, it became a necessity. Bartali hated school, but his father was determined that he would at least complete the sixth grade. The local schoolhouse ended in fifth grade, so Bartali would need to go into Florence for his final year. The only realistic way to commute was on a bicycle. His father told him he would need to earn the money to buy one. His mother, Giulia, found the twelve-year-old Bartali a job sorting raffia, long palm frond fibers used to make ties for grapevines and nursery plants. "From that pile of raffia that covered me up to my knees—my good father Torello would tell me—should come a solid bicycle with which to reach Florence every day as soon as autumn came," Bartali recalled. It was tedious work, but by end of summer he had almost enough lire and, with contributions from his father and sisters, was able to buy a rusty, extremely used bike. "You can imagine my joy," he remembered. "The first nights I kept tossing and turning in my bed from the desire for it to be day so that I could ride it."

Bartali was hooked. Every day he rode in and out of Florence with his friends, usually by the longest routes. One of his favorites was the difficult climb up to the Piazzale Michelangelo. "When I descended into Florence, the air was clear, one could smell the fresh perfume of the green from the trees and from the meadows," he remembered. "The water from the Arno was limpid, like the pure water of the creek in my native village, the Ema." The excitement of the city was magnetic. He particularly loved the bike shop where his older cousin Armandino Sizzi worked, a hub of activity where professionals and amateurs came for repairs and to compare notes.

Bartali always beat his friends to the top of hills, where he watched them struggle up breathlessly after him. Sometimes the boys would challenge amateur riders in training. "Despite their perfect bicycles, they didn't always beat us, even though the bikes we pedaled were like lumbering horse buggies." Bartali would overtake them on climbs. "At first, even I was astounded and embarrassed by this discovery." He was working three days a week in the local bicycle shop when its owner, Oscar Casamonti, heard rumors of Bartali's prowess and invited him on a fifty-five-mile ride. Everyone besides Bartali had a racing bike. Halfway through, Casamonti sprinted out in front. When he turned around, only Gino had been able to keep up, not even pushing himself. "I didn't want to disrespect him, he was my boss!" Bartali admitted.

Casamonti was stunned. He took the boy home and told Torello and Giulia Bartali that Gino could be a champion. In the 1920s cycling was one of the world's most popular spectator sports, particularly in Europe. The Tour de France and its Italian equivalent, the Giro d'Italia, were major events and had made some of the cyclists wealthy celebrities. "They took a bicycle and conquered the world on the back of that fragile steel seahorse," one journalist wrote. Bartali now avidly followed the sport, "enchanted." The cyclists, with their spare tires slung over their shoulders and their large goggles, were his heroes. Now his boss was telling his parents that he too could be a star.

But they would have none of it. The Florentine papers were filled with stories of bicycle accidents. Even professionals were occasionally killed in competition and his parents were terrified. When a friend attached a pair of curved racing handlebars to Bartali's bike, Torello told his son that if he "didn't remove it immediately from his sight, he would have it reduced to scrap metal in five minutes." The Bartalis were convinced that Gino was too weak for the sport, a feeling exacerbated in 1929 when he took six months to recover from severe pneumonia. Torello told Casamonti, "One day you will bring him back in pieces."

Bartali worked relentlessly to get into good physical condition and recruited others, including the local priest, to join Casamonti in pleading with his parents. Finally, on his seventeenth birthday, they relented. "My heart leapt," he wrote. "It was one of the best presents I had ever gotten in my life." The next day he won a competition. His racing career had begun.

Bartali woke up at dawn every morning to exercise. He became obsessed with nutrition, deciding that a combination of pasta and bananas was best. He went on long training rides, teaching himself to go with as little water as possible, and logged his progress so carefully that he was nicknamed the Accountant. He joined a local amateur club called L'Aquila and refined his technique, developing what he believed was the most important skill, a tolerance for pain or what he called his "capacity for suffering." Although he had a slight frame, rarely weighing more than one hundred and fifty pounds, Bartali considered himself made of hard wood "like the olive trees in the fields around Siena where my father was born." He had a signature style, repeatedly bursting out in front, slowing down, and then speeding up again. As he bounced up and down, "he looked like he was being electrocuted," recalled a competitor. It worked well, and in 1935 he turned professional, initially paying his dues as a supporting rider in the peloton. Shortly thereafter he won a race in Spain and became captain of a team sponsored by the bicycle manufacturer Legnano.

Soon Batali was earning enough to build a two-story home with a garden for his parents. He was often stopped for his autograph and hired a press secretary to handle his fan mail. But he was most focused on Adriana Bani, a teenage brunette he caught sight of from his friend Emilio Berti's pastry shop on Via del Corso, directly across the street from the fabric store where she worked. Women he did not know sent him passionate love letters, but when Bartali finally got up the nerve to speak to Adriana, she had never heard of him. "He was so embarrassed and funny in his shyness that it was sweet," she remembered. "And I fell in love with that, his purity of soul and his ingenuousness in everyday life." Adriana was the daughter of a conservative railway administrator, and her courtship was highly supervised. When Bartali visited, the sitting-room door would remain open at all times, and they could only go out in groups.

Adriana's mother was skeptical of someone earning a stable living on a bicycle. Adriana too was worried about Bartali's career. However, he was on the brink of stardom. On June 7, 1936, he wore the pink leader's jersey as he crossed the finish line of the Giro d'Italia in Milan, winning the 2,300-mile, three-week race considered the second most prestigious Grand Tour event. He was instantly the most celebrated cyclist in Italy.

Sadly, he did not have time to enjoy it. A week later, on June 14, his brother Giulio, a highly successful amateur, crashed into a car during a race in Turin at full speed. Bartali rushed to the hospital. The following day he prayed for hours at a nearby chapel while Giulio underwent surgery. It did not go well. Giulio died holding Bartali's hand.

"The deepest sadness fell on us like lead," Bartali recalled. "We went from the greatest joy to the most terrible pain." His parents' worst nightmares had come true, only the victim was their younger son. His mother begged Bartali to stop cycling. Racked with guilt, he fled to a small cabin by the sea, determined not to race again.

Friends and teammates begged him to reconsider. Fan letters poured in, and his press secretary himself wrote him his own letter, urging him not to end his career. One of his sisters even brought by his bicycle. In the end, it was Adriana who prevailed on him not to throw away his career at the age of twenty-two. Rather, he should race to honor his brother's memory. Bartali once again returned to his bicycle.

After his brother's death, Bartali became even more devout. He was an active member of Catholic Action, a lay group with six hundred thousand members that sponsored activities from Bible classes to summer camps. The church was thrilled, and Bartali spoke about the importance of his faith in his success. Catholic newspapers gave him fawning coverage, poets sang his praises, and a play was produced about his life. When the Fascist press mocked him as "the Little Monk," many journalists came to his defense. The Catholic Church was, perhaps, the only institution in Italy that could hold its own with the regime.

Bartali preferred not to become involved in politics, but in Italy at that time it was hard not to. His father had briefly flirted with socialism over a decade earlier, until one of his employers was murdered in his bed by Fascists. Terrified, Torello had asked Bartali to hide some pamphlets in the attic. However noble the goal, it was not worth it. "Politics is a trap," he warned Bartali darkly. "Keep your distance."

———

In 1937 Bartali set a goal to do something no one had ever done before. Not only did he want to win the Tour de France, but he wanted to win the Giro d'Italia in the same year. It seemed impossible: to ride over two thousand miles throughout Italy, followed by an even longer race through France—a distance comparable to that between Paris and Beijing—with only a few weeks off in between and a fresh set of world-class competitors in both contests.

The season did not start auspiciously. During a training ride, Bartali was caught in a snowstorm and developed bronchial pneumonia. Amazingly, six weeks later, in May 1937, he again won the Giro. The Fascist press began to trumpet the dream of winning the Giro and the Tour in the same year. But Bartali now was concerned about his health and began to speak about skipping the Tour. Mussolini would have none of it. His newspaper, *Il popolo d'Italia*, declared that Bartali needed "to understand that at the Tour de France the national honor of our cycling is at stake." It planted a rumor that Bartali was holding out for two hundred thousand lire to compete. "A soldier who defends his flag leaves the trenches, risking his life without thinking of his bank account," it declared. The head of the Fascist-controlled Italian Cycling Federation, a general, soon visited Bartali to ensure his participation. Bartali announced twelve days before the Tour that he would race.

Bartali was an exceptional mountain racer, and the Tour had two legendary passes through the Alps and the Pyrenees. Bartali made his move in the former, and after the Galibier mountain pass he was in the lead. The Italian delegation, dressed in suits and monocles, believed him on the way to victory, and his fans were beside themselves. But the next day, as he swerved to avoid hitting a teammate skidding over a bridge in the rain, Bartali was hurled into a frigid river. He got back on his bicycle with help from a teammate and finished the stage, clutching his injured torso, but he had lost nine minutes. He decided to continue and seemed to be gaining strength. But then suddenly, with the leader seventeen minutes ahead, the Italian Cycling Federation announced Bartali's withdrawal for health reasons.

Bartali believed it was because he was not a Party member, but it may have simply been that the federation believed that he had no chance of winning, and the risk of injury was not worth it. Bartali was in tears. To add further indignity, he was forced to pay his own way home, borrowing money for a train ticket. "I had such great dreams for the Tour," he said years later. "When the doctor didn't want me to race, 'they' made me race; when I should have withdrawn, they made me continue; when, after the four difficult stages, I was getting better, they sent me home." When he arrived, he was greeted by his fans' applause in the train station. He would always consider his forced withdrawal "the greatest injustice suffered during my career."

A few months later Bartali was summoned to meet with the regime's national sports directors. They told him that it was imperative that an Italian win the Tour de France. He was informed that he would not be competing in the 1938 Giro d'Italia so he could focus exclusively on the French competition. When he objected that he was sure he could win both, they were unmoved. "There was nothing else to say," he wrote later. "I had to grin and bear it." Feeling massive pressure, he found himself regularly visiting his brother's tomb.

On July 5 the Tour began. After an epic performance in the Alps in the mountain passes of the Col d'Allos, the Col de Vars, and the Col d'Izoard, he stormed to the lead in Briançon and never gave it up. On August 1 he rode into the Parc des Princes stadium in Paris and crossed the finish line the winner. It was his last major racing triumph before the war.

During the Tour, the first legal persecution of Italy's Jews emerged. In May, Hitler had visited Mussolini to much fanfare, making a whirlwind tour of Italy. The dictators had not always been allies, but had recently collaborated during the Spanish Civil War, with Il Duce declaring that their relationship would be the "axis" around which Europe would revolve. After Mussolini visited Germany in 1937, the führer decided to reciprocate just weeks after the annexation of Austria. The final stop of the trip was Florence, where a fortune was spent cleaning and refurbishing the city's main attractions. When Hitler and his entourage arrived, Nazi flags flew and crowds cheered the motorcade. Hitler visited the Uffizi and the Palazzo Pitti and was treated to an opera by Verdi. "Now no force can ever separate us," Mussolini told him when they said goodbye at the train station.

In retrospect, it would be a turning point for the Jews of Italy. Many Jews had fought for Italian unification and were well incorporated into Italian society. Indeed, Mussolini had previously publicly criticized the Nazis' anti-Semitism. But now, with Germany in the ascendant, Mussolini moved to ingratiate himself with Hitler. On the day of Bartali's triumph in the Pyrenees, the government published the *Manifesto of the Racial Scientists*, declaring that Italians were Aryan, and that Jews did not belong to the Italian race. It was an ominous moment for the forty-seven thousand Italian Jews and the ten thousand others who had fled there from elsewhere. The manifesto heralded the introduction of a series of anti-Jewish laws during the next months. The Fascist Grand Council stripped Jews who had arrived after 1919 of their citizenship, prohibited all Jews from certain professions or from owning property over a certain value, and banned Jewish children from public schools. Twenty-five Jewish generals and five admirals were dismissed from the Italian military. Especially in the north, anti-Semitism became rampant. Signs declared Jews and dogs not welcome in stores and cafés, and Jews were banned from parks, sports facilities, and other recreational establishments.

The regime also banned marriages between Jews and gentiles, and later refused to recognize Jewish conversions to Catholicism. Pope Pius XI publicly criticized the *Manifesto* several times in the weeks after its publication. While the pope's successor, Pius XII, would say disturbingly little publicly, senior members of the church would in fact take individual stands. During Hitler's visit to Florence, one man in particular was conspicuously absent from the ceremonies: Bartali's close friend Cardinal Elia Dalla Costa, archbishop of Florence, who had refused to put any decorations on the red, white, and green marble of the Duomo, perhaps the city's most famous site. When the two dictators arrived at another church, they found the front door locked and were forced to go in through the service entrance. Dalla Costa spent the day in the city's prisons, visiting dissidents.

After his 1938 win at the Tour, Bartali lost at the road cycling world championships in the Netherlands. An informant told the German Ministry of the Interior that Bartali might have lost intentionally, to avoid a win being used as propaganda by the regime. At an event in Milan, where he wore the Tour yellow jersey, he was booed and shouted back at the crowd. "The pedestal of fame is neither very comfortable, nor is it very secure," he observed. In 1939, as relations deteriorated between Italy and France, Bartali was not allowed to defend his title at the Tour. A new rival was also emerging, a nineteen-year-old Turinese named Fausto Coppi, "reed-thin" and "more like a thin, starving goat" than a cyclist according to his coach. Bartali was dominant during the spring season and led the Giro d'Italia after the first stage, until he crashed into a dog that suddenly darted in front of him. Coppi went on to win the Giro. It was the start of a legendary rivalry.

The day after, Mussolini walked out onto the balcony of his headquarters at the Piazza Venezia in Rome and declared war on England and France, which were already fighting Nazi Germany. "A great tragedy," Bartali later wrote, "was to befall us all."

———

When Bartali was hanging around his cousin Armandino Sizzi's bicycle shop as a teenager, he was introduced to a bespectacled man in his mid-thirties named Giacomo Goldenberg. Goldenberg was born in Kishinev and in the years before the First World War moved to Italy, where he obtained citizenship. He became fluent in Italian, graduated from an Italian university, and owned a textile shop. Goldenberg and Sizzi became friends during the two years he lived in Florence. In the late 1920s Goldenberg moved to work in the port city of Fiume for a Florentine lumber merchant, Giorgio Roifer, a Zionist whose company owned a swath of the Black Forest in Bärental. There he married a Jewish Italian girl, Elvira Beck.

Soon after Bartali won the Tour, Goldenberg returned from a seaside vacation with his wife and two children. His six-year-old son, Giorgio, excitedly dressed in his school uniform, had been pulled aside on the first day of school, along with the other Jewish students. A policeman had informed the children that they were permanently expelled and forbidden to ever come to the building again. "I started to cry because I couldn't understand why I could not go to my school," Giorgio Goldenberg remembered decades later. In June 1940, with the declaration of war, police arrived at the villa the Goldenbergs shared with their cousins the Kleins as part of a sweep. By luck, the Goldenbergs were not at home, but the Kleins were not so fortunate and only their older son, Aurelio, escaped the dragnet by jumping out the back window. Thousands of foreign Jews were interned across Italy in hastily established concentration camps, the largest of which was Ferramonti di Tarsia in the south.

Packing only what they could carry, the Goldenbergs took a train the next morning for Florence. Giacomo found someone willing to lease him a small house in Fiesole, a hill town overlooking Florence. The home was near the well-preserved ruins of a Roman theater and down the street from the Villa San Michele, a former monastery that claimed a facade by Michelangelo. The family was quickly understood to be Jewish, but the locals were not particularly militant in enforcing Fascist regulations. Giacomo was required to check in with the police once a week but was largely left alone. Giorgio was enrolled in a local Jewish school, where he stayed until the end of 1942 and played with non-Jewish friends. As an Italian, Elvira Goldenberg could go freely into Florence, but Giacomo, who had by then lost his citizenship, was not allowed to leave the village. He could, however, have visitors from the city and soon reconnected with Armandino Sizzi, who regularly came by on his bicycle, often with his son Marello, who became a friend of Giorgio's.

One day when Bartali came along to visit Goldenberg with Sizzi, Giorgio was starstruck. As the men chatted, word spread throughout the village, and a crowd began gathering. Bartali handed out signed photographs. He inscribed one specially for Giorgio and then presented him with a small blue bicycle he had brought with him as a gift. Giorgio would keep the precious photograph with him for decades, a head shot of Bartali, signed and dated July 16, 1941. "Bartali was a kind of demigod," Giorgio explained later. He didn't know it at the time, but his father's friendship with Bartali and his cousin would save the entire family's lives. Two years later, Giacomo was arrested and interned in the Notaresco concentration camp near Rimini, leaving his wife and children stranded in Fiesole.

———

On October 9, 1940, Bartali was called up for active service and assigned as a courier. When he had a small accident, the examining doctor was surprised to find an irregular heartbeat and brought in a colonel for a second opinion. The colonel deemed Bartali unfit for military service, but so as not to appear to be giving the cyclist preferential treatment, he stationed Bartali as a messenger close by a seaplane factory near Castiglione del Lago on Lake Trasimeno, seventy-five miles outside Florence. One of his superiors, Olesindo Salmi, was an admirer and allowed Bartali to use his bicycle instead of a moped so that he could train, and granted him leave to compete in the handful of races still being staged in Italy. Bartali hated the army, hated carrying a gun, and hated talking about the war. When he was in the barracks, he spent his time reading the lives of saints.

On his visits to see her, Adriana was agitated. Her brother's ship had been sunk on its way to Albania, killing those on board. She refused to accept that her brother was dead and was in a panic about Bartali's safety, aware he could be called away at any time. He decided to accelerate his plans to marry her. "Better a widow than a girlfriend," he told her. He obtained a short leave and, on November 14, 1940, they were married by Cardinal Dalla Costa in a small ceremony. They managed a brief honeymoon in Rome, where they met the pope, a passionate *bartalini*, as the cyclist's fans were called. In February they had a few happy days on the Italian Riviera, where they were painted in formal dress on a tandem bicycle near the seaside before Bartali returned to the barracks.

Bartali's life was now a strange combination of messenger work for the military, domestic life, and competition. His and Adriana's first son, Andrea, was born in October 1941. That year and the year after, Bartali competed in more than a dozen races, although all prize money was donated to the war effort. After the Allies invaded North Africa at the end of 1942, the tide of the war began to shift in western Europe. Italy sent more troops to Tunisia in March, including Coppi, whose regiment was captured by the British; he would spend the rest of the Second World War in prisoner-of-war camps. Just after midnight on July 10, 1943, Allied forces landed in Sicily, and on July 25, the day after a no-confidence vote against Mussolini by the Fascist Grand Council, King Victor Emmanuel III announced that he had arrested the dictator as he left the royal residence. Crowds celebrated everywhere, and over the following weeks streets were renamed and Il Duce's picture was removed throughout the country. On September 3 Allied troops landed on the mainland, and five days later the new government under Marshal Pietro Badoglio signed an armistice, surrendering. Italians throughout the country again cheered. Bartali filed his discharge papers, looking forward to leaving the military for good.

The jubilation was short-lived. Two days later, Germans troops occupied Rome, Naples, and northern Italy and the king fled south to Brindisi. On September 12 German paratroopers landed in gliders at the Hotel Campo Imperatore where Mussolini was imprisoned in the Gran Sasso mountains and flew him to Vienna. A new Fascist government was established in the Lombard town of Salò, with Mussolini again in charge. Field Marshal Alfred Kesselring and the Wehrmacht dug in along lines south of Rome. The reinstated regime tried to impress its soldiers back into service, interning hundreds of thousands of deserters. Bartali fled with his family to an isolated mountain village in Perugia but was quickly recognized. Afraid of endangering his hosts, he made plans to go elsewhere but then returned to Florence to brave the bombings and food shortages. As luck would have it, Bartali's resignation papers landed on the desk of a cycling fan, who excused him from further service, although at one point he would be detained for several days as a suspected deserter.

The arrival of the Germans brought a new level of peril to the forty-three thousand Jews, both Italian and foreign, trapped in northern Italy. In November the Fascists formalized the *Carta di Verona*, which essentially declared Jews enemies of the state. This was not mere discrimination; Jews were now in mortal danger of deportation. Giacomo Goldenberg had been released from internment after the armistice and returned to Fiesole. Now he was desperate to go into hiding. The local police had his name on a list of Jews. Finding an apartment would be extremely difficult and would put the family at the mercy of anyone who might want to take advantage of the bounties offered by the Nazis for turning in Jews.

Goldenberg reached out to Armandino Sizzi. He had already put his eleven-year-old son Giorgio into hiding at the Santa Marta Institute in Settignano, a boardinghouse for children run by nuns. But he needed a place to hide with his wife and their six-year-old daughter, Tea. Bartali offered shelter in the basement of an apartment he owned on Via del Bandino, where he also lived, away from the center of town. "The Germans were killing everybody who was hiding Jews," Giorgio Goldenberg recalled. "[Bartali] was risking not only his life, but also his family." The grateful Goldenbergs moved in. While Elvira, who had blue eyes and looked Italian, could occasionally leave, it was too dangerous for Giacomo or Tea to even go outside.

In November 1943 the Goldenbergs' twenty-two-year-old nephew Aurelio Klein, who had escaped the 1940 roundup that caught his parents and younger brother, came to Florence, where he had been told it was easier to get false identification papers. He was allowed to stay in the apartment as well. "I spent most of my time waiting," recalled Aurelio. One day, there was a scare when a man warned of Fascists nearby, and the entire group fled over the rooftops. Klein eventually received papers in January and took a train to the Swiss border, where he crossed over with a group of cigarette smugglers from Lake Maggiore and found work as a watchmaker in Lausanne.

The Goldenbergs were not the only ones that Bartali and Sizzi sheltered. One day Bartali was at his cousin's bike shop on Via Pietrapiana, not far from the synagogue, when there was a roundup. "With quick reflexes and cool heads," Bartali's son later wrote, Bartali and Sizzi rushed outside, pushed several people who were fleeing into the store, and quickly pulled down the rolling metal shutters. When night fell, most made their way home, but two remained. One was Jewish. The other was a Romani—subject to similar persecution by the Nazis—who had fallen in love with a Florentine woman. They were both terrified to leave. Bartali and Sizzi allowed them to remain there until the liberation, bringing food and hiding the entrance by parking bicycles in front of the door.

———

It is likely that when Goldenberg approached Sizzi, Bartali had already gotten involved in broader efforts to help Jews and others running for their lives. Prior to the Germans' arrival, much of the work of dealing with the influx of foreign refugees in Italy had been handled by the Delegation for the Assistance of Jewish Emigrants (DELASEM). Established by Jews based in Genoa, DELASEM was supported by donations from overseas, particularly from the American Jewish community, and was authorized by the government, which was pleased to both delegate the humanitarian issue and take a commission on all funds the organization raised. DELASEM also helped thousands of Jews find a route out of Italy to safety in neutral countries.

But in 1943 DELASEM's Jewish leadership was forced underground, and many of its members were arrested. They turned to the cardinal of Genoa, Pietro Boetto, who directed his secretary Francesco Repetto to coordinate with DELASEM and essentially have the church take over its activities. A clandestine network of church officials quickly developed throughout northern Italy, not only providing financial support to Jews but helping to hide them or smuggle them out of the occupied zone.

Cardinal Dalla Costa was the leader of the effort for the church in Florence, where he had been approached by the local Jewish community, including its young chief rabbi, Nathan Cassuto. As archbishop of Florence, the seventy-one-year-old Dalla Costa had been rumored as a possible successor to Pius XI before the last conclave. He too deputized his personal secretary, Monsignor Giacomo Meneghello, to oversee clandestine activities for the curate and serve as liaison to the underground. Orders were given to the diocese's convents to open their doors to Jewish women and children, and a number of priests also hid Jews in churches and orphanages. The cardinal led by example and himself hid Jews on the run in his home, just as Bartali was doing with the Goldenbergs. Meetings of the underground were also hosted in an archbishopric palace at Via Pucci, 2, where in November 1943, Cassuto and a Catholic priest were arrested during a raid.

At around this time, Padre Rufino Salvatore Niccacci, the thirty-two-year-old father superior of the San Damiano monastery in Assisi, met with Dalla Costa. Niccacci's superior, Giuseppe Placido Nicolini, the Benedictine archbishop of Assisi, had instructed him to work with Nicolini's own secretary, Father Aldo Brunacci, to help hide Jews and others who had fled to Assisi. This legendary home of Saint Francis 120 miles north of Rome had a population of just five thousand, including a thousand monks, nuns, and priests. "Bishop Nicolini was really a father for all the Jews who passed through Assisi," Brunacci recalled years later. He and Niccacci arranged for clothing, housing in twenty-six convents and monasteries, and false identity papers. Though Niccacci had never seen a Jew before—indeed it was said that no Jew had ever lived in Assisi—he threw himself fully into the task. Over the course of the war he would hide hundreds of Jews. Not one who came to Assisi was apprehended in the nine months of its occupation.

Routes of escape were becoming more challenging, and Niccacci had been sent to ask Dalla Costa for help with some Roman Jews who had fled to Assisi. Dalla Costa explained that he had his own group of Jews stranded from Perugia, and over forty thousand more were estimated to be in the northern sector. He warned that the Swiss border was now largely sealed, and the Germans kept a close eye on the port of Genoa, from which boats had departed for the Americas with refugees. The only hope for those on the run was to either stay in hiding for the duration or try to escape to the unoccupied southern zone. Dalla Costa believed that the mountainous areas of Tuscany and Umbria were a good place for Jews and others to hide or to escape across the front lines. Critical to the effort were false identity cards and Assisi was quickly becoming a counterfeiting center. Dalla Costa asked for help procuring false papers for Jews in hiding. He would provide photographs, he told

Niccacci, and would also arrange for the documents to be picked up by couriers.

It is reported that Dalla Costa personally recruited Bartali for the effort. He reached out to him through Emilio Berti, the pastry-shop owner also active in Catholic Action, who brought the cyclist to the cardinal. Dalla Costa was Bartali's priest, spiritual guide, and close friend. And although he wasn't the only courier in the underground, Bartali was uniquely placed as one of the few people in Italy with an excuse to travel long distances by bicycle; he would, indeed, ride forty thousand kilometers a year on his training routes. Now, he could save lives too. "I put myself to work with my friend Berti to help Jews flee the country," he told his biographer.

Bartali would leave early in the morning, dressed in biking shorts and a jersey with his name emblazoned on the back. He did not need anyone to ride with him. An exceptional mechanic, he carried a screwdriver, wrench, and other tools, a little bit of cash, and a spare tire to handle any contingency. He would first ride from his home to the center of Florence to pick up the photographs and papers to be made into false identity cards. Sometimes he would get them from Berti. Other times they would come from a clergy member. Often Dalla Costa's secretary, Monsignor Giacomo Meneghello, himself hid the cache under a pew at the cathedral.

Bartali would stash the documents under the seat of his bicycle or unscrew its frame, roll them up, and stuff them inside. Then he would head out on the 250-kilometer ride to Assisi. Incredibly, he would often return home the same day. His wife did not understand where he was going, but he assured her that he was just training. "He would leave the home almost daily to train," Adriana recalled later, and "sometimes he was away two or three days. I think he hid the truth about saving Jews to protect his family." His admonition that she should tell anyone looking for him that he had an emergency or was going to get medicine for the baby did little to calm her fears. "As a child everything seemed normal," his son Andrea remembered. "Sometimes the less you know the better." Bartali himself was given only limited information about the network of which he was now a part. He did not want to know the details of what the documents in his bicycle were, he recalled, "in case they catch me."

Bartali would cycle on the often-damaged roads as far as Genoa and Rome. In Genoa, he would deliver forged documents, many used to help those fleeing for the United States and elsewhere, and pick up money that had arrived from Switzerland for the Curia in Florence. In Rome, he would see contacts in the Vatican. But Assisi was perhaps the most critical destination. It was one of the most important Catholic cities in the world, a destination for two hundred thousand pilgrims each year. Bartali admired Nicolini, and the bishop had once presented the cyclist with the gift of a chalice for the private chapel in his home.

Even in a religious town like Assisi, it would be very difficult for a celebrity like Bartali to go unrecognized, so riding by day, hiding in plain sight, was generally safer. At checkpoints he would be waved through or subjected to light chitchat about cycling. His legend had long ago made its way even into the cloisters behind the rose-colored stone buildings in Assisi. Pier Damiano, a twenty-year-old student of Niccacci's at the monastery, remembered being stunned to see Bartali standing by a side door as he came out of his room one day, after which Damiano was sworn to secrecy by the father superior.

Bartali was frequently at the convent of San Quirico, where the mother superior, Giuseppina Biviglia, hid dozens of Jews in the guesthouse and served as a conduit for false identification papers. He would ring the doorbell and head upstairs to drop off his parcels. Two nuns, Sisters Alfonsina and Eleonora, recalled Bartali coming dozens of times during the war. "He would arrive with his bicycle and would ask for the mother superior," remembered Alfonsina. They would meet privately. "I can still see him. He was tall, strong, suntanned and had short pants." Many of the nuns only heard Bartali's voice in their cloister, as he left his packages in the wooden *ruata* (wheel) used to deliver items from the outside world in the guesthouse. Sometimes he would leave his bicycle at the convent and go to meet others in the center of Assisi. Other times he had barley coffee with Niccacci at the monastery, where he sometimes spent the night.

Mother Giuseppina would record Bartali's visits in her private diary. An active member of the underground, she personally prevented the Nazis from breaking into her convent. She had initially been afraid to put the convent in danger by housing refugees, including Jews, partisans, and deserters being hunted by the military, but she saw little choice. "We just acted spontaneously every time these desperate human beings came knocking on our door under threat of arrest, concentration camps, shootings and worse," she recalled. At the behest of Father Niccacci, she made the dramatic decision to hide Jews, including men, in the cloister. The Germans regularly searched monasteries and convents. "More than once the Germans would knock on the door and ask to enter the cloister, threatening the Reverend Mother to take her to a concentration camp," Eleonora recalled, but Giuseppina stood firm. When there was acute danger, the refugees would flee to the old Roman tunnels underneath the convent and into the Roman caves carved into the Assisi hillsides. They would also be hidden in woodsheds, or in the cloisters, dressed as monks and nuns. After the smuggling route to the southern zone was closed, they dug in for the duration.

Having dropped off documents, Bartali would hide batches of false identity papers made in a nearby printshop in the crossbar or handlebars of his bicycle. The counterfeiting ring in Assisi had quickly become a well-oiled machine. Sixty-eight-year-old Luigi Brizi owned a small stone-walled souvenir store on Via Santa Chiara, in a piazza opposite the Basilica di Santa Chiara, from which he also ran a foot-operated printing press. A lifelong atheist, he nonetheless played a friendly game of checkers at the Café Minerva each Wednesday with Niccacci, who one day appealed to him to make counterfeit papers for

Jews in hiding or trying to escape. At that moment, the priest confided, at least fifty Jews were hiding in Assisi, and he estimated he would need 150 false identification cards. He struck a chord when he reminded Brizi, whose ancestors had been important local members of the Risorgimento, of the Jews' contribution to the movement for Italian unification and independence, and of their patriotism.

Brizi agreed, but he did not want to involve his twenty-eight-year-old son, Trento, who had just returned safely from the Yugoslavian front. Several days later the young man asked his father what he was so intently working on. Brizi confessed but begged him not to get involved. "I fought for three years on the front," Trento said. "I heard the bullets that were whistling around me and by now I am no longer afraid of anything. If you are doing something, I will do it too." He was an expert at making the municipal rubber stamps necessary for each card. "While several of my friends climbed up into the mountains and became partisans," Trento recalled, "I decided to stay at my print shop. My weapons against the Nazis were ink and paper."

Father and son were nearly surprised as they were finishing the first false card by a German soldier and Italian Fascist sharing a cigarette outside. "What a scare," Trento remembered. "I wanted to throw everything away." Despite the curfew, he rushed over to San Damiano and delivered the card to Niccacci, who complimented him and told him that they would need many more. Eventually hundreds of Jews would be hidden all over Assisi, including in private homes as the monasteries filled up.

The first document was for a well-to-do Jewish engineering student from Trieste, Enrico Maionica, who became Enrico Martorana of Caserta, a city in the liberated zone. A member of the partisans, Maionica himself joined the effort, hiding with Niccacci's help in a former laboratory in the cloisters of San Quirico, where he would finish the identity documents the Brizis printed by filling in information, forging signatures, and perfecting the art of applying fake seals. They created stamps for places like Sicily, Calabria, Lecce, Bari, Naples, Foggia, Taranto, and Caserta, all located behind Allied lines. Maionica and his helpers also picked names from southern Italian phone books to create pseudonyms that could not be checked. Thus the Jews using the documents would "pretend to be evacuees who have lost their houses in the bombings." Maionica procured ornate House of Savoy stamps, which he had seen on many old identification cards and which were available only to authorized printers. He also bought postage-stamp-size license tags for a few lire from Italians who no longer had cars and expertly transferred them onto the cards by soaking off the ink and regluing them. "I put three- or four-year-old tags to give them more authenticity," he recalled. The documents would then be given to Father Niccacci or to Mother Giuseppina for Bartali to pick up, Maionica testified.

Eventually the Brizis were churning out hundreds of identity cards. After the first batch—recalled by Trento as "a brutal job, done . . . in an atmosphere of continual terror"—the need only increased. When on October 3 Assisi was declared off limits to combat as a religious town with little industrial, topographical, or strategic value, it was flooded by refugees and convalescents, doubling its population. "If the Nazis were to single out our print shop, we would be shot," Trento realized. In early 1944 he was working on a batch of identity cards in the back of the shop and forgot to close the curtains when two German soldiers suddenly walked in. He froze with terror as one of them asked to buy images of Saint Clare for their wives. Relieved, Trento found two wooden carvings and refused payment, "a gift from Assisi to our German friends."

Panicked, Trento rushed over to San Damiano to tell Padre Niccacci that he wanted out. "Instead, as soon as I arrived in the convent, something happened that made me forget the fear I had felt shortly before." He was let in a side door by another monk and asked to wait in the courtyard. There, he caught sight of Niccacci talking with a young man he judged to be around thirty, leaning on the handlebars of a magnificent bicycle and wearing short pants over muscular legs. "I saw him get on the seat of his bicycle and race off, from the main door, at a great speed."

A stunned Trento asked if he had just seen Gino Bartali. Niccacci confessed that he had. He told him he must keep it a secret, and that Bartali had carried many of the Brizis' documents to Perugia and Florence. "No one dares stop him," he explained. Years later, Trento remembered the moment. "The idea of taking part in an organization that could boast of a champion like Gino Bartali among its ranks filled me with such pride that my fear took a back seat."

Allied bombing brought new risks. Bartali always kept his bicycle polished and shiny. One day he left it outside in the sun, and it attracted fire from an Allied pilot. From then on Bartali let the bike get dirty, and even covered it with mud. Another time he had to hurl himself into a drainage pipe during an air raid and traumatized Adriana when he arrived home covered in sewage. In Rome, while he was visiting his friend Bartolo Paschetta, who ran the Vatican bookstore and was his intermediary with the pope, the two men were caught in the bombing of the library and "escaped by pure miracle," Bartali's son wrote.

Bartali also went on scouting missions for the underground and the partisans. On the road, he would make careful note of checkpoints and roadblocks and also relayed information from friends in the Resistance like Gennaro Cellai, the famous cobbler who made his custom biking shoes. It is also said that he served as the go-between with smugglers from Abruzzi, helping people cross the border into the Allied zone. He would be called upon by the partisans if they had an urgent warning that the OVRA (Opera Volontaria di Repressione Antifascista), Mussolini's secret police, was about to arrest someone. "I was the only one," he told his son, "that could move about at night with a certain degree of safety in Florence. My bike was in order. There were no loose screws. It was very quiet. I knew the city streets very well, I could cross it at a speed of 50 kilometers an hour. Just like in racing and despite the tram tracks, in just five minutes I could reach and give warning to anyone. Three or four times they shot at me at a checkpoint, but they never got me because I would arrive suddenly and silently and before they could realize what was happening, I was out of there."

At least once Bartali stopped at Terontola, about halfway along the route from Florence to Assisi. The railway station at this small Tuscan town between Arezzo and Perugia was extremely busy, an intersection where Jews and dissidents on the run had to change trains. As elsewhere in Europe, train stations were the bane of a refugee's existence, generally crawling with uniformed Fascist and German police who paced the platforms.

As part of a coordinated effort with local partisans, Bartali glided on his bicycle to the station. "My father would play the part of the great cycling champion," his son explained. As soon as he walked in, news spread quickly throughout the town. While he greeted his friends—including Leo Pipparelli, who owned the bar in the train station, and Dino Magara, the local tailor—crowds began to form and press toward the superstar. As he signed autographs, he was offered a panini and cappuccino, and more and more people would appear. In response to the tumult, the patrolling officers would approach to control the crowd (or perhaps get a glimpse themselves). While they were distracted, the partisans quickly moved the refugees from one train to another. "It was easier for the Jews to find an escape route in the midst of this artfully created bustle," Andrea Bartali wrote. By the time the station had returned to normal and Bartali had ridden off, they were safely on their way.

———

By the spring of 1944, more than sixty-five hundred Jews had been deported, among them a thousand rounded up in one day in Rome, one of the world's oldest Jewish communities, and another thousand in Florence, including fifty orphans. The Goldenbergs decided to retrieve their son Giorgio and bring him into hiding with them. Living under the name Giorgio Goldini, he was one of ten Jewish boys, none of whom knew of the others' real religion at the time, who were hidden by the nuns in the Catholic boardinghouse of Santa Marta outside Florence, along with twenty Jewish girls.

Like the nuns in Assisi, one of whom cooked a huge meal for hidden Jews to break the fast on Yom Kippur, the sisters had a respect for the religious beliefs of their wards. Only the mother superior allegedly knew they were Jewish, although others clearly did as well; as Goldenberg recalled, "it's not logical that an Italian child between eight and ten doesn't know any Catholic prayers." The sons of the chief rabbi of Genoa were also hidden there, and the nun who put them to bed each night, Mother Marta Folcia, would tell them to secretly kiss her finger rather than the cross she held and then to say the Shema Yisrael quietly before falling asleep. When German soldiers inspected the boardinghouse every few months, looking for Jewish children, the boys carefully recited Catholic prayers such as the Ave Maria and Pater Noster that had been drilled into them several times a day at the convent. The mother superior stood behind the officer, mouthing the words, in case any of the children forgot in their panic.

Elvira Goldenberg came to get Giorgio, who joined his parents and younger sister in the *cantina* (cellar) of Bartali's apartment. It was barely ten by ten feet, with no windows, a closed door, and stone walls. There was no electricity or running water, it was cold and dark, and the Goldenbergs shared one double bed that barely fit in the room. Behind the cellar was a courtyard with some trees. The fair, Italian-looking Elvira Goldenberg was still the only one who went out to buy food, carrying two buckets with her to retrieve water. The boredom was incredible. "What can you do if you are closed in a room twenty-four hours a day without permission to go out?" Giorgio recalled. "My sister and I sat counting flies." The sounds of the night remained with the siblings for years. Tea would later confide to her husband that the German boots on the stone streets still haunted her dreams. Her brother Giorgio remembered the air raid sirens and the bombings.

During his trips to Genoa, Bartali sometimes stopped at the Certosa di Farneta Monestery near Lucca, home to Carthusian monks including his friend Father Gabriele Costa, a devout bald man in his forties who had previously served in Spain. The monastery was part of the underground network and served as a gathering point for refugees on their way to Genoa. The monks took in Jews, partisans, Communists, and dissidents and then moved them to villages in the hills, where Costa often brought them food. On September 2, 1944, German SS officers appeared at the door. Forcing their way in, they came upon the monks praying and singing a Gregorian chant. They seized six, including Costa, six lay brothers, and over one hundred refugees. They were all driven to a warehouse nearby in Nocchi, where several days later Costa and over forty others were machine-gunned near a hillside. The massacre was so traumatic for Bartali, he could not bring himself after the war to visit the monastery.

"These are terrible times," Bartali noted. "But a sense of duty and human solidarity keeps us going." One day he received a summons to appear with his friend Emilio Berti before Major Mario Carità of the secret police, who, along with two hundred underlings, assisted the Nazis in pursuing Jews and partisans. Bartali was terrified when he arrived at Carità's headquarters in a repurposed luxury apartment building on Via Bolognese, nicknamed the Villa Triste because of the cries heard from inside. Carità, it was said, made a spectacle of torture, interrogating prisoners as he indulged in gluttonous feasts, drank wine, and had Neapolitan songs played on the piano.

Bartali was taken downstairs into the coal bunkers that served as prison cells, where an array of torture instruments were on display and the sounds of screaming echoed in the air. He noticed a pile of letters addressed to him that seemed to have been intercepted by the police, and was panicked as to what they could be. Eventually Carità confronted him. After an anti-Catholic tirade, he angrily read aloud a letter from the Vatican thanking Bartali for his help. In his free time, Bartali would gather food in the countryside for the poor and send it to the Vatican, but Carità accused him of sending them weapons.

Bartali denied it, telling him that he had sent flour, sugar, and coffee to needy people. He didn't even know how to shoot, he told Carità, and always kept his pistol unloaded in the military.

Carità looked at him. "It's not true," he declared. Bartali insisted it was, and Carità threw him back into the dungeon to consider his position. Bartali remained there for some time, terrified. "These were times when life was not highly valued," he remembered. "You could easily disappear as a result of hatred, a vendetta, rumor, slander, or ideological fanaticism."

On the third day Carità once again called him for interrogation. Bartali again explained he had just gathered food and sent it to the Vatican. Carità still did not believe him.

It was at this point that one of Carità's men stepped out of the shadows. It was Olesindo Salmi, Bartali's former supervisor in Castiglione del Lago, who had authorized his use of a bicycle when he was in the army. "If Bartali says coffee, flour and sugar," Salmi declared, "then it was coffee, flour and sugar. He doesn't lie."

Bartali was stunned by the intervention, then further shocked as Carità backed off and released him. Carità told him they would meet again and ordered him to remain in Florence.

"I hope I never see you again," Bartali mumbled.

"I think that was one of the few times that he was really scared," his son wrote later. "Following the meeting with Carità, he didn't feel safe anymore." He and his family moved in with Berti in Via del Corso, in the heart of Florence near the Palazzo Vecchio, an area they believed less likely to be bombed.

Bartali did participate in one daring operation at the very end of the war. A friend in the partisans had told him that forty-nine British soldiers were trapped in a villa between Florence and Bartali's hometown of Ponte a Ema. Both entrances to Florence—the old Roman Via Cassia and the Via Chiantigiana—were under heavy German artillery bombardment. Bartali put on a Fascist black shirt and rode his bicycle with his unloaded musket down to the villa. There he slowly marched the British prisoners through rural roads, their hands raised and with white sheets, and turned them safely over to the protection of the partisans in San Marcellino. When Florence was liberated, General Harold Alexander asked to meet Bartali to shake his hand.

On May 11, 1944, the Allies began their attack on Monte Cassino, after which the road north to Rome was open. On June 4 the Eternal City was liberated. In the final, dangerous days of the occupation in Florence, as the Allies approached the historic city, rumors circulated that the Germans would take vengeance. All those who lived along the Arno were ordered to evacuate their homes. On August 3, the German commander ordered that no one was to leave their house or approach their window and the electricity was cut off. Loud blasts were heard, and the sky turned crimson. Bartali felt his house shake and told his small son that it was just a thunderstorm. Outside, the Germans were destroying all the historic bridges in Florence except for the Ponte Vecchio as they retreated. The next day, Allied troops arrived.

"A bleak spectacle presented itself before our eyes," recalled Bartali of the devastated Florence. Some Florentines who came out of hiding to celebrate were killed by mines left behind by the Germans. Snipers still in the city killed others. Fearing the violence, Bartali took his family to the edge of Florence. On August 11 the bells atop the Bargello in central Florence rang to announce the liberation. In Bartali's apartment on Via del Bandino, the Goldenbergs heard local boys shouting that the English had arrived. Giorgio came outside and saw a British soldier standing on the street next to the building, a Star of

David on his shoulder. The boy did not speak English but began to sing "Hatikvah." The soldier immediately began to speak excitedly, and Giorgio ran downstairs to get his father, who came upstairs and spoke with the man animatedly in Yiddish. His son was profoundly relieved. "For me, that was the end of the war," he recalled.

———

Almost immediately after the liberation, Bartali wanted to get his career going. He had a wife, a young son, and aging parents, and his savings had evaporated. He had lost many of the best years of his career, during which the Tour and the Giro had been canceled. The war had taken its toll, financially, emotionally, and physically. "You feel like you have gotten much older than if you could have led a normal life," he reflected. His country was a disaster. One day he rode up to Milan on an old bicycle to get supplies. By coincidence, he came upon a large crowd gaping at the bodies of Mussolini and his mistress, hung upside down by their ankles in a gas station in the Piazzale Loreto. "This is not the Italy I dreamed of for myself and for my family," he thought. "It was an obscene spectacle, a savage testimony of the cruelty of the times."

A group of ten cyclists banded together to create an improvised tour, riding around in an old truck. They were, Bartali recalled, "like clowns in a traveling circus." They competed for livestock and passed a hat to spectators. The glory of the prewar days was gone. "It seemed like they had been lost in that deafening uproar that had shattered nature and souls," Bartali wrote. "People had forgotten about us. They had other things on their minds, and those who still followed sports considered our generation already 'old.' So we had to struggle a great deal to make our comeback." Well off his peak condition, Bartali found himself forced to withdraw from his first real race. He began losing his temper with reporters, earning the nickname Ginettaccio, "Gino the terrible." As he confessed later, "I ended up completely demoralized. Any kind of dignified resumption of our activity seemed impossible."

But as Italy climbed out of the literal rubble of the war, its love of cycling also revived. The country was still bike-mad, and bicycles were still a critical part of everyday life. In the Neorealist cinematic masterpiece *Bicycle Thieves*, the young son of the protagonist decorates his room with pictures of famous cyclists. Amid massive unemployment and bubbling unrest, the races provided a welcome distraction. In 1946 the first real Giro d'Italia in years was staged, an epic struggle between Coppi and Bartali, who won in the final stretch by a mere forty-seven seconds. Bartali was triumphant once again, although once again he was struggling by the next season.

The political situation in Italy rapidly deteriorated. With the economy devastated, it was unclear what direction the nation would take. The center-right Christian Democrats were led by Alcide De Gasperi, an honest but colorless politician who was a friend of Bartali's. Their main opposition were the Communists, led by Palmiro Togliatti, a corpulent and charismatic bon vivant. Bartali hated politics and had hoped, like his father, to leave them behind after the war. But while the government would no longer meddle in his athletic career, he was pressed into service by the Christian Democrats and their allies in the church. The first parliamentary elections of the postwar period were held in April 1948, and both the United States and the Soviet Union secretly funneled millions of dollars into the contest, an opening salvo in the Cold War. The rhetoric was ugly, but the result was a landslide for the Christian Democrats. When Bartali sent a cable of congratulations to De Gasperi, his message was plastered on walls by the victors. He would be used for politics again, whether he liked it or not.

Bartali focused on the Tour de France. The race had been held the prior year, but many countries, including Italy, had not participated, and the race had been won by a five-foot-three Frenchman, Jean Robic. Coppi insisted he should lead the Italian team. When it became apparent, however, that Bartali would be allowed to defend his title from a decade earlier, Coppi announced that he had no intention of riding and withdrew. Few thought Bartali, who would turn thirty-four during the Tour, had a real chance, and only fourteen Italian journalists bothered to make the trip.

The race started on June 30. Bartali was competitive in the beginning of the Tour, but at the halfway point, he seemed to be falling behind. In a mountainous stage between San Remo and Cannes on July 13, Bartali held his own in hundred-degree heat but suffered a burst tire. As he crossed the stage's finish line under the palm trees of the Mediterranean coast, he was over twenty-one minutes behind. The Tour director declared Bartali could not win. The Italian press, too, threw in the towel: "Bartali, the old king of the mountains, is no longer the king today. These are bad times for monarchies, and kings also pass away in the world of sport."

The next day, July 14, was a rest day, and Bartali spent his time giving interviews at the Hotel Carlton as France celebrated the Bastille. Back in Italy, however, things suddenly exploded when the Communist leader Togliatti was shot by a young extremist outside the Chamber of Deputies and rushed to the hospital. Thousands took to the streets, and fourteen people were killed and two hundred injured in the ensuing riots. De Gasperi called Bartali and asked if he thought he would win the Tour. Bartali promised he was doing his best, and De Gasperi is said to have told him it was important for all Italians.

Bartali slept that evening with his bicycle in his hotel room. Banners with "Viva Italia" and "Viva Bartali" greeted him at the starting line, and the French movie star Maurice Chevalier was in the crowd. The Frenchman Louison Bobet pulled out to a large initial lead, but Bartali—the King of the Mountains—narrowed it to thirty seconds at the top of the Vars and zoomed by Bobet on the decline. "The good Lord took a pair of wings from one of his angels to put them on the back of Bartali," a journalist wrote.

Bartali crossed the finish line in Briançon as Giacomo Puccini's *Tosca* played on the loudspeakers, winning the stage by six minutes. In Italy the chamber erupted in applause at the news. At the hospital, Tagliotti awoke from surgery. Among his first words, those present noted, were "What happened at the Tour? How did Bartali do?"

The next day was another Alpine stage, soaring eight thousand feet at the Galibier, and Bartali took the yellow jersey from Bobet. He was racing at twice the speed of his competitors. "I feel like a lion," Bartali thought as he crossed the finish line. The rest of the Tour was a glide to victory. Ten thousand Italians cheered him outside his hotel when the race crossed into Liège in Belgium. "Bartali wrote in these last two days—if one can write with pedal strokes and drops of sweat—perhaps the most beautiful page of his career," one journalist declared.

In Paris, Bartali rode to the finish line in the Parc des Princes velodrome before forty thousand cheering spectators. He had been on his bicycle for a hundred and fifty hours. "I have won the most beautiful race in the world," he said. "With this, I will enter into history." It was a pinnacle for Bartali, one of the oldest men to win the Tour, as he had done ten years and a lifetime earlier. "Everyone in their life has his own particular way of expressing life's purposes—the lawyer his eloquence, the painter his palette, and the man of letters his pen from which the quick words of his story flow," he reflected. "I have my bicycle."

People have credited Bartali with averting civil war. Bartali was more modest. "I don't know if I saved the country," he said, "but I gave it back its smile." It would be the final summit of his career. He retired in February 1955 at the age of forty. "For a quarter of a century my mother has been waiting for me to stop racing," Bartali announced. "Now she will finally have a bit of peace."

Bartali settled into family life. He and Adriana welcomed a second son, Luigi, and a daughter, Bianca Maria. He proved less successful as a businessman than an athlete, with attempts to launch a line of bicycles and a professional team floundering. After failed ventures in shaving products, wine, and sewing machines, he went to work as a cycling commentator for RAI, the national television station, and did appearances for the Coca-Cola Company. While cycling never regained the popularity it had in the immediate postwar period, Bartali remained a beloved figure, immortalized in a song by Paolo Conte. He entered the pantheon of international celebrity and became a friend of more than one pope. At the Florence opera, he met Maria Callas, who was a fan.

Things were finally calm for Gino Bartali.

———

Shortly after the war, rumors were already circulating among the Florentine Jewish community about Bartali's involvement as a courier in the underground. In 1978 Alexander Ramati, a Polish soldier and reporter who had been present at the liberation of Assisi, published *The Assisi Underground*, which told the tale of the underground from the perspective of Father Niccacci and included the story of Gino Bartali. "I want to be remembered for my success in sport," Bartali told his son, "not as a war hero. Others are war heroes, those who suffered in their limbs, their minds, and their hearts. I limited myself to doing what I knew how to do best. Riding a bicycle."

One should do good but not talk about it, he believed. "These are things that are meant to be hidden," Bartali once said of his wartime heroics. To discuss it would be to debase it, he believed, to benefit from others' misfortunes. When a film starring Maximilian Schell and James Mason was made from the book, he even threatened to sue Italian television for airing it. "I don't want to talk about it or act like a hero," he said once when asked about his wartime exploits during a broadcast. "Heroes are those who died, who were injured, who spent many months in prison."

In his later years, Bartali's health began to fail. "Life is like a Giro d'Italia, which seems never-ending, but at a certain point you reach the final stage," he told a reporter. "Yes, I'll soon be called and I'll go up there." He was at peace. "Heaven should be a happy place, like those green summits of the Dolomite Mountains, after you've rounded a hundred curves, pedaling all the way." On May 5, 2000, he passed away at home, surrounded by his family, at the age of eighty-five. Pope John Paul II remembered him as a "great sportsman." A fan recalled the postwar period: "When we were poor and weary, he gave us back our honor." He was buried in the family tomb next to his parents and his brother.

Bartali had confided his story to his son Andrea, who remembered his father wanting to return to Assisi to see the Giotto frescoes or to visit Nicolini at San Damiano. After repeated questioning, Bartali shared details about his work during the war with his son on long trips together in Italy, Germany, the United States, Canada, and elsewhere. But he told Andrea he could not tell anyone. Andrea eventually asked why his father had confided in him. "When the time comes to talk about these things, you will understand it by yourself," he told him.

In 2004, when a young cyclist, Paolo Alberati, wrote his thesis on Bartali's exploits, Andrea decided the time was right. In 2006 he published a book about his father. That year, on Liberation Day in April, the president of the Italian Republic awarded Bartali the Civilian Gold Medal for his actions. In 2013 Gino Bartali joined other members of the Assisi underground—including Niccacci and Dalla Costa—in being named as a Righteous Among the Nations by Yad Vashem. In 2018, in a unique tribute, Bartali was made an honorary citizen of Israel, and the first three stages of the Giro d'Italia were held in the Holy Land, the first time they had ever been held outside Europe. Before the race began, a memorial ride was taken in Bartali's honor.

Over 7,600 Italian Jews were deported, some 17 percent of the total. But the survival rate was much higher than in almost all of the rest of occupied Europe, and wherever the Italians were the occupying forces, Jews were not rounded up. When Ramati entered Assisi on its liberation, he was greeted by a banner hoisted by the Brizis with a quote attributed to Giuseppe Mazzini: "The Jews of Italy have Italian blood, Italian souls and Italian genius." It is estimated that DELASEM and the underground networks rescued over nine thousand Jews during the occupation. The Assisi underground, with its twenty-six convents and abbeys, directly sheltered several hundred Jews and other refugees and provided false identities to thousands.

Precisely how many owed their lives to Gino Bartali will never be known, but it is likely several hundred. One he certainly saved was Giorgio Goldenberg, who moved to Israel after the war and eventually became a grandfather. "Gino Bartali saved my life and saved the life of my family," Goldenberg remembered. "He is a hero." Bartali's friend, the Vatican bookseller Bartolo Paschetta, had called Andrea down to Rome and confided in him on his deathbed, "You had a great father. You can't know how many people he and we saved." For Bartali, his heroics seem to have been something private and very much connected to his faith. "If you're good at a sport, they attach the medals to your shirts and then they shine in some museum," he told his son. But good deeds were of a different type, he believed. "These are medals that are pinned to the soul and will be recognized in the Heavenly Kingdom, not on this earth."

5

Samurai Spirit

KOVNO,[*] THE SECOND LARGEST CITY IN LITHUANIA, WAS A STRANGE PLACE TO open a Japanese consulate since no Japanese citizens lived there or ever visited. But in the late summer of 1939 the diplomat Chiune Sugihara was sent to do just that. His real mission was not diplomatic at all but espionage. Kovno was the perfect location to monitor Russian and German troop activity on the borderlands, information that had become critical since the Japanese were stunned, along with the rest of the world, by the news of a nonaggression pact between the Soviet Union and Nazi Germany on August 23, and the outbreak of the Second World War a week later, when the two behemoths invaded and partitioned Poland.

The two mortal enemies might have come to a rapprochement, but Japanese strategists in Tokyo were convinced they would eventually fall out again. The Japanese ambassador to Berlin, Hiroshi Oshima, was an ardent pro-Nazi militarist and had heard rumblings from Hitler himself of potential plans to invade the Soviet Union. Such a move would be of profound importance to the war, and more particularly for the Japanese military, allowing it to immediately transfer elite troops on the Manchurian border with the Soviet Union to the southern islands

---

* I have used the Russian name Kovno, by which the city was widely known at the time. Since Lithuania's independence in 1991, it has been more commonly known as Kaunas, its German name.

of the Pacific. Unsure whether the information was true, the general staff pushed for "new eyes in Lithuania" with a new consulate in Kovno, and particularly suggested Sugihara for the job.

Fluent in Russian and German, Sugihara had years of experience in both diplomacy and espionage. In Kovno, he would have few diplomatic obligations to distract him from intelligence gathering. "My main task was to establish the foreseeable date of the German attack on Russia quickly and correctly," he later admitted. And given the sensitivity of the mission, he would also report directly to the Foreign Ministry in Tokyo, not to the Japanese ambassador in Riga.

When Sugihara arrived, he beheld a Kovno filled with medieval architecture and ornate churches. The alluvial plain on which it sat was ringed by ancient castles and fortresses. For a small, quiet city, it had a surprisingly cosmopolitan feel, with a rich café culture and wide boulevards lined with tall chestnut trees. It was an ambiance that would appeal to the worldly Sugihara, a bon vivant who enjoyed well-tailored suits and gourmet food. Unusually for a man of his generation, Sugihara had spent a large part of his life outside his native Japan. He had been sent to Europe a year earlier and was already at ease on the Continent. He was kindly and courtly, as befitted a good diplomat, but behind his large eyes he had the keen intellect of an intelligence officer.

Sugihara was born the second of six children, five boys and a girl, in Yaotsu, a small town in the mountains of Gifu, on January 1, 1900. All his life he would be extremely proud to be the exact same age as the century. His early childhood, set against the mixing of the traditional and the contemporary that marked a Japan rapidly modernizing under Emperor Meiji, was idyllic. He wore a brightly colored kimono with clogs and fished with bamboo poles, as Japanese children had for centuries, but also spent afternoons playing baseball. Sugihara got his taste for the modern from his father, an imperial tax collector who enjoyed Western attire, movies, and dances. On his mother's side, he was descended from old samurai stock and deeply imbued with the ethics of the *bushido*, its chivalric warrior code.

Sugihara's family moved several times for his father's career, and he did well in the various schools he attended. He wanted to study English and become a teacher, but his father was adamant he become a doctor. Sugihara dutifully sat for the medical school exam, but less dutifully left the entire test blank. Incensed, his father cut off his allowance, and Sugihara moved to Tokyo to enroll in the High-Normal School at Waseda University. He did his best to support himself, working as a tutor, newspaper delivery boy, longshoreman, and even rickshaw driver, but struggled to make ends meet even with money his mother sent him secretly. "Chiune, come back to us," she begged him in a letter. "I'll apologize to your father for you."

Realizing that the situation was untenable, Sugihara sat in July 1919 for the highly competitive Foreign Service examination, which offered fourteen students the opportunity to study abroad with government subsidies. He passed and, on the advice of someone at the ministry, opted to study Russian, which was increasing in importance given the fraught Russo-Japanese relationship. There were also fringe benefits: Sugihara loved Russian literature and would become a connoisseur of vodka.

In the fall of 1919 Sugihara moved to Harbin, Manchuria, where he would live for the next fifteen years. Harbin's nickname, Little St. Petersburg, suited it well; Orthodox churches dotted its landscape, and it was home to some 120,000 White Russians, many of whom had fled the recent Bolshevik Revolution. The vast majority of the population was Chinese, but there was both a Japanese and a Russian Jewish community. "The cosmopolitan nature of Harbin opened Chiune's eyes to the diversity and excitement of the world," Sugihara's wife later wrote.

Sugihara enrolled in Harbin Gakuin, a national academy where he soon became fluent in Russian. His gift for languages would extend to English, Chinese, French, and German, and he continued to enjoy foreign pastimes, like baseball, hockey, and the Chinese game of Go. After graduating with high honors, he was asked to teach Russian part-time and eventually made a professor. By some accounts, he was tasked by the military to use his language skills to gather intelligence on the Soviets. In February 1924 he officially joined the Foreign Ministry, and the next month he was also commissioned as a second lieutenant.

After a stint as an interpreter in Tokyo, he returned to Harbin, where he fell in love with Klaudia Apollonova, a sixteen-year-old Russian waitress and daughter of a formerly wealthy White Russian colonel who had fled the revolution and now worked as a guard on the Chinese Eastern Railway. Sugihara married Klaudia a few months later and converted to Russian Orthodoxy. The couple hosted glittering parties at their home. "He was very influenced by the West," his son reflected, "and his behavior was not like Japanese men. He said what he thought."

In September 1931 Japan invaded Manchuria, and the following March officially declared it to be the puppet state of Manchukuo. Sugihara was soon the head of the North Manchurian mission office and section chief in charge of all Russian issues, putting him in 1933 at the center of tensions between Japan and Russia over the fate of the Chinese Eastern Railway. Difficult negotiations lasted twenty-one months before a deal was eventually reached to buy out the Soviets at less than half the price they had demanded, averting a second Russo-Japanese war. Sugihara's information proved vital to a successful Japanese strategy, and he was promoted to the number-two position in the Manchukuo Foreign Affairs Ministry.

But then his life suddenly changed completely. He abruptly requested to leave Manchukuo and was assigned to the information department of the Foreign Ministry in Tokyo. "I resigned from my post in the Foreign Ministry because the Japanese dealt with the Chinese so cruelly," he admitted in his diary. Then he and Klaudia divorced over her opposition to having children. Shortly thereafter he met Yukiko Kikuchi, the twenty-one-year-old younger sister of a friend. At five feet,

Yukiko was five inches shorter than Sugihara and thirteen years his junior, but like him she had wavy brown hair. They were married in early 1936 in a Russian Orthodox ceremony after Yukiko also converted. In mid-September their first son, Hiroki, was born.

Sugihara was then assigned to the Soviet Union as a translator, but the Russians, without explanation—perhaps still smarting over his work on the railroad negotiations—denied him a visa. The Foreign Ministry knew Sugihara's value as an intelligence operative and decided instead to send him to keep an eye on the Soviets from the other side of their vast country, assigning him to Finland. As he could not traverse Russia, the Sugiharas went the long way to Europe, across the Pacific, the continental United States, and the Atlantic.

They would remember their year in Helsinki fondly. The twenty-four-year-old Yukiko began her duties as a diplomatic hostess, learning German and French, taking etiquette and dance classes, and entertaining constantly, often in her kimono. Her younger sister Setsuko accompanied her to Europe and helped with the baby. Sugihara learned to drive and practiced at night. The Sugiharas loved the opera, and a highlight of their stay was an audience with the Finnish composer Jean Sibelius, who presented them with a record of his opus *Finlandia*. They had a second son they named Chiaki, and rented a cottage in a white birch forest outside the city where the children could play and enjoy the long summer nights. When the ambassador was suddenly transferred to another posting, Sugihara became acting minister and was very busy handling his duties on top of gathering critical intelligence.

It was then that war broke out, and Sugihara was given the mission to Kovno. He found a three-story house at 30 Vaizgantas Street in the embassy district on the eastern end of the city. Perched halfway up a hill, the white stucco building had a lovely view of the town, and its black wrought-iron gate opened onto a curved staircase at its entrance. Its garden would bloom with crocuses and daffodils, where Sugihara could work early in the morning in his knickerbockers before going to his office. He opened the consulate on September 20 and less than a month later, the family moved in.

Sugihara quickly hired a staff, including a valet, two maids, and two secretaries, employing only locals. The consulate was a hothouse of espionage. At least two of the hires were secretly working for foreign intelligence. Wolfgang Gudze, a German aide to Sugihara, was actually a Gestapo plant, and the butler, Borislav Rõžyki, was an informant for Polish intelligence. Sugihara maintained close contacts with the Poles, with whom the Japanese had a long history of cooperation from a shared wariness of both the Soviet Union and Germany. In Kovno, Sugihara provided diplomatic cover for Polish agents and smuggled information to the government-in-exile in London. At least one mysterious gentleman—who the family called "the Crow"—regularly came to get information from Sugihara.

The Sugiharas made an exotic addition to town. "The people there had never seen a Japanese person before," Sugihara later recalled. The family continued to grow, Yukiko giving birth to a third son, Haruki, in May 1940. They also continued to enjoy excursions that served as cover for Sugihara's clandestine activities. The consul often drove his family himself for picnics in his black Buick. "We would go to out-of-the-way places, following the tracks of tanks or trucks," Hiroki later recalled. "My father was always looking around and taking pictures. I didn't realize this at the time, but he was gathering information on Russian and German activities."

Sugihara also noticed a continued increase in Jewish refugees from Poland, who believed neutral and independent Lithuania to be a haven from both the Soviets and the Nazis. There was already a significant Lithuanian Jewish population there of 32,000, and a community had been present since at least 1280. The city featured some forty synagogues, four Jewish high schools, and a thriving Zionist community. By May 1940 at least ten thousand additional Jews had fled from Poland into Lithuania. They could be seen by the side of the roads, carrying their belongings and speaking a mélange of Yiddish, Polish, Russian, and German. Many slept in the streets or in the railway station. There was also a growing presence of Soviet troops. Yukiko noted that "an eerie atmosphere of uneasy quiet pervaded our new city. Each morning when I woke up, I hoped nothing bad would happen to us."

Sugihara was concerned about the plight of the Jews, both refugees and the local Lithuanians, who seemed oblivious to the danger they faced if the Germans arrived. Many were frozen as they contemplated the threat from the Germans and the Russians—trapped "between the jaws of two lions," as one put it—and in denial that Lithuanian neutrality could be threatened. The previous December Sugihara had met Solly Ganor, the eleven-year-old nephew of the proprietress of a specialty shop where he bought imported delicacies like French champagne and Beluga caviar. The boy invited Sugihara to his house for a Hanukkah party, and the consul had accepted, arriving on a snowy night with Yukiko and Setsuko.

A refugee from Poland, Jacob Rosenblatt, and his eight-year-old daughter, Lea, were temporarily living with the boy's family, and Rosenblatt told the gathering that his wife and older daughter had been killed by the Germans and he had fled south. "You are crazy to stay here," he warned his hosts, and Sugihara asked him about the situation in Poland in great detail. He was horrified. Ganor's father, Chaim, had visas for America, where his brother and sister lived, and was trying to sell his restaurant supply business. "If I were you, I wouldn't worry too much about the business," Sugihara advised him.

In the spring, Sugihara invited the boy to the consulate. Solly had told him at the party about his passion for stamp collecting, and Sugihara presented him with a package of exotic Japanese stamps in different shapes and sizes, many with the emperor's portrait. He asked the boy about Rosenblatt and then told him to give a message to his father. "Tell him," Sugihara said, "the time to leave is now." Soon Sugihara would decide to offer more than just informed advice.

———

As the Nazis and the Red Army were on the march, diplomats throughout Europe scrambled to respond to rapidly developing events. In the middle of June the Dutch businessman Jan Zwartendijk was appointed honorary consul general of the Netherlands in Kovno. The forty-three-year-old Zwartendijk was entirely new to diplomacy. He ran the local division of Philips Electronics, the large Dutch radio and lighting company, and had no experience outside the business world. Born in Rotterdam and educated in England, he had, like Sugihara, spent a significant amount of time abroad. During the First World War he had served in the army before decamping to Argentina and then Paraguay for better prospects. After time as a cowboy on a large cattle ranch, he returned home in the mid-1920s.

Zwartendijk's business ethos was decidedly old-world. His father had run a family tobacco and tea trading firm and taught his twin sons that business was done on a handshake, and that a man's integrity was everything. Zwartendijk developed an instinctive distaste for unethical people.

He found the Netherlands damp and claustrophobic, and went to work in Prague as a commercial agent for a Dutch export firm, where he could make use of his fluency in four languages. There he met his wife, Erna Christianus, and had a son and daughter. After a brief time living in Hamburg, he returned home and in 1936 joined Philips with the goal of another overseas posting. In 1939 he got his wish and arrived in Kovno to oversee the office there. A third child was born in September, the same month war broke out next door in Poland, and around the time the Sugiharas arrived.

On May 10, 1940, the Germans invaded the Netherlands. The Dutch ambassador in Riga, L. P. J. de Dekker, immediately relieved the prior consul of his duties, in part due to his known Nazi sympathies. De Dekker initially planned to leave the position vacant, but a few weeks later he changed his mind and asked a reluctant Zwartendijk to assume the post.

Zwartendijk ran the consulate out of his office. The day after his appointment, on June 15, the Red Army marched into Lithuania. The new government immediately shuttered banks and business came to a standstill. Zwartendijk cabled the head office: "Commercially we are finished here, whatever the further developments may be. It can only become bad or still worse." The local American emissary noted in his diary, "A veritable pall has descended over the country."

There were very few Dutch citizens in Lithuania, and Zwartendijk expected little work on visa matters. But he was soon contacted by a Jewish refugee for help leaving Lithuania. Pressla "Peppy" Lewin had been a Dutch citizen until her marriage in 1935 to the Polish historian Isaac Lewin, and the couple had fled Poland through the forest at night with their three-year-old son, Peppy's mother, and her brother. She contacted both Zwartendijk and De Dekker to see if she might get visas for the Dutch East Indies, but these were no longer being issued. In late June 1940 she again wrote to De Dekker with another proposal: perhaps she might get a visa for one of the Dutch territories in the Americas, either Suriname or Curaçao,* a small Caribbean island offshore of South America known mostly for its strategic Shell refinery that processed Venezuelan oil. De Dekker replied that no visas were ever issued for those colonies, as entrance was only by the consent of the local governor.

Peppy Lewin wrote back with the clever suggestion that perhaps De Dekker could just note that no visa was required for the colonies—which was technically true—and simply omit mention of the required landing permit. She was not planning on going to the West Indies, anyway. She only needed the papers as proof of a final destination to obtain a transit visa, which would allow her to cross another country.

---

* The Dutch West Indies included Curaçao, Aruba, Bonaire, Saba, Sint Eustatius, and Dutch Half Sint Maarten.

"Send me your passport," De Dekker wrote back. He returned it with the truncated language she had requested in handwritten French: "For the admission of aliens to Surinam, Curaçao, and other Dutch possessions in the Americas, an entry visa is not required." The visa was dated July 11. Eleven days later Zwartendijk copied the same language, which became known as the "Curaçao formula," into her husband's safe-conduct pass, allowing them to leave Lithuania with their son, and also gave visas to her relatives.

Almost simultaneously, a twenty-three-year-old student named Nathan Gutwirth approached Zwartendijk with the same idea. The two had become acquainted being among the few Dutchmen in Lithuania when Zwartendijk first arrived in Kovno. The Russians had closed Jewish shops and the yeshiva in Telz, where Gutwirth had been studying for three years, and he no longer felt safe. Thousands were being arrested. "We were more afraid of the Russians than of the Germans," Gutwirth recalled. Going home was no longer an option, since the Nazis occupied the Netherlands. But Gutwirth recalled Curaçao, and remembered that the Caribbean territory was still loyal to the government-in-exile. (By coincidence, it was also home to the oldest synagogue in the Western Hemisphere and eight hundred Jewish families.)

Gutwirth and Zwartendijk appealed to De Dekker to approve the same annotation as he had used for the Lewins, which the ambassador did immediately. In fact, as a Dutch citizen, Gutwirth did not actually need the visa, but he wanted it to make sure there was no ambiguity. On July 23 Zwartendijk used his inkwell with silver antlers to add the "Curaçao formula" to Gutwirth's passport, along with those of two other Dutch nationals. "My office carpet is being worn out by Dutchmen who for some reason or another are in the soup," Zwartendijk reported home. "As Consul, I must try to help them."

Gutwirth then asked Zwartendijk if he could provide Curaçao visas—with the truncated language—for ten Lithuanian classmates, even though they were foreigners. De Dekker again gave his approval.

When word of this reached Zerah Warhaftig, an energetic leader in the religious Zionist Mizrahi movement, he implored Gutwirth to ask Zwartendijk to also help the hundreds of trapped Polish Jews. De Dekker had by now left for Stockholm, and Zwartendijk was forced to act entirely on his own. Without hesitation he agreed to issue Curaçao visas "to everybody who applied."

"An unexpected chain reaction followed," Gutwirth recalled. The news spread like wildfire through the yeshivas and the refugee gathering places at the Café Métropole and Alexander Restaurant. Soon hundreds were pushing and shoving in line at the Philips offices. Over the next four days, before the consulate closed for Sunday, Zwartendijk issued over thirteen hundred visas. When it reopened, he issued another thousand. The refugees had procured a green ink rubber stamp in Vilnius with the Royal Dutch crest that added to his efficiency. He charged no more than the small administrative fee of eleven lit, and waived it if necessary. On August 2, the last day the Dutch consulate was open, Zwartendijk wrote visa number 2,345, the final one, for Eliasz Zupinski. The next day the Soviets "allowed the workers" to take over the office, and the consulate was permanently closed.

"He knew he was in a position to possibly prevent great suffering," Zwartendijk's son later wrote of his father. He had previously had limited contacts with Jews, but he could not watch their persecution. A humanist Protestant with a fascination for Eastern mysticism, he was horrified by cruelty and touched by the Jews' desperation, and he had an instinctive dislike for the Nazis, who "enraged him from the start." But Gutwirth was sure that a week earlier, Zwartendijk "could have had no inkling" that there would soon be two thousand visas under his name.

With now a theoretical place to go, in order to leave Lithuania those holding the Curaçao papers needed to get transit permits for the countries they would cross on their way to freedom. The only possible direction was east. On the other side of the Soviet Union was the land of the rising sun.

———

It was early in the morning and still chilly outside. Sugihara was already downstairs in his office, after his usual light breakfast. A heater warmed the sitting room where Yukiko was reading and listening to the birds singing in the garden. She had only read about ten lines when her husband suddenly appeared and rushed to the window. He had heard a "humming noise" outside the consulate, he later wrote. He opened the curtain to reveal a crowd of refugees forming an uneven line outside the gate. "This was indeed an extraordinary sight because our street was usually empty and quiet," Yukiko recalled. The noise got progressively louder. "People looked frightened and even desperate. They looked hungry and dirty. These people were terrified."

Sugihara sent the houseman Borislav to find out what was going on. He returned with the news that over a hundred Jews were outside, and many thousands more would likely arrive in the coming days. Many had trekked "for many days under severe conditions," Sugihara wrote in his notebook, some all the way from Poland, "dragging themselves on painful feet and enduring countless hardships." Sugihara had issued a handful of transit visas in the previous two weeks to Jewish refugees seeking to escape through Russia, and word had spread of his actions.

Yukiko and Setsuko peered out the window, and shouting erupted as the crowd caught sight of them. Setsuko instinctively snapped a few photographs with her camera. "It was an upsetting sight," Yukiko wrote, "and we felt badly for everyone. We saw the desperate faces of Jewish fathers and mothers holding their children in fear and anticipation. The eyes of tiny children were filled with hunger and fear." They clung to their parents' hands and wore heavy winter coats in layers despite the heat.

Borislav and Gudze, Sugihara's secretary, went back outside to try to keep order. Some people tried to climb over the fence. When the maid went out to buy groceries, the crowd tried to rush in. Sugihara told his children they could not go outside that day as they normally did to play in a huge park near their home. He issued a few dozen visas, but the chaos was substantial. Eventually he went outside and addressed the crowd from the steps, asking them to select five men to speak with him. Shortly thereafter a delegation of Russian speakers, led by Warhaftig, gathered in his office. "Those five men told me about the horrors they would have to face if they didn't get away from the Nazis," Sugihara wrote in his notebook, "and I believe them." Warhaftig and the others told their harrowing stories of escape. "With tears in their eyes, they asked for Japanese visa[s]," Sugihara remembered. Warhaftig explained that for them to use the Dutch visas from Zwartendijk, the only possible route was through the Soviet Union, and to take it they needed to prove they had permission to go directly to a bordering country. A Japanese transit visa, giving the holder permission to stay for ten days, would work perfectly.

Sugihara listened politely and sympathetically. He had, in fact, already issued a handful of visas to Jewish refugees and Polish officers as far back as January, but this was different. He was candid, explaining that while he could issue a few visas on his own, he would need permission from the Ministry of Foreign Affairs to provide them to hundreds of people.

When the men had left, Sugihara sat alone in his office for a few minutes. Then he came upstairs, sat at a table quietly, and drank coffee with Yukiko. The situation was even more complicated, he confided, for he had received notice from the Soviets that he would have to close the consulate by early August. The new Communist government, elected with 99 percent of the vote, had on July 21 formally requested annexation of Lithuania, which would thus cease to be an independent country. Throughout Kovno, consulates were shuttering in compliance with the order. If he followed suit, all hope for the refugees would disappear.

"That night was one of the most upsetting of Chiune's life," Yukiko recalled. He tossed and turned, unable to sleep. The next day, he determined to act. The consulate was closed, and he composed a cable to the Foreign Ministry about the situation on the ground. He reported that the Communists, with help from the Red Army and the secret police, were committing "acts of terrorism." They had stormed the headquarters of political opponents and arrested several thousand people, targeting Poles, White Russians, socialists, Bundists, and Jews. The recently deposed prime minister and foreign minister of Lithuania themselves had been deported to Moscow with their families. In closing, he noted, "Daily, hundreds of Jews are thronging our building asking for visas to go to the US or Japan."

With a diplomatic sleight of hand, he had informed his superiors of the unfolding crisis without actually asking for instructions. He was aware that a few days earlier, on July 23, the Foreign Ministry had circulated a telegram reporting a significant uptick in Jewish refugees passing through Japan on their way to the United States, and that over six hundred people had already booked passage in Berlin on the Japanese NYK Lines. "More and more requests are coming in," Yōsuke Matsuoka, the minister of foreign affairs, wrote, "and unless all arrangements have been completed concerning destination and entrance permits, I want you to be careful not to grant any visas for passage through our country." The telegram put consulates—including presumably Kovno—on notice to ensure that transit visas were only issued to those who had satisfied the entry requirements for their ultimate destination.

Japan had a complicated view of Jews, going back to Jacob Schiff's critical financing of their war against Russia in 1904. Various plans had been hatched in recent years to attract Jewish immigrants and capital, in part because a number of policymakers believed classic anti-Semitic tropes about Jews controlling the world, so they sought to co-opt them. In December 1938 the government had attempted a nuanced policy, avoiding antagonizing the Germans by welcoming Jews but also preserving flexibility to attract those who might be beneficial to Japan. Exceptions could be made for businessmen, engineers, and others with potential value for the nation. But for the moment, the Foreign Ministry seemed focused on avoiding a refugee crisis.

Outside the crowd continued to grow. "They came to my office in waves," Sugihara recalled later. He spoke of an old Japanese proverb: "Even the hunter cannot kill a bird that came to him for refuge." There were women, children, and elderly people. Sugihara wondered if they even had anywhere to sleep. Many were terrified to eat or go to the bathroom for fear of losing their place in line. "Chiune really wanted to help them," Yukiko remembered.

Sugihara was tormented by the Japanese policy. "Tokyo stubbornly refused to allow it," Sugihara remembered. "We had thousands of people hanging around the windows of the residence." At night, he was still not sleeping. "I cannot allow these people to die," he remembered thinking, "people who have come to me for help with death staring them in the eyes." He did not wait for a response to his cable. Determined to act, he went outside and addressed the crowd.

"I will issue visas to each and every one of you to the last," he told them softly. "So, please wait patiently."

A hush came over the refugees as Borislav translated Sugihara's words. After a moment, an electricity seemed to flow through the crowd. People embraced and kissed one another. Mothers picked up their children in joy. Some reached toward the sky in quiet jubilation. "The magic of the moment filled me with gladness," Yukiko wrote.

Sugihara set up a makeshift office in the garage, and when the door opened, the refugees pushed forward in such excitement that they almost crushed the consul against the wall. Borislav moved the crowd back, and Sugihara instructed him to write numbered cards and hand them out to refugees in the order in which they had lined up. Then Sugihara drank several cups of coffee and began work.

Sugihara personally interviewed each refugee, taking down all the required details, from their name and age to their port of entry and proof of funds. He did his best to put them all at ease, quietly nodding as he took down the information. He introduced himself as "Sempo," which was easier to pronounce than his unusual given name, and served them tea. Among his first transit visas had been for the Lewin family on July 26, who had presented their Curaçao papers the day before the crowd showed up. Gutwirth got his visa on August 6. Many others also arrived with Curaçao visas from Zwartendijk, around a third of the total Sugihara would help. "I had to look up where it was and found it in South America near Cuba," Sugihara later recalled. Others were headed to America, New Zealand, Australia, Palestine, and Brazil, or at least their papers said so. At the end of the interview, Sugihara sometimes advised the refugees to say "Banzai Nippon!" ("Long live Japan!") to the Japanese customs officials who would inspect their papers on the other side. Then he looked into their eyes and wished them luck.

By the time he sent a second and third cable to Tokyo for instructions on specific cases, Sugihara had issued over 525 visas in just a few days. The Japanese government would not tolerate disobedience well, he knew, but to him the choice was clear. "I had to do something. There was no place else for them to go," he later recalled. "I decided to halt pointless exchanges with Tokyo which had become a waste of time, especially because I had my work cut out with closing down the consulate. Whatever punishment may be imposed on me, I know I should follow my conscience." The Sugiharas knew that he could be dismissed from the ministry. There was also the physical threat from the Nazis, who would not view his actions lightly. "It was very dangerous," Yukiko later wrote. "You cannot hide such a crowd. The Germans must have known."

Sugihara's expertise in all things Russian also again proved decisive. Without Soviet consent, a Japanese transit visa was useless. He drove his Buick, the small Japanese flags flapping over the tires, to the Soviet consulate to confirm that they would permit the refugees to transit across their country. It was a serious matter, and one that needed approval from ten Soviet senior officials, including Stalin himself. After a few days Sugihara was given the go-ahead by an apparatchik. The Russians would honor the Japanese stamps.

"Chiune was very persuasive with the Soviet officials," Yukiko wrote. "He returned, his face glowing with happiness." It is likely that Sugihara arranged a special deal with the Soviets, who were always eager for hard currency and agreed to sell tickets on the Trans-Siberian Railroad to refugees at extortionate prices. Perhaps getting rid of hundreds of religious Jews was an added inducement.

The refugees kept coming to the consulate. Perhaps the most dramatic request made of both Sugihara and Zwartendijk was papers for the entire Mirrer yeshiva. Founded in Belarus more than a century earlier, it was the only such institution to survive the war intact. Gutwirth took the Mirrer's request for three hundred Curaçao visas to Zwartendijk, who immediately agreed to issue them. One of the students had obtained Polish safe-passage papers for everyone from the British consulate, and these were dropped off by five boys at Zwartendijk's office. When they picked them up shortly thereafter, all three hundred were stamped and signed.

The scholars still needed transit visas, and they headed to Sugihara. Twenty-year-old Moshe Zupnik, who could recite Goethe in perfect German, was chosen as spokesman, dressed in a borrowed pin-striped suit. When he arrived at the Japanese consulate, he initially could not get past Borislav, but was eventually taken around the back door and presented to Gudze, Sugihara's German aide.

Gudze was stunned by the request for three hundred transit visas. There was no way Sugihara could do that, he told Zupnik. "The consul will never allow this."

Zupnik begged to speak to Sugihara directly. Gudze looked at him carefully. "All right," he finally said, "talk to the consul."

When Zupnik entered Sugihara's office, the consul was seated at his desk. Zupnik could hear Gudze explaining the request in Russian.

"Who are you?" Sugihara asked Zupnik in broken English.

"We are a rabbinical seminary with over three hundred people, and we want to go to Curaçao," Zupnik said.

"How could I be responsible to my government giving out so many visas in one time?" Sugihara asked. If the group tried to remain in Japan unlawfully, it would be a disaster.

Zupnik quickly improvised a story about an American rabbi who was providing ships and money and with whom they communicated by secret code.

Sugihara studied Zupnik, barely older than a teenager, in his desperation. "All right," he said finally. "I believe you."

In the hallway, Gudze stopped Sugihara. "How can I handle such a crowd?" he asked.

Zupnik offered to help. Sugihara accepted without hesitation. "He simply handed over the consular stamp and allowed me to make visas," Zupnik remembered.

Zupnik and Gudze set up chairs in the corridor outside Sugihara's office and worked for the next fourteen days straight, stamping visas into passports as the consul conducted interviews and handwrote the necessary portions. They stamped all the Mirrer visas and hundreds of others, at one point even passing papers out of the window. "Whatever came in, I stamped," Zupnik recalled.

Gudze was a former wine salesman and, as they worked, he talked in German with Zupnik. Gudze confessed that he had opposed Hitler and disagreed strongly with the führer about the Jews. He had previously had a romance with a Jewish girl whose family would not allow her to marry him, which actually only increased his respect for them. Gestapo informant or not, Gudze was, in Zupnik's view, "a tzaddik"—a righteous person.

———

When he began, Sugihara kept a log of each visa, assisted by Gudze. The work was painstaking. The ornate, vertical, almost calligraphic Japanese script could not be done quickly, and Sugihara had to write most of the transit permit—the equivalent of several long paragraphs—by hand before the official stamp of Japan was affixed. As his ink began to run out, he mixed it with water to try to make it last. His words became fainter, and as he pressed down on the pen, it finally snapped. Even when one of the staff procured a rubber stamp, the required handwriting was still enormous.

Sugihara worked methodically, often in his shirtsleeves, from eight in the morning to late at night. There were so many Jews crowded into his office that Yukiko could not get him lunch, and he often skipped meals. He reappeared upstairs every evening, eyes bloodshot, hair disheveled, and collapsed on his bed. His children barely saw him. Yukiko tried to keep the baby quiet and massaged Sugihara's hands, which were racked with pain, sometimes even after he had fallen asleep.

"He was in a hurry for he knew, sooner or later, he would have to close the consulate," Yukiko wrote. At one point he stopped keeping a list of the refugees or taking the time to charge the nominal processing fee. Eventually he even halted detailed interviews.

Sugihara quickly realized that many of the refugees did not have anything close to adequate papers or financial resources. Many had forged documents, expired or invalidated Polish passports, suspect Czech documents, dubious visas to Palestine, or nothing at all. But

Sugihara helped them regardless. He was not even under any illusions about the usefulness of the Curaçao visas. (As it happened, none of the refugees actually went to Curaçao, and it was a good thing: the governor of Curaçao later told Warhaftig he would have turned away any boatload of refugees that showed up.) "I'd say more than half of them had no passport. Under the conditions they had to deal with when they left their homeland it seemed understandable," Sugihara remembered. "So we accepted anything." Even blank sheets of paper with Curaçao visas on them were allowed.

Conditions were difficult for everyone. Yukiko was under such stress that she was unable to breastfeed. They did not go out of the consulate for food and were surviving on rice soup. The volume of refugees pouring into Lithuania caused food shortages, with bread tripling in price, and sporadic violence occasionally broke out. The line outside the consulate stretched two hundred meters. Some refugees pitched tents, and many slept in the park to get a spot near the front of the line. Ludvik Salomon, a refugee from Kraków, had stood on line for several days without eating before Sugihara served him tea and stamped his passport.

The staff was periodically sent outside to control the crowd. The girl who lived upstairs served Jews sandwiches in her flat and allowed them to lie down on the sofa for a few minutes to rest. "They were in a panic that they would not get visas," she recalled. "We tried to calm them down. 'Sugihara is a wonderful man,' we would tell them. 'He would not refuse you help.'"

"The world says that America is civilized," Sugihara told the thirty-year-old rabbi Eliezer Portnoy when he gave him a visa. "I will show the world that Japan is more civilized." Many refugees were struck and comforted by Sugihara's gentle manner when they finally got to see him. Two teenage Polish girls, Chaya and Feiga Szepsenwol, were terrified when they confessed to Sugihara that their father was dead and their mother did not have valid papers. "He looked very sympathetic, he looked like such a kind man," one recalled later. As he wrote their visas, the sisters kept saying "Thank you" over and over in Polish until Sugihara finally raised his hand "to let us know it's okay and smiled at us." They burst out crying, shaking as they left. A number of witnesses even saw refugees bend down and kiss Sugihara's feet in gratitude. Once Sugihara saw a woman waiting by herself on the line and sent a messenger to tell her to go home and rest and he would have her visa ready the next day. He did this for women and children. "I thought that he was a real gentleman," she said years later.

By the middle of August, some of the refugees had begun to arrive at the other end of the Soviet Union, asking for entrance to Japan. A cable—No. 22—arrived on August 18 from the Japanese foreign minister, complaining that refugees from Lithuania on their way to the United States or Canada were arriving with visas signed by Sugihara but without enough money and proper destination visas. "We cannot permit them to land here and we are troubled as to how to deal with this," the cable read. Sugihara was warned, therefore, "to deny transit visas to such individuals who lack sufficient funds to stay in Japan and who have not completed the entry procedures for their destinations."

Sugihara composed a telegram in response that was as close to heartfelt as diplomatic formalities would permit. The refugees had no other choice, he explained. There were no Central or South American consulates nearby, and so Japan was "the only country left to transit." There was desperation, as the refugees knew the consulate was soon to close, and a Japanese visa was necessary for the Soviet Union to allow transit on the way to the United States and other havens. He assured his superiors in Tokyo, moreover, that he would only issue visas contingent on all the requirements being in place, including financial guarantees, and to those who were well recommended to him. Those who did not comply could always be stopped in Vladivostok, he suggested. Of course, as he well knew, that was precisely the problem. While he managed to send off a cable on August 24 about a particular refugee named

Leon Polak, he did not send his reply to cable no. 22 until September 1. By then an urgent telegram had arrived from the Foreign Ministry: "Close the Consulate and go to Berlin at once." The Soviets were pressuring Tokyo to shutter the consulate, and the ministry feared an international incident.

When Sugihara finally sent his cable on September 1, the response arrived two days later, again titled "Handling Refugees." Tokyo was not pleased. Sugihara was putting them in an untenable situation. The shipping company in Vladivostok could not deny boarding to the holder of a Japanese visa, and the Soviets in any event were insisting the papers be honored. "From now on please keep under the conditions of telegram No. 22." Tokyo, it seemed, understood that Sugihara knew exactly what he was doing.

Zupnik came to get his things and say goodbye. He found Sugihara in his office, writing a visa for an elderly Polish couple. When Sugihara saw Zupnik, he grabbed the young man by the shoulders, thanked him for his help, and wished him good luck.

Zupnik bade farewell to Gudze as well. "Wolfgang," he said, "how can I thank you?"

"Remember the world is like a *rad* [wheel]," Gudze told him. "Whoever is on top today, tomorrow might be down. Don't forget what I did for you."

"Those were the best two weeks of my life," Zupnik later said.

———

The night before they left the consulate, clouds of pale blue smoke wafted upstairs from Sugihara's office. Rushing downstairs, Yukiko pounded on the door and discovered Sugihara burning his confidential papers. The next morning, the family prepared to leave. The bags were packed, the furniture covered with sheets for transport, and important files and the official seal already sent on to Berlin. "I will never forget the look of despair on the faces of the Jews who did not get visas as we left our consulate," Yukiko wrote in her memoirs. Yukiko, Setsuko, and the children waited in the car as Sugihara made one final inspection of the consulate and then came outside with his briefcase for one last look at his garden. Before he got into the car, he posted a sign on the wrought-iron gate and then was driven off.

The sign said that Sugihara would be staying at the Hotel Metropolis until his departure. By the time he had checked into his room, he was told a crowd of people in the lobby was hoping to see him. He came downstairs and again set up shop in a large stuffed chair, where a line quickly formed. He no longer had the official seal or the rubber stamp but wrote out impromptu visas—"Permission papers"—on official consulate stationery.

He wrote visas for several more days—"To the very last minute," Yukiko recalled. Eventually she came downstairs to tell him their train would be departing soon and they had to leave.

"Please forgive me," Sugihara said sadly to the refugees. "I cannot write anymore. I wish you the best." He then bowed deeply and left the hotel.

"They stood frozen before our eyes," Yukiko remembered, "as all hope faded from their faces."

The crowd followed him to Kovno Station, where special international trains for diplomats waited for departure. The platform was packed with refugees, travelers, Red Army soldiers, and merchants selling to all of them. Refugees swarmed around Sugihara. "I didn't know what to do for I just couldn't say no to them," he said. "I signed papers for five or six people on the platform." Even on the train, he scribbled furiously, passing visas through the window.

"Don't go, please!" shouted a refugee. "Don't forsake us!"

As the train gained speed, refugees ran alongside. Sugihara finally handed the remaining stack of stationery to them through the window.

Yukiko wrote, "I was sad for the people left behind at the station without visas. I will not forget their eyes for the rest of my life."

Soon the train was surrounded by thick pine woods.

"Father, are we going to Berlin?" five-year-old Hiroki asked.

The consul nodded and then fell fast asleep.

———

In Kovno, many of the refugees with papers remained stuck as the Soviets, despite the assurances to Sugihara about issuing transit visas, were very slow to do so. Only a trickle of Jews arrived in Japan in the autumn. "Nobody dreamt the Russians would permit us to go," Zupnik recalled. But then in November, the Soviets suddenly opened the gates. Gutwirth, who had been so early in getting his papers, finally left Lithuania on December 8 and arrived in Japan about two weeks later. Over the following months, hundreds of Jews departed with their Japanese transit visas, making the eleven-day journey to Vladivostok on the Trans-Siberian Railroad, courtesy of Intourist, the Soviet travel bureau. From there they took the three-day voyage on cargo ships over often-rough seas in the Sea of Japan to Tsuruga.

Zwartendijk too had been in limbo, unable to get a Soviet exit visa after trying for several weeks over the summer because the Netherlands and the Soviet Union did not recognize each other diplomatically. His alarm increased dramatically when his landlord, a professor of history who lived downstairs, appeared at the door with his wife and five-year-old daughter. "They were tearful and terrified, having been told by the Soviets to get ready within a very few hours to leave for Siberia (his sin was being an intellectual)," Zwartendijk's daughter recalled. Such intellectuals everywhere were being eliminated. "There wasn't a tree without someone hanging from it" in the local park, his son remembered. Zwartendijk fled to a house sixty miles outside town on the Memel River, only to discover a Russian base being erected nearby. Finally in September the family's papers came through, to their great relief, and they left immediately by train.

Zwartendijk feared for his safety back in the Netherlands under Nazi rule. The Gestapo would certainly not look well on his work rescuing Torah scholars. Heinrich Himmler was so concerned about a "renaissance of Jewish learning" in the United States that he had specifically targeted Polish Talmudic scholars for elimination. Ominously, the Gestapo headquarters was next door to the Zwartendijks' home, and one day two officers showed up at their door. They had tortured a close Jewish friend of his to death during an interrogation—"Trying to escape," as the euphemism went—and found Zwartendijk's name and address in the man's pocket. As it happened, they had not in fact learned anything about the visas, and any Gestapo file on Zwartendijk had remained in Lithuania. But his actions in Kovno had been very public. As his son Jan later remarked, "It is the more astonishing that the German security forces did not catch up with my father for having undermined their master plan. A little vengeance could have been expected." The family survived hardship during the war, selling their grand piano for food and enduring bombing. Zwartendijk could not breathe easily until the Netherlands was liberated in September 1944.

———

After reporting in Berlin after leaving Kovno, Sugihara was appointed consul in Prague. Life for diplomats there was once again enjoyable, and the Sugiharas took up residence in a grand Rococo building on the Moldau River, supported by a staff of ten. As always, they took drives into the countryside, and there was even time for trips to Rome, Venice, and Switzerland.

On February 4 the foreign minister cabled Sugihara for an accounting of the visas he had "issued to Jewish refugees . . . in Kovno." Sugihara responded the next day that he had issued 2,132 visas, some for entire families, of which he estimated 1,500 were for Jews. The list was incomplete because he had issued as many as 80 additional visas to mostly German Jews on the run in Prague as well. On February 28, he sent a final tally.

Sugihara was now being viewed with "caution" by the Germans, most likely because of his espionage activities. His reputation was not helped when in early 1941 he confronted German foreign minister Joachim von Ribbentrop at a meeting of the Prague diplomatic community. Seated at a large desk beneath a photo of Hitler, Ribbentrop had ordered the diplomats to leave the now annexed Czechoslovak territory, much as the Soviets had done in Kovno. Sugihara alone had spoken up, calmly stating that the Germans' Japanese allies could not be ordered around. "I feel good today," Sugihara told Yukiko after the meeting.

On February 15 Sugihara was summoned to Berlin and ordered to close the Prague consulate. He was made head of a new consulate in the snowy town of Königsberg, the legendary home of Immanuel Kant, which he opened on March 6. The location was once again chosen as an observation post. The family moved into a large two-story home with a pear and apple orchard where the children fed peanuts to the squirrels. Sugihara quietly issued at least thirty-two more visas, and he again often drove into the countryside, noting German troops arriving by train, steamships in port, tanks mobilizing, and officers being taught basic Russian and how to read maps. His conclusion that war between Russia and Germany was imminent was proven right in June, when the Nazis invaded the Soviet Union.

The following autumn, he was appointed ambassador in Bucharest. The current ambassador ended up unable to leave, so Sugihara instead spent his time helping out as a translator. The family lived in a grand mansion and spent the next two years enjoying a "gorgeous life." The children learned to play instruments and enjoyed Romanian animal performances on the street, complete with dancing bears. When the Allies began bombing the city, the family moved for safety to the countryside, where they skied and made snowmen and Sugihara worked in a rose garden.

Things became dangerous, however, as the bombings escalated, destroying large parts of Bucharest. In March 1944 Sugihara made preparations to leave as the Red Army drew nearer to the city. When Yukiko went into town to retrieve some belongings, she was caught in the final fighting and forced to hide in a forest in the Carpathian Mountains, separated from her panicked family for eight harrowing days.

The Nazis were finally repelled from Bucharest in September. They surrendered to the Allies eight months later on May 8, 1945. The Soviets finally declared war on Japan on August 8, two days after Hiroshima, making the Sugiharas now enemy citizens. They were escorted by armed guard to the Soviet military officers' residence and placed under house arrest there. They could not leave but were treated reasonably well. The Romanian guards even gave the children a turtle and allowed them to play in the fresh air.

Shortly after the Japanese surrender, the Soviets transferred the Sugiharas to an old army barracks on the outskirts of Bucharest. They were put into two drafty rooms heated only by a coal stove, and slept on uncomfortable straw mattresses thrown on a dirt floor. As diplomatic prisoners, they were not forced to work but had little to do. The food was terrible. Sugihara was repeatedly interrogated. "I'm not a spy," he insisted.

They remained in the barracks for over a year. In December 1946 the Russians finally informed Sugihara that he would be permitted to return to Japan, leaving immediately. Yukiko dressed the children in fur coats and hats for the trip through the Russian winter, and they were driven in a frozen truck to the train station and boarded onto a passenger train crowded with Soviet soldiers. The glacial trip across Russia took several weeks. Massive white birch forests and golden-onion-domed churches drifted past the windows, though some of the time all they saw were massive expanses of snow. It was the same long trip of over nine thousand kilometers that many of the refugees had taken to Vladivostok and the rough voyage across the Sea of Japan to the port of Tsuruga. Outside it was forty-five degrees below zero, and the Sugiharas' eyelashes froze. Showering was forbidden, and the children were soon tormented by fleas and lice.

For several weeks they were interned in Odessa on the Black Sea. From there, they were transferred from camp to camp over the next three months, subsisting on meager rations. Their thirty-six pieces of baggage were repeatedly searched, each time more of their belongings disappearing, including many of their photographs from Kovno.

When they finally arrived at Nakhodka on the Sea of Japan, home felt imminent. It was March and still bitter cold, but their journey was almost done. They were once again interned for a month in a barracks where they saw ordinary Japanese prisoners working as lumberers outside. In April 1947 they were at last given permission to leave and boarded a small cargo vessel. "The excitement I felt climbing up the ladder onto the ship was much greater than any I could have experienced if I were taking a cruise on a deluxe ocean liner," Yukiko wrote in her memoirs. Two days later, on April 10, they arrived in Vladivostok and boarded the *Koan-maru*. Everyone on the ship was Japanese, and the sound of so many people speaking the language was strange, almost foreign.

When the ship entered the port of Hakata in Kyushu, it had been ten years since the Sugiharas were last home. "We have come back to Japan," Yukiko kept repeating to her children as she pointed to the land.

From the boat, the family could see cherry blossoms, and Yukiko burst into tears.

The Sugiharas had almost no money when they arrived home. Sugihara sold some property he had in Gifu to buy a house in Kanagawa Prefecture, south of Tokyo. In July he was summoned to Tokyo to report in to the Foreign Ministry. He dressed for the appointment at the Gaimusho and was excited to return to diplomatic work, this time in a peaceful world. But in an ominous sign, Vice Minister Katsuo Okazaki kept his back to him when he respectfully knocked on his office door.

"Thank you, Mr. Sugihara, for your service," Okazaki finally said to him coldly. "As we no longer have a post for you, please resign. We can no longer take you under our wing!" Sugihara later admitted to Yukiko that Okazaki had mentioned his refusal to follow orders in Kovno. "If I admit your way, I am to set a bad example to the others," Okazaki told him. He prepared a pension for him, advising him to rest and "start a new life." Then he went back to reading the newspaper.

Sugihara duly submitted his resignation on May 28. He was devastated. As time went on, he had dared to believe that his actions in Kovno would perhaps be forgotten. His modest severance and retirement allowance were set at prewar rates, and the higher cost of living meant the money was soon exhausted as the Sugiharas were forced to burn through their savings. Particularly painful too were the rumors circulating through the Foreign Ministry that Sugihara had taken bribes from Jews to issue visas. "In the days after the war, Chiune was very depressed," Yukiko wrote. "It was as if a shadow had crossed Chiune's face. I often found it difficult to look at him because of this."

Shortly thereafter, in December 1947, the Sugiharas' youngest son, Haruki, came home from a school trip with an excruciating headache and massive nosebleed. He was dead the next day. Sugihara stood in his garden, devastated, "helpless and vacant-eyed." They blamed the war, convinced the stress of life in the internment camps in Lithuania and the severe Siberian cold had taken a toll on the child. The year after they lost Haruki, Yukiko's sister Setsuko died of a kidney ailment that would have been treatable in normal times. Life in Japan after the war was difficult. There were shortages of everything. Work was hard to find. Sugihara periodically traveled to the countryside in Gifu to bring back rice to feed his family. He was forced to work for a time selling lightbulbs door-to-door, as a purchasing agent for the occupation forces, and at a Ginza department store that catered to American GIs.

Some measure of brightness finally returned in 1951 with a newborn son they named Nobuki. Eventually Sugihara's language skills served as a fallback, and he worked as a teacher, then as a translator for an American textile company, for the NHK Radio translating Russian reports into Japanese, and for the Science and Technology Agency. In 1960 he was asked by Kawakami Trading to work in Moscow. He decided to go alone, concerned about the effect of the bleak, bitter weather on Yukiko's health.

He remained there for fifteen years. During his time in Russia, he was able to return to Japan only a few times a year but kept up a constant stream of letters to his wife and children. When his son Chiaki visited, he found his father living in a small room where the bathroom served as a kitchen and a toilet seat as a cutting board. "He never used money for himself," Chiaki recalled. He sent it all home and managed to send the two elder boys to college in the United States.

Sugihara often wondered what had happened to the refugees. Then, during a trip home in August 1968, he was invited to the Israeli embassy in Tokyo to meet the new commercial attaché, who had asked to see him. A bit confused, he brought his son Nobuki with him. When they got to the embassy, the attaché introduced himself as Yehoshua Nishri and explained that he had last met Sugihara as a young man when the consul had given him a visa in Kovno. He was, in fact, one of the boys whose papers Sugihara had signed at the train station on his departure.

Nishri grabbed Sugihara by the hands, tears welling, and told him that none of the refugees had been able to find him for years. Sugihara had told them to call him "Sempo"—it was easier to pronounce—and for years no one could track down "Sempo Sugihara." The Foreign Ministry had records of no such person. With emotion, Nishri showed Sugihara his carefully preserved visa, now a "very old and worn out piece of paper." Sugihara had always been skeptical his visas would do much good, assuming most had been worthless to the refugees, given the profound difficulties, risk, and expense of actually getting out of Lithuania. Now he learned that at least some refugees had been saved.

As a gesture of thanks, the Israeli embassy arranged for a scholarship to Hebrew University for Nobuki, and Sugihara visited him there the following year on his way to Moscow. He posed for a picture on a camel beside the Dead Sea and enjoyed a three-day tour of the country. He met a couple of survivors as well—the vice mayor of Tel Aviv and, in Jerusalem, Warhaftig, now the minister of religion and a signer of the new state's declaration of independence in 1948. Warhaftig had twenty-five grandchildren, all of them alive because of Sugihara, and he called the consul an "emissary of G-d."

"I am proud to have issued visas to the Jews," Sugihara reflected to an interviewer during the trip. "My act may have been questionable as a diplomat, but I'm sure what I did was not wrong at all seen from a humanitarian point of view. If I face the same situation, I would do the same thing."

In the Netherlands, Jan Zwartendijk had said virtually nothing about his activities in Kovno when he returned home. Even his youngest son was entirely ignorant of what his father had done until he was in his thirties. After the war, Zwartendijk spent ten years in Athens as director for Philips Electronics and then retired to Rotterdam. In 1963 an article appeared in a Los Angeles Jewish newspaper about the "Angel of Curaçao," and the Dutch Foreign Ministry contacted him. What archives there were had gone up in smoke when Zwartendijk and his eleven-year-old son had destroyed his papers before leaving

Kovno. Zwartendijk was thrilled to hear that some people had actually escaped, a question that had plagued him for years. As with Sugihara, the refugees did not know Zwartendijk's real name, some calling him "Swarthout" and others only "Mr. Philip Reyda" (recalling the Philips Radio sign on his office), and so had been unable to find him.

His inquiries for further information went unanswered. In 1964, he was stunned when he was summoned to the Dutch Foreign Ministry and formally reprimanded for his actions, then informed that he could never receive a government medal because he had broken the rules by issuing false visas. In 1971 Gutwirth, who was living in Antwerp, tracked him down to thank him, one of the few. But Zwartendijk eventually dropped the matter again. "He did not wish to appear to be looking for praise or glory, because he was not," one of his sons wrote later. "He did not wish to be honored for simply being decent, any more than he would have accepted a reward for being honest." His other son said, "He just wanted to do good for people." And he did not like being called the "Angel of Curaçao."

His son ignored his modesty, however, and in 1976 found a historian who informed Zwartendijk that he had saved the lives of over two thousand people. In September a Kobe rabbi dispatched a letter with the names and details of 2,178 Jews who had gotten safely to Japan on Curaçao visas. Zwartendijk died peacefully two days before it arrived.

In 1975 Sugihara finally came home from Russia. He had developed heart problems and retired to a house in the mountains in Kamakura, a Tokyo suburb. He took walks and played the piano and on Sundays worked in the garden. Survivors came to visit him to share stories about their children and grandchildren. In November 1984 a cedar grove was planted on a hill on Beit Shamesh in Jerusalem in his honor. His son Nobuki represented the family and wrote to his parents that meeting the survivors and hearing their stories made it the best day of his life. Two months later, Sugihara was made a Righteous Among the Nations, the first Asian person to receive that title, but was too sick to attend the ceremony. On July 31, 1986, Sugihara passed away from heart failure.

There was an outpouring of grief when news of his death was made public. In 1991 the Gaimusho rehabilitated Sugihara, and the vice foreign minister, Muneo Suzuki, paid Yukiko a visit of respect. The next year Sugihara received the Nagasaki Peace Prize and a monument at his birthplace in Yaotsu—the "Hill of Humanity"—was dedicated to him. The monument was in the shape of a bamboo pipe organ on a lotus pond whose ripples, Yukiko declared, "symbolize the ripple effect of one pebble and its impact on the entire world." Streets and monuments have been named for Sugihara in Lithuania, Israel, Japan, and the United States. In 2000, the hundredth anniversary of his birth, a plaque was installed in the Foreign Ministry archives, honoring him for his "courageous and humanitarian act." In 2001 two hundred cherry trees were planted along the Neris River in Kovno. In 2006 schoolchildren in his hometown folded six thousand origami cranes from visas, one for each of the Sugihara refugees, and sent one thousand to Yad Vashem. One man rescued by Sugihara said, "He took us out from hell and put us in heaven." A sixteen-year-old refugee later reflected similarly, "I think he was a man sent by God. If he had issued earlier or later, the visa would have become no use."

"There's a choice to be made in your life," Zwartendijk's younger son reflected, "and you have to make the right choice, not the easy choice. This was not an easy decision, not for my father, not for Sugihara." In the end, it is estimated that Sugihara saved several thousand people from the Nazis. His actions during a few weeks in Kovno in the summer of 1940 echo through the tens of thousands of descendants of those he saved who are alive today. "I didn't do anything special," he once said of the days in Kovno. "I made my own decisions, that's all. I followed my own conscience and listened to it." Yet Sugihara always felt the need to rationalize his disobedience. "What I did as a diplomat who disobeyed his country's orders while serving his government may have been wrong," he told Yukiko toward the end of his life, "but I could not, in good conscience, ignore the pleas of thousands of people who sought my help. Therefore, I conclude that I did the only right thing, as any decent human being would have done. In the end, history will be the true judge."

Nobuki once asked his father why he did what he did. "I felt pity for the people," he told him. "Simple, nothing dramatic." His son Hiroki saw his father's samurai blood at work. "My father told me that a samurai warrior is not only strong and brave, but is also very kind and always ready to help those in need," he said. "My father was a real samurai."

6

Miracle on the Øresund

GEORG FERDINAND DUCKWITZ WAS PERHAPS AN UNLIKELY HERO OF THE RESIS-
tance. He had been, after all, a card-carrying member of the Nazi Party
since November 1932. Born into a well-to-do German family in 1904 in
Bremen, Duckwitz had studied as a lawyer and an economist and first
came to Denmark as a twenty-five-year-old employee of Kaffee Hag, a
German coffee trading firm. It was to be a lifelong love affair with the
country he would refer to as his "chosen fatherland." For several years
in the early 1930s, he was an expert on shipping and maritime trade
in the region for the Foreign Ministry before returning to the private
sector as an executive for the Hamburg America Line, one of the largest
cargo and passenger shipping companies in the world. At the outbreak
of the Second World War, Duckwitz was living in New York as the
firm's representative. But after hostilities began, he was sought after
for his expertise, and the company seconded him back to the Foreign
Ministry, which posted him to Copenhagen on a murky assignment in
collaboration with the Abwehr, the German intelligence service.

Denmark was extraordinarily important to Germany, sandwiched
between its northern border and the sea, and a year earlier the two nations had signed a nonaggression pact. As a result, the Danes had never
bothered to fortify their border, and at four in the morning on April 9,
1940, German troops crossed into Denmark while simultaneously invading Norway. They landed in fifteen different locations, including
the center of Copenhagen, by land, sea, and air. The fighting was over

within hours, with sporadic gunfire at the royal palace and around the country. Only thirteen soldiers were killed. But Denmark from the beginning would prove to be an exception in many ways under German occupation.

From the outset, Germany announced that it did "not intend now or in the future to interfere with Denmark's territorial integrity or political independence." Under Nazi ideology, the Danes were considered pure Aryan. Berlin decided to govern with a light touch what they hoped would be a "model protectorate" for the "Neuropa" Hitler envisioned. The Danes accepted the terms, as the king and his prime minister declared, "under protest." The Danish government was kept in place, the king remained on the throne, and even the military was left untouched. The only difference was the presence of German troops and officials.

All of this gave the Danes some leverage, and from the first day of the occupation, the treatment of the Danish Jews was a high-priority issue for the king and for the government. The oldest members of the Jewish community—the so-called Viking Jews—had lived in Denmark since 1622, and shortly thereafter the parliament had rejected the implementation of a ghetto as "inhuman." In 1814 all religious discrimination was declared illegal. The several thousand Danish Jews were thoroughly integrated into the life of the nation, involved in all spheres from politics to the military to the economy. A strong condition of peaceful Danish accommodation was that the Jews were to be left alone, a demand that came directly from the king. Indeed, the well-known story of King Christian X wearing a yellow Star of David in solidarity with his Jewish subjects is apocryphal—because the king and his government would not permit the star to be mandated. "I considered our own Jews to be Danish citizens, and the Germans could not touch them," the king noted. "The prime minister shared my view and added that there could be no question about that."

Not wishing trouble, at first the Germans left the almost eight thousand Jews in Denmark alone. For three years after the invasion, things were calm. At the embassy Duckwitz kept his head down and continued to cultivate strong relationships across Denmark, including at the highest levels of political leadership. His fluency in Danish and elegant manners eased his orbit through local society, and he worked to soften some of the Germans' more extreme requests of the Danish shipping companies. His perfectly slicked-back jet-black hair gave him an air of sophistication, while his tweed suits and glasses implied an unthreatening, professorial presence.

Around him life went on. Schools, churches, and civil society all continued to function normally, while the economy boomed with agricultural exports to the Reich. The country appeared from the outside, as Churchill grumbled, "Hitler's canary." But resentment toward the Germans simmered just below the surface, and resistance erupted periodically in modest protests. The Danes were determined not to embrace what one member of parliament had called "the cloven hoof of Nazism." Anonymous graffiti mocked the Germans, there were frequent acts of vandalism, and the Danes generally adopted a cold politeness that they called "den kolde skulder" to the Germans.

Christian had asked Danes to show "an absolute correct and dignified behavior," although every morning he rode out on horseback to greet his subjects and made a point of ignoring the Germans in their midst. And to the irritation of the Nazis, the local Fascist Party, the National Socialist Workers, consistently polled at less than 2 percent and, despite pressure, the king repeatedly refused to include them in the government. The Danes were against totalitarianism of any kind—Fascist, Communist, or National Socialist—and remained so throughout the war.

Things finally unraveled quickly in October 1942 over the kind of petty incident for which the Nazis were notorious. When the king responded to a long and effusive birthday greeting from Hitler with only a terse five-word response—"My utmost thanks, Christian Rex"—the führer was enraged. Determined to put the Danes in their place, he appointed as plenipotentiary the thirty-nine-year-old SS Gruppenführer Werner Best, who would take a much firmer hand in policing and overseeing the country. From his time in France overseeing the deportation of foreign Jews, Best was known as the Bloodhound of Paris. And to further emphasize the point, Hitler replaced the local Wehrmacht commander with General Hermann von Hanneken, known as a strong enforcer of order.

The arrival of Best was a positive for Duckwitz. His new boss valued his knowledge of and contacts among the Danes highly, often calling on him to act as an intermediary. Despite his reputation, Best agreed with the "policy of accommodation" to keep things under control. A lawyer by education, he tried to cultivate a gentlemanly, courtly demeanor despite his status as the third in command of the SS. He relied on Duckwitz to arrange meetings, often at his own house, where Best could informally interact with Danish leaders. Accordingly, Duckwitz quickly became part of Best's inner circle, increasingly so as the local situation deteriorated over the following months.

Another member of the inner circle was Paul Kanstein, a forty-three-year-old SS Brigadeführer who had highly secret contacts with the anti-Hitler resistance and who over time detected enough of Duckwitz's sympathies to confide in him. (Duckwitz had joined the Nazi Party at the instigation of Gregor Strasser, one of its early leaders killed in the purge on the Night of the Long Knives, and had remained a member, although he had fairly quickly soured on its ideology, in particular its use of terror and its persecution of the Jews.) Both Duckwitz and Kanstein would try to be moderating influences on the dark instincts of Best.

The German defeat at Stalingrad in February 1943 and word of their surrender in North Africa broadcast Nazi vulnerability to the world and seemed to signal a turning of the tide of war toward an eventual Axis defeat. Best allowed a general election to go forward in March in Denmark, which resulted in a humiliation for the Germans, with almost 98 percent of the population voting for a coalition of non-Fascist mainstream parties. The Danish Resistance became much bolder, engaging in daring acts of sabotage and encouraging mass strikes that periodically paralyzed the country. At the end of July a German minesweeper under construction was destroyed two days before it was to leave the shipyard. Then on August 24 a young delivery boy smuggled explosives inside beer crates to disguised Resistance operatives in a convention center in Frederiksberg that had been turned into a Wehrmacht barracks. The blast completely destroyed the building.

The Danes had now exhausted the Nazis' patience. Four days later, on August 28, Best declared a state of emergency. Public meetings and strikes were banned, strict censorship was put in place, and a curfew was declared. Special courts were set up with orders for the summary execution of anyone engaging in sabotage or found with weapons. The king and government sent word that they would not be a party to these measures, which "would ruin the government's possibilities of keeping the people calm." In response, the Germans turned the dial up even further the next day, declaring martial law.

Fighting now broke out as Germans attacked the Danish army. By morning, German troops could be found everywhere and telephone and mail service had been cut. General Hanneken instructed the government to resign, but first to order all civil servants to continue their work. In a final act of defiance, the cabinet declared it was no longer in power to do so. The Germans would have to rely on the willingness of each civil servant to stay at his post of his own volition, creating a highly precarious situation for the administration, given the Danish bureaucracy's lack of affection for the Nazi hierarchy. Best blamed the press "in this ridiculous little country" for portraying Germany as weak. At a press conference he barked, "Last night you got your reward."

Duckwitz was devastated at the turn of events. "It has finally happened and here, too, everything has gone to pieces. One has to try very hard not to lose one's composure and not to weep. Four years of hard work is for naught—because of stupidity and unreasonableness," he wrote in his diary. "Now the inhabitants of the [last] country in Europe will hate us from the bottom of their hearts. It is very difficult to be German."

Best, on the other hand, saw an opportunity to finally take actions to liquidate the Danish Jews. On September 8, he sent cable no. 1032 to German foreign minister Joachim von Ribbentrop. "It is my opinion that measures should be taken towards a solution of the problems of the Jews and the Freemasons," he wrote. "The necessary steps should be taken so long as the present state of emergency exists, for afterward they will be liable to cause reaction in the country." Once civilian rule was restored, he explained, any move against the Jews would likely result in refusal by the king and parliament to participate in government, and mass unrest and strikes among the population. In fact, Best predicted, the appointment of any Danish government after the deportation of the Jews might become impossible, and it would be necessary to set up an administrative council to rule by decree. The operation would require real support. "In order to arrest and deport some 6,000 Jews in one fell swoop (including women and children) it is necessary to have the police forces I requested in my telegram No. 1001 of 9/1. Almost all of them should be put to work in greater Copenhagen where the majority of the local Jews live. Supplementary forces should be provided by the German military commander in Denmark. For transportation, ships must be considered a prime necessity and should be ordered in time."

Three days later, Best told Duckwitz about the cable. Outraged, Duckwitz threatened to resign in what he described as "a very heated discussion." Unwilling to be part of an atrocity, he informed Best that a friend in the Foreign Ministry, Undersecretary A. Hencke, had offered him a transfer to Sweden. Best urged him to reconsider, and many of Duckwitz's Danish friends convinced him he could do more good by staying at his post. His Swiss wife, Annemarie, agreed. "She was my best moral support, willing to go with me through thick and thin," he wrote. "We never regretted our decision."

Duckwitz now began a frenzied two weeks of trying to prevent the deportation of the Jews. The next day, with Best's permission, he flew to Berlin and contacted Hencke to try to intercept the cable. It had, unfortunately, been sent on to Hitler by Ribbentrop, who summarized the needed resources and Best's view of potential blowback in a cover note.

Back in Copenhagen, Duckwitz sat down for another long meeting with Best, strongly warning about the dire consequences of acting against the Jews. Duckwitz was one of those who could see the good in anyone, writing in his diary that Best secretly agreed with him: "Deep down he's decent."

On September 17 Hitler ordered the implementation of the Final Solution in Denmark, and preparations began under Heinrich Himmler. Many of the Nazis, recognizing the need to maintain order locally, were hesitant, likely anticipating the mass resignation of those civil servants who had remained in place and on whom the entire administration of the country depended. Franklin Roosevelt had announced that the Allies would try those responsible for atrocities, so some may also have been trying to avoid such a reckoning for crimes after the war ended.

For its part, however, the Gestapo remained untroubled by any of these considerations. That day, plainclothes police stormed the Jewish Community Center and seized the names and addresses of Jews at gunpoint. It was an ominous sign, and a tactical error that caused rumors to swirl. Alarmed, Duckwitz confided to Danish friends that he was convinced action was being prepared against the Jews. He did not know the date, but advised that "all that can be done is to be prepared."

On September 19, Best informed Duckwitz that Hitler had approved the operation and that it would happen during the state of emergency. The wheels were in motion. That night, Duckwitz wrote in his diary, "Now I know what I have to do."

The next day he contacted Niels Eric Ekblad, a Swedish diplomat passing through Copenhagen, who arranged for a travel visa for Duckwitz with the Swedish ambassador Gustav von Dardel. Following the occupation of Denmark and Norway, Sweden had maintained a quiet neutrality, allowing German troops passage through their territory and trying to remain as uncontroversial as possible to avoid invasion. But after Stalingrad, the Swedes began to move decidedly toward the Allies, and news of the liquidation of the Jews of Norway had shocked its people. One pastor captured the mood when he declared in a sermon, "If we were to stay silent, the stones would cry out." In late August Sweden had requisitioned a castle in southern Skåne, across from Copenhagen, to receive the refugees who had begun arriving. These were mostly soldiers trying to make their way to England to join the Allies, but also included a few Jews. In Copenhagen, Dardel was given permission to loosen the standards for visas, but even these more lenient requirements only applied to the few Jews with existing ties to Sweden.

Duckwitz had more ambitious ideas for the Swedes. On September 21 he traveled on an overnight train to Stockholm. His wife stayed behind, spending the night at the home of a Jewish friend, Liselot Morescu. The next evening his friend Ekblad hosted a three-hour meeting at his home in Stockholm between Duckwitz and Swedish prime minister Per Albin Hansson. Hansson agreed to inform the Germans of Sweden's willingness to receive and intern the Danish Jews on their soil, an offer that the Nazis did not even acknowledge. Ekblad would also accompany Duckwitz back to Copenhagen, where he and Dardel would keep the government in Stockholm apprised of all developments in real time. No record of the conversation survives, but subsequent events strongly imply an understanding that the Swedes agreed to assist any attempted evacuation of Jewish refugees that Duckwitz might precipitate. Before returning home, Duckwitz stopped off to see a Dr. Reinsberg, his counterpart as maritime expert at the German embassy in Stockholm. The two former Hamburg America colleagues worked out a secret code that rescuers and refugees could use to communicate in the certain chaos that would surround any rescue operation.

Back in Copenhagen, Duckwitz confided in his diary once more: "Everything I do, I do fully conscious of my own responsibility. Here, I am assisted by my rock-solid belief that good deeds can never be wrong. Therefore, I need to get to work and to muster all my courage."

On September 25 Duckwitz again met with Best for an update. Three hundred "specialists" from the SS had arrived under the command of SS Standartenführer Rudolf Mildner, who had been in charge of courts martial at Auschwitz. The increased presence of the Gestapo severely shook Duckwitz. Quietly, he told Ekblad that "something was up in the air." That night, his mood was black. "No power in the world can absolve RB [Best] from his heavy burden of guilt," he wrote in his diary.

The next day, Duckwitz went to see Kanstein, urging him to press Hanneken to object to this "dirty business" as a violation of the Wehrmacht's "sense of honor." Without the army, Duckwitz believed the local police force would not be able to carry out the roundup, and the result would be a postponement "for the duration." The secretly anti-Hitler Kanstein was concerned for Duckwitz, to whom he had grown close. As Duckwitz recalled in his diary, Kanstein offered what he called "friendly advice": stop trying to countermand Hitler's orders. He was sure the SS viewed Duckwitz as suspicious and would capitalize on any pretense to "remove" him, a sinister outcome in the parlance of the day. Duckwitz told his friend that he was fully aware of the potential consequences to himself and would nevertheless do anything to stop the deportation. Kanstein, he recalled, left him "as if he had just said his last goodbye to a cherished child that had been seized by temporary insanity."

Duckwitz's instinct to appeal to the military was sound. In fact, Hanneken and the army were not at all enthusiastic about the round-up, and they had already complained about it. Hanneken's primary concern was to protect against a potential Allied invasion on Jutland's west coast. When he heard of Best's cable on September 20, the day before Duckwitz went to Sweden, Hanneken cabled Berlin to ask that the action be canceled. "The operation," he wrote, "will place a heavy burden on the army which will not be able to act vigorously, particularly since it will be necessary in Copenhagen and on the island of Fyn to use new recruits. The benefits of the deportation strike me as doubtful." The civil administration and police force would cease working with the Germans, he predicted, and food supply and armament manufacture would be severely undermined. "Disturbances requiring use of military force must be expected."

Perhaps surprisingly, even the Gestapo developed serious concerns about the operation. Mildner's primary goal was to combat the Resistance, and he almost immediately concluded that a roundup of the Jews would cause serious complications. Not only would the Danish police and population refuse to help such an effort, they would almost surely become even more inflamed against the occupiers. So Mildner, who had previously been stationed at Auschwitz, recommended to his superiors that the operation be canceled or postponed. But Hitler would have none of it. He immediately dispatched Sturmbannführer Rolf Gunther, Adolf Eichmann's deputy, to ensure that the action was implemented with sufficient intensity.

Next on Duckwitz's list to contact were some old friends in the German navy, which had even less interest in being part of the deportation than the army or the SS. Two old friends of his from the Hamburg America Line were now stationed as harbormasters. Captain Richard Camman and Lieutenant Commander Friedrich Wilhelm Lubke were both Iron Cross veterans of the First World War. Camman had been serving as captain of a large passenger ship when he was recalled to serve in Copenhagen at age fifty, while Lubke was assigned to Aarhus. They were entirely in sympathy with Duckwitz. The biggest risk to any evacuation was the German vessels patrolling both land and sea along the coast. When the time came, Camman would ensure that the coast-guard ships remained quietly in drydock. In doing so, Duckwitz later wrote, "He took great personal risk, but he did so without hesitation." For his part, Lubke colluded with Heinrich Bertram, the captain of a large hospital ship that had been dispatched to carry Jews away, to pretend that the vessel's engines were damaged, further slowing the operation.

Meanwhile, at the Swedish embassy, frenzied efforts to provide exit visas continued. Even as he rushed around gathering support for an evacuation, Duckwitz also spent hours working with Ekblad and Dardel, trying to secure papers for Jewish friends. On Friday evening he went home and spoke again with his wife. With a moment to reflect, he wrote in his diary, "It is good that Annemarie shares my conviction. There will be no detour from the road I have taken. Only once in a while the responsibility seems unbearable. But those moments pass. There are, after all, higher laws. I will submit to them."

On Tuesday, September 28, Best received the order to launch the Final Solution. The roundup was scheduled for the coming Friday evening, October 1—which was also Rosh Hashanah, the Jewish New Year—and was targeted for completion by the next day. Best called Duckwitz into his office and briefed him on the plans. Duckwitz listened and left the meeting. And then he sprang into action one last, remarkable time.

Among Duckwitz's closest political contacts were Hans Hedtoft, the head of Denmark's Social Democratic Party and future prime minister, and Vilhelm Buhl, the powerful former prime minister. Duckwitz had often provided the Danes with critical information about Nazi plans and deliberations, some of which was passed on to British intelligence. More generally, he had confided to Hedtoft that most of the

Germans outside the Gestapo were "in their innermost hearts" against a roundup, and more recently he had begun sharing his concerns that it would happen anyway.

Duckwitz telephoned Hedtoft and asked to meet him urgently. Hedtoft invited him to a secret meeting then under way with Ekblad at the Workers' Assembly Building at Rømersgade 22 in Copenhagen, a "cabin of trust." Gathered there were Hedtoft, Buhl, and a number of other Danish leaders, including H. C. Hansen and Herman Dedichen. Hedtoft recalled Duckwitz, normally a calm, bespectacled presence, as "white with indignation and shame."

"Now the disaster is about to occur," Duckwitz said. "Everything is planned in detail. Ships will anchor at the mooring off Copenhagen. Those of your poor Jewish countrymen who get caught by the Gestapo will be forcibly brought on board the ships and transported to an unknown fate."

The Danes were stunned. Although Hedtoft was used to shocking messages from Duckwitz, he recalled being temporarily speechless this time. "This was too diabolic," he wrote. "I just managed to say: 'Thank you for the news.'" Duckwitz then disappeared.

The Danes moved quickly to act on Duckwitz's warning. Through underground contacts with the police department, they requisitioned cars. Each went in a different direction to warn the heads of the Jewish community, many of whom, despite the rumors, could not at first bring themselves to believe the news.

Hedtoft went immediately to the Charlottenlund home of Carl Bernard Henriques, a prominent attorney and Jewish community president. The men knew each other slightly, and Hedtoft asked to see Henriques alone. "Henriques, a great disaster is going to happen now," he blurted. "The feared action against the Jews in Denmark is about to come." The Dane then provided all the details Duckwitz had given him, including the raid planned for the night of October 1. "You must immediately do everything in order to warn every single Jew in the city," he said. "Obviously, we are ready to help you with everything you need."

Henriques was in shock. "You are lying," he stammered. He had, Henriques told Hedtoft, just heard these very rumors debunked by the Danish foreign minister, Nils Svenningsen, who himself had been lied to by Best. Hedtoft explained that Svenningsen spoke in good faith but was misled, and begged Henriques to believe him. As part of Best's inner circle, Duckwitz was about as reliable a source as could be found, and the warning had come directly from him. Eventually the information about the pending roundup sank in. In despair, Henriques kept repeating, "I do not understand how it can be true."

On Wednesday, Duckwitz turned thirty-nine. By now his warning was spreading like wildfire across the country as Danes from all walks of life—from politicians to journalists to priests to businesspeople—told their Jewish neighbors of the impending action. "Everything is dark and hopeless. The preparations for the actions against the Jews are proceeding at great haste. New people have arrived—experts in this tawdry enterprise," Duckwitz wrote in his diary. Then he added, presumably with some satisfaction, "They will not find many victims."

The next morning, Rabbi Marcus Melchior led the prayers at the early morning services in the synagogue on the Krystalgade. He then announced that the High Holiday services the next day were canceled. "I have very important news to tell you," he said from the pulpit. "Last night I received word that the Germans plan to raid Jewish homes throughout Copenhagen to arrest all Danish Jews for shipment to concentration camps. They know that tomorrow is Rosh Hashanah and our families will be home." Duckwitz's warning had now reached a significant part of the Jewish community, which immediately began to go underground. The seventy-two-hour head start he provided proved lifesaving.

What transpired over the next days across Denmark was undoubtedly one of the greatest humanitarian actions of the twentieth century. King Christian X presented an official protest to Best against the intended deportation of the Jews, "to emphasize to you that special actions taken against a group of people who for more than 100 years have enjoyed full civil rights in Denmark could have the utmost serious consequences." Simultaneously, thousands of the king's subjects undertook thousands of actions and thousands of kindnesses across his realm.

Hundreds of Danes opened their homes to Jews who were hiding from the Gestapo. Teachers warned students, friends warned their neighbors, workers warned their colleagues. Priests sheltered rabbis. On Sunday, Copenhagen University decided to close for a week so that its students could assist in the evacuation. Aarhus University did the same. That day a letter was read in churches across the nation: "We understand by freedom of religion the right to exercise our faith in God in such a way that race and religion can never in themselves be reason for depriving a man of his rights, freedom or property. Despite different religious views, we shall therefore struggle to ensure the continued guarantee to our Jewish brothers and sisters of the same freedom we ourselves treasure more than life itself."

Jews found shelter in schools and hospitals. The Bispebjerg Hospital in Copenhagen was the center of particular heroism. Medical students and doctors went door to door to warn Jews of the danger and bring them to the hospital. There they were hidden and given fake names and diagnoses before being smuggled out to other hospitals. From there ambulances and other vehicles took Jews down to the waterfront for embarkation. In the end, some two thousand Jews were saved through the hospital's efforts. The ambulances joined the nonstop fleet of taxis that also transported the Jews down to the docks, not one of whose drivers denounced their passengers.

The armada that formed across the Øresund, the narrow stretch of water between Denmark and Sweden, is now legendary. From more than fifty points across the coast from Zealand to Moen, from Falster to Gilleleje to Naes, some three hundred vessels—fishing boats, motorboats, rowboats, pleasure boats, even racing boats—would undertake more than one thousand crossings. It was perhaps the greatest amateur flotilla since the great evacuation at Dunkirk, and as heroic. Some of the crossings lasted less than an hour, some more than a day, depending on the elements and drifting mines. While the fishermen generally charged for passage, Danes all over the country contributed to pay the fare for poorer Jews. In the end, no one was turned away for lack of funds. Many, of course, did not charge at all.

———

One remarkable vessel was the rowboat oared by Knud Marstrand Christiansen, which made eighteen trips back and forth across the Øresund. Tall and handsome, with blue eyes and blond hair, Christiansen had recently turned twenty-nine. He had competed as a rower for Denmark in the 1936 Berlin Olympics, where he witnessed firsthand the evil of the Third Reich. His wife, Karen, was the daughter of Dr. Holger Rasmussen, the Danish navy's chief physician, who also served as personal doctor to the king. She had a similar experience in Berlin a few years earlier when she went to study cooking. While there, she lived with a Jewish family and was so aghast at the "horrible brutalization" of the Jews that she left her studies midway through to return to Denmark.

Both Karen and Knud joined the Resistance during the occupation, maintaining appearances by continuing to run a ski pole and leather goods manufacturing concern. They lived quietly with their small children at their spacious home on the Havnegade, where senior Nazi officials also lived, overlooking the canals and harbor. Knud became part of the Danish Freedom Fighters (which planned acts of sabotage), the Danish Resistance, and other such groups and remained in shape as part of the Danish Rowing Club. Karen, a champion sharp-shooter, for five years published *Das Warheit*, an underground news-letter, and translated BBC broadcasts into German to clandestinely inform local Wehrmacht soldiers about Nazi atrocities and reports of Allied advances. Even Knud's mother, Alida Marstrand, who owned a famous chocolate shop in Copenhagen on Bredgade, offered her store as a Resistance drop point. Alida and her twenty-three-year-old daugh-ter, Tove, ran an ammunition depot there for the freedom fighters and held their breath any time German soldiers came in for sweets. A soda bottle placed upside down in the window was the signal that the coast was clear.

The Christiansens had learned through the underground about the impending deportation, and Knud was afraid that the roundup was imminent when he saw two German freighters out of his apartment window. "I called my colleagues in the resistance and told them that I feared the Jews were going to be picked up," he recalled. Karen printed hundreds of leaflets warning the Jews to flee. Knud told two Jewish friends in his weekly bridge game, the blacksmith Ludvig Philipson and his brother, that they were in danger and offered to shelter them. They ignored the warning, not wanting to believe it, and were arrested and interned at the Horserød camp. Knud immediately went to the camp and asked the commandant for their release, claiming they were only "half-Jewish" and offering him a tub of butter as well. The man turned him down, telling him that "Hitler would hang me!"

Remarkably, Knud then obtained an appointment to see Best. As a former celebrated athlete, he was granted an audience. In as ingra-tiating a manner as he could muster, he made a deal with Best: as an Olympian, he would make a propaganda film praising the Germans as friends of Denmark in return for his friends' release. The men were put on a bus and arrived back in Copenhagen, where Knud arranged for their flight to Sweden. (The film, of course, was never made.)

Then, along with his wife, his brother Jørgen, and his father-in-law

Dr. Rasmussen, Knud personally escorted dozens of Jews into hiding places. More than forty at a time, including the president of the Danish Central Bank, filled the Christiansens' own apartment before moving on by train, truck, or ambulance, often to Dr. Rasmussen's home in Espergærde, a village thirty-five kilometers north of Copenhagen on the coast. A young woman from Amaliegade made bowl after bowl of delicious soup for the refugees. The children were told their guests were their visiting aunts and uncles, in case the Gestapo should arrive.

Knud realized that his greatest skill—his rowing—gave him the ability to save lives. He made his way to Espergærde and his father-in-law's villa, about a kilometer from the beach. The doctor lived comfortably there, having stocked up over a thousand bottles of gin and whisky before the occupation, and commuted into the city daily to see surgical patients. During those harrowing days of the evacuation, Dr. Rasmussen also treated sick and wounded Jews in the villa and his home became one of the embarkation points for the great exodus. From Espergærde, Knud personally rowed back and forth to Sweden in his boat, carrying Jews to safety. Under cover of night, as his younger brother stood lookout on the beach, he would tirelessly ferry them until enough larger boats had arrived on the scene. Later, Knud recalled, he got use of a motorboat. "It was faster!" he observed.

———

One of those Knud rescued was Max Rawitscher, a young divinity student who had fled his home in Dresden five years earlier. When he arrived in Denmark, a kindly railway worker had smuggled him on board the Gedser ferry from Warnemunde, hidden him from a German raid, and then sent him to Copenhagen with a ten-kroner bill and advice to find the local Jewish community. Instead, immigration officials quarantined him, but he offered to work and found employment on a farm in northern Zealand. There he learned to speak Danish. His isolation helped him during the German occupation, although he still managed in the summer of 1943 to meet a Swedish girl in a Copenhagen ice cream shop named Anne-Marie who worked at a carton factory. They were engaged the next month, during harvest time.

Anne-Marie was part of the Resistance and heard that the Jews were to be rounded up imminently. She was told to immediately warn her fiancé. When she arrived, the word had already gotten out up north, and Max was being hidden by a clerk at a tannery where Knud bought leather for his business. The clerk asked Knud to help get Max out to Sweden. Max boarded a train for Copenhagen. In Ringsted or Næstved (Max could never recall), he was met by a young Resistance member who bandaged his head and one of his arms so he looked like an invalid. Then the young man escorted him on the train to Næstved Station outside Copenhagen, where an ambulance waited to escort him to a safe house. After meeting Knud and Karen at their home, he was hidden in a small apartment that served as the tannery's showroom until the time was right to escape.

Max was terrified. When the bachelor who lived in the apartment went out, he was instructed to make no noise. He could not turn the faucet, flush the toilet, go near the window, or turn on the radio. Footsteps on the stairway outside and imagined noises inside the walls spurred uncontrolled fear. "The thoughts flew through my overheated brain," Max remembered. Maybe the Nazis were watching him through an invisible trapdoor.

For one entire unbearable day he waited. His host came with food and told him, "Tonight it will not work." Then another day crawled by. Then at five in the afternoon on the third day a young man from the Resistance arrived. It was Jørgen Christiansen, Knud's younger brother. "Tonight we shall try to get you to Sweden," he told Max. Jørgen pulled out a razor and shaved Max's dark hair, which looked out of place in Denmark. Max shaved six or seven times, desperate to hide his dark whiskers. German soldiers were everywhere outside. "I knew from Germany that on only the slightest suspicion they could arrest a man and my appearance would leave no one in doubt that I was Jewish," he said. Jørgen then took out powder and patted it onto the rest of Max's hair and his stubble to lighten it further. Jørgen replaced Max's hat, pulling it down over his forehead. The start of the journey was by rail to Espergærde. "First we have to get to the train station looking relaxed," Jørgen told him. "Keep a cool head!"

Easier said than done. Two hours later they went down onto the street and strode toward the Østerport Station with a determined stride. It was a bright day. Jørgen walked a few meters in front of Max, Anne-Marie a few meters behind, a precaution should any one of them be arrested. They heard hard boot steps and passed some Germans en route. Max's heart stood still, but his legs moved forward like an automaton in a dreamlike state. He remained in a trance, the people blurring together into phantoms, as Jørgen hid him in a bathroom at the station. As the train began to leave, Max was rushed out at the last moment by Jørgen and the train conductor and smuggled on board. As the train moved upland, they passed the magical and legendary castle of Kronborg on the very northernmost tip of Zealand, better known as Elsinore, the home of Shakespeare's Hamlet.

In Espergærde, Jørgen took Max to Dr. Rasmussen's villa. When the young man entered the room, he was frightened by the foreboding darkness caused by the blackout curtains required for curfews and air raids. But he exhaled when he saw that the house was filled with other refugees, and a beautifully laid out table had been set for all of them. "It was as if we were going to a party," he remembered.

"You will not leave here before you eat well," Dr. Rasmussen told him. "You will not go to Sweden hungry."

Max sat down but ate almost nothing. "I had to eat a little bit but it was difficult, so difficult that only someone who is face to face with death could understand."

Knud then appeared. He put his arm on Max's shoulder and motioned for him to follow. "In a minute we will be leaving," he said.

Jørgen had been sent to the beach on his usual job of lookout. He would wait thirty minutes after a ship or person passed before returning with an all-clear. Since he did not have a watch, he would drink a beer; when he had to run to the bathroom, he knew that thirty minutes had passed. Now he walked in the door to report that the time was right.

Knud, Karen, and Jørgen all left with Max, following the seaside road down to the edge of a forest. On the way, German patrol cars with searchlights swept over them, and more than once they fell to the ground to avoid being seen.

Jørgen and Knud unearthed a sleek racing scull from under brush and leaves. Jørgen took off his shoes and socks and launched the boat into the water down at the shore. Across the dark water, Max could see the blinking lights of the opposite coast. There was a small bathing pier nearby, with a couple of wooden huts at the end of it. He was convinced the Germans were waiting there. "Are we going to Sweden in that boat?" he said. "That will not work. I'm not doing it. I refuse to be shot or thrown in the water."

Jørgen picked up the terrified Max, carried him out over the water to the boat, where Knud was waiting, and sat him in the passenger seat. Max eyed the hut in terror. "I was scared, knotted in pain with an agonizing panic," he remembered.

Knud's back was to the Swedish coast. He pointed to a green light, which could be seen in the distance from Helsingborg. "See the light there?" he said cheerfully. "That is where we are going!"

Then he began to row. With his expert stroke, the boat moved smoothly and silently across the darkness of the water. There was silence, and the Danish coast disappeared into the night. It was a cloudy night, but the stars were visible. The Danes had given Max a package of food, warm gloves, and a sweater—but he had forgotten his overcoat in the rush to leave. The cold air came up off the water and he shivered.

Knud stopped rowing for a moment, took off his coat, and handed it to Max. "You are cold but I keep warm from rowing," he said. "Have my jacket."

Time crawled forward. Max had a sudden impulse to scream, but he controlled it. Knud slowed his rowing for a moment, leaned forward, and paddled with his hand for a moment to keep the light boat from capsizing.

He had rowed for two hours. They were now in international waters, he said. They had passed the island of Ven, and the green light came closer and closer as Helsingborg approached. It had felt like an eternity.

A Swedish boat filled with soldiers approached them and towed them to the wharf. A crowd stood watching. Suddenly Max was pulled from the boat and his feet touched Swedish soil. He was safe.

"I was saved!" Max remembered thinking. "After a while the numbness left. I looked around. Where had my rescuer gone? 'Where is the man who brought me here?' I called. I had not said good-bye to him, didn't say thank you."

Knud was already on his way back to Denmark. He had to row another two hours home. Karen was waiting for him on the beach when he returned at one in the morning.

Max had never gotten his name.

———

There were thousands like Knud Christiansen risking their lives for their neighbors. That night alone, Max later heard, six hundred Jews made it across to Sweden. Duckwitz had set in motion the rescue of almost the entire Danish Jewish population. Over the next week, an entire nation warned, sheltered, protected, and smuggled out their Jewish neighbors. Taxi drivers, doctors, teachers, students, farmers, and clerks all took part. The Danish police were intimately involved in the operation: one evacuee recalled an officer escorting her to a ship and telling her to "have a good trip." In the end, fisherman and captains transported over seven thousand Jews across the Øresund as well as almost seven hundred of their non-Jewish relatives. Schooners and sailboats made their way across the sound. Among those rescued in the flotilla was Niels Bohr, the Nobel Prize winner who had pioneered quantum mechanics, one of the giants of twentieth-century science.

Across the straits, Swedish naval vessels stood guard, and fishermen were given fuel to head out and collect the refugees from the Danish ships coming in the opposite direction. "Welcome to Sweden" were often the first words refugees heard from the authorities. There the Jews were given shelter, medical care, and food, schooling was provided for children, and vast numbers of the citizenry, including the royal family, donated to their support. "Sweden is open to all," Dardel had announced when the roundup was imminent, emboldening many to make the trip. In the end some 95 percent of Danish Jews made it to safety in Sweden, where they would wait out the war.

Many of the rescuers and refugees noticed a remarkable lack of activity on the part of many German soldiers in attempting to stop the escape. The navy was almost completely quiet, and, due in part to the efforts of Duckwitz's friend Captain Camman, the harbormaster, no German patrol boat interfered with the evacuation. As Christiansen recalled later, many soldiers were not interested in the war; they "were very young and wanted nothing to do with the killing of the Jews." Even the Gestapo to some extent pulled its punches. To Sturmbannführer Gunther's enormous frustration, Mildner remained convinced of the folly of the operation and ordered his agents not to violently enter Jewish homes, on the grounds that it could lead to "looting." In the end, only the most rabid of the SS went about their monomaniacal mission.

Unfortunately, not all of the Jews were able to make it out. Some

498 did end up arrested by the Nazis. Two hundred were elderly residents of an old-age home. A group of young Zionists as well as German children of the Youth Aliyah, both groups that had taken refuge in Denmark with hopes of going on to Palestine, were captured. So too were Jews in the countryside who did not get the warning in time, as well as a group of eighty surprised by the Gestapo as they hid in the loft of a church, waiting for a fishing boat to pick them up. They had been betrayed by a girl who was in love with a German soldier.

These unlucky few were sent to Theresienstadt, forty miles north of Prague, a concentration camp holding some 150,000 inmates, 10 percent of whom were children. While it was not itself a death camp, the conditions were horrendous. Rations were meager, lice and vermin infested everything, and prisoners were forced to wear the yellow star. Many died of malnutrition or infectious diseases, and many more were eventually shipped on to be murdered at Auschwitz and other death camps in the east.

But once again, the Danish Jews experienced a different outcome. Three weeks after the deportation, the Danish chargé d'affaires in Berlin filed a formal request with the German embassy to send packages to their Jewish citizens in Theresienstadt and to visit the camp. The government continued to put pressure on the Germans, keeping up a relentless campaign to check up on the Danish Jews. In time, they would be able to send food, vitamins, clothing, and even books. On June 23, 1944, two members of the Danish government and a Swiss representative of the International Red Cross were allowed to inspect their conditions. Theresienstadt was "beautified" to create the false impression of a model camp, complete with fresh paint, rose bushes, and even a preschool for toddlers. The three inspectors wrote up a report attesting to the camp's cleanliness, but later testified that they had not been fooled by the Potemkin village. At least they saw that the Danish Jews were being better treated. Their visit was an enormous boon for prisoner morale as well. As one captive recalled, he felt "redeemed as a human being in my own eyes. Once again I have certain value as a man. These Danes have given it back to me."

Many of the inmates of Theresienstadt would be shipped off to Auschwitz, but the Danish Jews were exempted. In the end, the Nazis hesitated to murder the Danes with their government watching. By April of the next year, with the last offensive against Nazi Germany almost complete, Himmler at last acceded to the Danish government's request to transfer its Jewish citizens to Sweden. On April 12 a convoy of thirty-five white buses flying the Swedish and Red Cross flags pulled up at Theresienstadt. The Danish Jews were told to pack their bags. Two days later they were boarded onto the buses. In a surreal scene, a camp band played in the central square. As one rabbi recalled, "The gate was opened—and we were free men. No one said a word." All but fifty-three Danish Jews survived Theresienstadt.

Two days later the convoy arrived briefly in Denmark, where thousands of citizens waved flags, cheered, and threw candy and cigarettes. It quickly moved on to Sweden, where the Jews were interned for several weeks, until German forces surrendered in Norway and Denmark on May 4, 1945. Duckwitz had remained in Copenhagen, urging Best and the other Nazis to exercise restraint in responding to the continued activities of the Resistance. After the failed assassination attempt against Hitler and subsequent purges, he carried cyanide pills, afraid that his connections with the underground opposition would become known. Not until after the war would he know that he had in fact been on a Nazi hit list. It would not have deterred him. "One does not think of personal danger in such circumstances," he said. "The fate of six thousand persons was at stake." Of the German surrender, he said, "When I heard the news I experienced one of those rare happy moments in my life that assured me that I had not lived in vain." And when it came time to arrest Best, the honor fell to none other than Knud Christiansen, the heroic Olympic rower.

The Danish Jews were in for one final surprise. All across the country, they largely found their homes untouched when they came back. In many cases their plants had been watered and their pets fed, their homes painted and filled with flowers. Some discovered that their neighbors had even managed their businesses for them in anticipation of their return. As Rabbi Melchior noted, "In most cases in Europe saying 'good-bye' was easier than saying 'welcome back.' But when we returned, our fellow Danes *did* say 'welcome back.' And *how* they said it—emotionally, with open arms and hearts. Our homes, our businesses, our property, and money had been taken care of and returned to us. You cannot imagine how happy it made us feel to be back home."

Max Rawitscher eventually tracked down Knud and Karen Christiansen with the help of a Danish television station. In December 1955, a rapt audience in Denmark and Sweden watched as Knud and Max were reunited. Max presented Knud with the most beautiful Orrefors bowl he could find.

"How could you risk all," Max asked him, "to help me, a total stranger?"

"It was my duty!" Knud told him.

"Why did you disappear?"

"I saw you safely to freedom. Then my mission was complete."

"Words cannot say what I feel," Max said as both men wept. "I owe you my life and I stand here and cannot find the words that can express my gratitude."

Karen and Knud eventually moved to New York, where he opened a clock repair shop. He continued to exercise on the rowing machine at the Jewish Community Center on Amsterdam Avenue. At age ninety-one, he was made a Righteous Among the Nations, with Karen also receiving the honor posthumously.

The story of the Danish Jews is remarkable in its uniqueness. The country is the only one whose entire population has been recognized as a Righteous Among the Nations by Yad Vashem. When an entire nation decided they would not permit atrocities in their midst, even the

Nazis found themselves hamstrung. As the king noted, "I had noticed that when we were determined, the Germans backed off." Eichmann later complained in frustration, "Denmark created greater difficulties for us than any other nation. The king intervened for the Jews there and most of them escaped." In the end, 99 percent of the 7,800 Jews in Denmark survived the Holocaust.

As for Duckwitz, he was arrested by British troops under Field Marshal Bernard Montgomery for six hours and then released. He was permitted to stay in Denmark and subsequently joined the West German government as a senior diplomat under Konrad Adenauer, the great postwar statesman and first chancellor of the new nation. In an appointment that must have been extraordinarily sweet, in 1955 he became West Germany's ambassador to the country he loved so much, Denmark. He remained a senior Foreign Ministry official, including a stint as ambassador to India, until his retirement in 1970. He was, Hedtoft said, "one of those men who made one put one's faith in a new Germany." Years later, in 1971, he too was recognized as a Righteous Among the Nations and a tree was planted in his honor at Yad Vashem. In a unique position to issue his fateful warning, close to the Danes and close enough to the SS to ensure that his message was taken seriously, he had risen to the occasion. Without Duckwitz, the miracle of Denmark could never have taken place. He remains an object lesson in adhering to the light of an inner morality, which burned as bright as the green light Max saw in the dead of that autumn Danish night when Knud rowed him to safety.

7

Beneath the Apple Tree

MANY OF THE TRULY NIGHTMARISH LANDSCAPES CONJURED UP BY THE HOLO-
caust are in Poland. Within Polish territory were six major death
camps—Auschwitz, Treblinka, Chelmno, Sobibor, Majdanek, and
Belzec—and the Warsaw Ghetto saw half a million Jews barricaded in
inhuman conditions in an area of just a few city blocks. Yet amidst this
hell, one fiery young woman, standing just under five feet tall, with an
ailing mother in her apartment and an estranged husband in a prisoner-
of-war camp, found a way to enter and leave the ghetto on a daily basis.
For several years she oversaw a network of mostly young women, some
still in their teens, who risked and sometimes gave their lives to rescue
hundreds of Jews, most of them infants, toddlers, and children.

Irena Sendler was born Irena Krzyżanowska on February 15,
1910. Her father, Stanislaw, was an infectious disease doctor who had
been expelled from the universities in Warsaw and Kraków for Socialist Party activities and participated in the Russian Revolution of 1905.
He married an attractive girl named Janina Grzybowski and finished
his studies in the Ukraine. After his graduation, the young couple returned to Warsaw, where Irena was born. When the child developed
whooping cough at age two, the family moved to Otwock, a village at
the edge of a beautiful pine forest on the bank of the Vistula River.
There Irena's father opened up a clinic for tuberculosis patients in a
large wooden home where the family also lived.

Unlike other Polish doctors, Irena's father treated anyone in need of care, including the poorest, many of whom were Jewish. Irena quickly had many Jewish friends and playmates and spoke some Yiddish by the age of six. "I grew up with these people," she remembered. "Their culture and traditions were not foreign to me."

It was a happy time for Irena, and her father adored her. "Don't spoil her," her aunts warned him. "We don't know what her life will be like," the doctor had replied. "Maybe my hugs will be her best memory."

When Irena was six her father caught typhus from one of his impoverished Jewish patients. A number of his colleagues from St. Spirit Hospital came to examine him and left the room, sadly mumbling. Irena's mother had told her that her father would recover but that the two of them would go to Warsaw until the epidemic passed. They packed five suitcases for a few days, and when Irena went to say goodbye to her father, a doctor ordered her to stay away from the bed and not to touch or kiss him. In the light of a candle, her father looked half asleep, yellowish, with red spots on his arm. Four days later, he died. Five days after that, Irena turned seven.

Her mother was left with very little money. Educating Irena would be a struggle, but she turned down an offer of assistance from the Jewish community. The following year, Irena nearly died of a brain abscess that developed when she caught the Spanish flu. Her mother then moved with her to Piotrków Trybunalski, a busy market town near Warsaw, where they lived in a small apartment. Irena joined the Girl Scouts there and had a normal childhood.

Irena became friends with Mietek Sendler, a boy who took her ice-skating in high school. They were both accepted to Warsaw University and decided to marry after graduation. In 1927 Irena and her mother moved to Warsaw so she could live at home during her studies. Mietek focused on classics and Irena planned to study philology. After she graduated in 1931, she married Mietek and became Irena Sendler.

The couple moved into a one-room apartment and Mietek got a job as a faculty assistant at the university.

Irena decided to pursue a graduate degree in social welfare at the University of Warsaw. "My father was a doctor," she reflected, "a humanist—and my mother loved people and helped him in his social work a great deal." Irena had long had a dislike for bigotry and for its most common manifestation in Poland, anti-Semitism. Her willingness to stand up to it had often gotten her into trouble. At thirteen, she had intervened to protect her only Jewish classmate from a beating by two other girls. She enraged her teacher in her senior year with an essay criticizing anti-Semitism and supporting tolerance.

When Irena arrived at Warsaw University, it had become a hotbed of anger and unrest. Gangs of young students in the ultranationalist Obóz Wielkiej Polski, a student group, proudly wore green ribbons and physically attacked classmates, preying especially on young Jewish women. A segregated bench was set up where Jewish students were forced to sit, and grade books were stamped "Aryan" or "Jew." Horrified, Irena crossed out her Aryan stamp and one day took her seat on the ghetto bench with her Jewish classmates. "I was beaten by anti-Semites together with Jewish students," she remembered. The next day she was called to the dean's office. After a two-hour wait, she was suspended for dishonoring the university.

In September 1932 she found work at the Department of Assistance to Mother and Child at the Citizens' Committee of Social Work, helping single mothers in need of support. She was electrified. "Everyone here was dedicated and true to their goals: everything that I had been taught seemed to come to use." When Mietek was offered a teaching position in Poznan, several hours away, Irena decided to stay in Warsaw. The mother-and-child committee closed when it ran out of funding, but Irena found a new job in the city's municipal welfare services. In 1938 a sympathetic professor intervened to have Irena reinstated at the University of Warsaw, where she completed her thesis and finally graduated the following spring.

———

When the Nazis invaded Poland on September 1, 1939, Irena rushed to an air raid shelter. When the all-clear sounded, she took her gas mask and headed immediately to her office. Some of her colleagues were also there: her boss Jan Dobraczyński, the director of social welfare and a staunch Catholic; his assistant Jaga Piotrowska; and Irena's former supervisor and close friend Irena Schultz, the other one of the "two Irenas," as they were known. Irena had first met Schultz in 1935 when the latter noticed her altering minor details about her clients—the size of an apartment, the age of a child—to get around severe restrictions for Jews and Roma enacted by the right-wing National Democratic Party. A tall blonde who towered over the four-foot-eleven brunette, Schultz joined forces with Irena, and together they found myriad ways to subtly circumvent the raft of discriminatory laws passed by the government and bring food and money into the Jewish quarter as the situation deteriorated.

Irena Sendler was given responsibility for many of the families arriving daily from the western front. As the German army advanced and artillery began to hammer Warsaw, the refugee crisis exploded. She ran dozens of canteens and shelters across the city that were set up quickly for orphans, the elderly, and the poor. Life was extremely dangerous; buildings were regularly bombed, killing all inside. In mid-September, three large families under Irena's watch were starving, even though the warehouse was full of food and the welfare office's bank accounts filled with zloty. Desperate, Irena forged Dobraczyński's last name on food vouchers and bank receipts. When she went to the warehouse to collect the goods, no one scrutinized the documents: the young clerk merely wanted to rush back down to the shelter where he had been hiding as bombs fell. One day Dobraczyński, a known anti-Semite, came into Irena's office and left a folder on her desk. Inside were blank documents: birth certificates, baptismal certificates, marriage licenses, and other forms. More could be provided. Dobraczyński knew of her "creative social work," his assistant Jaga explained, and that Irena knew what to do with the papers to help Jewish refugees.

The Germans steamrolled the Polish armed forces, who rode out on horseback against Nazi tanks. Seventy thousand men were killed, and over six hundred thousand, including Irena's husband Mietek, taken prisoner by the Germans and the Soviets. The bombing reached a crescendo at the end of September, and Irena slept in the shelter each night. On September 27, 1939, Warsaw capitulated. The devastation was terrible, buildings everywhere reduced to rubble and people starving or dead in the streets. Forty thousand residents of Warsaw had been killed. The Jewish areas had been hit doubly hard by the Luftwaffe.

German troops began pouring into the city, and Hitler paid a visit on October 5. Even before the führer's arrival, the Germans began issuing anti-Jewish decrees, limiting property rights, and declaring a census and a curfew. Irena saw Jews kicked out of shops and thrown off moving trams. Poles beat Jews on the streets and terrorized them. Irena even witnessed shootings. "Our streets were flooded with blood," she recalled. "And in this sea of blood, the Jews were drowning the most, especially the children."

Social welfare aid to Jews was strictly forbidden. All Dobraczyński could tell Jews who asked for help was that their sole recourse was the Judenrat, the committee of Jews set up to administer the community. Forced labor was instituted, and all Jews over the age of ten were required to wear a four-inch white armband with a blue Star of David on their right sleeve. Jews were banned from the post office; their schools were closed, and their synagogues shuttered. Radios were forbidden throughout the city, on pain of death. Strict food rationing began. While Germans were entitled to 2,613 calories per day, Jews were limited to 184, a starvation level. "There were families where one herring was shared amongst six children during Sabbath," Irena reported. The only way to stay alive was to buy food on the black market, an offense itself punishable by death.

At the end of October, barbed wire began appearing around the Jewish district, which was declared a quarantine area. The Germans were well known for their obsessive fear of infectious diseases such as typhoid, tuberculosis, and typhus, which they were convinced the Jews carried. Irena noted that by creating conditions of malnutrition, overcrowding, infestation, and horrendous sanitation, they actually fostered an epidemic. That winter was brutal, and heating scarce. The two Irenas quickly developed a trusted network of other social workers, nine women and one man, each in a different office, who also began altering documents and distributing forged papers. "The basis of receiving social assistance was collecting data and statistics from the communities," Irena said. "So we forged these statistics and interviews—meaning we listed made-up names, and in this way were able to secure money, food items, clothing."

In March 1940 wooden quarantine fences were erected along eight streets. On October 12, Yom Kippur, the Germans declared that all Jews in Warsaw must move into the Jewish district with only what they could carry. The district comprised only 4 percent of the total area of Warsaw but would now house one-third of the city's population. The entire ghetto was sealed on November 15. From her office at the edge on Zlota Street, Irena watched the sad parade of families as children carried pillowcases stuffed with their belongings. Of her three thousand clients, 90 percent were now in the ghetto.

"With the creation of the ghetto, the entire aid system that we were building with so much effort was destroyed," Irena wrote. Over the next few days, she sprang into a frenzy of action. "We made contact with our friend, Ewa Rechtman, who organized an underground unit consisting of women employed in the Jewish charity organization Centos in the ghetto," Irena wrote. Jewish teenagers in the Youth Circles hid sacks of food in basements and attics. Irena found false identities and hiding places for Jews who were wanted by the authorities.

By April there were more than five hundred cases of typhus in the Jewish district. Dr. Juliusz Majkowski, the head of the Zakladow Sanitarium's Sanitary Epidemiological Station, gave the two Irenas epidemic control passes, authentic documents with which they could go in and out of the Jewish district at will to help those on the inside. These would prove critical.

The two women dressed in nurse's uniforms, with white caps and red crosses, and were able to go in and out of the twenty-two gates. "At first, I was driven mainly by emotional impulses: I knew the suffering of the people rotting away behind the walls, and I wanted to help my old friends," Irena said. She smuggled money and documents sewn into her clothing or in the false bottom of a canvas nurse's bag beneath soiled dressings placed to keep the Germans away. She brought vaccine for typhus and even handmade dolls for children, lovingly crafted by one of her former professors, Dr. Witwicki, who was himself in hiding. Sometimes Irena wore a Star of David armband, as much to show solidarity as to blend in.

"The first time I went into the ghetto, it made a hellish impression on me," Irena noted. The sight of skeletal children reaching out their arms, barely eking out the plea "bread" in a whisper, would stay with her. "I'd go out on my rounds in the morning and see a starving child lying there. I'd come back a few hours later, and he would already be dead, covered with a newspaper." Eight people were crammed into each room in some apartments. No motor vehicles were allowed except for police, and a heavy pall of silence hung over the area. Rickshaws were the primary form of transportation. There were no parks and no greenery, and children fought desperately on the streets over scraps of food. Some were shot by soldiers; others were picked up by the Jewish police tasked with keeping order and sent to Gensia Prison, from which most did not return.

"One thing is certain," Irena declared. "Whoever did not live through the ghetto, who didn't see it, can't imagine what it was like." The Wehrmacht and SS patrolled the area with help from Polish Blues and Ukrainians, and there was constant random violence. "By order of Hitler, Himmler, both adults and children were dying in the streets with the silent consent of the whole world," Irena wrote. She got in contact with around twenty-five trusted people on the Aryan side who were willing to shelter any children she might bring out of the ghetto. "It was hard not to be concerned when they were shooting at children," she said.

In October 1941 the Germans began to shrink the ghetto, cutting off sections. Typhus was now raging terribly, with thousands of new cases a month. As winter descended, furs were banned and the gas mains turned off. Shortly after the ghetto was shrunk, another wave of destitute refugees arrived, swelling the population to half a million. The Germans were maniacal about escape. On November 10, 1941, the district governor decreed death for anyone "who knowingly provides shelter or assists in other ways" any Jew trying to leave the ghetto, "such as offering a bed for the night, upkeep, providing transportation and the like. No mercy will be shown." In December eight Jews were executed for leaving the ghetto, including six women trying to get food for their families.

In January, SS lieutenant colonel Ludwig Hahn arrived at the social welfare office and demanded to see Dobraczyński. The Nazis were upset about legions of children—most of them not Jewish—begging on the Aryan side of the wall, an embarrassment to the Third Reich. Hahn demanded they be removed, disinfected, and kept off the street. If Do-braczyński and Irena did not do it, the Germans had other methods.

The next day, social welfare trucks began gathering children on the streets of Warsaw. Dobraczyński had the two Irenas supervise the de-lousing of the twenty-five skeletal and shivering children, mostly boys between five and fifteen, who arrived in the first truck. Hahn arrived and ordered the children to remove all their clothes except for their shoes. Irena realized he was looking for circumcised males and stepped forward with her epidemic control pass, objecting that it was unsafe to inspect the children before they showered and were deloused.

The children put their clothes in a pile at the communal shower. Irena saw that two of the boys, probably brothers, were Jewish and whispered to them in Polish and then Yiddish to cover themselves as they slipped into a hallway, where her pass got her to a pile of cotton pants and shirts. The back door opened onto a courtyard and alley-ways, and a bribe to a Polish Blue guard allowed them to escape. She hailed a horse-drawn carriage on Ogrodowa Street and, not knowing where to go, took the boys to her friend Jaga's apartment. When Irena returned to the bathhouse, another twenty-five children had arrived. By the end of the day, she had separated thirty-two Jewish boys without papers and arranged for emergency shelter for them.

But then Dobraczyński called Irena into his office. A German police officer had arrived earlier that day and told Dobraczyński that thirty-two beggars were missing. For two thousand zloty and confir-mation that the children had been returned to the ghetto, the officer would drop the matter. Otherwise, the consequences were dire. Now, at Dobraczyński's insistence, Irena had to do the unthinkable: smuggle the children *back* into the ghetto. She appealed to the legendary Dr. Janusz Korczak, who ran an orphanage for two hundred children in the ghetto on Sliska and Sienna Streets, to provide housing for the children now being forced to return. Korczak was probably the most famous children's educator in Poland, and his book *King Matt the First* was a beloved best seller. The doctor was "like a ray of sun in the dark despair of the ghetto," Irena believed. He had actually turned down an opportunity to flee Poland to remain with the children at the orphanage.

Irena met the next day with Korczak, who walked with a cane after a severe beating from the Gestapo.

Irena explained the situation. "Why are you doing this, Pani Sendler?" he asked. "You could be executed."

"I can't bear the suffering," she confessed, "and no one suffers as much as the Jewish children."

Korczak said her request was very expensive and dangerous, but she assured him she would find a way. That night, Korczak said by telephone that he would take the children the next night and would send a trusted smuggler named Hirsch to meet Irena. Irena's friends picked up the children from their hiding places and brought them to a rendezvous point at the Church of the Annunciation, alongside the wall of the ghetto in the Aryan quarter. Irena bribed the night watchman and was stunned to find that Hirsch, who declared himself "an important friend of Dr. Korczak," was only ten years old. She waited with Hirsch and the boys silently until curfew began.

There was barely a crescent of a moon as Hirsch led the boys single file out the back of the church to a place where there were loose bricks in the wall. He threw a pebble over the wall and another pebble came back. Bricks began to move, and Hirsch and Irena helped create a small hole, then pushed each child through carefully. Irena heard a whisper and saw a hand appear and squeeze hers.

"Pani Sendler, I hope we meet again," Korczak said, "under more favorable circumstances."

All the boys arrived that night safely at the orphanage.

———

For several days in February, Irena noticed a young girl in rags, no more than six years old, at the corner of Karmelicka and Leszno just outside the ghetto. She could barely sit up, and Irena came over and shook her to make sure she was still alive. Irena pulled her friend Jaga, who had come with her that day, into a doorway. Their friend Izabella Kuczkowska, who worked as a legal specialist with Irena, had recently realized that the courthouse that straddled the ghetto had an entrance on the inside and another on the Aryan side. The janitor there, Jozef, had offered to help smuggle children out through a warren of basement tunnels. Irena thought they should try the route for this child. They could hide her with Sister Matylda Getter who had taken a boy into her convent and had offered to take more children, although the girl would need to be temporarily housed. Jaga agreed to take the child into her apartment before she was transferred to the convent.

When Irena picked up the little girl, she asked for her mother. The girl weighed almost nothing. Speaking to her in Yiddish, Irena discovered that her name was Beryl. She sang her a lullaby until Jaga returned and signaled that the tunnel route was usable at that moment.

Irena carried Beryl into the courthouse, where Jews and Poles crowded beneath a high vaulted ceiling supported by marble columns. She identified Jozef at the end of the enormous room by his broom handle and made her way over. He led her down a back staircase, leaving the noise of the lobby behind them. He unlocked a door, led Irena down another short staircase to a dark hallway, and gave her directions. She tried to give him fifty zloty, but he refused to take it.

"God bless you," Irena said.

"No," he said, turning off his flashlight, "God bless you," and locked the door behind her.

Beryl slept in Irena's arms as she made her way through cobwebs to an unlocked door. She pushed it open and saw Jaga standing with a *droshky** on Biala Street. They got off a short distance from Jaga's apartment, cut through a back alley to her front door, and took Beryl upstairs. Jaga told her ten-year-old daughter that if anyone asked, the girl was a sick cousin from Poznan staying with them for a few days.

Irena accelerated her work smuggling out orphans. In spring 1942 some four thousand children were living alone on the streets outside the ghetto, many of them left there by smugglers their desperate parents had used. One day Irena Schultz even found a little girl climbing out of the sewer with a single-digit number on a piece of paper pinned to her dress—her age. Irena worked to find them all safe places. Particularly helpful were convents like the Sisters of the Family of Mary and Father Boduen's children's home, founded in 1736 by a French priest as a home for abandoned children and now under the leadership of Dr. Maria Prokopowicz-Wierzbowska. The efforts were further helped by a stroke of luck when, in autumn of 1941, Irena Schultz obtained a stack of blank birth certificates—a gold mine—from a local priest in Lwów and smuggled them back to Warsaw on the train.

Particularly problematic were children who had what were known in the ghetto as "bad looks"—dark hair and obviously Semitic features. Blond and blue-eyed children could more easily assimilate into orphanages and refuges, provided they had appropriate papers. But those who looked "Jewish" needed to go into deeper hiding with individual foster families. Many of these children arrived in burlap sacks at Father Boduen's and then moved after a few hours to temporary homes in "emergency care centers" with one of the senior network operators. They provided initial care, washing the children, feeding and clothing them, and obtaining medical care. If they had "bad looks," their hair might be lightened, and little boys might be dressed as little Polish girls. They also did their best to teach the children the Polish language as well as

---

* A four-wheeled, open horse-drawn carriage with a low bench common in the former Russian empire.

the Catholic catechism, which Nazis loved to test children on to try to discover hidden Jews. "I was teaching them little prayers that every child knows, in Polish," recalled Magda Rusinek, one of Irena's teenage volunteers. "I would wake them up during the night to say the prayer."

Many of the children were terrified of being identified, a fear, Irena observed, "doubled by the tragedies of leaving their mother and their father." Forced to grow up quickly, they often wept at night. "Sometimes these small hearts couldn't take these problems." Irena recalled one child, Rachel, who began waiting for her mother every night at the door, begging to be taken home. The children were subjected to sudden Gestapo raids, forced to hide in a closet or attic, clutching a doll or teddy bear. Sometimes after a raid, the child would have to be moved elsewhere, giving up their foster family. "How many mothers can I have?" Irena once remembered a boy asking her as he cried. "It's the third."

The women in the network eventually asked Jan Dobraczyński for help. An active member of the Resistance, he had excellent contacts in the church. "Jan Dobraczyński came to an understanding with the underground which agreed to guide the Jewish children to centers," Irena remembered. He arranged to personally sign papers as a special signal so that the nuns who ran children's homes would accept any Jewish child sent to them. If the Germans had caught him, he would have been executed. Nuns and priests issued fake certificates and hid children. One convent had as many as thirty Jewish children under its roof. Some of the nuns risked their lives accompanying Jewish children to convents outside the city in Chotomow and Turkowice, often boys with "bad looks."

One of Irena's couriers, a nineteen-year-old girl named Helena, was caught with poorly forged papers and a four-year-old boy who began to cry for his mother in Yiddish. The boy was sent to Gensia Prison, where he died, and Helena to the notorious Pawiak Prison, where almost all inmates were brutally tortured and then executed. For a while, it was unclear how much of the network had been compromised. Irena immediately shut down all its activities and burned a few forged identity documents. But the most dangerous document was a list that she personally kept of the children's real names, Polish aliases, and the addresses where they were hidden. It was an extraordinarily risky ledger, and she had been warned against it. But Irena had insisted, although she did encrypt it. "There had to be some record where these children were, otherwise they couldn't be returned to the Jewish community," she said. They also needed the addresses to deliver the monthly food stipends to foster families who needed assistance. But she also believed, as she put it, that every child deserved a name. She wanted their families to be able to retrieve them after the war or, at least, if they were the only survivors in their families, for the children to know that they were Jewish.

Soon the news was posted that Helena had been killed at Pawiak. Irena was devastated and felt responsible. Shortly thereafter, rescue operations began again. The courthouse route was now compromised, so Jewish couriers delivered orphans to their Aryan counterparts through new escape routes. One boy escaped inside a man's coat. Children were hidden in garbage, which was taken to the city dump, where they were then retrieved. Others were taken out in fire trucks or sedated and hidden among corpses in hearses. New routes were developed in the underground labyrinths beneath the buildings and in the sewer system, where Irena obtained help from the Jewish underground to navigate the same mazes where they surreptitiously moved throughout the ghetto.

———

In April 1942, on the "Night of Blood," sixty prominent Jews with connections to underground newspapers were executed in the street. The

Nazis were trying to control rumors about Jews being packed into cattle cars and deported to extermination camps or murdered in the forest. News arrived that thirty thousand Jews in Lwów had been deported and that the ghetto in Kraków had been liquidated. Ominously, a new camp called Treblinka was being erected sixty miles outside Warsaw, without barracks and with brick smokestacks. The Nazis aggressively spread the word that Jews would merely be relocated for resettlement and labor in the east.

More families began to hand their children over to Irena to be smuggled to safety, knowing they might never see them again. The perimeter outside the ghetto was rife with blackmailers who would come up behind Jews and begin meowing, a signal that if they were not paid, they would denounce them. Irena and her network learned how to navigate the peril more and more creatively. She timed her exits with the evening return of forced labor brigades coming in the other direction which absorbed the guards' attention. Sometimes she would add Jewish adults and teenagers to the work brigades themselves and have them disappear into the Aryan side, bribing the gendarmes who counted the groups when they returned through the gates.

In May, Irena tried a new escape route with the help of Leon Szeszko, who drove a tram that originated in the Muranowski depot inside the ghetto. One of Irena's teenage girls picked up a three-month-old baby before dawn, sang him to sleep, and then wrapped him in a cardboard box with air holes. Szeszko had left the door to his tram ajar and the girl left the package under a seat. An hour later, at six in the morning, Szeszko checked the box and then drove the tram outside the ghetto, where Irena was the first passenger to get on and took the seat above the package. She got off at the next stop with the package, and eventually the boy arrived at the Sisters of the Family of Mary convent.

———

On July 22, 1942—the ninth of Av—the Germans announced that all Jews, excluding those working for the Germans and a few others, would be deported. They could bring up to thirty-three pounds of valuables, including gold, jewelry, and cash. When Irena arrived in the ghetto, there was a rainfall of feathers as bedding was emptied to make room for caches that were, in fact, destined for confiscation. Along with several young women serving as couriers, Irena began appearing at houses to offer to take children to safety. "Very quickly," Irena noted, "we realized that the only way to save the children was to get them out." With some advance warning from the Jewish police of which neighborhoods were being targeted, she went to the areas likely to be rounded up first. With as many routes as possible now in use, children arrived at eleven different emergency centers. At the end of the first day, Irena's list had over 250 names, and she worried how they would all be supported. Some six thousand Jews had already been seized and marched to the Umschlagplatz, where they were loaded onto cattle cars, one hundred in each, and shipped to Treblinka. Those who protested were shot. Each day more Jews would be arrested for deportation, a quota of several thousand. The numbers would reach over ten thousand some days, and there were sometimes not even enough train cars to transport the Jews.

On the second day of the roundups, July 23, the head of the Judenrat, Adam Czerniaków, swallowed cyanide in his office. Very few now voluntarily agreed to be relocated, so the Germans and their collaborators began forcibly marching random victims to the trains. The first to be targeted were those who could not work, including the sick, the elderly, and, of course, children. Many parents kept their children home, and the youth circles became much smaller. The orphans had no one to protect them and were being rounded up quickly.

"We witnessed Dantesque scenes," Irena recalled of the agonizing decisions forced on desperate parents. She could offer no guarantees to them other than to try to get their children out of the ghetto. "The father of the child was okay and the mother was not. The grandmother was really close with the child, with tears in her eyes. And she was saying, 'No, no, we cannot give her away.'" When Irena would return, it was often too late. "Frequently all of them were already on the Umschlagplatz."

A backlog was developing among the emergency houses, and Irena was desperately trying to solve the bottleneck. In the Aryan quarter, she looked for any and all hiding places. A number of children found temporary refuge at the Warsaw Zoo, run by Jan Żabiński and his wife Antonina, active members of the Polish underground who hid dozens in their empty animal cages. Irena herself had eight to ten apartments under her own direct care, hiding Jews and providing financial aid.

Danger was constant. One day Irena took eight-year-old Guta Etinger through the now reopened courthouse tunnels. On Ogrodowa Street they got on the tram, where a young man chivalrously gave Irena his seat. She quietly reminded Guta that her name was now Zofia Wacek. The girl buried her face in Irena's coat. Then she suddenly looked up and burst into tears.

"Hab Rakhmunes!" the girl cried in Yiddish.

Irena froze. Passengers began looking at her and whispering. The girl continued to sob.

Before anyone could move, the tram screeched to a halt as the operator pulled the brake. He yelled that something was terribly wrong with the vehicle and ordered all the passengers out immediately. As he rushed up the aisle, begging people to leave as quickly as possible, he stopped Irena and whispered to her to stay.

When the passengers were all out, he closed the door and told Irena to kneel down on the floor as the girl continued to cry. He started the tram again, running it as quickly as possible, rushing around corners. After a rocky ride, he stopped in a quiet neighborhood.

"You're safe now," he told Irena. "God be with you."

"Why did you do it?" Irena stammered.

"I don't know," he admitted. "I just did it without thinking. You better go."

Irena walked with Guta to the Praga district. She bought the stunned girl a pastry with sugar frosting and then took her into hiding.

———

Shortly thereafter, Irena heard that Korczak's orphanage was to be liquidated. By the time she arrived, Ukrainian solders under SS command had already herded the children outside, where they were lined up in groups of four, dressed in their blue denim holiday uniforms, many clutching the homemade dolls Irena had smuggled in to them. The doctor moved up and down the group, trying to calm and reassure the almost two hundred children as the Nazis called the roll. Each child carried a flask of water, and Korczak told them that they were going for a picnic at the pine and birch trees, just like summer camp, and they would all be pretend birds and squirrels and rabbits. "At last they would be able to exchange the horrible, suffocating city walls for meadows of flowers, streams where they could bathe, woods full of berries and mushrooms," Wladyslaw Szpilman recalled Korczak telling the children in his memoir *The Pianist*. One of the boys held the green flag of King Matt, the hero of Korczak's popular children's book. An SS officer ordered a twelve-year-old boy to play music on the violin.

Irena watched as the doctor gave the signal and the children began a two-mile march to the Umschlagplatz. Korczak carried a five-year-old and held the hand of a ten-year-old boy and led the children, singing a marching song: "Though the storm howls around us, let us keep our heads high." A Pole shouted out, "Good riddance, Jews!" as the column passed over the wooden footbridge over Chlodna Street. Dr. Korczak "kept walking," Irena remembered. "And all the while, what was waiting for them at the end of their journey was the great German invention

Zyklon-B." Hundreds of people lined the streets to watch the solemn march as word ripped through the ghetto. Some children began to tire of terrible thirst under the blazing sun, and Irena heard Korczak shout encouragement. After three hours, the group finally arrived at the Umschlagplatz, where a crowd waited for deportation.

Eventually the children were ordered onto the train. As the older ones began helping the younger board, a German SS officer stormed through the crowd to Korczak. He handed the doctor a document that the old man slowly opened and read with his spectacles. Someone very high up had offered to free the doctor, given his celebrity.

Korczak shook his head. "I will stay with the children," he said in Polish and then in German. Then he calmly got on the train for Treblinka. "It was not a simple boarding of the freight cars—it was an organized silent protest against this barbarism," noted one witness.

"Remembering that tragic procession of innocent children marching to their death," Irena said, "I really wonder how the hearts of the eyewitnesses, myself included, did not break in two." When she staggered home, she was so distraught by what she had seen that her mother had to call an ambulance. Of all the horrors Irena saw and experienced in the ghetto—and there were many unspeakable atrocities—"Not one," Irena reflected, "left so great an impression on me as the sight of Korczak and his children marching to their death."

———

Deportations ended on September 21, Yom Kippur, with only thirty thousand Jewish workers officially left in the ghetto. A similar number, it was believed, lived underground in the sewers, bunkers, and other secret places within the abandoned ghetto—the "wild area." Eighty-five percent of the original approximately 450,000 had been deported. Organized resistance was emerging in and out of the ghetto.

The Żydowska Organizacja Bojowa (ZOB), the Jewish resistance, announced on October 30 that they considered the Judenrat and other Jews working with Germans to be traitors. The day before, the deputy commander of the Jewish police had been assassinated as he walked home.

Meanwhile, a new group, known as Żegota, was formed in September 1942 to help the Jews. Its founders were two women who were both Catholic but quite different: Zofia Kossak-Szczucka was a well-known author and far-right nationalist who had been openly anti-Semitic before the war but who could not abide the sin of genocide. She published a manifesto entitled *Protest*, describing the liquidation of the ghetto, the murder of the Jews, the trains to Treblinka, and the innocent people killed for the crime of being born Jewish. "Poland is silent. Dying Jews are surrounded by a host of Pilates washing their hands in innocence," she wrote. "Whoever remains silent in the face of murder becomes an accomplice of the murder. He who does not condemn, condones. We are required by God to protest."

Her cofounder was Wanda Krahelska-Fikipowiczowa, a liberal socialist whose husband had been Poland's ambassador to the United States. The women created their new organization as a Catholic group originally called the Aid Committee for Jews and then the Jewish Relief Council. To maintain secrecy, the group eventually took the name of an imaginary man named Konrad Żegota, who was soon at the top of the Gestapo's most-wanted list.* In December the group was reorganized to include groups across the political spectrum (except Communists), and both Jews and non-Jews, all of whom agreed on nothing but saving the innocent. Its chairman was a socialist social worker from Lodz, Julian Grobelny, and the group maintained close links with the Polish

---

* Zofia Kossak claimed the name came from an archaic Polish word—*zegot*—which meant "to burn," symbolizing the group as keepers of the flame.

underground and the Home Army, which by then claimed one hundred thousand members.

Irena had recently been given an important mission for the Resistance, escorting Jan Karski, secret emissary of the government-in-exile, on an inspection of the ghetto. Afterward he had observed mass killings near Belzec and then traveled to London, where he met with Foreign Secretary Anthony Eden, and to Washington for an audience in the Oval Office with Franklin Roosevelt. His report was largely ignored, but Irena's exceptional work was noted. In early November a coworker, Marek Tarctuyński, contacted Irena, telling her that Żegota could help her by providing the large sums of money needed for "keeping cats." Irena was intrigued. As the mass deportations had continued in 1942, the project was enormous: "to lead as many Jews as possible, and above all Jewish children, outside the ghetto walls." But she was running out of money as the Germans clamped down on social services that needed to be replaced and the rapidly spiraling price inflation on the black market ate up what remained. Soon she would not be able to continue if she did not find other resources.

Irena was taken to a third-floor apartment at 24 Zurawia Street, where she was greeted by Halina Grobelny, a small, kindly woman who led her through a labyrinth of corridors to her husband's small room. In the bare apartment, a thin, tubercular man with wild eyebrows introduced himself as Julian Grobelny, the chairman of Żegota. He was, Irena noted, "a man with a big heart, devoted wholeheartedly to the matter of saving the most unfortunate people from the ghetto during the occupation." Grobelny told Irena he had known her father from the old socialist days, and asked how many children she had rescued. The plight of children was important to him, and as Irena would learn, no matter how difficult things became, he would often personally rescue them.

Żegota, Grobelny explained, was well funded by the government-in-exile. But their efforts at smuggling Jewish children out of the ghetto were less effective than Irena's. They had heard about the tremendous success of her informal network of social workers. "You know the people, we have the money," he said. They could provide one hundred thousand zloty a month and help find shelters among the clergy and wealthy estate owners. Irena could pick up funds from various "postboxes" all over Warsaw, and of course be protected by Żegota's safe houses. They wanted Irena to merge her operation into Żegota.

Irena instinctively trusted the group and agreed. Grobelny told her to pick a code name. His was Trojan. Irena told him she already had one: Jolanta.

In the fall of 1942, Irena took control of the child welfare division of Żegota, a position which now gave her more opportunities to help. Over the next ten months Irena and Żegota worked to take out hundreds of children. More money allowed her to operate on a bigger scale. "Vast sums passed through my hands," she noted. She made sure meticulous records were kept. Her monthly budget was as much as 250,000 zloty as funds were parachuted into Żegota from the government-in-exile and American organizations like the American Jewish Joint Distribution Committee.

"I'm a good organizer," Irena admitted. "But time did not count! We worked day and night. Very often, we had things to do in the shadow of the night. It was too risky in the daylight." She rented two old buildings, which she declared tuberculosis clinics but which functioned as safe houses. Young Jewish women were secretly placed as domestic helpers or nannies. A hundred young people were spirited away to join the partisan resistance in the forest. Jolanta was soon being hunted by the Gestapo. The penalty, Irena noted, "for harboring a Jew" was death, as a thousand posters plastered all over the city proclaimed.

On January 18, 1943, the SS moved to round up Jews living in the "wild areas." As they marched a group to the Umschlagplatz and reached the corner of Mila and Zamenhofa, young ZOB operatives embedded among the prisoners opened fire and threw hand grenades. The fighters seized German weapons and disappeared back underground as the crowd fled in panic. The next four days saw brutal guerrilla fighting as Jewish rebels used whatever weapons they could find. While many ZOB members were killed during what came to be known as the January Uprising, so were many Germans. The Polish underground now began to funnel weapons to the ZOB, viewing them as viable allies instead of helpless victims. Throughout Warsaw the symbol of Polish resistance—a combined P and W standing for "Polska Walczaca" ("Poland is Fighting")—appeared on walls.

Irena was barred from the ghetto during the fighting, but on the fifth day she was able to get back in. The ZOB now worked intensely with her to smuggle children through the network. There were now only four open gates into the ghetto, heavily guarded by unbribable Germans, and the only way out was now through the sewers or hidden holes in the wall. On February 16 deportations began again.

Not every one of Irena's missions was a success. She arrived one day to take an infant, Isek Rosner, out of the ghetto. The parents also agreed to let her take Isek's older sister, Mirjam, but asked that she come back the following day so they did not have to lose both their children at once. Irena noticed the little girl holding back tears, and her hairpin was the same one she herself had as a child. As Irena took Isek, the mother screamed a terrible wail and grabbed the baby while Mirjam looked forlornly into the empty cradle. After a moment, the father took his son and left with Irena. The baby was quickly taken away by Irena's colleague to be met in the Aryan quarter by Irena Schultz.

"I'll come for Mirjam tomorrow," she told the weeping father gently. When she arrived the next morning at Wolynska Street, she saw debris everywhere, a child's shoe, a cane, smashed furniture thrown from windows. The Rosners' apartment was empty, the door ajar, the mezuzah ripped from its place on the doorpost. There was broken glass on the floor. Next to the empty cradle, she saw Mirjam's hairpin.

————

Irena's mother Janina was growing weaker, and the wartime conditions exacerbated her heart condition. She seemed worried about Irena and confronted her about rumors that she was on a Gestapo list. "What you're doing is God's work," her mother said. "What your father did was God's work. I bless you both. For being so decent, so courageous. But I lost my husband. You lost your father. I can't bear to lose you." Irena knew that she was not only risking her own life but putting her mother through a daily terror. Not only was anyone caught helping Jews executed along with those they assisted, but the rescuer's entire family was generally immediately shot by the Germans, their bodies left on the street as a warning to others.

One night at three in the morning, a teenage girl appeared the door of Irena's apartment at 6 Ludwiki Street, shivering in a black coat. She had four small children with her, covered with sewage. Irena pulled the group inside the apartment, and as she closed her door, she saw her neighbor across the hall looking at her. Their eyes met, and the neighbor quickly closed the door. Mrs. Marzec was a polite woman, but of German origin. Irena may now have been compromised.

Irena ordered the entire group into the bathroom, where they removed their filthy clothes. The grime itself was a typhus risk to everyone. The children, aged four to seven, were so skinny that they all fit into the bathtub at once.

Irena and the girl were washing the children when Irena's mother walked in and gasped at the smell. Irena told her they were Jews from the sewer, but they would be out by the time her mother's helper arrived at seven in the morning.

Janina simply began to help with the bath.

"I'm sorry, Mother," Irena said. "I didn't mean for this to happen."

Then they realized that they were out of soap. It was a disaster: the smell of sewage was a dead giveaway. Irena suddenly went across the hall and knocked on her neighbor's door. She had no choice. She told Mrs. Marzec she couldn't sleep and was doing her laundry and had run out of soap. The shocked woman handed her a bar of soap and then locked her door. Terrified, Irena returned to her apartment. By seven in the morning the girl and the four children had left in clean clothes, with 1,200 zloty, fake papers, and the smell of sewage removed, on their way to the convent at Pludy.

When Irena returned from the ghetto later that day, her mother reported that Mrs. Marzec had told her Irena had gone crazy and was doing her laundry in the middle of the night. Janina responded that Irena cried all the time about her husband, who was in a prisoner-of-war camp. Doing the wash was the only way she could forget. "I felt sorry for you, because your daughter is already quite bad," the woman said. "There must be something wrong with her head."

———

Children continued to get out in groups of five and ten through the drainage system all winter. But on April 19, the first night of Passover and Palm Sunday, Irena noticed large numbers of German, Polish, Lithuanian, and Ukrainian policemen and troops in the ghetto. When she arrived at the Nalewki Street gate the next day, there had been explosions and gunshots overnight, and smoke rose over the ghetto. Young Jews had been preparing for some time, smuggling in dynamite and guns and manufacturing Molotov cocktails. Irena saw a unit of SS troops preparing to enter the ghetto and could hear gunfire. A large howitzer stood in the square, firing over the wall every minute. Curious onlookers had gathered to watch when suddenly the gate swung open and a group of terrified storm troopers rushed out, dragging others behind them. The Germans had moved in for the final clearing of the ghetto, and the Jews of the ZOB had fought back. Two hundred

Jews were killed in action, but many more Germans fell. The Warsaw Ghetto uprising had begun.

One of Irena's couriers reported back to her that pitched battles were going on between the ZOB and SS, and that the Jews had largely disappeared underground. German planes dropped incendiary bombs into the ghetto, and as the fighting spread, the Germans began burning entire blocks. "The ghetto was on fire!" Irena wrote, noting the surreal mingling of gunfire on one side of the wall and church bells on the other. The sky glowed red, and the howitzer continued to pound the ghetto. The ZOB fought hard, and German soldiers moved around in military formation. Irena was moved by the desperate struggle. "Every day, every hour, every minute of the long years spent in that hell was a battle," she said of the young people. "And when they finally realized that there was no hope for them, they heroically took up arms to fight."

On Easter Sunday Irena was stunned to see a carnival erected directly next to the ghetto in Krasinski Square, crowded with families in their finest. An organ grinder mixed with the sound of machine-gun fire, tank artillery, and small weapons just over the ghetto wall. A Ferris wheel provided rides to Polish children who, at the top of the arc, could see the battle going on. The world had gone mad.

The Nazis thought it would take five days to clear the ghetto. Three weeks later, they were still fighting. On May 8 the Germans captured the headquarters of the ZOB at 18 Mila Street, where many committed suicide rather than surrender. "There was no air, only black choking smoke and heavy, burning heat radiating from red-hot walls, from the glowing stone stairs," ZOB fighter Marek Edelman wrote in his diary. "The flames cling to our clothes, which now start smoldering. The pavement melts under our feet." Parents leaped out of windows to their deaths, holding their children. Over the next few days, the Nazis brutally executed most of the remaining fighters as they ran out of water and ammunition. Fewer than two hundred made it to safety. Grobelny asked Irena to find shelter for anyone escaping the ghetto.

On May 16, German commander Jürgen Stroop ordered the destruction of the Great Synagogue of Warsaw on Tlomackie Square, and at 8:15 a huge explosion was heard throughout the city. The next day Irena saw the magnificent domed Neo-Renaissance building in rubble. "The former Jewish Quarter in Warsaw is no more," Stroop wrote in his daily report to Berlin. Seven thousand Jews had died in the fighting, and seven thousand more were captured and sent to Treblinka. The remaining forty-two thousand Jews were deported to forced-labor camps, and the vast majority were killed in a two-day shooting operation in November code-named Operation Harvest Festival.

The ghetto was now quiet. There would be no more rescues. For every child Irena had smuggled out, probably one hundred had lost their lives. But there were some twenty thousand Jews still in hiding in the Aryan part of Warsaw, of which more than 10 percent were Irena's children. The network turned its focus to helping support those in hiding. Irena spent the next five months tirelessly visiting foster families, bringing zloty and identification documents sewn into the lining of her coat.

———

October 20 was Saint Irene's Day—Irena's naming day, often a more important occasion for a Pole than a birthday—and one of her aunts and her friend Janina Grabowska came to celebrate with Irena and her mother. They stayed up late into the night, long past curfew, so Irena set up cots for them to stay the night. Before they went to bed, Irena put two pages of the secret tissue-paper list of names on a table in the middle of the room near the window as a precaution. If anything happened, she could quickly throw them out the window into the garden. "During the occupation, all underground agents had to be prepared to be arrested," Irena wrote.

Two hours later, very early in the morning, there was loud banging at the door and Irena heard Germans demanding she open up. She instinctively grabbed the list of names, but when she went to throw them out the window as planned, she saw German SS officers in the courtyard.

Janina took the lists and stuffed them in her bra. "They came to your house. They're looking for you, not me," she told Irena.

Irena realized she had left a large amount of cash for the convent at Pludy under her bed, as well as fake identification papers. The Germans continued to pound, and it was too late to hide the incriminating hoard. Irena asked Janina to stay with her mother and answered the door. Eleven SS officers stormed in. Irena asked them to be gentle with her mother, explaining that she had a bad heart. The SS officers ransacked the apartment. They pulled out all the drawers, ripped down mirrors and pictures, threw dishes from cupboards, and pulled up the carpets. The commander, clad in a leather coat, walked in arrogantly and stared at Irena. He looked around the two-room apartment and ordered Irena's mother off the bed, which one of the SS soldiers then bayoneted, causing it to erupt with clouds of feathers. The commander then clicked his heels and told her mother to sit down and stay still; he was not there for her.

In the other room, an SS officer pointed a gun at Irena and Janina as the destruction continued. "It went on for two hours," Irena remembered. Amazingly, Irena's bed collapsed onto the hidden documents, so the Germans did not find them. Irena was more concerned at that moment about her mother seeing her be killed than she was about dying herself.

The commander ordered Irena to get dressed. Knowing that she should not show any fear, she demanded to know where she was being taken. She was given the address of the notorious Gestapo interrogation headquarters at Aleja Szucha 25. It was close to a death sentence. Irena took cold comfort in one thing: "As they arrested me and took me away, I was sure of one thing: the list had not got into their hands." She put her jacket on and went out with the SS officers, still wearing her bedroom slippers. Janina came running after her with her shoes, and the commander allowed Irena to change her footwear on the cobblestone street. Irena's mother then watched in horror as her daughter was loaded into the back of a police wagon with several SS soldiers.

Sitting on one of the officer's laps, Irena looked out a wire-mesh window at her mother, possibly for the last time, as the wagon pulled away. As the young officer dozed, she realized that she still had one tissue-paper list in her pocket. Pretending to be crying, she turned her back, tore the paper into scraps, and let the breeze take it through the window. No one noticed. Her head was pounding, and she began crying for real.

At Szucha 25, a low gray compound, she was put into a holding cell with several people and then brought into a windowless room. A tall SS officer came in, sat down at a desk, and began to read her file. Neither of them wanted to be there, he assured her, but it was necessary, and the Gestapo would find out everything anyway. He told her that if she told him what she knew about Żegota, she would be free to go home to her sick mother.

Irena had prepared for the moment. She told him she was merely a zealous social worker with an ill mother whose care took up all her time.

The officer told her to stop the charade and demanded information. He handed her the file, which contained signed confessions about rescued children, her name underlined in black all over them. On the front page, she learned that one of her network's meeting places—a laundry on Bracka Street—had been compromised. "The owner was arrested, she could not stand the torture and issued my name," she noted. The only positive was that the file did not identify Żegota, or indicate that Irena was a senior member of the organization.

Irena tried to sound airily dumb. "I'll tell you everything I know," she said, "but I don't know much."

The officer said the SS believed she was an intermediary, perhaps being taken advantage of by criminal elements. He presented her with a list, asking if she recognized any names and again promising to send her home. She was stunned to see detailed information about Żegota, its meetings and operations. Kossak-Szczuck and Grobelny were at the top of a list, and Irena was tagged as a "conspirator."

The officer told her that she would be questioned more intensely at Pawiak Prison, the macabre jail that was one of the few remaining buildings standing in the ghetto. Her next interrogator would be far less reasonable, he warned.

"I can only tell you the truth," Irena said.

She was transported in silence with ten other prisoners to the castle that housed Pawiak, originally built in 1835 by the Russians as a prison for Poles fighting the czars. In the Gestapo wagon, a man lay unconscious and bleeding. In front of the floodlit barbed wire of the prison, she was unloaded and taken through the courtyard into the women's section. After exchanging her nightgown for a gray-and-black-striped prisoner's uniform, she was thrown into an eight-by-twelve foot cell with seven other women. She had been awake for almost two days, and she briefly fell asleep. When she woke up, she met her cellmates, including an older woman named Basia, who told Irena she had heard about her heroics.

On the second day, Irena was hauled before another German SS officer, a heavyset man with black-framed glasses, stubble, and a tunic he could not entirely close. He smelled like alcohol and tobacco and, unlike her prior interrogator, did not speak Polish but used an interpreter. He introduced himself as Herr Bach—he liked to think he was a distant cousin of the composer, he told her—and then demanded names, addresses, code names, and other information. He showed her a black whip and explained that while he did not normally beat women, if she did not confess, he would likely be sent to the eastern front, so he had no choice. Irena told him she was a simple social worker. He did not beat her, but told her he would the next time.

When she was not being interrogated, she worked at a sink for twelve hours, scrubbing underwear with a wire brush. Twice a day she was taken to the bathroom, a quasi-outhouse where she was humiliated as she was watched by German matrons. Pawiak was a chamber of horrors. Through the window of the laundry, she watched an SS officer give a Jewish toddler candy, pat him on the head, and then shoot him in the back with his Luger when the boy walked away happily. At the start of her second week in prison, she was awakened by a German commandant reading out a list of twelve names. She heard the voices of women crying out and wailing as they were dragged past the cell. Basia explained to her that they were being taken to the firing squad. It always happened first thing in the morning, and if someone's name was not called, she was safe for that day.

Irena was regularly strapped by her arms and legs to a chair by Bach. Every time, he asked her the same questions. He began the beatings lightly, hitting her legs and feet with a truncheon. Eventually he began whipping her feet and legs, an excruciating exercise. After an hour the matron would take Irena to the laundry, where she was forced to stand for ten hours with her legs throbbing and bleeding. The interrogations and beatings continued most days, with different severity depending on Bach's mood. Irena prepared herself before each session, determined to think of other things to distract herself from the pain, even as she heard herself scream. She thought of her mother and her father, of holding her father's hand and walking along the Vistula as a child. She reminded herself of her father's name, her mother's maiden name, of playing with her cat behind her father's sanitorium, of her grandfather who had been tortured by the Russians. On the thirty-fifth day, the beating was so intense that she passed out and woke up in the bathroom in a pool of her own blood.

The women in the laundry sometimes tore the soiled Gestapo underwear as they struggled to clean it. One day, four prison officers arrived, ordered the twenty women, including Irena, out into the courtyard, and lined them up. One of them held aloft a pair of underwear with holes as another man read off the names of ten women who were told to take a step back. Irena's heart was pounding as she heard a pistol shot behind her, and a woman fell to the ground. Nine more shots followed. Irena was in tears as the bodies were pulled to the side of the courtyard and she was sent back to the laundry.

One day, Irena's cell was disinfected. One of the women in the sanitary group, Jadwiga Jedrzejowska, an old school friend, told her to report to the dentist. Irena obeyed, thinking it ordinary prison procedure. The dentist, Hania Sipowicz, drilled a healthy tooth and whispered to her that she was putting a tissue into her cheek; she should write what she was accused of on it, and give it to Jedrzejowska. Soon she received a message back. "Don't worry," it read. "We are doing everything we can to save you. Żegota." Irena tore off the name Żegota, swallowed it, and then sent a message back to them through Sipowicz that the lists were safe. "They valued my work and they were searching for a way to get me out of there," Irena reflected. "They knew that with my death, the register of all the children would disappear. "

Then, on January 20, the SS Hauptsturmführer strode into the corridor and read the list of those condemned for execution. "Irena Sendlerowa!" he yelled.

Irena felt like she was falling off a mountain. She was led with a group of other women and loaded roughly by Germans into a truck. A Polish guard gently helped her. "Be careful," he told her. "Don't hit your head. I'll pray for you." She was being transported back to Szucha 25, where many executions were carried out. Irena was pleased that at least she had not broken and given up names. When they arrived, the women were pushed off the truck into the entryway. Some of them began to cry. One fainted as each was led, one by one, through the door to the left, and gunshots were heard. Irena wished she had cyanide.

When they called Irena's name, she was brought to a door on the right, where an SS Untersturmführer pushed her onto her knees. Her legs were so swollen, she felt her skin would burst. A guard at the door looked impassively at her, and the officer dismissed him. It seemed like another interrogation. Irena felt her heart sink. She could not endure any more pain, she thought.

The officer quickly lifted Irena and helped her across the room. Then he unlocked a door that led into an alleyway. "I remember feeling the chill of a crisp January morning," she wrote. "I had not seen the sun for 100 days, and when it came out from behind a cloud it blinded me." The SS officer grabbed her hard under the arm and lifted her, leading her across the Aleja Ujazdowska, past the park where Irena had once picnicked with her mother.

"I was confused," she remembered. "He turned me around a corner, onto quiet Wiejskiej Street, where he released his brutal grip on my arm and I almost fell. Then he said, in Polish, 'You are free. Get out of here as fast as you can.'"

In shock, Irena leaned against a lamppost, thinking she was dreaming or dead. The man shook her by the shoulders. "Don't you understand?" he said agitatedly. "Get out of here."

Irena wondered if he was real. He turned and started to walk away. "I need my *Kennkarte* [civilian ID card]," she suddenly shouted at him.

"He looked back," she remembered, "dumbfounded. I felt my strength return and insisted. 'Give me my *Kennkarte!*'

"He marched up close to me and I saw his apprehension turn savage. He slapped me hard across the face with his black gloved hand and now I fell to the ground, tasting blood. He walked away."

Żegota had bribed the man to obtain Irena's release. She later learned that several weeks later, he was arrested and sent to the eastern front for the crime. It was one of the largest bribes Żegota ever paid and was delivered in cash by the fourteen-year-old daughter of her friends. "It was," she said later, "a miracle."

She pulled herself up and looked around. The street was deserted, and she found a pharmacy a few meters away. There were no customers, and the pharmacist, a young woman, took her immediately to the back of the store. Irena was wearing a prisoner's uniform, and the woman did not ask her any questions, introducing herself as Helena and giving her a glass of water and some medicine to calm down. "Slowly, I felt myself waking from an interminable nightmare," Irena remembered.

Helena combed Irena's hair, washed her, and dabbed cologne on her face, neck, arms, and stomach. Her legs stung too much to tolerate it. She gave Irena old clothing to cover her uniform, a cane, and money for the tram. After resting for an hour, without giving it much thought, Irena boarded the No. 5 tram for home. Her heart was racing. "Luckily I found a seat on the tram, exhausted, my legs on fire, my mind confused. I stared out the window, the rocking tram relaxing me, the normality of life returning. Like a lost child, I thought of nothing but finding my way home."

Suddenly a newspaper boy jumped on board and shouted that the Gestapo were seizing people at the next stop. Irena had no papers and could easily have been arrested again. People were jumping off the tram as it moved, and a man helped Irena. She fell to the ground onto her hands and knees, which began bleeding. She could only walk with a limp that would stay with her the rest of her life. She found another tram and finally arrived at her apartment. Her mother was there, and they embraced, crying and laughing. "I was so naïve," she wrote, "that I spent several nights at home, in the same apartment where the Gestapo had arrested me."

While Irena was in prison, Janina's heart failure had gotten worse, and she had become depressed. "I was so exhausted and confused that I fell asleep in my bed without noticing how sickly Mother had become while I was in Pawiak," Irena remembered. It weighed upon her. "One of the burdens I carry is the full knowledge that my illegal activities put my entire family at risk of execution," Irena reflected. "I had to choose between my mission and my mother, and, God forgive me, I chose my mission."

Although posters around Warsaw announced that Irena had been executed for aiding Jews, the Gestapo soon discovered that she had escaped and began looking for her. After being interrogated in her apartment, her mother sent a note upstairs, where Irena was hiding with a cousin: "You are not even allowed to come in to say goodbye to me. Run away as soon as possible." Żegota gave her a new identity as Klara Dabrowska. Irena recuperated, dyed her hair red, and stayed at a different safe house each night. For a few days she was hidden by the Żabińskis at the Warsaw Zoo, along with an armadillo and fox kits that had been nursed by a cat. Irena secretly visited her mother when she could, with a friend standing lookout in the stairwell. The doctor told Irena that her mother was not responding to her heart medication. The priest began to visit as well. One day her mother made Irena promise that she would not come to her funeral. "They'll be looking for you," she told her daughter. Irena argued but then agreed.

When she recovered her strength, Irena asked to resume her work for Żegota. "There were no more children to rescue," she remembered, "but thousands of children to support in hiding." They agreed to let her help distribute money and forged papers, but she could not return to her office, which was under Gestapo surveillance. On March 30, 1944, Irena's mother died in her sleep at a safe house. Irena was with her.

In July the Gestapo tightened its noose around the Resistance as the Red Army approached Warsaw. At five in the afternoon on August 1 the underground Polish Home Army began the Warsaw Uprising, with implied support from the Russians. Himmler ordered that the Germans kill all the inhabitants of Warsaw and bulldoze the city. The Russians halted and did nothing, hoping the Nazis would annihilate the population for them in advance of their occupation.

One night, after Jaga's daughter Hanna had gone to bed, she and Irena quietly went down the wooden stairs into Jaga's backyard, carrying a carbide lamp. Beneath a beautiful apple tree, they dug in the soil, first with a spade that proved too noisy, and then with a spoon. They placed the lists of children, written in barely legible pencil on thin rolls of tissue paper, inside a glass milk jar and buried it in the ground. They decided they would dig up and update the lists once a month as necessary, on the new moon when the sky was darkest. It was a secret they would share with no one else. "In case of my death," Irena recalled, "she could find it and give it to whom could use it."

The Luftwaffe began bombing, and over the next two weeks almost seventy thousand people, including small children, were executed. "Almost all Warsaw is a sea of flames," Governor-General Hans Frank recorded in his diary. Irena hid with friends at a construction site at 51–53 Łowicka Street. On September 9 leaflets fell from German planes, ordering Warsaw residents to report to processing centers or be executed. The group of thirty with Irena decided not to move. Two days later German troops arrived with flame throwers to burn every building. The group bribed a German guard, who directed them to an abandoned airfield at the army barracks in Okęcie.

On October 2 the Warsaw Uprising was finally put down by the Germans. The city was in ruins, and two hundred thousand Varsovians were dead. As the fighting stopped, the true magnitude of the war's tragedy became apparent. It is estimated that eight hundred thousand people perished at Treblinka from July 1942 to August 1943. Ninety percent of the families of those children Irena rescued did not survive the war. Fifteen percent of all Poles—six million people—were dead, including 90 percent of the Jewish population, more than three million souls. One million of them were children, and now there were, by one estimate, only five thousand left alive.

———

In the spring following the war, Irena went to Jaga's house. Every day since the war had ended, she had thought about the jars and the lists of names. "I had promised all those mothers and fathers and grand-parents," Irena recalled. "It was the only guarantee I could give them." The two women went out to the apple tree, this time in broad daylight, and dug up the earth. Irena's shoes and dress were covered in dirt by the time the jars emerged, but the soil smelled rich to her, "full of the promise of peace." As long as the jars were buried, Irena reflected, they did not have to admit that the children's parents were mostly dead. "I think memory is like that—we bury it to keep from hurting, but always it needs to be dug up."

With 95 percent of the population of the city displaced, the ad-dresses she had so painstakingly recorded were largely useless. It was a massive undertaking to track down surviving relatives. The new Soviet regime had no interest in helping. "We now began to realize the un-anticipated implications of finding living relatives," Irena remembered. There would be more trauma, especially for the younger children. They would be taken from the only family that they had ever known and re-turned to a surviving, often distant relative. But it had to be done." She contacted Adolf Berman, the president of the Central Committee of Polish Jews, who promised to do all he could to reunite families. A few years later, when he moved to Israel, he took copies of the unencrypted list there. Irena never knew what happened to it after that, although she did stay in touch with a number of children she had rescued.

The return to normal life was difficult for Irena. She and Mietek divorced when he returned home. She married Stefan Zgrzembski, a Jewish lawyer also in the underground whom she had rescued along with his mother and sister. She returned to the city welfare office and was appointed director of citywide welfare services and later joined the Ministry of Education. Two Jewish children lived with her for a time.

In March 1947 Irena gave birth to a daughter, who she named after her mother.

Under the Communist regime in Poland, it was not a good thing to have been a wartime rescuer of Jews. Those who participated in the Warsaw Uprising were persecuted. Many members of Żegota were put on trial, and some were sent to Siberia or executed because they had been sponsored by the Western Allies. Irena was repeatedly interrogated by the Polish Communist secret police and nearly sentenced to death. She miscarried a child, convinced it was due to the stress. Although she gave birth to a son, Adam, her family life was difficult, and her second husband died suddenly a few years after they were divorced. Finding renewed interest in religion, she remarried Mietek, although they eventually divorced again. "It is hard to be for the world and for your own family," her daughter later reflected.

Irena was named a Righteous Among the Nations in 1965, the first time her children had really heard anything of her wartime heroics. An olive tree was planted in her honor at Yad Vashem. The Communist government barred her from traveling to Israel to get her medal. Her daughter, Janka, then seventeen, had her admission to Warsaw University revoked. Two years later, her son, Adam, was not permitted to enroll either. "What sins have you got on your conscience?" her daughter asked her. In 1968 the president of Poland gave a diatribe against the Jews. Irena told a man she had rescued as a four-year-old that her network was ready to act again. "You and your family can count on us," she said to him. "Obviously those words meant a lot to me," he later reflected. "For me, Irena is like a good fairy."

In March 1979 Irena attended a reunion with Jaga Piotrowska, Izabella Kuczkowska, and Wanda Drozdowska-Rogowiczowa, three of her most active comrades, who had also worked as social workers. The four women drew up a statement trying to quantify how many children had been saved by the network and Żegota. Although 25 percent of the lists had been damaged, they confirmed Irena's estimate that 2,500 children had been rescued. "We think that there are many more rescued children from the war than this register because there were many ways to help outside the organization," they declared. It is estimated that Żegota provided aid to over a hundred thousand Jews and supported four thousand in hiding.

In the late 1980s Irena finally traveled to Israel, where she met a number of the children she had rescued. But the story remained silenced in Poland and virtually unknown around the world. In 1999 her son, Adam, died suddenly at the age of forty-five. Shortly afterward, three teenage girls from rural Kansas—Elizabeth Cambers, Megan Stewart, and Sabrina Coons—began to research Irena's story for a National History Day competition. Their project became a play entitled *Life in a Jar.* They traveled to Warsaw and visited the apple tree—which still bore fruit—the ghetto, and Pawiak. They met with survivors. And they met Irena, who was ninety years old. When asked why she had saved Jewish children, she always answered, "It was a need of my heart." Her parents had taught her that all people are the same, regardless of race or religion. She had simply followed her father's direction: "When someone is drowning, give him your hand. And I simply tried to extend my hand to the Jewish people."

The story of Irena's heroics at least became more widely known. In 2003 she received the Jan Karski Award for Valor and Compassion, named for the man she had escorted through the Warsaw Ghetto, from the American Center of Polish Culture. Too frail to attend, she wrote a letter that was read aloud at the ceremony: "I only did what any decent person would do in such horrible times. I do not consider myself a hero. The true heroes were the mothers and fathers who gave me their children. I only did what my heart commanded. A hero is someone doing extraordinary things. What I did was not extraordinary. It was a normal thing to do. I was just being decent." A week later, the president of Poland bestowed on her the nation's highest honor, the Order of the White Eagle.

As diabetes began to destroy her eyesight, she moved in with her daughter-in-law, with her daughter and granddaughter nearby. She still suffered from pain in her legs from the Gestapo's beatings. "I am a veteran of war," she noted. Even more profoundly, she suffered from nightmares of the painful scenes of the separation of families. "I still hear mothers and children crying," she said. She could not get rid of a feeling of guilt. "My biggest failure is that I didn't do more—that I couldn't save more children." She stayed in touch with those she rescued, always telling them that they were the heroes of their mothers' hearts. She died peacefully at age ninety-eight in the presence of one of the children she had rescued.

Irena was always also emphatic in pointing out that she had not worked alone but had help from at least twenty-five other people. "I could not have achieved anything were it not for that group of women I trusted who were with me in the ghetto every day and who transformed their homes into care centers for the children," she said. "These were exceptionally brave and noble people."

When she received the Order of the White Eagle, Irena shared her thoughts on the war. "Every child saved with my help is the justification of my existence on this Earth, and not a title to glory. Over a half-century has passed since the hell of the Holocaust, but its specter still hangs over the world and doesn't allow us to forget the tragedy. Let us build a civilization of good, of life, not of death."

8

The Ivy Leaguers

HIRAM BINGHAM IV HAD A GREAT DEAL TO LIVE UP TO. HARRY, AS HE WAS KNOWN, was the second of the seven sons and namesake of Hiram Bingham III, renowned discoverer of the lost ruins of Machu Picchu. The original Hiram Bingham was one of the first Protestant missionaries to Hawaii, and his son, Hiram Bingham II, expanded the family business to Micronesia and the Gilbert Islands. But both were overshadowed by Hiram Bingham III, a swashbuckling academic who taught at Harvard, Princeton, and Yale, his alma mater. In 1911 he led the expedition that rediscovered the ancient Inca city and became world-famous. Then, during the First World War, he distinguished himself as a lieutenant colonel in the new US Army Air Service and followed it up with successful campaigns for governor and senator from Connecticut.*

Hiram III married Alfreda Mitchell, granddaughter of Charles Lewis Tiffany, founder of Tiffany & Co., and niece of the designer Louis Comfort Tiffany. They lived in a large mansion in New Haven, where Harry was born on July 17, 1903. The boy attended Groton and then Yale and, after a stint as a secretary in the US Embassy in Beijing and travel to Egypt and India, he went to Harvard Law School. His passion for travel and diplomacy drove him to sit for the Foreign

---

* In 1924 the elder Bingham was elected Connecticut's governor, only to have a Senate seat open up before he took up office. He successfully ran for Senate and became simultaneously governor- and senator-elect. He then served in the state house for one day before going to Washington, adding yet another unusual accomplishment to his long list.

Service exam, placing third. He joined the State Department and was sent to Kobe, Japan. Tall, handsome, spectacled "like a sage old owl," he was the embodiment of an aristocratic American abroad.

His next stops were Warsaw and then the prestigious American embassy in London, where one of his tasks was escorting young American debutantes. In June he accompanied Rose Lawton Morrison, age twenty-five, when she was presented to Queen Mary at Buckingham Palace. The niece of James Hamilton Lewis, the first Senate whip, Rose had been a guest in the Senate chamber for the inauguration of Franklin Roosevelt. Harry fell for her immediately. They were married shortly after at Grace Episcopal Church in Waycross, Georgia. They honeymooned briefly at his parents' country home in Connecticut, then returned to England.

In 1937 Bingham was made vice consul with oversight of visas at the consulate in Marseille, the second largest city in France. Its magnificent bay on the Mediterranean had first attracted Greek settlers in 600 BCE, but it was now an industrial city that lacked the charm and glamour of the other cities strung along the Côte d'Azur. It was known instead for its dangerous docks and Corsican gangsters. Although Rose was disappointed to leave the glittering parties of London, the Binghams soon befriended many of the local elite, and Harry became a regular fixture at the tennis club.

The South of France, like Paris, had been a magnet for refugees from Germany, Austria, and other occupied countries. Most thought it impossible that France would ever be occupied, but some eventually started to emigrate, although getting a visa was not easy. In February 1940 Bingham had a glimpse of what was to come. A nineteen-year-old Viennese Jew, Jacques Bodner, arrived at the consulate, intending to sail for the United States. He told Bingham that he had fled the Anschluss two years earlier and had twice been imprisoned, most recently at Camp-des-Milles in Aix-en-Provence. He was emaciated and Bingham immediately issued him a visa. When he returned a month later to depart France, he was escorted by a French gendarme and was in leg irons, handcuffs, and prison clothes. They had kept him in jail the entire time, and he had not showered in three weeks. Bingham was incensed. He had seen Nazi persecution of Jews firsthand when he and Rose visited Germany several years earlier. He ordered the boy released and instructed his secretary to provide him with a bath and new clothes. Then he personally took him down to the dock and saw him aboard the SS *Champlain*. It would be the first of many such interventions.

After the invasion of June 1940, France was divided into an occupied zone and a "free" zone, overseen by collaborators in Vichy. Marseille was the largest city in the latter, and the American consulate became ground zero for anyone seeking exit papers. Lines of refugees stood all day in the hot sun outside the building, but very few were successful.

Many senior officials in the US Department of State did not want to allow Jews and other "undesirables" into the United States. Immigration matters had recently been transferred to State from the more sympathetic Department of Labor, and the month before Bingham issued Bodner his visa, Franklin Roosevelt had appointed Breckinridge Long as assistant secretary of state with a broad portfolio, including the visa division. A member of a prominent southern political family, the Princeton-educated Long was overtly anti-Semitic. A personal friend of Roosevelt's, he served as ambassador to Italy in 1933, where he was impressed with Benito Mussolini and successfully advocated against imposing sanctions on Il Duce for his invasion of Ethiopia.

Long was determined that Jews would not come to America. "We can delay and effectively stop for a temporary period of indefinite length the number of immigrants into the United States," Long wrote in a memorandum ten days after France fell. "We can do this by simply advising our consuls to put every obstacle in the way and require additional evidence and to resort to various administrative devices which would postpone and postpone and postpone the granting of visas." Long also made deft use of the "public charge" criterion, which impeded refugees who could not demonstrate financial independence, and also made the absurd argument that German Jews were potential Nazi spies. The year before his appointment, the United States had filled its entire quota of Germans for the first time since 1933. After Long took over, it was never filled again.

At the consulate in Marseille, most were in agreement with the policy. Consul general John P. Hurley was against visas for Jews. "The Germans are going to win the war. Why should we do anything to offend them?" he told Bingham. Bingham's immediate boss, Hugh Fullerton, was more sympathetic to the refugees but terrified of defying orders or antagonizing his hosts in Vichy. As one refugee wrote later, "Visas were granted in the merest trickle, in a manner so criminally stingy that thousands upon thousands of real victims, all fine human beings, were left to the mercies of the Nazis." Bingham took a more liberal view than Fullerton. Bingham told his granddaughter the most important thing was "getting as many visas as I could to as many people" as possible. As one Resistance worker put it, "Fullerton took the bad way and Bingham the good."

The terms of the armistice with Germany were dire for refugees in France, which had always been a haven. Article 19 in particular was bleak, declaring, "The French Government is obligated to surrender on demand all Germans named by the German Government in France as well as in French possessions, colonies, protectorate territories and mandates." The Gestapo could now order the French to seize and hand over anyone they desired.

———

It was because of the surrender-on-demand clause that another young Ivy Leaguer, Varian Fry, soon arrived in Marseille. Thin and proper with hazel-green eyes, horn-rimmed glasses, and dark, curly hair, Fry was an intellectual with a degree in classics and a passionate devotee of the arts who had started a literary magazine at Harvard with Lincoln Kirstein, *Hound & Horn*. Fry knew all about the Nazis. Five years earlier he had been eyewitness to a Nazi-sponsored event in front of his hotel on the Kurfürstendamm in Berlin. As Fry reported in a dispatch to the *New York Times*, a large crowd pulled Jews out of cars and beat them, shouting "When Jewish blood spurts around the knife, then everything will be fine in Germany." Plate-glass windows were smashed as a crowd of men and women, young and old, many well-bred, gleefully chanted "The best Jew is a dead Jew" and beat Jewish passersby. In a nearby café a Nazi stabbed a Jewish man in the hand, pinning it to a wooden table before laughing and swaggering away, telling Fry as he passed, 'This is a holiday for us.'"

Paul Hagen, a German exile Fry met working on Spanish Civil War relief, told him that the Nazis maintained long lists of enemies, including prominent politicians, intellectuals, and cultural figures. Hagen was convinced that Europe was no longer safe for these men and women, and the two men determined to act. They organized a high-profile luncheon for two hundred guests at the Commodore Hotel in New York City three days after the armistice was signed. Erika Mann, the daughter of Nobel Prize–winning writer Thomas Mann, declared, "We mustn't forget that money alone is not going to rescue those people. Most of them are trapped without visas, without passports that they dare use. They can't just get on a boat and leave. Somebody has to be there who can get them out." She suggested a new organization be formed, and the Emergency Rescue Committee (ERC) came into being.

Fry and Hagen assembled a list, soliciting input from whoever they could, including exiles plugged into the "refugee telegraph" of information. Thomas Mann contributed a list of writers, and Alfred Barr, director of the Museum of Modern Art, compiled a list of artists.

Soon there were two hundred names of cultural and political figures in known danger, people Fry called his "clients."

Eleanor Roosevelt immediately gave her support. She had recently been disturbed by a photograph—actually sent by Harry Bingham—of the renowned novelist Lion Feuchtwanger behind barbed wire in the Les Milles internment camp. Fry volunteered to travel to France. The YMCA gave him affiliation as a cover story, and Eleanor Roosevelt got him a letter of introduction from undersecretary of state Sumner Welles. Fry had visions of a three-week jaunt in the south of France, riding a bicycle and handing out visas. He took a month-long leave of absence from his job as a book editor, packed a few Brooks Brothers dress shirts, his Patek Philippe watch, cuff links, his homburg, and a Burberry raincoat, kissed his wife, Eileen, goodbye, and boarded a four-engine Pan American Clipper at La Guardia Field. He carried his travel documents, the list of his clients, an agreed code, and three thousand dollars in cash strapped to his leg. Thirty-six hours later he was in Lisbon, and several days later he arrived in Marseille.

Fry initially did not connect with Bingham. On his first day he headed to the American consulate on the place Félix Baret to introduce himself and was told the visa division had been relocated to the suburb of Montredon after Italian planes dropped bombs a block from its prior location. The next morning he met Frank Bohn, who had been sent over by the American Federation of Labor on a parallel mission to help European political leaders and ran his operation from a third-floor room in the Hotel Splendide, assisted by a handful of German refugees. Bohn oriented Fry in the travails of visas, passports, and escape routes. For the moment, he explained, chaos was playing to their favor: neither the French police nor the Germans seemed focused on refugees. Some sympathetic officials were also still in their posts. For a brief time "it was a complete mess at the border," as one witness put it, and anyone could pass through. With overseas visas and Spanish and Portuguese transit papers, foreigners could still even sneak out without the required French exit visa. Bohn thought things would soon get tougher, and they should move fast.

They agreed to divide their clients up, with Bohn taking the trade unionists and socialists while Fry focused on artists, writers, and younger activists.

Near the top of Fry's list was Feuchtwanger. One of the German refugees told Fry that the novelist had been interned, but he had escaped and not been heard from since.

———

The fifty-six-year-old Feuchtwanger, a Bavarian Jew, was one of the most popular writers in the world. He was also an outspoken critic of the Nazis, and his 1930 novel *Erfolg* was a thinly veiled critique of the failed Beer Hall Putsch. On January 30, 1933, the day Hitler became chancellor, Feuchtwanger was in the United States being honored at the German embassy, hosted by ambassador Friedrich Wilhelm von Prittwitz und Gaffron. Von Prittwitz resigned in protest the day after, and advised Feuchtwanger not to return to Germany, where his home had been raided. Feuchtwanger's wife, Marta, was skiing in the Alps, and he went to meet her there. In May his books were burned in the infamous bonfire in the square before the State Opera in Berlin. In August he was one of thirty-three Germans stripped of citizenship.

Feuchtwanger and Marta headed for the South of France and began a new life in the pretty town of Sanary-sur-Mer, living comfortably on his royalties. Feuchtwanger was a complainer, a rumpled intellectual who suffered from chronic ulcers and a double hernia. But he was a bundle of mental energy, working feverishly and holding forth on any and all subjects, and soon the couple attracted a powerful circle of literati to the picturesque fishing town. Thomas Mann arrived, living in the Villa Tranquille, as did his brother Heinrich, who settled in nearby

Nice. Bertolt Brecht, Alfred Döblin, Joseph Roth, and Arthur Koestler all came to live in Sanary. D. H. Lawrence was a resident, as was Aldous Huxley, who wrote *Brave New World* there, and a young naval officer, Jacques Cousteau, who worked on diving experiments from his home in the village.

The Feuchtwangers lived for seven years in the Villa Valmer on a hill with a commanding view of the Mediterranean. "I had my books around me," he wrote later. "Olive-groves sloped down to a deep azure sea. I was content. I had not the remotest idea of ever moving from that house." But when France declared war on Germany, the Feuchtwangers were interned with other German exiles as potential fifth columnists. After a protest from the British, they were released a few days later with an apology, but Feuchtwanger's request for an exit visa was ominously denied. In May, Germany invaded, and they were again ordered to report for internment. "We had been celebrated on our arrival some years before," he wrote bitterly. "The newspapers had published editorials of cordial and appreciative welcome. . . . Now they were locking us up!"

On May 21 Feuchtwanger waited in front of Les Milles, the former tile factory near Aix-en-Provence, before entering at precisely five o'clock in the afternoon. Three thousand foreign men crammed into the makeshift barracks. Other than roll call, life in Les Milles was more uncomfortable than anything else, with long stretches of boredom and horrific sanitary conditions. But news of German advances toward the Rhône Valley were terrifying. The Nazis had attacked many of the men at Les Milles in newspapers and on the radio, and if they were apprehended, it was certain death. The French did not mistreat the prisoners, but they did little to help. "There was never a case of beating, of punching, of verbal abuse," Feuchtwanger wrote. "The Devil in France was a friendly, polite Devil. The devilishness in his character showed itself solely in his genteel indifference to the sufferings of others."

On June 21 Feuchtwanger and two thousand others were finally sent to an area south of Nîmes, where the famous Roman amphitheater was filled with refugees. The sight of the Mediterranean was joyous. "It lay in the sunshine," Feuchtwanger wrote, "lustrous dark blue with bursts of spray leaping in delicate white lines from the surface. Our spirits rose." Word arrived about the Armistice, bringing profound relief that they were now deep in unoccupied France. The men walked along a stony path over blue hills, along ravines and rivers, and through growths of holly oak. They eventually came to an abandoned farm called San Nicola. There were vast open fields and a broad meadow with mulberry trees and the conical white tents used by French colonials in North Africa. The whole scene soon took on a carnivalesque atmosphere as townspeople made their way up from Nîmes to hawk cigarettes, chocolate, and bonbons to the prisoners at extortionate prices.

Pointing out the surrender-on-demand clause, two young men recommended that Feuchtwanger try to escape, but he was too timid. "Plato places courage in the lowest order among the virtues," he quipped. Barbed wire arrived almost immediately. But very quickly it was stretched in several places so that anyone could get out if they were willing to stoop low and risk a tear to their clothing or skin. Guards largely watched with indifference.

Feuchtwanger decided to walk out of the camp through the exit, head held high. He was immediately halted by a guard.

"No further, there!" the man shouted.

"What would you do if I didn't stop?" Feuchtwanger asked him. "Would you shoot?"

"I'm not that crazy," the guard told him, "but why not make it easy for yourself and for me and crawl through the wire?"

The problem was rather where to go. Those who escaped were often picked up and brought back in handcuffs. After a while the men simply satisfied themselves with "going to town," taking surreptitious trips to Nîmes for a meal at a restaurant followed by a warm bath and good night's sleep in a hotel before taking a taxi back to the camp. The more enterprising loaded up with provisions and engaged in a brisk trade. One could buy condensed milk, fried chicken with cucumber and tomato salad, fountain pens, Swiss and Parisian newspapers, brown leather shoes, forged Polish passports, and even old masters at the camp. Illegal restaurants opened there of such quality that the officers in charge not only dined there but brought guests from Nîmes.

But it was still an internment camp. Dysentery soon was rampant, and veils of red and green gauze were everywhere to combat the plague of mosquitos. One renowned German chemist wandered about in soiled tennis clothes and a monocle, a dose of cyanide in his pocket. For all its festivity, it reminded Feuchtwanger of a Breughel painting of hell. "What wore a man down most was not so much the ever-present and very real menace of the extradition clause, as the forced inactivity, the crushingly patent senselessness of our detention there," he wrote. He confided to the Surrealist artist Max Ernst that he sometimes wished he were dead.

Then Feuchtwanger fell seriously ill in his tent, with intense stomach cramps and a high fever. He began to hallucinate bats and horrible images that seemed straight from Goya and recited a Hebrew prayer he had learned as a child against the terrors of the night. Drenched in sweat, he ran back and forth from the latrine to his tent. "It was a July night less than seven hours long," he wrote. "To me it was seven years long and more than that." He drifted in and out of consciousness, treated with a mix of tea, morphine, and alcohol. Finally, on the fourth day, his fever broke. When he stumbled out of the tent, his appearance shocked the others.

A few days later he was summoned to the commandant's office. A telephone call had come in.

"I wanted to make sure you were about," the Frenchman told him. "Take my advice, don't leave the camp." When Feuchtwanger pushed for more information, the commandant cut him off.

The skies turned gray in Feuchtwanger's imagination as he went over the mysterious conversation endlessly. Soon he was in a depression.

As he was walking in a field the next day, a voice called out that his wife was there. He ran to his tent and found Marta sitting on a bench under the trees with several of his friends. She had recently escaped her own internment and immediately made her way to Nîmes, where she had gone to the military authorities. A kindly officer had called the commandant: the cryptic message had been a friendly gesture to ensure that Feuchtwanger would be there when Marta arrived.

Marta stayed in Nîmes for four days, appealing to officials to let her husband go. He looked terrible and was in serious danger. Then she went to the American consulate in Montredon. She wrote her name on a piece of paper and convinced a guard to hand it to a consular official. By sheer luck, it was given to Bingham's deputy Myles Standish, a student of literature and direct descendant of the eponymous captain who accompanied the Pilgrims on the *Mayflower*. He recognized Marta's last name and brought her in, telling her that he and Bingham would be pleased to help, and that Eleanor Roosevelt had specifically authorized them to assist the Feuchtwangers if they could be found.

Bingham gave Standish his car to drive to Nîmes, where, on Marta's suggestion, he met with Madame Nanette Lekich, a doctor's wife who had regular access to San Nicola, to prepare a rescue. That morning Feuchtwanger had gone swimming in a river with a few friends and to lunch at a restaurant. After a nap in the meadow, Feuchtwanger headed back and ran into Madame Lekich.

"They told me that you had gone bathing," she told him quickly. "I have some news for you from your wife." She handed him a note from Marta.

Feuchtwanger looked at her, confused. "Thank you," he said, taking the letter.

"But read it," Madame Lekich instructed him. "Read it at once."

Feuchtwanger tore it open and read a message in French in Marta's handwriting: "Do exactly as you are told. Do not stop to consider. It is all straightforward and perfectly sure."

He reread the note and then looked at Madame Lekich, who pointed to a red car parked by the side of the road. Standish was getting out of the car, dressed elegantly in a white summer suit and knitted gloves. "Don't ask any questions," Standish told him in English. "Just get in. Don't delay. I will explain everything on the way."

Feuchtwanger looked at him and then instinctively down at his own tattered clothes.

"Get in please," Standish said insistently. "There is a coat in the car."

The writer got into the automobile, and Madame Lekich climbed in after him. Standish told Feuchtwanger to put on a light woman's coat with an English badge as well as dark glasses and a shawl, and then drove off at high speed. When they were stopped by a gendarme at the next town, Standish casually explained he was out for a drive with his wife and mother-in-law. They stopped to eat in Nîmes and then picked up Bingham on the way to Marseille and Bingham's villa, where Marta was already hiding. Efforts were underway to get them both out of France. "The good-natured, embarrassed Bingham gradually explains to me several details about the escape plan that do not sound very promising," Feuchtwanger confided to his journal.

Bingham lived in a two-story yellow stucco villa on the rue du Commandant Rolland, an avenue behind the Corniche, the picturesque road running along the seashore. The villa was an oasis, with an overgrown garden and a nice pond for swimming. "Our house was pretty isolated from other houses," Bingham recalled. "It would be a safe place to hide." In addition to Lion and Marta, a refugee named Joachim was also hiding there. Soon Thomas Mann's son Golo arrived, having decided, with "a very, very heavy heart," to leave Europe. Marta and Lion exhaled, feeling safe on what they believed to be the American soil of the consulate (only later would they learn that diplomatic immunity did not extend to Bingham's villa).

For his own safety, Bingham banned Feuchtwanger from going outside, except for a few steps of exercise at night, and instructed him to wear the shawl and sunglasses Standish had given him. The vice consul told his neighbors and the Boy Scouts who came to swim in the pond that Feuchtwanger was his mother-in-law from Georgia, who knew not a word of French. Feuchtwanger worked on the final chapters of his trilogy on Josephus and disappeared into his writing and his reading. "The servants are bad and not very friendly," he noted. Bingham's Czech maid warned Marta that the Swiss housekeeper had a sister who was a Nazi. Marta made every effort to court her favor, buying her gifts and helping out in the kitchen.

Initially Feuchtwanger was concerned about Bingham's moodiness. Bingham had sent Rose and his children back to the United States when war broke out. "Bingham is an awkward, friendly, puritanical, dutiful, somewhat sad New Englander," Feuchtwanger observed in his diary, who was "very attached to his wife" and missed her and his children. "I miss you so much," Bingham wrote on a postcard to his son. "We will have such fun when I can be with you all again." He confided in Marta and Feuchtwanger about his work trying to help refugees and the frustrating position he was in, powerless to help the streams of people begging for papers daily at the consulate. "The whole world around us has the disease which we've feared for so long," he wrote to Rose.

Things were dangerous in Marseille. When he returned from escorting Rose and their four children to Genoa and their ship home, Bingham had narrowly escaped a bombing at the glass-domed train station, coming outside to the red flares of anti-aircraft fire, as if it were the Fourth of July. Soon he was used to it, even playing tennis as air raid sirens went off. But he kept a gas mask at his office and stopped smoking.

Bingham started to work on getting the Feuchtwangers out of France. The Spanish border authorities did not recognize the French identity papers given to stateless persons, so Bingham issued them not only visas but also "affidavits in lieu of passport." Feuchtwanger was too high-profile to travel under his own name. "Bingham had a great idea," Marta remembered. "He asked Lion whether he had ever published under a pseudonym." As it turned out, he had published American ballads years earlier under the name J. L. Wetcheek, the English translation of his last name. Bingham loved it, and "James Wetcheek" was duly issued a visa for the United States.

Meanwhile, Fry and Bohn had been talking with Bingham about other high-profile German refugees at the top of Hitler's enemies list. Bohn had told Fry when he first arrived that Bingham "has a heart of gold. He does everything he can do to help us," and this proved quickly true. Fry managed to get the German Nobel laureate Otto Meyerhof, who he met in the Hotel Splendide, out of France and to America. Two writers in serious danger were Heinrich Mann and Franz Werfel. Mann, the older brother of Thomas, was an outspoken opponent of the Nazis and fascism. He was seen as a hero during the Weimar Republic, and in the early 1930s he and Albert Einstein had signed letters criticizing the Nazis and calling on voters not to support them. In 1932 he was even considered a serious candidate for president. But after Hitler seized power, Mann's works joined Feuchtwanger's in the book burnings, and he too was stripped of citizenship.

The sixty-two-year-old Mann had immediately fled Germany with his young wife Nelly Kroeger, a cabaret singer. Like his brother, he took the precaution of accepting honorary Czechoslovakian citizenship. But unlike Thomas, who went to America, he was determined to wait out Hitler on the promenade des Anglais in Nice, believing that the "use of power which is not filled with goodness and kindness will not last." He wrote and continued his political activity in exile, broadcasting on French radio and smuggling antifascist essays into Germany.

When his nephew Golo learned about Article 19, he reached out to his uncle from his hiding place in Bingham's villa, urging him to get in touch with his host and Fry.

The poet and writer Franz Werfel, born in Prague, then part of the Austro-Hungarian Empire, had also attracted the wrath of Hitler. His novel *The Forty Days of Musa Dagh*, about the Armenian genocide of 1915, did not sit well with the Nazis. He too lost his citizenship in 1935 and went to live in Austria with his wife, Alma Mahler, considered by many in her youth the most beautiful woman in Vienna. "Her name alone," one of Fry's team wrote, "brought back the last great era of German music, conjured up a jumble of images of the brief Weimar Renaissance, the last days of Vienna, before the Anschluss, the last days of Prague." She had been romantically linked with a series of artistic geniuses, including the artists Gustav Klimt and Oskar Kokoschka and the composer Gustav Mahler, her first husband. Mahler was devastated when she began an affair with the Bauhaus architect Walter Gropius, whom she also married, and sought counsel from Sigmund Freud. Then during the First World War she met and fell in love with Werfel. He was twelve years younger and obese, with thick glasses, unattractive features, and a bald head. But Alma saw only his genius, declaring that his face had "sensuous lips and large beautiful blue eyes under a Goethean forehead," and married him in 1929.

Fry went to see the Werfels in their hotel room at the Hotel du Louvre et de la Paix, where the poet lounged in a silk dressing gown and slippers. "Werfel looked exactly like his photographs: large, dumpy and pallid, like a half-filled sack of flour. His hair was thin on top and too long on the sides," Fry wrote. Over dinner the Werfels recounted their harrowing flight from Vienna through Italy to Paris, where the highly nervous Werfel suffered a heart attack. His health had been a constant source of concern for Alma ever since. When the Germans invaded, the Werfels briefly took refuge in the Hotel Vatican in Lourdes after finding Bordeaux overrun with refugees. Werfel was Jewish but had a proclivity for Catholicism. He visited the Grotto of Our Lady of Lourdes twice a day, convinced the spring water had healing powers, and began work on his novel *The Song of Bernadette*. When the Werfels had returned to Marseille, they received word that Bingham had issued them visas to the United States. But they were still stuck without exit papers.

Bohn, meanwhile, had been working on a grand scheme to have a boat surreptitiously pick up thirty refugees in the harbor at night. Fry decided to put the Werfels, Feuchtwangers, and Manns on board. There were also a few politicians he wanted to send, though they were even more difficult to handle. Rudolf Breitscheid, the wanted leader of the Social Democratic Party in Germany and a rival of Hitler's, sat every day at the Café Sélect on the boulevard d'Athènes with Rudolf Hilferding, the former Weimar finance minister, debating what to do in broad daylight. And the Italian Socialist Party leader Giuseppe Modigliani, the brother of the painter Amedeo Modigliani, who had fled the anti-Jewish laws, refused to do anything illegal or to shave his trademark beard, viewing it as an insult to the labor movement.

The Werfels and the Manns were immediately game for the plan. Bingham brought Bohn to the villa to explain the scheme to the Feuchtwangers and Golo Mann. "The prospect of escape lifts my mood, but the impending hardships and dangers make me nervous," Feuchtwanger wrote in his diary. On Saturday, August 17, Bohn and Fry went to the villa for dinner and talked over logistics. Feuchtwanger was ebullient, chatting with Bingham well into the night. Everything was in place.

Around ten days later, Fry got a panicked morning call from Bohn. The captain had been seen loading provisions onto the ship, attracting suspicion. "Half the refugees in Marseille had known about it days before the Italian Armistice Commission woke up to it," Fry wrote. Italian soldiers seized the ship and prevented anyone from getting near it. The boat plan was off.

It was getting dark when Fry and Bohn opened the gate to Bingham's villa. Bingham was finishing a swim in the fishpond, and Feuchtwanger was sitting at a small iron table on a gravel terrace. Bingham and Fry were impressed by how Feuchtwanger handled the news. "All through dinner he talked and joked as if nothing more serious had happened to him than the last-minute postponement of a long-planned vacation," Fry wrote in his memoir. After dinner they repaired to the drawing room for coffee and cognac. Fry told them that people were going to Spain without exit visas, and asked Feuchtwanger if he was willing to try as well.

"If you will come with me, of course I will," he said. Fry agreed to escort him and Marta. They would leave in mid-September, a couple of weeks away.

"I am in a good mood because finally there is a tangible plan," Feuchtwanger wrote that night.

The Werfels still had no exit visas. Franz briefly considered sneaking aboard a troop transport to Casablanca disguised as a soldier, an absurd idea for an overweight aesthete his age. But he did obtain letters of introduction from the Czech consul and French church officials to add to the visas from Bingham, so he was willing to try his luck crossing into Spain with the Feuchtwangers. The biggest issue was the thought of climbing the Pyrenees. The Werfels, Fry wrote, "never went around the block without taking a taxi, if they could help it." But Fry assured them there was a decent chance he could get them through without having to get off the train. Fry also invited Heinrich and Nelly Mann and Golo to join them. Heinrich Mann was extremely concerned about taking his large, handwritten diary with him, so Bingham sent it by diplomatic pouch in exchange for a promise to donate it to the Library of Congress.

The departure date was set for September 12. At the last minute, word filtered back from the frontier that the Spaniards were no longer letting those who were *apatrides*—that is, without nationality—through. The Werfels and Manns had Czech passports, but the Feuchtwangers were stateless. Fry decided that it was too dangerous for them to attempt the crossing. He would instead first assess the situation on the ground himself when the others went, and then telegram back whether the Feuchtwangers could risk the trip.

Fry arrived at the Gare Saint-Charles at a few minutes before five in the morning with a map identifying minefields and a code based on the poems of Thomas Carlyle. He had brought along his gopher Justus Rosenberg, a Jewish teenager with Aryan looks from Danzig, as well as Leon Ball, a Montana native known as Dick whose years in France had done nothing to help his French but who had been escorting refugees across the border every few days. The Werfels and the three Manns were already there, as was the Werfels' dog Heinrich, who had not been expected.

Fry was stunned when he saw Alma Mahler's twelve suitcases. She declared them all essential, and he was not about to argue with her. She also carried a satchel that contained the first draft of *Song of Bernadette*, the score of Mahler's unfinished Symphony no. 10, his final composition, as well as the manuscript of Anton Bruckner's Third Symphony and some of her jewelry. She was also wearing sandals, "the most sensible walking gear" she possessed. The group boarded the first-class compartment, where they would be ignored by the gendarmes, and departed on time at five thirty. Fry duly instructed Ball and Rosenberg to make sure the mountain of luggage got "on and off the train with no problems."

After a three-hour stop to change trains in Perpignan, they arrived in Cerbère at the foot of the Pyrenees twelve hours later. It was now dark, and they could see the entrance of the tunnel to Spain. At that hour, they assumed they would just walk through the station onto the street, but froze when they saw passengers lined up in front of the frontier police to have their travel documents inspected. "Panic seized us then," Fry admitted. He was the only one with an exit visa and therefore the only one traveling legally.

Ball confidently took the passports and went into the police office. When he came out, he looked deflated. He told them everything was fine, that they should go get rooms at the local hotel and come back the next day and see if they could go through. On the way, he dropped back to talk privately with Fry. Ball was concerned. The *commissaire* had been pleasant but said that he had strict orders not to let anyone through without an exit visa. Ball had convinced him to think it over. The train for Portbou in Spain did not leave until two thirty the next day, so they would have the morning to make their case.

They were back at the station for breakfast early, and Ball went in to talk again to the *commissaire*, who confessed that his supervisor, a stickler, was there for several days and advised Ball to send the group over the hills on foot. He insisted they not wait any longer, saying that Vichy could issue arrest warrants any day. He seemed to know something, Ball told Fry, and had even come out on the platform to point out the best way to cross the mountains.

Fry looked at the big hill with the hot sun beating down on it, skeptical that Mann or Werfel could make it. Ball could go to Perpignan to try to get exit visas, but it would take several days. They returned to the station and brought the group outside to explain the situation. Fry gave his strong advice that they attempt the crossing that day. The decision, however, was theirs.

Heinrich Mann, Golo, and Alma immediately decided to go. Werfel looked at the hill with a sigh. He remembered it was Friday the thirteenth and began to tremble.

"It's an unlucky day," he moaned. "Don't you think we'd better wait until tomorrow?"

"This is nonsense, Franz," Alma told him sharply, and Werfel lapsed into sullen and silent agreement.

Nelly Mann also wavered. "Listen, Heinrich," she said in German,

"Mr. Fry is a very nice young man. He *says* he comes to save us. But how do we know? Maybe he is a spy come to lead us into a trap. I think we ought not to do what he advises."

"Excuse me, Mrs. Mann," Fry told her in her own language, "but maybe you do not know that I understand German."

"Mrs. Mann blushed crimson at this," Fry wrote later, "and we heard no more from her."

Fry would continue on the train with the luggage while the others would climb over the hill and meet him at the railway station in Portbou. The Werfels would use their Czech passports, and Golo would use his American papers. Given Heinrich's prominence, the Manns and Fry decided not to risk using their authentic Czech documents; instead they would rely on the papers Bingham had provided in the name of Mr. and Mrs. Heinrich Ludwig. Fry had them search their pockets for anything—calling cards, letters, documents—that might bear the name Mann. He asked for Mann's hat and scratched his initials out of the band with his penknife.

"We are obliged to act like real criminals," Mann said sadly.

Fry bought a dozen packages of Gauloises cigarettes to bribe the Spanish guards if necessary. Then he left the group just beyond the local schoolhouse. It was a very difficult climb for Heinrich Mann. He did not complain, but Ball and Golo had to carry him most of the way over the foothills because he could not handle the incline. Nelly sipped from a small flask of brandy every so often, and Alma's white dress billowed conspicuously as she clutched the satchel containing the precious manuscripts. "It was sheer, slippery terrain that we crawled up," she recalled later. "Mountain goats could hardly have kept their footing on the glassy, shimmering slate. If you skidded, there was nothing but thistles to hold on to."

At the top of the hill, Ball took them a few hundred years farther, until they could see the Spanish sentry house. There was a brief moment of awkwardness when Werfel tried to tip him. Ball shook their hands, and they walked to the border crossing.

The Spanish guard carefully examined their passports beneath his Napoleon-style hat. Golo's "affidavit in lieu of passport" stated that he was going to visit his father at Princeton University.

"So you are the son of Thomas Mann?" the sentry asked.

Golo was sure he was doomed. "Yes," he answered defiantly. "Does that displease you?"

"On the contrary," said the sentry. "I am honored to make the acquaintance of the son of so great a man." He warmly shook Golo's hand and then called down to the station for a car to transport the group. Fry, meanwhile, had waited until afternoon for the next train. To his amusement, the French customs guard seemed to have little interest in a lone man traveling with seventeen pieces of luggage filled with women's clothes. On the train, he burned the Manns' Czech passports, almost asphyxiating himself in the bathroom.

After they had all reunited and had a celebratory dinner at a hotel (where they learned that they were sitting next to the chief of the Spanish secret police), Fry got the Manns the last two seats on a flight to Lisbon from Barcelona. The rest of the group took the train to Madrid and were able to find two seats on another plane for Portugal for the Werfels. Golo Mann took the opportunity to visit the Prado and then took the train to Lisbon.

———

Back in Marseille, Lena Fischmann, Fry's young polyglot Polish assistant, received a telegram from her boss. There was no ban on *apatrides* at the Spanish border. Fry reported that it was fine for "Harry's friends"—code for the Feuchtwangers—to come over, after all.

They were ready to try. An American couple had recently come to Bingham's villa to see Feuchtwanger. Reverend Waitstill Sharp was the minister of the Unitarian Church in Wellesley Hills, Massachusetts, and he and his wife, Martha, were working for the Unitarian Service Committee. They looked after refugees in Lisbon when they arrived there. Eleanor Roosevelt, they explained, had sent them specifically to rescue Feuchtwanger.

The Sharps hatched an escape plan with Bingham. Marta Feuchtwanger memorized a map of the area, as it was dangerous to carry one. Bingham told her that Camel cigarettes could be a magic currency and filled her backpack and pockets with packages. Martha Sharp rented a room at a hotel built into the Gare Saint-Charles, which connected through a tunnel to the platform. The Feuchtwangers left Bingham's villa after dark, went to Martha Sharp's hotel room, and then rushed with her through the passage to the station at around five in the morning. Waitstill Sharp met them there to take the train to Cerbère.

When they arrived at the border, they too headed over the hills. Marta was a skilled mountaineer and had even once forced Feuchtwanger to climb Mount Etna. She led him through vineyards and mountainous terrain strewn with boulders. They eventually heard voices below and made it to the same customs house where the Manns and Werfels had recently crossed. There was no guarantee of as smooth a passage, however. Fry had learned that arrests did in fact regularly happen. At around this time the writer and philosopher Walter Benjamin, who had received a visa from Bingham, was successfully guided to Spain, only to be informed in his hotel that anyone without a French exit visa would be returned the next day. In despair, Benjamin committed suicide by swallowing morphine pills.

As their identification papers did not match each other's, they decided to go separately. Feuchtwanger went first. From her hiding place, Marta saw him enter the customs house and then appear a few minutes later, looking satisfied and walking down the mountain. She strode into the building and presented her identity card. As instructed, she announced that she had heard there was a high duty on cigarettes. In a flourish, she said she preferred to abandon hers there and threw a large pile of Camel packages onto the table. "Once again, Bingham proved his worth," she wrote later. "They all pounced, and one of them hastily stamped my papers without even a glance at my name or me. I have never gone down a mountain so fast in my life."

The Sharps bought Feuchtwanger a ticket for first class, where papers were checked much more superficially, and a third-class ticket for Marta. They all boarded the train and pretended not to know each other. Sharp gave Feuchtwanger his briefcase, marked "Red Cross" in large letters. When the writer went to the men's room, he met a Nazi officer who, spotting the logo, asked about America. They exchanged brief small talk in English, the officer speaking in a Prussian accent and Feuchtwanger in a Bavarian. The conversation ended without incident.

At the Portuguese border, there was another frightening moment. On the platform, a young American journalist rushed up to Marta. She had heard that Lion Feuchtwanger was on the train and wanted to know if it was true. Marta played dumb and asked who Feuchtwanger was. Sharp pulled the girl aside. "Shut up," he told her. "Someone might lose his life." The group eventually made it to Lisbon and checked into the Hotel Métropole. Charles Joy, a Boston Unitarian minister, advised Feuchtwanger to get to America as soon as he could, as the Nazis were illegally abducting people off the streets in the Portuguese capital. The Sharps had already booked passage to New York for themselves on the *Excalibur*, and Martha gave Feuchtwanger her berth. She and Marta followed two weeks later.

On October 6, Feuchtwanger arrived in New York and met reporters at the dock. "The author spoke repeatedly of unidentified American friends who seemed to turn up miraculously in various parts of France to aid him at crucial moments in the flight," the *New York Times* reported. "He guarded the names of these men carefully . . . explaining that he wanted to say nothing that would hamper further rescue work in France."

Eight days later, the Werfels and the Manns arrived in Hoboken. Thomas Mann was waiting for them at the pier. When he heard about their escape, the Nobel laureate wrote a letter of thanks to Bingham. His family "have repeatedly spoken to me about your exceptional kindness and incalculable help to them in their recent need and danger," he said. "I want particularly to be able to thank you personally for your sympathetic help to many men and women including members of my own family, who had turned to you for assistance." On his transatlantic trip, Feuchtwanger also wrote a heartfelt letter to Bingham in broken English. "It was a great chance that it was not Mr. X or Mr. Y, in whose house I had to face these bad days, but yours. I ever shall remember with pleasure those some good talks we had. When you get this letter, you certainly will be informed how all happened. It was a great stress all at all, I feel a little exhausted, I miss my things, I have only this famous rucksack, but I feel happy." He signed it, "Yours forever, Wetcheek."

———

In addition to his work with Fry, Bingham assisted a number of other organizations helping refugees, and at the end of 1940 he made a tour of the deplorable conditions in five internment camps, which he summarized in a memorandum for the State Department. He gave papers to refugees on Bohn's list as well as to those assisted by the Quaker American Friends' Service Committee, the American Red Cross, the Mennonite Committee, the Unitarian Service Committee, and the United States Committee for the Care of European Children. Most refugees, especially Jews, were not eligible for emergency papers, as Fry's famous clients were, but Bingham often issued them visas within hours of their request. The Hebrew Immigrant Aid Society reported in 1940 that the consulate in Marseille was issuing thirty to forty visas per day: it is likely Bingham personally issued visas to hundreds of refugees. In one case, Bingham issued papers for all fifty-two members of the Zucker family and then arranged for them to obtain Spanish transit visas. He also provided safe transit to refugees interned in camps, allowing them to travel to the consulate, where he could give them papers for entry into the United States.

Hans Schlesinger was interned in Gurs and then Les Milles in 1940. Toward the end of the year, he received a letter from the American consulate in Marseille, strongly urging him to present himself as soon as possible. With help from a local friend, he somehow managed to obtain a one-week permit—then sometimes possible from Les Milles—to leave the camp in February 1941. When he arrived at the consulate, he was welcomed on the stairs by "a tall, good looking gentleman" who put his hand on Schlesinger's shoulder and told him he was glad to see him. "I was completely flabbergasted," he wrote later. Bingham took him into his office and asked him what kind of visa he wanted. In disbelief, Schlesinger offered to show his identification. "Not necessary," Bingham told him. "I know all about you." He also arranged for the French underground to smuggle Schlesinger's wife out of Belgium and obtain a visa as well.

"God, it was such a relief," another Jewish refugee who escaped from Les Milles, Fred Buch, remembered of meeting Bingham. "Such a sweet voice. Such a wonderful man. He looked like an angel, only without wings. And you felt so safe there in the consulate when he was there, so safe and . . . you felt that new life could start. . . . He was the angel of freedom." On March 6, 1941, Bingham gave him the papers that allowed him to escape. "He was," Buch declared, "a mensch."

"I could write a treatise about what Consul Hiram Bingham did to save refugees during his posting as consul at the American Consulate in Marseille," wrote Ralph Hockley, whose entire family got visas when he was fifteen. Joseph Schachter was ten years old when Bingham saved him, his parents, and three siblings in February 1941. "When he reaches paradise he will find a multitude of greeters welcoming him and thanking him!" he said decades later. For years the Schachter family lit a candle in Bingham's memory.

———

Fry moved from the Hotel Splendide, which had been subject to raids, to a real office under the name Centre Américain de Secours, which served as a cover for the clandestine work by also providing food, clothing, and money to refugees. Fry had in short order assembled a group of fellow idealists to help him, which soon numbered more than a dozen. His aide-de-camp was Otto Albert Hirschman, a French-speaking German Jewish veteran of the Spanish Civil War who later became a celebrated economist. Beamish, as Fry nicknamed him, met the American the day he arrived from Lisbon and was instantly impressed, volunteering to help. Fry was, he felt, "a bit of an innocent abroad," while Hirschman was adept at undercover work, even, if necessary, dealing with local gangsters on the black market, where the foreign exchange rates were five times more favorable than the official one. Tall, with large gray eyes, Hirschman became Fry's right-hand man, the partner who "knew how to do, and did, all of the things that Varian knew little about and was better off not doing," wrote another member of the team.

Beamish recruited Bill Freier, a little Viennese cartoonist who had escaped internment and was an exceptional forger of identity papers. There was also Franz von Hildebrand, an American-educated Austrian monarchist who helped process Catholic refugees, and Heinz Ernst Oppenheimer, who dealt with the books and records of the ERC, cleverly characterizing some of its murkier transactions. The German Jewish poet, novelist, and translator Hans Sahl was also a client and helped with the authors who came to the center, as did the exiled

German poet Walter Mehring, whose satires had cost him his citizenship.

When Mehring first told Sahl that a young American had arrived in Marseille to rescue him, he thought he was joking. When Fry told him he would arrange for his escape and gave him money for new clothes, Sahl burst into tears. As for the high-profile Mehring ("Joseph Goebbels is personally interested in me," he had confided in a panic), there were several failed attempts to get him to safety, including by chartering a fishing boat or smuggling him by rail over the border, where he was briefly arrested at the train station because of his vagabond appearance. On another occasion Bingham arrived at the Hotel Splendide in the nick of time to save Mehring just as he was being taken into custody.

There were also some colorful American expatriates in Fry's crew. Charlie Fawcett was a twenty-one-year-old southerner descended from three US presidents who had already traveled the Far East, learned trumpet from Louis Armstrong, and volunteered for the French ambulance corps. Jovial and courtly, he served as the doorman, keeping both order and calm. Fawcett once managed to smuggle out an entire squad of British soldiers, at one point hiding them in Henri Matisse's barn. He also married quite a few Jewish women in weddings of convenience so they could escape France. Bingham was his comrade in this enterprise, issuing visas and certifying that the recipient was married to an American. Suddenly there were myriad Mrs. Fawcetts proliferating in Lisbon with visas issued by the American vice consul in perfect order.

Twenty-five-year-old Miriam Davenport, a graduate of Smith College studying art history at the Sorbonne, had introduced her Paris neighbor Mehring to Fry. Fry immediately sensed a kindred spirit and hired her. With her pale blond hair piled in two braids atop her head, she chain-smoked, coughed, and giggled her way through refugee interviews for the ERC. She also convinced Fry to hire her friend, Mary Jayne Gold, a blond midwestern heiress who used her own plane to fly to the nicest ski slopes and summer resorts in Europe. Fry was initially reluctant, assuming that she was a dilettante who likely hobnobbed with Fascist aristocrats. But she became a crucial source of dollars for the ERC, funding many of the expenses for those who did not meet the celebrity criterion for the initial list but were nonetheless in a desperate situation. Davenport also introduced Fry to Justus Rosenberg, the young refugee who had helped with Alma Mahler's luggage and who was soon entrusted with special missions like escorting André Malraux.

The mood in Marseille was "the worst that you can imagine," Hirschman recalled. "It was despair about what had happened and foreboding about what might happen." Every morning the interviewers spent four hours with desperate refugees on the verge of tears and nervous breakdowns, knowing that they could not help most of them. "There were very often terrible decisions to make, triage-type decisions." Fawcett was so distraught he was ready to quit. "It was terribly sad, you really saw these people were desperate," he recalled. Fry moved him from the door to the field. Himself a refugee, Rosenberg was traumatized for highly personal reasons, seeing the lines of people in front of the office: "I saw myself sitting there," he recalled.

In the summer of 1941 Fry and Bingham undertook one of their most consequential rescues. The forty-two-year-old lawyer and civil servant Jean Moulin had arrived in Marseille, where he took the nom de guerre Joseph Jean Mercier. Moulin had been arrested and beaten by the Germans in the early days of the invasion, and the Americans got him out through Spain and Portugal. He made his way to London, where he offered his services to Charles de Gaulle, who charged him with organizing the emerging French Resistance. After parachuting back into France, Moulin brought eight separate groups together in the Conseil National de la Résistance and became perhaps the most important Resistance leader behind enemy lines. His impact before his capture and execution by the Nazis was enormous. He was, de Gaulle wrote, "a great man. Great in every way."

————

While Fry was away in Lisbon, Vichy authorities came to the American consulate and complained. Consul General Hurley advised Fry, on his return, to leave France before he was arrested and expelled. He refused to tell Fry what the French prefect had said, or the contents of the report he had sent back to Washington. He did, however, show him the State Department's return cable, signed by Secretary Cordell Hull himself:

> THIS GOVERNMENT CANNOT REPEAT CANNOT COUNTENANCE THE ACTIVITIES AS REPORTED OF DR. BOHN AND MR. FRY AND OTHER PERSONS, HOWEVER WELL-MEANING THEIR MOTIVES MAY BE, IN CARRYING ON ACTIVITIES EVADING THE LAWS OF COUNTRIES WITH WHICH THE UNITED STATES MAINTAINS FRIENDLY RELATIONS.

His colleague had advised Washington that the situation was "in danger of becoming a public scandal." The embassy was further instructed to inform the prefect in Marseille of the State Department's position. In the first week of October, Bohn was recalled to the United States.

News soon came that the Spanish had closed their frontier, leaving only one way out: by boat to Oran and Algiers, a route almost impossible to take unless you were a French official. "Now, it seemed, the refugees were really trapped," Fry wrote. "They were to be kept in France as cattle are kept in the pens of a slaughterhouse, and the Gestapo had only to come and get them. There would be no more escapes." The noose was tightening: the Kundt Commission, a group of German officers and Gestapo agents, was making the rounds at the concentration camps, seizing wanted prisoners and sending them to Germany.

In mid-December 1940 rumors swirled that the Germans would occupy Marseille. Francisco Largo Caballero, the former prime minister of the Spanish Republic, was arrested by Vichy officials on the heels of the incarceration of the Jewish former prime minister of France, Léon Blum. The former director of the Bibliothèque Nationale, Julien Cain, was snatched off the streets and deported to Buchenwald in February. The ERC also had their first extradition among its clients, a German art student who made the mistake of asking the Gestapo for an exit visa. Ominously, even the industrialist Fritz Thyssen—one of the Nazis' biggest initial supporters, who had subsequently broken with them—was arrested by Vichy authorities at the Hôtel Montfleury in Cannes and sent to Germany. Anyone who thought they were safe in unoccupied France was disabused of that notion.

Fry detected even darker clouds gathering. "The atmosphere is the atmosphere of death," he wrote his mother. "It's hard to realize sitting here in a quiet café on the old *quai* that in another corner of Europe and across the sun-touched Mediterranean, a titanic struggle is going on, a struggle which will determine the future not only of the actual combatants, but also of this same France which watches, inactive and impotent, from the sidelines. It is a bitter thing to see a people defeated."

It was clear that the next likely targets were the two Rudolfs, Breitscheid and Hilferding, the anti-Hitler politicians. Fry sent word to them in Arles that they needed to escape on a ship he had booked to Martinique. To his surprise, they agreed. Unfortunately, they refused to follow his directions, insisting on using exit visas given to them by Vichy in addition to their American papers from Bingham. Breitscheid—though not Hilferding—also declined to travel in steerage, the only class available. Sadly, by the time he changed his mind, Vichy had canceled their visas and extradited them. The US embassy declined to intervene, pointing to Article 19, and would not even meet Breitscheid's wife. Hilferding was found dead in a prison cell at La Santé Prison the next day. Breitscheid was deported to Buchenwald, where he was killed in August 1944.

The Americans in Marseille did not know any of this, but when Hilferding did not show for the ship sailing, on February 4, they decided to try one more time to get Walter Mehring out with his ticket. The poet waited nervously at the port until he was interviewed by a representative of the Sûreté Nationale. The officer carefully examined his papers, then quietly opened a box and removed a card, which he showed to Mehring. It bore Mehring's name and a legend reading: "Forbidden to Leave France, Decision of the Kundt Commission."

"I'm afraid you'll have to wait a few minutes," the officer said. "I'll have to look into this."

Mehring collapsed onto a bench, convinced he was finally caught. The policeman went into another room and called the prefecture on the telephone. Ten minutes later he returned and handed Mehring his papers.

The man smiled. "I guess it must be another Walter Mehring," he said and winked. It was one of those quiet gestures of kindness that meant life for those on the run. Mehring scrambled on board the ship. Within weeks, he was in Florida. Within a month, he was in New York.

———

The lovely villa where Bingham lived soon inspired his fellow Americans to find their own oasis. Miriam Davenport and Mary Jayne Gold stumbled upon a three-story, eighteen-room nineteenth-century house covered in ivy in the country east of Marseille. Situated on eighty-five acres a quarter mile from the road, it had a charming overgrown formal garden, a swimming pool, and a view of a landscape dotted with red and pink roofs, leading down to the sea. It was called the Villa Air-Bel, and Fry was giddy from the minute he walked on the black-and-white checkerboard tiles of the enormous living room. He loved everything from the gilded furniture to the horrendous landscape paintings to the gigantic old-fashioned kitchen that opened onto the only bathtub in the house, one that reminded him of the one where Marat was murdered.

"I have never before lived in such a beautiful place," he wrote. "I wonder if I ever shall again." He wrote his father of "one of those magnificent views that only the Mediterranean area can boast, a view of pine trees and olive trees, dark green and light, of soft red-tiled roofs, of mist and the fascination of distance, and back of it the rugged grey limestone mountains which surround the Marseilles area like a great amphitheater."

Other than electricity, there were no modern conveniences, no central heating, not even a telephone (to Beamish's frustration). But it was enormous, and the three Americans invited others to come stay with them and Fry's standard poodle puppy Clovis and Gold's dog Dagobert. Two young Alsatian men working with Fry moved in: Jean Gemähling and Danny Bénédite, an idealistic young former policeman, along with Bénédite's wife, a British girl named Théodora Prinz, and their young son and nanny. Théodora also found a cook who brought with her an alcoholic cleaning woman. Miriam Davenport's client the Russian novelist Victor Serge came with his girlfriend and twenty-year-old son Vlady. He had been a member of the Comintern but sided with Leon Trotsky and regaled his housemates with stories about the insides of the Russian gulags and the details of the various European secret police organizations. He was also an expert on reading between the lines of the propagandist press. And things got even more exciting when another of Davenport's clients, André Breton, the poet and author of the Surrealist Manifesto, moved in with his beautiful wife Jacqueline, who wore a fake bird and bits of colored glass in her hair and a necklace of tiger claws around her neck, and their five-year-old daughter Aube.

Serge put up a sign at the gate reading "Château Espère-Visa," as half the residents were waiting for exit papers. They all ate outside when the weather was warm, laughing and talking spiritedly, and Breton placed live praying mantises as a centerpiece on the dining-room table. On Sundays Surrealists flocked to the Villa Air-Bel. The poets

Benjamin Péret and Tristan Tzara, and the artists Oscar Dominguez, André Masson, Max Ernst, and Wifredo Lam, the Cuban Chinese protégé of Pablo Picasso, were all regulars and almost all clients of Fry. Breton handed out old magazines, colored paper and pencils, pastels, scissors and paste for montages, drawings, and paper dolls, and led sessions of the legendary Surrealist drawing game Exquisite Corpses, in which select guests were allowed to participate. The Surrealists even made their own deck of oversized, hand-painted playing cards they called the *Le Jeu de Marseille.*

Davenport had seen the Air-Bel as "a splendid, private hotel for the right people," though she left France a few days after they moved in to join her ailing fiancé in Yugoslavia. At some points food was scarce, but the mediocre wine was plentiful, and they grew fresh fruit and vegetables in the garden. Guests flowed in and out. The American writer Kay Boyle was often there, as was the artist Victor Brauner. The heiress and collector Peggy Guggenheim also moved in for a while, as did the aviator and writer Antoine de Saint-Exupéry's wife, Consuelo. A photograph of Fry with her in a plane tree, laughing and talking, shows him about as happy as he probably ever was in Marseille.

————

It was something of a party until December 3, when Harry Bingham received word that Fry and most of the Villa Air-Bel had been arrested and were being held on a ship in the harbor. Bingham had suspected that the house was under surveillance, just like the offices of the Centre Américain de Secours, and he had been too busy to ever make it out there. Marshal Pétain was to be in Marseille that day. "In my experience, when a head of state comes to town in a fascist state, I like to get out," Hirschman recalled. Fry had been working from the villa the previous morning with his assistant when a squad of five plainclothes police arrived, just as a peaceful fog had settled on the valley. A cat-and-mouse game followed, both comic and frightening, as the residents took turns distracting the officers while others got rid of anything suspicious. Fry burned his address books and ledgers in the fireplace. The police found Serge's pearl-handled revolver and an inflammatory drawing by Breton of a rooster named Pétain. After the housekeeper served everyone coffee, the police announced they were all going to the station. The officers allowed the children, their mothers, and the servants to stay behind. "It will only be a short time," one said. "You will all be back before nightfall. A mere formality." To Fry he had been even more apologetic. "There is absolutely nothing against you," he said. "No suspicion of any sort."

Ten hours later they were still sitting in the station in the Hotel de l'Evéché, unable to contact their lawyers or the consulate, when they were herded into a van and driven to the harbor. "I have to admit that I began now to feel that sense of high indignation which Americans sometimes feel when they are not treated as superior beings in foreign lands," Fry wrote. They were boarded onto the SS *Sinaïa* at Mole G on the Bassin Président-Wilson, along with six hundred others. The women were given third-class cabins, the men bunk beds. Exhausted, they slept in their clothes on burlap bags stuffed with straw.

In the morning they were put into groups of ten and asked to elect a leader. Breton was chosen and came back in half an hour with half a loaf of black bread and a tin pail half full of coffee. They asked to speak to the American consulate and were refused. In the afternoon they were all ordered into the hold and a rumor went around that they were being taken to a concentration camp in Africa. But it turned out that it was just Pétain passing by on a coast-guard cutter.

In the evening boys came to the side of the ship to take orders for food. Fry wrote a note to the American consul, wrapped it around a ten-franc note, and threw it to one of them while the guard had his back turned. Shockingly, the note found its way to the consulate, and

Bingham immediately sent a large package of sandwiches down to the boat with the calling card of the American consul general. He began calling the prefecture to find out what was going on, but all the senior officials were out with Pétain.

The next day the Air-Bel group sat singing French songs. Fry and Mary Jayne Gold sent a message to the captain of the ship, asking to speak to him. They were escorted up, and the captain apologized to them as Americans. When Fry told him he had crossed the Atlantic as a college student on the *Sinaïa* (a coincidence that had delighted Breton), the captain was very distressed, telling him, "I am sorry you should have had to see it again under such very different circumstances." As they talked, a cabin boy announced that M. le Consul des États-Unis was waiting below. A few moments later Harry Bingham walked through the door, warmly shaking hands with Fry and Mary Jayne. Impressed, the captain poured four glasses of cognac.

Fry and his friends were relieved to see him. Bingham told them at least seven thousand people had been arrested, including the six hundred on board the *Sinaïa*, and would likely be released within a few days. He had had to fight with the police to get on board and could not find out the specific charges. He was doing everything he could to get them out as soon as possible. The experience of being held without explanation and incommunicado was "one of the most surprising and shocking experiences of my life," Fry wrote his wife. He planned to lodge a complaint against the *commissaire* in charge of the roundup. "He'll find me a mighty tough customer," Fry wrote to Miriam Davenport. "This is precisely the sort of treatment I never forget or forgive." The group now had an even further heightened sympathy for those in internment camps, and were determined to "redouble our efforts in their behalf."

The next day at noon, after Pétain had left town, they were released. They later learned they had been swept up in the dragnet because eight years earlier an anarchist had left a bomb near the Villa

Air-Bel where the railroad cut across the property in an attempt to blow up the Prince of Wales' train. When Jacqueline Breton's sister showed up on Sunday night (the day before Pétain's arrival) with a large suitcase at a house recently rented by a group of foreigners, the police had become very suspicious.

As the liberated group now walked through the streets, they saw workers cleaning debris from the parade, and flags and bunting were everywhere. It was the height of Pétain's popularity, and members of the Garde du Maréchal proudly swaggered about with their leather helmets and riding breeches. Anyone suspiciously foreign had been impounded for the event. Fascism had truly come to France.

At the beginning of October 1940, Pétain had issued a series of anti-Jewish laws, and at the end of the month he shook hands with Hitler at Montoire. Fry wrote to the painter Marc Chagall and the sculptor Jacques Lipchitz, both Jewish, and to André Masson, whose wife was Jewish. None was prepared to leave France, although Masson did throw up when he read the racial laws. The Russian Chagall was a naturalized French citizen, and had lived in France on and off since 1922. He had moved south with his wife and muse Bella and fallen in love with the Riviera, and he did not see why he should leave his adopted homeland. "He was just comfortable where he was," Bingham recalled. "It was hard in the peaceful French countryside to imagine that there would be all this trouble." His work was both highly modern and infused with religious and traditional Jewish imagery. As a "degenerate artist" with Jewish subject matter, he was a prime target of the Nazis, who mocked his work, as one scholar has explained, as "green, purple and red Jews shooting out of the earth, fiddling on violins, flying through the air . . . representing an assault on Western civilization."

As things deteriorated, Fry kept pestering Chagall. As reality sunk in, he finally changed his mind. He and Bella came down to Marseille on December 29 and met with Fry and Bingham to plan their emigration. Over dinner at a restaurant, Chagall had nervously asked, "Are there cows in America?" No sooner had Fry assured him that there were than the lights went out, the blackout shades were drawn, and a candle was lit. The air raid that followed removed any lingering doubts the Chagalls might have had. The Museum of Modern Art had requested an emergency visa for Chagall in November, but it had still not been issued. So at the consulate Bingham gave the Chagalls visas, even though they did not have the required affidavits other than one from Fry attesting to Chagall's moral character and financial independence. Fry also bought the Chagalls two tickets to New York.

On March 8 Bingham drove Fry to Gordes, the charming and difficult-to-access village northwest of Marseille where the Chagalls lived in a stone cottage, to spend the weekend and make further preparations. They were struck by the magnificence of the landscape—"beautiful beyond belief." "The almond trees are in bloom, a delicate pink against the soft gray-green and sage-green and dark cypress-green of the Provençal landscape," Fry wrote in his journal. "In this, of all places, it is hard to believe that men, given the beautiful world to live in, can sully and destroy it by war. . . . I can see why they didn't want to leave; it is an enchanted place." Chagall had already begun to pack, and he told them they could have the house after he left to hide people in.

Chagall was a voluble and gracious host, childlike, talking about his paintings and about the world. Dressed informally, with creased old pants and a dark blue shirt, he showed off his studio. Bingham brought along his movie camera and filmed the visit. The Chagalls posed for a photograph with Bingham beaming behind them as Fry intensely studied an easel. Bingham talked with Chagall about his great-uncle, the great window maker Louis Comfort Tiffany, a conversation he believed influenced the artist in his later work in stained glass.

Despite having to return to Marseille in a hailstorm, Fry and Bingham adored the visit. Chagall sent a note to Bingham shortly after: "Thank you with all our hearts. We had a great deal of pleasure in spending these last two days with you."

In April the Chagalls came to Marseille to prepare to leave and checked in to the Hotel Moderne. By then Vichy had its own commissioner-general of Jewish affairs. A few days later there was a massive roundup of Jews early in the morning. Bella immediately called Fry and Bingham in a panic. Fry telephoned the police station and told them they had just arrested M. Marc Chagall.

"If, by any chance, the news of his arrest should leak out," Fry told the man answering the phone, "the whole world would be shocked, Vichy would be gravely embarrassed, and you would probably be severely reprimanded."

"Thank you very much for calling me," the man said quickly. "I shall look into the case at once."

Bingham too called, using the full weight of his authority and the prestige of the US government to press for Chagall's immediate release. As the painter's granddaughter later said, "Through sheer audacity, Fry and Bingham cajoled and threatened police officials to release him."

Thirty minutes later Chagall had returned to the hotel. He came around to thank them in the afternoon. "All the reluctance he used to feel to leave France has disappeared," Fry wrote in his journal. "Now he is rarin' to go."

On May 7 the Chagalls went by train through Spain. They arrived in Lisbon four days later and continued on to America. Many of the paintings in Chagall's studio followed after them, carefully identified in small sketches by the artist on the back of a copy of Le matin, rolled up by a Resistance fighter, and shipped in a diplomatic pouch arranged by Bingham. When they left, Chagall gave Fry a drawing of a goat holding a violin. The Chagalls settled in Connecticut, with some of the artist's greatest work, particularly his monumental stained-glass windows and his commissions for the Paris Opéra and Metropolitan Opera House, ahead of him.

The Cubist sculptor Jacques Lipchitz was another Russian Jew who had settled in Paris, where he lived with his wife, the poet Berthe Kitrosser. Friends had all but forced him to flee Paris as the Germans bore down, and he was on the brink of suicide when the Spanish border closed in front of him with the Armistice. He found a studio in Toulouse, where he received a letter from Fry asking what the ERC could do for him. Lipchitz asked Fry to send his last drawings to the Museum of Modern Art. When Fry explained that he could get him out to America, Lipchitz demurred. The treeless canyons of skyscrapers there would surely kill him, he declared. He preferred to die in France.

Fry convinced him to come to Marseille to talk it over. While there, he arranged for a physical and for emergency visas they could pick up from the American consulate. "When you are ready," Fry told him, "you come here. We will send you to America." For a while Lipchitz did nothing, and Fry finally sent him a blunt letter, telling him that he would love to reclaim his papers because others were "crazy to go to America," while he was wasting his golden opportunity. As the artist recalled, his friends now threw him out of his studio, warning him Hitler would soon occupy France and he would be killed. Finally he relented. "In some ways I owe him my life," Lipchitz later reflected. "I did not want to go away from France. It was his severe and clairvoyant letters which helped me finally to do so." Now Lipchitz followed Fry's directions clearly, and in May 1941 he sailed for America. Fry wrote his wife at the time, "Lipchitz is the best of the lot: polite, intelligent, and enormously grateful."

Perhaps the two most celebrated artists in France were Pablo Picasso and Henri Matisse, both on Fry's list. Picasso opted to stay in Paris. His antifascist credentials were impeccable—he was the painter of *Guernica*—and although he was forbidden to exhibit and periodically harassed by German authorities, he was generally left alone due to his fame. Matisse lived in Cimiez, a wealthy suburb of Nice, and Fry paid him a visit, offering to help him go to the United States. Matisse was not interested. "If all the talented people left France, the country would be much poorer," he told Fry. "I began an artist's life very poor and am not afraid to be poor again. I will lock myself up in Nice with my 200 birds and paint." Fry photographed Matisse in his studio, working on *Nymph in the Forest*, and was a bit bemused by the old man. "With all his genius, he was the successful *bourgeois* at heart, happy in the comfort he had surrounded himself with and proud of his collection of African masks and sculpture, plants and tropical birds." On the trip, Fry ran into the writer André Malraux in Nice, who also declined to leave: he was joining the Resistance.

Fry then made a pilgrimage to see André Gide, the seventy-year-old writer considered the dean of French letters, at his home near Cannes. They spent an hour and a half together over tea and dry biscuits. Nursing a cold and dressed in heavy tweed with a thick scarf, Gide confided his gloom, saying he could only write in his journal and was spending most of his time rereading Charles Dickens. He would never betray France, he told Fry, and like Matisse refused to leave, believing his place was there. They both did agree to lend their names to the *comité de patronage* in support of the ERC.

The route to Martinique that Mehring had taken soon became a vital exit. Fry and Bingham managed to get out as many as eighty refugees, including André, Jacqueline, and Aube Breton; Victor Serge and his son; André Masson and his family; Hilferding's wife; and Breitscheid's secretary. Fry wrote in his journal that Bingham "has worked very hard, minimizing the formalities and always showing a sympathetic attitude towards candidates for immigration." By spring, the requests for help were overwhelming. Well over a thousand people came to the Centre Américain's offices to plead for help in the space of two weeks, including an unknown young philosopher named Hannah Arendt who they helped escape.

Three of the members of the White Rose, a group of German students who tried to inspire resistence to the Nazis: siblings Hans and Sophie Scholl with Christoph Probst *(right)*, July 23, 1942. *(© George (Jürgen) Wittenstein/akg-images)*

Aristides de Sousa Mendes, the Portuguese consul general in Bordeaux, was responsible for the largest rescue by a single individual during the Holocaust. *(Courtesy Sousa Mendes Foundation)*

Medical student and White Rose member Alexander Schmorell was one of the first to try to publicize the Holocaust within Germany. *(Sueddeutsche Zeitung Photo/Alamy Stock Photo)*

Above: Angelina and Aristides de Sousa Mendes pose in France with several of their fourteen children in front of the special car they commissioned—the "Expresso dos Montes Herminios"—to carry the family. *(Courtesy Sousa Mendes Foundation)*

Left: Sousa Mendes with Chaim Kruger, the young Polish rabbi whose request for visas began Sousa Mendes's rescue campaign. *(Courtesy Sousa Mendes Foundation)*

Visa issued in Bordeaux, France by Aristides de Sousa Mendes to Dutch refugee Ella de Winter on May 24, 1940. *(Courtesy Sousa Mendes Foundation)*

Ringmaster Adolf Althoff and his wife, Maria, hid a Jewish family of four in their circus for several years. *(Courtesy Yad Vashem)*

Jewish acrobat Irene Danner, hidden at the Althoffs' circus, with some of her fellow performers. *(Courtesy Yad Vashem)*

Rescuer Maria Althoff with two of her elephants. *(Courtesy Yad Vashem)*

Before being murdered by the Nazis, Irene's family, the Lorches, performed for Ringling Brothers in the United States as the highest paid circus performers in the world. *(Bridgeman Images)*

"I have made my cross": Archbishop Damaskinos led efforts to save Jews in Athens and the surrounding areas during the occupation and was the only head of church to officially speak out against the Shoah.

Great-granddaughter of Queen Victoria, cousin of Kaiser Wilhelm, niece of Tsarina Alexandra, and mother-in-law of Queen Elizabeth II: Princess Alice of Greece hid a Jewish family in her home in Athens during the occupation.

Athens chief of police Angelos Evert issued hundreds of false identity papers to Jews in hiding during the occupation. (*Courtesy Yad Vashem*)

Cycling legend and underground operative Gino Bartali racing at the 1938 Tour de France, which he went on to win. He refused to dedicate his victory to Mussolini.

The Basilica of Saint Francis in Assisi, the legendary pilgrim city where a network of Catholic clergy and residents saved hundreds of Jews. As part of the Assisi underground, Bartali secretly delivered life-saving false identification papers hidden in his bicycle. (*Berthold Werner, 2009*)

Photograph inscribed by Bartali to nine-year-old Giorgio Goldenberg. Bartali would hide Goldenberg and his family from the Nazis in the basement of an apartment he owned in Florence. (*Courtesy Eric Saul/Visas for Life*)

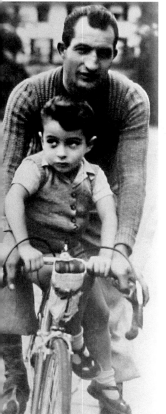

Gino Bartali with his son Andrea. Years after the war, Bartali would finally confide in his son about his heroics during the war. (*Courtesy Yad Vashem*)

The Goldenbergs, a family of four, were hidden in the basement of an apartment owned by Gino Bartali on via Bandino in Florence.

Diplomat Chiune Sugihara issued Japanese transit visas to thousands of Jewish refugees in Kovno, Lithuania. *(Courtesy Eric Saul/Visas for Life)*

The Sugihara family poses in front of the consulate in Kovno. The window behind them is where they would shortly see hundreds of Jewish refugees lining up for help. *(Courtesy Eric Saul/Visas for Life)*

As desperate Jewish refugees lined up outside the Japanese consulate in Kovno, Sugihara's sister-in-law Setsuko Kikuchi snapped this photograph. *(Courtesy Eric Saul/Visas for Life)*

Chinue and Yukiko Sugihara pose in traditional Japanese outfits in Bucharest. After the war, Sugihara would be dismissed from his job for helping refugees. (*Courtesy Eric Saul/Visas for Life*)

utch businessman Jan Zwartendijk with vo of his children in Kovno. As honorary onsul, his visas to Curaçao in the Caribbean ere lifesaving to thousands. (*Courtesy United ates Holocaust Memorial Museum*)

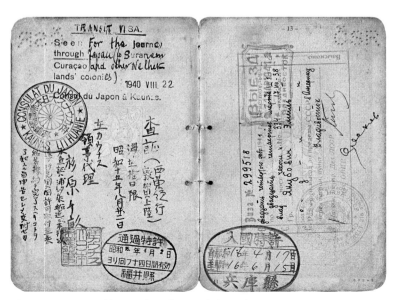

A transit visa issued by Sugihara for travel through Japan to Curaçao.

Maritime expert and Nazi Party member Georg Duckwitz provided an advance warning to the Danish Jewish community of an impending round-up, saving almost all the Jews of Denmark. *(Courtesy Yad Vashem)*

Danish King Christian rode daily on horseback in Copenhagen among his countrymen as a sign of resistance. He worked tirelessly to protect his Jewish subjects.

One of hundreds of Danish boats taking their Jewish fellow countrymen to safety in Sweden in October 1943. *(Courtesy Eric Saul/Visas for Life)*

Olympic rower Knud Marstrand Christiansen and his wife, Karen, were active members of the Resistance in Denmark and helped evacuate Jews. Knud personally rowed refugees to safety across the Øresund.

Polish social worker Irena Sendler risked her life going in and out of the Warsaw Ghetto and smuggling children and infants to safety. She would save 2,500. *(Courtesy AF Fotografie/Alamy Stock Photo)*

Irena Sendler described the scene inside the Warsaw Ghetto as "Dantesque." Here, Jewish women and children are rounded up by the Nazis and their collaborators.

Janusz Korczak was a renowned children's book author who ran an orphanage in the Warsaw ghetto. Irena Sendler recalled its liquidation as the most traumatic of the many great horrors she witnessed. *(Courtesy United States Holocaust Memorial Museum)*

Irena Sendler gave the Polish resistence operative Jan Karski a tour of the Warsaw Ghetto before he smuggled himself into a death camp to bear witness to German atrocities. His subsequent report to FDR and others was largely ignored.

Irena Sendler and her friend Irena Schultz—the "two Irenas"—disguised themselves as nurses to go in and out of the Warsaw Ghetto to rescue children.

The intellectual Varian Fry accepted a mission to go to Marseille to rescue many of the leading lights of European culture. He saved several thousand before the American government shut down his efforts. *(Courtesy Eric Saul/Visas for Life)*

Varian Fry in Berlin in 1935 where he witnessed a Nazi pogrom and sent a dispatch back to the *New York Times* describing the scene. The experience would have a profound effect on him. *(Courtesy United States Holocaust Memorial Museum)*

This photograph of world-renowned author Lion Feuchtwanger behind barbed wire at the Les Mille internment camp triggered Eleanor Roosevelt to support the creation of the Emergency Rescue Committee, which sponsored Fry's mission.

Often working with Fry, American vice consul Harry Bingham saved hundreds of refugees, including many of the most famous artists and writers in the world, who were fleeing the Nazis. *(Courtesy Robert Kim Bingham)*

Varian Fry at the Villa Air-Bel with a group of the Surrealists, many of whom were saved by his efforts. *(Courtesy United States Holocaust Memorial Museum)*

Fry examines a canvas at Marc Chagall's studio as the artist and his wife, Bella, pose for the camera. Behind the Chagalls is Harry Bingham. *(Courtesy Eric Saul/Visas for Life)*

Varian Fry walking the streets of Marseille. *(Courtesy Eric Saul/Visas for Life)*

Five thousand refugees found haven in the Protestant village of Le-Chambon-sur-Lignon and the surrounding area in southeastern France during the war. *(Courtesy United States Holocaust Memorial Museum)*

Pastor Andre Trocmé with his Italian wife, Magda, and their four children. Major figures in the nonviolent movement, the Trocmés led the village of Le Chambon during the war in saving thousands of refugees, many of them children, from the Nazis. *(Courtesy Swarthmore College Peace Collection)*

Trocmé with his colleague Pastor Édouard Theis *(right)* and schoolmaster Roger Darcissac *(center)* on their release from prison.

Andre's cousin Daniel came to Le Chambon to run two children's houses. He was arrested by the Nazis with several of his students and died in Poland. *(Courtesy Swarthmore College Peace Collection)*

A group of hidden children pose at the La Guespy young people's home in Le Chambon. Many of the children hidden in the village recalled a semblance of a normal childhood. *(Courtesy United States Holocaust Memorial Museum)*

Albert Camus lived in Panelier in Le Mazet-Saint-Voy, a short walk from Le Chambon, during the early part of the war, where he composed *The Plague*.

Nine-year-old Sara Matuson beneath a sunflower during what she recalled as an idyllic childhood in Shavel, Lithuania.

Sara Matuson and her older sister, Hannah, in the years before the Nazi invasion. They would both endure the horrors of the camps and the death marches with their mother. (*Courtesy Yad Vashem*)

The Matuson family in 1937, two years before the war destroyed their life. (*Courtesy Yad Vashem*)

Sara Matuson Rigler was reunited in London in 1972 with the British prisoners of war who rescued her from a death march and hid her in a barn for three weeks. (*Courtesy Yad Vashem*)

One of the British POW's, Alan Edwards, in front of the barn where he and his comrades hid Sara Matuson from the death marches. (*Courtesy Yad Vashem*)

The American authorities decided to recall Bingham. On April 26, 1941, US secretary of state Cordell Hull cabled the embassy, ordering Bingham to move to Lisbon, the transfer "not made at his request nor for his convenience." On May 7 Bingham told Fry that he was closing up his house and packing his things for Lisbon. "His going will be a great loss to the refugees, and may seriously cripple our work," Fry wrote in his diary. "He has been the one man at the consulate who had always seemed to understand that his job now is not to apply the rules rigidly but to save lives whenever he could without actually violating United States law. Without his help, much of what we have done we could [not] have done. . . . His behavior has always been in sharp contrast to that of most other American Consuls in France. I hate to think what it is going to be like here after he has gone."

The loss of Bingham was in fact devastating. His successor at the embassy, a young man on his first posting, delighted in refusing visas. "He was also very weak on modern European history, but very strong on defending America against refugees he regarded as radicals," Fry wrote. Caballero had not yet been extradited, and Fry wanted to smuggle him out via Casablanca. The new vice consul had never heard of the former Spanish prime minister. When Fry explained who he was, the man then assumed he was a Communist. When Fry explained that Caballero was not a Communist, the vice consul was still adamant. "It doesn't make any difference to me what his politics are," he said. "If he has any political views at all, we don't want him."

In June, the State Department declared that all visas had to be approved in Washington and that none would be given to anyone with relatives in Germany, Italy, or any occupied area. The local police became emboldened in their harassment of the Centre Américain, periodically raiding their offices and the Villa Air-Bel. Fullerton warned Fry that Vichy had a detailed dossier on his activities. "Why do you have so many Jews on your staff?" he asked, telling him the Foreign Service had purged all but one Jewish worker. "The situation here is bad and getting worse," Fry wrote to Miriam Davenport of the tightening American and French regulations. "I think we are right in feeling that we are approaching the end of our work."

In January the consulate had refused to renew Fry's passport, instead confiscating it. Fullerton informed Fry that it could only be renewed for two weeks for direct travel back to the United States. One State Department memorandum referred to him as a "dirty skunk" and a likely Communist who "cares little or nothing for the committee over which he presides or the refugees whom he is pretending to protect." Continual pressure was put on the ERC to recall Fry. Ambassador William Leahy, who had been tasked by Roosevelt with maintaining good relations with Vichy, wrote to the Foreign Ministry to let them know that the State Department did not approve of Fry's activities. In May he repeated the same message. As summer arrived, Fullerton warned that the police had informed him that unless Fry left soon, they would arrest or expel him. The Gestapo was pressuring the French to take action. Shortly thereafter Fry was summoned by the chief of police, who said that if he did not leave, he would be placed under house arrest. On August 30 the police finally arrested him. After a night in jail, he was given two hours to pack and then was escorted by train to the border. The American consulate expedited his exit papers, and he was formally expelled into Spain.

After six weeks in Lisbon, Fry returned to the United States. His team in Marseille continued their work. The State Department issued even more byzantine visa requirements, but by the time the Centre's offices were finally closed on June 2, 1942, Fry's team had gotten out nearly three hundred more people, including the artist Marcel Duchamp. But France was now a death trap for those left behind. Almost immediately after the offices were ordered shuttered, the police began aggressively rounding up Jews, including French citizens. More than seventy-six thousand French Jews were deported east to concentration camps. In the end, almost all of them were murdered.

———

Bingham had arrived in Lisbon, where he continued to work on refugee issues, in May. In September he was reunited with his family in Waycross. He had been away for fourteen months, and his hair had gone entirely white. Harry and Rose renewed their wedding vows, and the next month they left for Buenos Aires, where Bingham took up a new post at the American embassy.

For the next few years, Bingham's life was quieter. But the Fascist government of Juan Perón reminded him of what he had seen in France. As the end of the war approached, he observed a steady stream of Nazi war criminals and looted gold making their way to Argentina. Outraged, he wrote several memoranda to senior department officials, urging them to take action. "Perón and his whole gang are completely unreliable, and whatever happens, all countries in South America will be seedbeds of Nazism after the war," he warned.

Bingham's career was in shambles—as he wrote in his diary, "blasted." His loud opinions and his insubordination in Marseille marred his reputation within the State Department. He was repeatedly passed over for promotion. By 1945, one hundred and fifty Foreign Service officers had passed him on the ladder. On May 15, seven days after the Nazi surrender, he vented into his diary: "PROMOTIONS! . . . but not for me!" Two days later, he mulled over leaving the State Department.

After a brief stay in Miami at his mother-in-law's home in late 1945, Bingham went to Washington to argue his case that Nazis were hiding in Argentina. He strongly urged a program to hunt down war criminals, going estate by estate in the countryside if necessary, and volunteered to lead the effort, rooting them out in Argentina, Paraguay, Chile, Ecuador, and Brazil. Instead he was offered a position in Havana, then a diplomatic backwater where monitoring the casinos was the major priority, a thinly disguised dismissal of his recommendations. He had now had enough.

Bingham resigned from the Foreign Service and moved with Rose and their children back to his home in Salem, Connecticut. In one last petty slight, the State Department mailed his final paycheck, along with his assignment to Havana, to the embassy in Buenos Aires, despite knowing full well he was now permanently in the United States.

Bingham had inherited the Mumford House on his grandparents' estate, where he had once spent his summers. The house dated to 1769 and had been in his family ever since. He and Rose moved in and continued to have children, eventually reaching eleven: seven boys and four girls. The growing family was quickly eating through their savings, and Bingham had foregone his pension when he resigned. Several business ventures failed. But Bingham continued to paint, making copies of El Greco and imitations of Chagall's work. He learned to play the cello. He rode an Arabian horse. An avid sportsman, he enjoyed inventing games for the children, including one he called "Florbol." He patented a multipurpose mini sports field he called the Sportatron that he hoped to install on rooftops. But after seventeen years, his dream ended when his patent expired.

Bingham spent hours in his study reading, intrigued by everything from tennis (at which he excelled) to birdsongs to economics to gravity. He became particularly fascinated with religion, the spiritualism of anthroposophy, and Eastern thought. He presided over grace every evening and told his children that there is "a spark of divinity in every human being." He taught them to have an open mind and tried to be a good moral example. "He was a man who stood for what was right, and he was always concerned about us doing what was right," his daughter Abigail recalled.

Bingham rarely talked about his experiences in Marseille. With Rose present, he would occasionally open up, talking about the lines of refugees in front of the consulate and sometimes telling the story of his rescue of Feuchtwanger, with whom he stayed close until the writer's death in 1958. But the war remained for him a difficult subject:

what he had seen, those he had been unable to help, and his callous treatment by his own government. He had stretched the law, but believed he had been correct in doing so. As he had learned at Harvard Law School, he explained to his children quietly, American policy and Vichy law may have dictated one thing, but when it contradicted international law and fundamental human rights, it was necessary to follow the latter. God was always watching, he believed. Those on the ground in Marseille, with atrocities everywhere, understood. Years later Charlie Fawcett told Bingham's son proudly, "Your father broke every rule in the book."

Varian Fry too had a difficult time when he returned home. "I do not think that I shall ever be quite the same person I was when I kissed you good-bye at the airport and went down the gangplank to the waiting Clipper. For the experiences of ten, fifteen, and even twenty years have been pressed into one," he had written to his wife on the way back. "I don't know whether you will like the change or not: I rather suspect you won't." The couple divorced in 1942.

Fry also fell out with the Emergency Rescue Committee, which distanced itself from him. He joined the staff of the *New Republic*, where in December 1942 he published "The Massacre of the Jews," a highly detailed and accurate article reporting that two million Jews had already been killed and that the Nazis meant to destroy them all. He eventually resigned from the magazine after he objected to an editorial condemning American and British abuse of power but ignoring the much worse Soviet atrocities. "I felt as though I wanted to vomit," he wrote in his resignation letter. Like Bingham, he too would try his hand in business, buying a small television production company called Cinemart. After he had spent seven years at the helm, it went bankrupt, in part because his FBI file erroneously said he was a Communist, causing him to lose military contracts.

Fry felt he had lived several lifetimes in one year doing a meaningful job, one he liked better than any he had ever had. As he processed the experience, allowing the important facts to emerge "like the stones left on the beach by the ebbing tide," he turned his pen to paper. In 1945 he published *Surrender on Demand*, his memoir of his time in Marseille. "Maybe I can become a normal human being again, exorcise the ghosts which haunt me, stop living in another world, come back to the world of America," he wrote on its publication. The *New York Times* gave a glowing review, editorializing, "Though it is probably not the thing for a book reviewer to say, Varian Fry is a good man. Through the people he has helped rescue—the doctors, the painters, the writers, the sculptors, the teachers—he has added to the sum total of the world's happiness." He married a much younger woman, Annette Riley, with whom he had three children, and moved to the Connecticut suburbs. For a while he worked as a freelancer for the Coca-Cola Company, a twelve-year engagement that ended when his client did not like the conclusions of an internal report he wrote.

Fry and Bingham kept in touch over the years, but their former closeness became more difficult because Rose Bingham took a distinct disliking to Fry, who she viewed as a bad influence on her husband. She suspected that Fry may have had too much fun in Marseille, perhaps bringing Bingham along for the ride, and she thought his liberal drinking very distasteful. She also found him to be crass and was offended by his sometimes off-color language, and his sullen side grated on her. "He'd complain a little about troubles he was having and frustrations," Bingham remembered. Over time, the two comrades drifted further apart.

Fry discovered a passion for teaching. He returned to his love of classics and began work on a book about the Trojan War. He was fascinated by Aeneas—one of the world's most famous refugees, who fled Troy to found Rome—pictures of whose adventures had decorated the wallpaper at the Villa Air-Bel. As the twenty-fifth anniversary of the events in Marseille approached, Fry proposed to the International Rescue Committee—the successor to the ERC—a portfolio of editioned work by celebrated artists to raise money. Lipchitz, with whom he remained close, encouraged the project and wrote to Picasso, calling Fry "a legendary hero" who had saved a great many lives. Over the years, Fry had received letters of thanks from many he had rescued, both famous and not. But some of his celebrity clients had shown themselves less than grateful, convinced perhaps that he was trying to bask in their reflected glory. "The more famous they were," Rosenberg had remembered of Marseille, "the more difficult they were to help or just to deal with."

On a trip to Europe, Fry was rebuffed repeatedly when he brought up his project, although Malraux, now minister of culture, did surprise him with the Légion d'Honneur. While Lipchitz, Masson, Chagall, Lam, and Joan Miró all participated in the portfolio, many artists he had saved dodged or declined his request. When he asked Breton to write an introduction, the poet had his secretary respond that he had already given Fry a book inscribed to him and that was enough.

Fry was devastated. His health had begun to fail, and he had become more and more depressed after the death of his father in 1958. His son Jim recalled manic moments and frightening outbursts, and Fry continued to have trouble getting along with others professionally. His wife believed he was never as happy as he had been at the Villa Air-Bel and during the raucous times at the Hotel Splendide. Max Ernst believed he was perhaps not fit for normal life, that he fed off righteous indignation.

"I think he was always barely holding himself together," Jim Fry reflected of his father. "I think you could make an argument that what he pulled off in France was something that a sane person probably would not have thought possible, and that it was inspired by a combination of mania and grandiosity." Fry had indeed been rejected for military service with a "severe case of psychoneurosis," and Justus Rosenberg believed "that today he would be considered to be bipolar." In 1967 he and Annette were divorced. He took a job as a classics teacher at a

Connecticut high school and lived nearby, where he could enjoy his life-long interest in birdwatching. Just after Labor Day of that year he was found in bed, where he had been working on a version of his memoirs for schoolchildren, dead of a cerebral hemorrhage.

———

As Bingham approached his eightieth birthday, he took stock of his life. He was proud of his time in the Foreign Service, his son Kim recalled, but sad that his career had been damaged. "There is no question that I have been blessed," he wrote, "—blessed with family and friends—my best friends are my family—at the center of which now is my adorable darling marvelous wife." He recalled his diplomatic career fondly and thought about how the lessons of religion and ethics he had learned at Yale and Groton—where he was nicknamed "the Righteous"—had marked his life. His whole life he had lived by the motto "Give the best that you have to the best that you know." Others' pain profoundly affected him. "My father was all about not wanting people to suffer," his youngest son recalled. "He believed you are put here by God to do good works. He could not turn his back on his beliefs or on the people who needed him." Near the end of his life, Bingham confided to his nephew that he had visions of the souls of those he had saved and those he could not. They told him that all was forgiven, that he had done good, that it was not his fault he could not save them all.

Several years after Bingham's death in 1988 at the age of eighty-four, his son William found a cache of documents wrapped in twine and hidden in a closet behind a fireplace that had been built in colonial times. It was labeled "H.B.—Personal Notes—Marseilles—1940." The contents—Bingham's journal, along with letters from those he had rescued—told the story of his heroism as well as his struggles with the State Department.

Fry's story too began to resurface. In 1991 he was awarded the Eisenhower Liberation Medal by the United States Holocaust Memorial Council, and in 1994 he became the first American honored as Righteous Among the Nations at Yad Vashem. At the ceremony Warren Christopher, the secretary of state, apologized for the State Department's treatment of Fry.

In 1996 Bingham was included in the exhibition *Visas for Life*, on righteous diplomats, and in 2002 the American Foreign Service Association posthumously awarded him the Constructive Dissent award, declaring that his actions in violating American policy displayed "his willingness to put humanity above his career." In presenting the award, Secretary of State Colin Powell praised Bingham for risking "his life and his career" to save hundreds of Jews and others. Bingham's son Kim, who had wonderful memories of collecting stamps with his father, spearheaded an effort to put Bingham on a postage stamp. He was first so honored in Israel, and in 2006 finally recognized by his own country with a commemorative stamp.

Bingham and Fry never got their due in their own lifetimes. Together, they rescued several thousand souls from the jaws of the Gestapo, including many of the leading lights of the arts and sciences. As Charles Fawcett said of Fry, "Look at what he gave to America. Some of the great intellectuals of the world. We should be very grateful for it." As Hertha Paul wrote, "He will always be the hero to whom we owe our lives."

Disappointed in the world around them, Fry and Bingham shared the bond of having done the right thing without ever hoping for recognition. They were, instead, punished for their actions. Sadly, Fry was never able to be free of the burden of his melancholy. As Lipchitz said of Fry, he became "like a racehorse hitched to a wagon load of stones." His team remained devoted to him and his memory, to their "loyal faithful friend who was so courageous, discreet, sympathetic and unfailingly upright," as Miriam Davenport put it. As she wrote in her memoirs,

Marseille at that moment was "a place where grief, consternation, dis-illusionment and anger had become the gentle servants of justice." And Fry had been, Harold Oram declared, "the man for the moment."

One day after the war, Bingham received a package from Fry. His daughter Abigail recalled him beaming when he opened it. "He was so proud," she remembered decades later.

Fry had sent him a copy of his memoir. Inside, he had inscribed the volume to "my partner in the crime of saving human lives."

9

The City of Refuge

ANDRÉ TROCMÉ'S INITIAL REACTION TO THE ISOLATED MOUNTAIN VILLAGE OF LE Chambon-sur-Lignon was not positive. "Dreary granite facades alternate with dilapidated hotels covered with dirty yellow or grey stucco," he remembered in his memoirs. "The whole thing looks unbearably sad." The commune was situated some three thousand feet up on the Vivarais-Lignon Plateau, in the Haute-Loire region of south-central France, dominated by the extinct volcano Mont Mézenc. André had spent his entire life in cities, and it was urban not rural problems that interested him. But when he arrived in 1934 with his aristocratic Italian wife, Magda, his choices were limited. The passionate but extremely controversial belief in nonviolence that defined his life limited his job prospects. "Le Chambon was a take-it-or-leave-it situation," André wrote. "I took it." As it turned out, the Trocmés would stay sixteen years.

André was born in 1901 in Saint-Quentin in Picardy near the Belgian border, the son of devout Protestants in overwhelmingly Catholic France. His father was a successful lace curtain manufacturer, and André grew up in an eighteen-room mansion. When he was just ten years old, his mother was killed next to him in the family automobile on a ride in the country. His father had become enraged when a small vehicle cut him off, and he lost control of his car, smashing into a pile of construction stones. At the memorial service, his father cried repeatedly, "I killed her." André agreed. A profound horror of violence never left him.

"When I was still a young child," André recalled, "I learned to hate evil: not the evil you see others do, but the evil that you do yourself."

Three years later, the First World War broke out. German troops flooded into Saint-Quentin. Barbed wire surrounded the city and food became scarce. The town smelled like carbonic phenol acid and gangrene, and trainloads of corpses came every night from the Somme twenty-five miles to the northwest. One day, André saw three wounded German soldiers. "The one in the middle was unable to see, stumbling along with help from the others, and his entire head was basically a bandaged ball," he remembered. The man's lower jaw had been shot off, leaving only rags with strings of clotted blood. "My heart stopped when I discovered that's what war was like"

The war also threw André into much closer touch with the poor. He began attending the Young Men's Christian Union of his church, most of whose members were working-class children. The Germans nearly ruined his father by requisitioning his factories, and then, in February 1917, evacuated all civilians from Saint-Quentin. On a snowy day, André's family was loaded into unlit cattle cars with thousands of others and taken to a small Flemish farming village west of the Meuse River in Belgium. Despite food shortages, the townspeople set up a soup kitchen. "The experience was like a purifying bath, a dive into the working-class world where I was just like everyone else because my silver lining had vanished."

At the war's end, 80 percent of Saint-Quentin had been destroyed. André's father recovered his fortune in Belgium, but the Trocmé home would take five years to rebuild. The family boarded the first train for Paris and found an apartment in the Latin Quarter. André excelled as a student. He enrolled in the Sorbonne to study theology, Hebrew, Greek, and church history, took classes in philosophy at the École alsacienne in the sixth arrondissement, and studied German, English, geography, and literature at home.

André joined the pacifist Fellowship of Reconciliation. Yet he also decided to immediately do his compulsory military service, inspired by a devout German telegrapher who had been billeted with his family during the occupation and had explained to the young André that he refused to kill the enemy or even carry a weapon. It had been an extraordinary revelation for the boy. André was assigned to the geodetic—or mapmaking—brigade, which generally saw little action, and sent to Morocco. When he left his rifle behind in storage while on patrol, his commanding officer explained that his action endangered everyone. "If every one of us reasoned the way you do, we would be massacred in no time at all." André knew that the lieutenant was correct, and he resolved that if ever he was drafted, he would refuse to serve.

Religious conscientious objection had long been considered a form of treason, but the Great War changed some minds. France had suffered more than any other country, with some 60 percent of its almost nine million mobilized soldiers killed or wounded. Back at the Sorbonne, André found a group of like-minded students, some of whom would become significant figures in the pacifist movement. One of his closest friends, a quiet, towering young man named Édouard Theis, had also enlisted as a nonviolent soldier in a medical unit in the Dardenelles. Another, Arnold Brémond, invited André to go to India to visit Mohandas Gandhi and Rabindranath Tagore. André decided to make the trip but postponed it for a year when he won a scholarship to study at the Union Theological Seminary in New York. Shortly after arriving in September 1925, he was recommended as a French tutor for the younger children of Abby and John D. Rockefeller Jr. The hours were minimal, and the salary of $175 a week would allow him to save money for his trip to see Gandhi.

Several days before Easter, a young Italian girl also living at the International House on a scholarship to study social work caught André's eye. The Trocmés were upper-class bourgeois, but Magda Lisa Larissa Grilli di Cortona was aristocratic on both sides of her family. Like André, she had also lost her mother at an early age, in her case just twenty-seven days after Magda's birth. The girl grew up with house-keepers whispering that she was "the child who killed her mother." Her father married a devout Catholic woman, who sent her stepdaughter to a convent. Her father never visited, and Magda supplemented the finishing-school curriculum—which featured embroidery and other domestic skills—by reading Dante by the light of candle stubs. She soon gravitated to the local Waldensian Protestant Church, less for its religious beliefs than for its focus on helping to feed and clothe the poor.

"Her face was harmonious, her forehead luminous and her eyes were dark and magnificent," André noted. "She laughed and the sound of her laughter rang marvelously in my ears." Magda and André found a shared passion for religion and for good works. When they soon became engaged, her father warned against Protestant ministers, his father against Italians.

André's father wrote that his plans to go to India were no longer responsible and that the Reformed Church needed him now in northern France. "And that was it!" Magda remembered. "His wish was our command. Farewell Gandhi, farewell Tagore, farewell our eastern dreams." After a few months traveling in the West with the Rockefellers, they returned to Europe for their wedding.

After a honeymoon in Italy, André took up his first assignment in early 1927 as assistant pastor in a small church in Sous-le-Bois, a northern steel town in the parish of Maubeuge. The rust-colored smoke from the mills covered everything: the rooftops, the walls, the ground, even the inside of houses. The Trocmés moved into an abandoned tavern with no running water, an outhouse, and a rotting floor. It was there they welcomed their first child, a daughter they called Nelly after Magda's Russian mother.

André was a nonjudgmental pastor, seeking to improve the lives of his flock both physically and spiritually. The existence of the locals was bleak. Alcoholism was a major problem, and André's efforts to help through the Croix Bleue, an early temperance organization, endeared him to his parishioners. He also noticed that people were afraid to speak in church and so began organizing informal kitchen meetings to talk about religion and everyday problems.

In the autumn of 1928 André was posted to Sin-le-Noble, another town in the Maubeuge parish, where the local industry was coal. Once again, the Trocmés' accommodations were meager, with no indoor water or heating, yet they managed to sustain a loving family that expanded to three sons, Jean-Pierre, Jacques, and Daniel. They eventually decided to leave Sin-le-Noble because the bad air from the mines was affecting their children. When André heard of an opening for assistant pastor in Clamart, a working-class Paris suburb, he jumped at the chance. After an excellent meeting with the council, he was invited to give a sermon. André had never preached pacifism from the pulpit, but his beliefs were not a secret. He was given an enthusiastic formal invitation by the pastor, subject only to the approval by the Paris Regional Council of the Church. Its president, Pierre Durand-Gasselin, put only one hostile question to him, demanding a yes or no answer: "In the case that war is declared, will you fight to defend France under the flag of your country?" When he could only answer no, he was denied the post.

André soon found another opportunity in a town near the Swiss border overlooking Lac Léman (Lake Geneva). The local council again gave its support. But one member knew of André's pacifist beliefs and abstained from the meeting, quickly informing the authorities in Paris, who once again blocked his hire. André once again began to look for an alternative, but he was running out of options.

Then a letter soon arrived from Roger Casalis, pastor at Le Chambon-sur-Lignon. He was seeking someone to take over his far-flung parish, where the rough terrain made it challenging for him to make the rounds due to health problems. With few prospects, André went to audition, giving a sermon to a stone-faced audience in the plain Protestant Temple, which sat five hundred. The inscription on the

Temple lintel read "Love One Another,"* and after the service André enjoyed a lively meeting with the church council. He felt obliged to alert them to his pacifist views and pledged not to preach them from the pulpit. But here no one seemed to really care. They quickly offered him the position, and he accepted. The Trocmés had found a new home.

———

The day the Trocmés arrived in Le Chambon in September 1934, a torrential downpour flooded the uneven stone streets. They moved into the five-bedroom *presbytère*, a spacious fifteenth-century building with three-foot-thick granite block walls. They warmed it with multicolored Basque and Algerian rugs, geraniums, and a parakeet. The house was soon abuzz with activity, crammed with family, unexpected houseguests, and neighbors, and the Trocmés enjoyed trips in an old Citroën C4 down to the orchards and vineyards of the Ardèche valley and further afield when they exchanged *presbytères* with ministers on the Côte d'Azur and the Swiss border.

André quickly fell in love with the region, comparing "it to a lush basket of forests and rushing water suspended at an altitude of a thousand metres." For centuries the remote plateau had been home to the pious Protestant descendants of Huguenots who had fled there to escape persecution when Louis XIV revoked the Edict of Nantes. "Here, you can see forever," André wrote. "Your eyes can travel over the vast, open territory, searching for a straight grey line on the horizon, resting on the spectacle in the foreground of a grassy rock in the middle of the short meadow grass, the sparkling water bubbling over smooth pebbles in a stream, the red glow of a pine trunk against a patch of blue sky, the austere, grey farm in a green valley."

———

* "Aimez-vous les uns les autres."

Unlike his prior assignments, the population of just under three thousand in Le Chambon was 95 percent Protestant, a stark contrast with the 2 to 3 percent nationally, and more than six thousand others lived across the various towns and cantons of the surrounding plateau. It seemed like time had stood still in the commune. Many of the locals shared their homes with their animals and engaged in traditional farming on the rocky soil, eking out a living with crops like rye, potatoes, cabbage, and carrots. Many had no more than a ninth-grade education, although they generally knew the Bible very deeply, reading it with their parents as they grew up. André at first found the people distrustful, sad, and superstitious, but he soon saw warmth, humor, and a strong set of beliefs. His personal style was a good match for the community, and he was soon visiting people's homes, organizing study groups, dazzling children with parable stories for the Protestant Temple Christmas celebration, and launching a choir and even a small folk museum.

André's sermons were extremely popular. At over six feet, with a large frame, he towered at the pulpit, but he never spoke down to his congregants. His oldest brother, Francis, a doctor, visited and was amazed. "He is an absolutely striking pulpit orator with an authority surpassing any preaching I have ever heard," he wrote their other brother, Robert. "He leads you up to the summit of religious thinking, to the boundaries of the ineffable; and once there, he makes you soar in veritable ecstasy." Afterward, his congregants were left with "eyes clouded with tears, as if one has been listening to music that has seized you by your entrails."

Magda too was a whirlwind of activity, inspired by the spirit of social conscience in the region. She organized everything from a history class for young women to informational brochures for expectant and new mothers. Her major initiative, however, was a preparatory school modeled on a centuries-old one she knew from northern Italy. André was thrilled at the idea. "I had long dreamed of starting a secondary school that would be free of the narrow-minded nationalist teaching of history, where students from every country of the world would come and learn about peace." The Trocmés hoped it could also prepare the local youth to enter French universities and provide an economic balance to the town's dependence on the brief three-month tourist season.

André got approval from the church council in the summer of 1936 for the École Nouvelle Cévenole.* He invited his old Sorbonne friend Édouard Theis, who had a classics degree and had worked as a teacher in the United States, Madagascar, and the Cameroons, to serve as director. André was charismatic and temperamental, Theis quiet and steady. "He has all the qualities I lack," André noted. There were initially just eighteen students and four teachers—Theis, his American wife Mildred, Mlle Hoefert, who gave German classes, and Magda, who taught Italian. In addition to a traditional curriculum, the École Nouvelle Cévenole inculcated the values of pacifism and actively reached out to foreign students. The school was coeducational, operated on the honor system, and for several years had no grades. By the second year, as the Second World War broke out, there were forty students and enough teachers for full accreditation. The looming war drew many to the school, as like-minded people flowed into Le Chambon, including refugees. The school's education, open and free for those who could not pay, was an antidote to Nazi ideology, and among the teachers would be many who had been denied positions in public schools as Jews, idealists, or pacifists. One of its wartime students from Germany, Alexander Grothendieck, would become one of the twentieth century's most important mathematicians.

As early as 1937 André had spoken out against the Nazi ideology, as well as the Communists, in whom he saw "a demonstration of the same

---

* Later renamed Collège Cévenol.

spirit." In March 1939, as war loomed, he called upon his congregants to help any refugee on the run from the Nazis, quoting Deuteronomy—"Therefore love the stranger, for you were strangers in the land of Egypt"—and recalling the suffering of their Huguenot ancestors centuries earlier. "Once more, atrocious persecution is taking place," he wrote. "In the midst of all this cruelty and indifference, the time has come for Christians to act."

When war arrived on September 1, 1939, André's pacifist beliefs forced a reckoning. He knew that he could not serve in the military. As he had said in his very first sermon in Le Chambon, "No government can force us to kill; we have to find the means of resisting Nazism without killing people." He and Theis preached resistance and believed neutrality was tantamount to complicity. But André believed that the power of love and of nonviolence could overcome what he called the "diabolical forces of Nazism." On September 4 he took a walk with Magda to talk over whether he should resign.

"Today, I am still prepared to serve my country, with all my strength, as long as this does not require me to do what God forbids: to take part in war," he wrote the next day. "I have tried, like so many others, to envision serving in another form, as a stretcher-bearer, a chaplain, an orderly. Every time, I was stopped by the appeal of my conscience." He did not view himself as superior to others and understood Hitler to be the incarnation of evil. He did not judge the leaders who were leading their nations into war. Nor did he want to stay safely in the parish. "I only ask to be allowed to serve those in danger, the most pitiful victims of the war: women and children in the cities being bombed. I ask that my service be exclusively of a civilian nature. I am happy to give my life as others give theirs." He gathered the church council and offered his resignation. Le Chambon, however, declined it. He and Theis tried to volunteer for the American Red Cross in Paris and Lyon, but were rejected.

On June 23, 1940, the day after the Armistice, André and Theis delivered a stirring declaration. "Let us humble ourselves as we think of our responsibility for this catastrophe. Let us bow our heads as we remember the trespasses we have committed and which we have allowed others to commit, for standing idly by, for our lack of courage that made it impossible to stand up against the impending storm," they declared. The effect was profound. "In the church," one fifteen-year-old girl recalled, "you could hear a pin drop."

Immediately after the Franco-German Armistice was signed in June 1940, Le Chambon began a campaign of quiet civil disobedience. "The peace that was concluded is not an honorable peace," Theis would declare. "We simply cannot accept it." Particularly horrid was the agreement to turn over any refugees the Germans asked for, the infamous Article 19. "For the Pétain regime we had nothing but contempt," said Theis. He refused orders to put up Pétain's portrait anywhere in the schools or sign an oath of allegiance to the old man. He also refused to hold the morning ceremony Vichy required: the students standing in a circle and offering a Fascist salute to the French flag. The Temple custodian also refused to ring the church bell for a Vichy celebration. "The bells don't belong to the Marshal," she declared, "they belong to God."

Almost immediately, anti-Semitic propaganda appeared all over Vichy. "Although we were supposedly living in the free zone, the Gestapo had its inspectors everywhere," André recalled. "Already, at the end of 1940, they were organizing the deportation of political enemies and Jews to Germany. Families were separated without mercy." Word that Le Chambon might offer safe haven quietly began to circulate.

The first Jewish refugee to knock on the Trocmés' door arrived one evening as Magda put wood into the stove. A German woman stood freezing in the wind blowing off the Lignon River, her shawl covered in snow. Magda brought her inside and fed her as the woman explained that she had fled to France and then kept going south of the demarcation line. She had heard that in Le Chambon there was a pastor who might help her. Magda made up a bed and put the woman's wet shoes, a pair of summer sandals, into the oven to dry.

Magda then headed over to the mayor's office to ask for help, concerned that the woman did not have proper papers. The mayor was livid. Worried that bringing in foreign Jews could endanger the whole town, he told Magda to send the woman away as soon as possible. Magda quickly returned home.

When she opened the stove to retrieve the woman's shoes, they were burned to a crisp. Obtaining shoes in wartime was almost impossible. Only children could buy a pair once a year on their birthday, and it was illegal for adults to get new ones. Somehow Magda found a solution. By the time the woman left in the morning, her feet were clad, the gift of a young war widow.

———

The tremendously overcrowded French refugee camps housed over fifty thousand people by November 1940, approximately 70 percent of them Jewish. One teenager who came to Le Chambon recalled one camp, Gurs, as "a horror. The food was rotted, the buildings were dilapidated and cold, infested with insects and swarming with fleas and rats as big as cats." Humanitarian efforts by overwhelmed organizations were underway to provide food and medicine under the aegis of the Comité de Nîmes, an umbrella coalition of twenty-nine religious and secular groups headed by the American Donald Lowrie of the YMCA that had negotiated permission with the Interior Ministry to send small teams of relief workers into the camps. While the refugees starved, André wrote, "We, in Le Chambon-sur-Lignon, had everything we needed and lived in peace." He asked for permission to become the church's appointee to serve in the camps, leaving Theis as pastor in his absence.

André went to the beige-and-black four-story building on the boulevard d'Athènes in Marseille, where the American Quakers occupied two floors. The pacifist Quakers had a long history of helping those in need, from slaves in the American South to children in the First World War, and were trusted by Vichy in the internment camps. André met with Burns Chalmers, the tall, thin man in charge of refugee issues, and volunteered to go into the camps. Chalmers had heard of André's leadership in the pacifist cause and sensed that he was the kind of loving leader who would give children hope. Chalmers's office was chaotic, and he suggested that they meet again soon in Nîmes, halfway between Marseille and Le Chambon, to continue the conversation.

There, at a modest restaurant near the Maison Carrée, they developed an inspired idea. Both men were focused on helping children, not only materially but also, they hoped, by showing them that adults outside their families cared for them. There were plenty of organizations providing supplies and moral support to families and children in the camps. As an isolated mountain village, Le Chambon could perhaps do something more. The humanitarian disaster at that time was becoming a public relations issue for Vichy, Chalmers explained, and it was possible under an agreement that the Comité de Nîmes had managed to negotiate for some inmates, including foreigners and Jews, to get released from the camps if a doctor declared them unfit for forced labor in Germany. The Quakers were trying to get as many medical certificates as possible. If parents were deported, they took charge of the children. But it was very difficult to find communities that would take in refugee children, some of whom were illegal.

"Do you wish to be that community?" Chalmers asked. If André could provide housing and volunteers to take care of the children, the Quakers and the Fellowship of Reconciliation would provide the funding. André rushed back to Le Chambon to present the idea. Like the biblical "cities of refuge" erected "lest innocent blood be shed in your land," Le Chambon could protect those whose lives were in danger. The town council approved the proposal in one meeting.

Le Chambon was twice perfect for the task. The commune and the broader plateau of which it was a part had for centuries been a haven for religious dissenters, and many of its residents were themselves descendants of the Protestants who had rebelled against the persecution of Louis XIV. Recently locals had protected a number of women and children fleeing the Spanish Civil War. After the Munich Agreement, the local mayor had written in the Vivarais-Lignon newsletter, "Keep your spare rooms free, stock up with provisions, we are going to have a flood of refugees." He proved prescient, and when war broke out, a number of visitors simply stayed. Some villagers were initially frightened to disobey Vichy, but almost all eventually did, "gradually persuaded of the righteousness of their actions."

The region also had the infrastructure to host children. In 1893 a minister from Saint-Étienne had begun to bring poor and sick children to the mountains for fresh air, exercise, and nutrition. The region and its cool summer breezes soon became attractive for wealthier families as well. By 1935 there were 3,700 children spending some time on the plateau. There were around a dozen *maisons d'enfants* (homes for children), all of whose directors prepared to take in refugees, and many hotels that were closed during the slow winter months could provide additional housing.

In May 1941 André, in partnership with the Comité Inter-Mouvements auprès des Évacués (Cimade) and the Swiss Secours Suisse aux Enfants, opened the plateau's first sponsored home, La Guespy,* which flew both the Swiss and the French flag and housed sixteen young people released from Gurs. In October the Swiss sent August Bohny, a twenty-one-year-old schoolteacher from Basel, to oversee an expanded effort. He opened a second home called L'Abric (*abric* meant "sheltered" in the local dialect) and saw its thirty children, again mostly from Gurs, through the brutal winter. In April Bohny went to Lyon to

---

* The Wasps' Nest.

turn an old castle into a home for children from the Rivesaltes internment camp. There he fell for Friedel Reiter, the Austrian relief worker who had escorted the children there. They returned together to Le Chambon and opened another home for fifty children called Faïdoli, after a popular Swiss children's song, as well as a carpentry workshop and an agricultural school.

Although Bohny was barely older than some of his charges, they knew him as Papa Gusti, and he did what he could to make life as normal as possible for them. He and Friedel made sure their houses were full of singing. A talented pianist with a repertoire that included everything from classical and religious music to Dixieland jazz, Bohny often played the accordion in the evening as the children sang. He mostly lived with the forty children in L'Abric, where the youngest child was five years old, and every evening he would say good night to each one by name and comfort those who were sad or homesick.

Some children were severely traumatized. One little Greek girl who had seen both her parents shot slept with her eyes open every night. Another little boy, who did his best to distract himself by learning scouts' knots and playing ball, recalled, "Fear was our companion at every moment." Bohny and the other adults in Le Chambon did their best to make the children feel safe and experience some semblance of a childhood, making sure that, despite the shortages, there was chocolate, cheese, halvah, and jam for them, as well as entertaining them with games, plays, and excursions. André and Theis even converted an abandoned blacksmith's workshop into a movie theater, and the schoolmaster Roger Darcissac, a tubercular Parisian, showed magic lantern stories to bring the Christmas stories to life in the Temple.

Peter Feigl, a thirteen-year-old boy, remembered that "there was enough love and caring to make us feel as members of a 'family.'" Magda would take children on picnics with her dog Fido, a Brittany spaniel with white spots. There were scout troops, basketball games, snowball fights, and hikes to pick mushrooms, blueberries, and wild strawberries.

"It may sound stupid but I had a good time," Feigl recalled. "It was a very pleasant good life."

The children were also kept very busy with their studies—"They kept our noses to the grindstone," Feigl recalled—and many enrolled at the École Nouvelle Cévenole and the village public school. Times were hard, of course, on the plateau. Conditions were not luxurious; there was no hot water at La Guespy in the winter, and food was a constant struggle. Townspeople were generous with clothing donations, which were then handed down to younger refugees as the children grew. Shoes were a particular problem, and many children, like the adults, had to wear wooden clogs called sabots to go outside.

The daily one o'clock train, an old-fashioned steam engine that puffed white smoke, brought refugees, who were often met by volunteers. As more people began arriving on trains at all hours, a committee formed to await each transport, even at midnight. For many new arrivals, the first stop was the Trocmés' residence, where they could wait until temporary shelter in the village or in more secluded locales on the surrounding farms was found. Magda was among those actively involved in finding homes, as was her friend Simone Mairesse, who had come to a nearby village when her husband was drafted and also traveled up and down the mountains looking for hiding places. Madeleine Dreyfus, a Jewish psychologist from Paris, worked with the Œuvre de Secours aux Enfants (OSE) in its effort to bring Jewish children to the plateau. Several times a month she brought a group from Lyon by the train, instructing them not to speak. Once the children were in hiding, she periodically brought money and, when possible, letters from the children's parents, who were often not told where their little ones were being hidden. Dreyfus hid her own children on the plateau.

The Trocmés personally set an example. Two Jewish girls—Micheline and Martine, who were studying at the École Nouvelle Cévenole—lived with them, as well as two other students who paid for their board, an ill-tempered cabinetmaker, and a German cook with limited skills who complained often. The money from the two students provided "an income very much needed for our survival," Nelly remembered. Their daily rations included some lumps of sugar and a thick triangular slice of bread. "We were very poor."

Madame Eyraud, whose husband was a senior member of the Resistance, kept around fourteen adolescent boys at any given time in her boardinghouse, sheltering several hundred over the course of the war. Another pension was run by the Marions, a Huguenot widow and her two daughters, who tried to provide as much of a normal life as possible to the adolescent girls they sheltered. And the Tante Soly pension was, remarkably, run by a Jewish man, Émile Sèches, the nephew of the chief rabbi of Lyon, and Solange, his non-Jewish wife. They sheltered over a dozen children in addition to their own three. Many of the non-Jewish homes tried to make the Jewish children as comfortable as possible, and the Trocmés facilitated religious services for them. There was even a Hanukkah party one year, with a menorah lit in Le Chambon, and one Orthodox Jewish woman actually managed to keep kosher during her stay.

Refugees also were hidden in all twelve parishes flung over twelve square miles, where other pastors, like André, provided leadership.* Some were there for a night; others stayed for years. Housepainter Ernest Chazot and his wife hid a Viennese mother and son, the Hamkers, for three years. When Vichy officials came to inspect, Madame

---

* Pastors on the plateau actively involved in hiding refugees included André Bettex (Freycenet), Daniel Curtet (Fay and Les Vastres), Henri Estoppey (Intres), André Chapal (Labatie-d'Andaure), André Morel (Devesset), George Grüner (Mars), Marcel Jeannet (Le Mazet-Saint-Voy), Raoul Cabrière and Daniel Besson (Montbuzat and Araules), Alphonse Peyronnel (Saint-Agrève), Roland Leenhardt (Tence), Marc Donadille (Les Tavas), and of course Theis and Trocmé in Le Chambon. The former mayor of Le Chambon, Pastor Charles Guillon, also became particularly active in smuggling and resistance activities, in helping prisoners of war and interned refugees, and was crucial in gaining government permission for children to leave the camps to come to the homes in Le Chambon. The former mayor Guillon was also critically adept at dealing with the local prefect Robert Bach, whom the American Tracy Strong from the ESRF found a "smooth devil."

Chazot shouted at them from their porch, "There are no refugees in here! And if there were, I wouldn't tell *you!*" The villagers were driven by their basic belief in right and wrong, not by politics. "The people of Le Chambon were very simple people," recalled one boy who was hidden there. "They did not read the daily newspapers, but they read their Bible daily." The Calvinist Protestants in the villages were generally sympathetic to Judaism and felt a kinship with the Jews. Many of the farmers were Darbyists, who believed Jews were the original people of God and that it was an honor to shelter them. One refugee remembered a Darbyist calling her family downstairs, gushing, "We have in our house now a *representative of the Chosen People!*"

For many, harboring refugees meant real financial hardship. One eleven-year-old girl hidden on a farm was stunned that there was no electricity and that her hosts washed from the same trough as the goat and cow and had never before seen a toothbrush. But there is no record that anyone was turned away. The farmers knew the children placed with them were Jewish, though they were often not explicitly told so for their own protection.

André, Magda, and Theis provided leadership and inspiration, but the effort was diffuse by necessity. To manage his far-flung parish, André had several years earlier organized thirteen young people he called *responsables*, meeting with them as a group every fortnight to study a Bible passage that they would in turn teach their own neighborhood discussion groups. Soon after the refugees began arriving, this core group became the natural leadership network and communication structure for a significant part of the rescue operation. "It was there that we received from God solutions to complex problems, problems we had to solve in order to shelter and to hide the Jews," André wrote. "Nonviolence was not a theory superimposed upon reality; it was an itinerary that we explored day after day in communal prayer and in obedience to the commands of the Spirit." The message was continually reinforced to the villagers that they were, as Madame Eyraud put it, "doing something of consequence." Much of the rescue was organic. It took place in living rooms and kitchens. "If it had been an organization, it could not have worked," Magda reflected. "When the refugees were there, on your doorstep, in danger, there were decisions that had to made then and there."

More people became experts in the clandestine arts. False identification was the lifeblood of the underground and a capital crime to manufacture. Schoolmaster Roger Darcissac would generally take photographs of newly arrived refugees that would then be used by several expert counterfeiters to make papers. The ring initially included Mireille Philip, Theis, Jacqueline Decourdemanche, and Pierre Piton. It was eventually run by Oscar Rosowsky, a German-born Latvian Jewish teenager operating under the nom de guerre Jean-Claude Plunne. Rosowsky lived in a barn on Emma and Henri Héritier's farm at La Fayolle, where he produced excellent fake identification papers, library cards, demobilization records, and ration cards along with a local boy, Samy Charles. With little more experience than a familiarity with typewriters, he used a primary-school mimeograph machine to excellent effect. Gabrielle Barraud, the daughter of friends of the Trocmés, helped devise this system and also became versed in the art, working from her house on the edge of town. Her brother and sister would come by bicycle with the information she needed. They all used the same technique: tracing the stamp from a real identity card onto the fake one, using a strip of cloth covered with gelatin and heated over a candle. It required precision to prevent the gelatin from dripping if heated too much, but the trace would not be successful if it was heated too little.

Many others assisted. The Héritiers hid Rosowsky's papers and equipment in two of their beehives, where a nine-year-old shepherd boy named Paul Majola often picked them up and distributed them at night. Mireille Philip—a mother of five whose husband, André, was interior minister of Charles de Gaulle's Free French government in London and a major opposition figure—constantly acquired blank forms, some of them parachuted in, and carried forged stamps carved into the bottom of spools of thread in her sewing basket. Magda once smuggled in a large parcel of North African stamps packed in oatmeal; the Maghreb became a less detectable fake birthplace for Jews after the Germans gained access to local municipal records in the south of France. Theis printed postcards of the Tower of Constance, where in the sixteenth century a large group of Huguenot women had been imprisoned, and would send them on to pastors in other villages in advance of Jews arriving. "I am sending you five Old Testaments today," he would write. "They were justified lies, told to save the lives of the persecuted," Magda recalled.

————

As more and more refugees came to Le Chambon, the town became a cosmopolitan mix of languages and backgrounds, adding a youthful energy in stark contrast to the quiet, somber locals. Only four or five of the thirty-five workers at the Swiss Red Cross were actually Swiss. There were Jews in the Scouts, Jewish doctors and teachers, and even Jews helping with rescue efforts. Nelly Trocmé's piano instructor was Jewish. There were the highly assimilated German and Austrian Jews who had seen their lives completely disrupted. There were the Eastern European Jews who were used to anti-Semitism and persecution. And then there were the French Jews who could not believe that their country had turned on them despite its long history of anti-Semitism and the notorious Dreyfus affair.

Elizabeth Koenig, the seventeen-year-old daughter of a prominent Jewish journalist, had grown up in Vienna and Berlin. After fleeing to Paris, the family was on the run again in the south of France when Elizabeth's former Latin teacher, Mlle Hoefert, wrote to her parents from Le Chambon. She had a job for Elizabeth as a summer au pair for André and Magda, and in the fall she would be able to go to school at the École Nouvelle Cévenole. Elizabeth was awestruck by her hosts. "In the few months that I had lived in their house I had learned moral principles that shaped my life," she remembered. Magda and André were constantly pulled in every direction, and Elizabeth's job consisted of chasing after the three Trocmé boys "from the moment they opened their eyes to the moment they closed their eyes," taking them on long walks and trying to keep the peace as they quarreled constantly. The chaos in the house, however, would quiet suddenly when André said prayers before eating. As they all sat around the table, "the whole rhythm of the day changed," she remembered. She almost cried the first time she heard his prayer: "You who have all things and give them to us each day, receive, O Father, our prayer of gratitude and love."

When the fall arrived, Magda asked Elizabeth to move into La Guespy to help look after a group of German Jewish children who had just arrived from Gurs. "I could be a bridge between the people of the village and the children," Elizabeth reflected. The children were terrified and disoriented. "They did not understand where they were," she remembered. "They knew they were somewhere in France without their parents." She slept in the girls' room on the second floor with the younger children for three months before receiving a letter from her father with the news that the family had visas to America, provided by the Emergency Rescue Committee. "I was torn," she admitted. "I felt I am betraying my little comrades." When she left, they all escorted her to the railroad station.

By August 1942, pressure on Jews began to ratchet up significantly. An early August confidential memorandum instructed regional prefects to transfer all Jews who had arrived after January 1, 1936, to the occupied zone. When the Nazis requested that all Jewish adults other than the elderly be deported, Pierre Laval himself ordered that children be transferred as well. By the end of August, almost six thousand Jews had been arrested and sent to the Drancy internment camp near Paris.

That same month Le Chambon played reluctant host to a senior member of the regime. A large Assumption Day celebration was held in Le Puy with Marshal Pétain. Robert Bach, the smarmy Protestant local prefect of the Haute-Loire, desperately wanted Pétain to visit the nearby plateau, but the marshal's advisers worried he might get a less than enthusiastic reception. Instead they sent Georges Lamirand, the dapper head of Les Compagnons de France, an organization modeled on the Hitler Youth, complete with blue shirts, salutes, and marching. The pastors refused to participate in planning the event. It was also a potentially dangerous situation, given the refugees hidden all over the village.

As Lamirand's motorcade pulled into town, no flags greeted him, and few bothered to look out the window. The formal banquet at the spartan, all-purpose summer camp consisted of the spare local food and was served by the Boy and Girl Scouts. André sat next to Lamirand and watched as fourteen-year-old Nelly accidentally spilled soup from the overfilled tureen down the back of the sporty tweed coat of his elegant riding outfit. Later, at the sports field, no one had planned a parade or receiving line for Lamirand. He made a short speech and shook hands with a disorganized group of children. The officials then went to the Temple, where both Theis and André refused to preach.

After the service, a group of older students from the École Nouvelle Cévenole presented Lamirand with a document that they read to him. It began by expressing horror at the notorious roundup three weeks earlier in Paris, when nine thousand French police had arrested over thirteen thousand Jews, including over four thousand children. They shut them inside the Vélodrome d'Hiver, blocks away from the Eiffel Tower, for five days without food or water. Those without families were sent to Drancy. "We want you to know that there are, among us, a certain number of Jews," the students declared to Lamirand. "Now, as far as we are concerned, we do not make any distinction between Jews and non-Jews. That would be contrary to the teaching of the Gospel. If our friends, whose only offense is to have been born in another religion, receive the order to let themselves be deported or even be subject to a census, they will disobey those orders, and we will do our best to hide them in our midst."

Lamirand turned pale and mumbled that the questions were not his affair but an issue for the prefect. He excused himself and returned to his car to drive off, leaving Bach, his host, humiliated.

"Pastor Trocmé, this day should be a day of national harmony. You sow division," Bach exploded.

"It cannot be a question of national harmony when our brothers are threatened with deportation," André snapped.

"Foreign Jews who live in the Haute-Loire are not your brothers. They do not belong to your church, nor to your country!" Bach told him. "In a few days my people will come to examine the Jews living in Le Chambon."

André became angry. "We do not know what a Jew is, we only know men."

"M. Trocmé," Bach responded, "you had best be careful. Seven of your fellow citizens have been writing to me regularly to keep me informed of your subversive activities." If he asked for a list of the Jews, he said, the pastor would have to comply. "M. Trocmé," Bach warned, "if you are not prudent, it is you whom I shall be obliged to have deported. To the good listener, warning." Then he turned and left.

Fifteen days after Lamirand's visit, several cars and four khaki-colored buses escorted by police motorcycles arrived in the village square. There were fifty policemen, led by the chief of police, and a French colonel from Corsica. Their first stop was L'Abric. Two officers told Bohny they had a list of seventy-two people to be taken, and demanded to inspect everyone's papers. Bohny argued with them for half an hour, warning that the children were under Swiss protection. Like good bureaucrats, the policemen said they would need further instructions. Bohny did not wait for them to return but woke the children, fed them breakfast, and dispersed them to be hidden in the forest by Mireille Philip. When the gendarmes returned, they were furious.

The chief of police also demanded to speak to André in the town hall. "You are hiding in this commune a certain number of Jews," he said. He was under orders to bring them to the prefecture for "a control," and he wanted it done without incident. He demanded a list of the Jews, and that André ensure they come along without trying to flee. André told him he did not know the names of the Jews—technically true, since he never wanted to know their real names. "But even if I had such a list," he told the police chief, "I would not pass it on to you. These people have come here seeking aid and protection from the Protestants of this region. I am their pastor, their shepherd. It is not the role of a shepherd to betray the sheep confided to his keeping." The police chief gave André an ultimatum, and the pastor walked away, heading straight for his home. He called the Boy Scouts into his office and put into motion the "disappearance of the Jews," a contingency operation he had been planning. The lighting system went down in the village, and in the darkness many Jews in hiding fled into the woods around Le Chambon and into the neighboring department of Ardèche, east of the plateau.

The next morning the police did not arrest André, as he had feared. The service at the Temple was completely full. André and Theis preached a sermon: "Do the will of God, not of men."

By late afternoon the police were in full dragnet mode. "They searched first the houses in the village and of the closely surrounding country," André recalled, "calling for identity papers from everyone, opening cupboards, going down into the cellars, climbing to the attics, knocking on walls to see whether they were hollow. They showed themselves polite, sometimes rough—but they found no one." On Monday they headed to the more distant farms, where the Jews had already had a full day to escape. "The entire village worked together," Bohny remembered.

Outmaneuvered, the police insisted on arresting an Austrian Jew, M. Steckler, who worked at La Guespy. He was loudly accompanied to the bus by a large group of neighbors to say an emotional goodbye. As Steckler sat alone in the bus, surrounded by twenty gendarmes, thirteen-year-old Jean-Pierre Trocmé handed him a piece of chocolate, a scarce commodity during the war. Other neighbors followed suit, handing Steckler their precious food, and smiling at him as they passed through the square. Soon Steckler, a small man, was sitting next to a pile of gifts almost as big as him. He was held overnight, but released because he was only partly Jewish. For many of the children in hiding, it was an emotional turning point. "I think we felt safe in the village, up to the point when the gendarmes came and wanted to take us away," recalled Hanne Hirsch, a teenager at La Guespy.

A few months later, on November 10, two days after the Allied invasion of North Africa, the Nazis occupied southern France. More and more refugees began arriving. The Gestapo took control of the roundups with help from their Vichy counterparts, the Milice. The Trocmés also now began receiving anonymous calls warning of roundups, triggering evacuations of the Jews into the forest. Some gendarmes would arrive early in the Café May for a glass of wine, speaking loudly of those they were there to arrest to give them a warning. Rank-and-file officers were being "converted," as André put it, part of what he and Theis called the "mystery of love."

Those who worked with the Jewish children did their best to shield them from the terror of their situation even when they were hiding. When a roundup was imminent, they would take them for hikes deep in the woods or on trips out of town. "They didn't tell us the reason, they just told us, we're going to go and pick mushrooms in the woods," Peter Feigl remembered. "Sometimes we would stay in the woods for six hours, eight hours or something like that and then we would come back to the house and everything was fine and dandy. We didn't know what was going on." Rudi Appel remembered one of his residence directors, Mlle Usach, periodically sending him into the woods with blankets, and his feeling of safety, knowing the villagers were protecting him. Bohny even had a gentle way of retrieving those in hiding. As he searched for them, he would take children along, singing, as a sign that danger had passed. "Those in hiding would hear them, reconnect with us, and could come back."

There were no occupying troops stationed in Le Chambon, but some wounded German soldiers convalesced at the Hôtel du Lignon. The hotel's owner remembered the soldiers coming back from their afternoon walks and saying, "This place is full of Jews." When he denied it and told the soldiers they had seen tourists, the Germans would laugh. "These soldiers had gone through hell on the Russian front," Peter Feigl recalled. "They didn't want to start hunting Jews or anybody else, just to be left alone." They were generally polite, and one of the soldiers once even helped Jean-Pierre Trocmé gather pine cones for kindling.

The locals helped many Jews escape France; in fact, large numbers came to the town for that express purpose. Geneva was just three hundred kilometers away, and the Vichy government noted that Le Chambon seemed to be "the head of the escape route for Jews into Switzerland." The critical organization was the Protestant youth organization Cimade, run almost entirely by women under the leadership of the lawyer Madeleine Barot, which worked from the summer of 1942 to smuggle Jews to safety. Their sponsored house, the Le Côteau Fleuri (Flower Hill), built near thick pine woods, with clear views of all approaches, was a critical refuge for many on their way to Switzerland.

The elderly, the sick, women, and small children were often sheltered there before teams could be arranged to conduct them over the Swiss border. The underground railroad efforts were spearheaded by Mireille Philip. Many others assisted as well, and Theis in particular was active in helping refugees escape to freedom.

There were many different methods of escape, but refugees were generally taken through a network of safe houses, church buildings, convents, and farms to the border, which was often at least two days away. One escapee remembered Theis and Philip personally guiding them to the border and then camping in the mountains until they saw their proteges safely in Switzerland. A seventeen-year-old recalled being taken with his belongings on a toboggan through an underground network of farmhouses and bus routes. Another boy, Hans Solomon, remembered Philip dressing him and his friends as French Boy Scouts to march through town, loudly singing songs, and continuing on for miles to cross the border.

Many young people helped. Uniformed Scouts escorted the refugees from safe house to safe house. Seventeen-year-old Pierre Piton, a scholarship student at the École Nouvelle Cévenole, helped refugees find temporary shelter on farms, transferring them from town a few at a time. They would be given fake identity cards and instructions in their native language, and then Pierre would guide them to the border with Switzerland. They were instructed not to speak to anyone on the train, avoid eye contact, feign sleep, and pretend they did not know Pierre, who dressed in his Scout uniform. When they reached the border, local guides would help them slip under the barbed wire fence between patrols or through ditches, culverts, and other passageways. Pierre made twenty successful trips before being caught, beaten, and arrested. Others took refugees along different routes, some through the Alps, some across part of Lac Léman, some under the cover of a fake soccer game. Gabrielle Barraud escorted some who looked too Jewish to travel openly through the woods on foot to a local guide.

Things became increasingly hard for the Trocmés, even physically. André's chronic back problems made walking painful. Magda lost a huge amount of weight and seemed to age rapidly. In a letter to his half brother in February 1943, André worried about Magda's mental and physical health. "And now I myself seem to have cracked," he confessed, having had to take time off after his mind blanked during a pre-Christmas sermon. "All this served as a warning to me," he wrote, "because I am obviously overworked." The recent death of another pastor with nine children shook him: "Somehow, we have to find a way out of this whirl-wind, but it seems impossible." The financial situation was dire. With the influx of people and wartime shortages, prices in Le Chambon sky-rocketed, and the Trocmés were sometimes forced to the gray market for food. "We are eating large mouthfuls of our savings," he wrote.

But he was proud of their work. With the arrival of the Germans, word had spread throughout the south of France about Le Chambon and the plateau. "From Nice to Toulouse, from Pau to Mâcon, from Lyon to Périgueux, by way of Saint-Étienne, dozens, even hundreds of Jews have headed to Le Chambon."

————

Magda and André became increasingly concerned that he would be ar-rested. At seven o'clock at night on February 13, 1943, two uniformed gendarmes knocked on the door of the *presbytère*. The police had cut off the telephone, and five cars circled the house outside. Magda man-aged to send the two Jews living with them to hide, one in the attic, one in the basement, before answering the door. Major Silvani, the Corsi-can chief of police, insisted on speaking to André directly on "a very personal matter." She showed them to the pastor's study to wait and closed the door.

André arrived home two hours later and stormed into his office to get his papers. He returned shortly thereafter to the dining room, where his wife was knitting. "Magda," he told her, "I am arrested."

Magda packed a suitcase for André while the policemen waited, assuring her that they were not in a hurry. Dinner was ready, and Magda invited the policemen to join them. "I didn't do it out of generosity," Magda said later. "It was time for our meal." As André gobbled down his food, aware it was likely his last good meal for a while, his four children stared wide-eyed at the police chief, who looked on the verge of tears. He told Magda he did not have the heart to eat, and when André asked him why he was being arrested, he stammered, "I don't know. I know nothing. I can say nothing."

Word spread rapidly throughout the village. Upset parishioners soon appeared in the *presbytère* to bid farewell to André and wish him luck. They brought gifts, scarce items that might make his ordeal a little lighter: candles, sardines, chocolate biscuits, warm stockings, and a roll of toilet paper that, André later discovered, had verses of consolation from the Bible written on the outer sheets. Magda handed André his suitcase and a pair of wooden shoes.

When the policemen walked outside into the dark night with André, villagers, refugees, and students lined both sides of the icy street in solidarity as a light snow swirled. As the three men headed west toward the village square, a woman began singing Martin Luther's hymn "A Mighty Fortress Is Our God," and the whole crowd soon burst into song as they followed behind. Silvani got into the front seat with the driver, and André was put in the back with the lieutenant.

The officers then arrested Theis at his home on the outskirts of town near the Cévenole school. Once he was in the backseat with André, they drove to pick up their third quarry, Roger Darcissac, the head of the public school, who was put into another car. Silvani brought the three men to Tence, where they were booked and transferred to Le Puy. On the way, Silvani tried to reassure the pastors. "Things will change," he told them. "You'll not be there for long."

After a night in a locked room without sheets or blankets, they were taken to Lyon under armed escort and put on another train for Limoges. The local police chief held them overnight for interrogation. Expressing shock at seeing two pastors and a teacher arrested, he demanded to know what they had done. The Chambonnais responded that they did not know, but perhaps it was because they had been helping Jews to escape.

"What? Jews?" the captain shouted. "We all know that they're the ones who have brought France down into the abyss. Well, you're going to pay for all the harm you've done to the marshal!"

The encounter changed André. Before, he had viewed the world as a battle between good and evil. Now he recognized a third kind of person, someone unintelligent and unthinkingly loyal to power without any interest in evidence or sensitivity to others' pain.

They were imprisoned in Saint-Paul d'Eyjeaux, near Limoges, where five hundred mostly Communists and violent resisters were held. They were fingerprinted and photographed. Barbed wire surrounded the premises, and armed guards manned the watchtowers. André had heard terrible stories at his *presbytère* table, but the camp was relatively lenient, and the men were allowed to receive mail and even packages of food and clothing.

They were held without charges and forbidden legal counsel. André did his best to keep busy, preparing programs and making drawings of his surroundings. Darcissac used a camera snuck into camp by his son Marco to take pictures. They asked the commandant for permission to conduct Protestant services. The Trocmé charisma was soon at work, with twenty or so congregants meeting in a study group, although the guards and Communists could not understand their commitment to nonviolence. But even André applauded the news of victory at Stalingrad from the contraband BBC broadcast.

On March 15 the commanding officer summoned the three men and informed them that they were free to leave on the ten o'clock train.

As part of the exit process, they were required to sign an oath to respect Pétain and to obey the Vichy government without question. As a government employee, Darcissac had already signed similar documents, and he did so again, afraid of leaving his family destitute if he lost his job. As André brought his pen to the paper, Theis pointed out the part requiring unquestioning obedience.

"We cannot sign this oath," André said. "It is contrary to our conscience."

The stunned officer told them Pétain only wished the good of France.

"On at least one point we disagree with the marshal and his National Revolution," André said. "He delivers the Jews to the Germans and thus to death. . . . When we get home, we shall certainly continue to be opposed, and we shall certainly continue to disobey orders from the government. How could we sign this now?"

The commandant exploded. "This is insane! You know as well as I do the vicious activities of the Jews." Then he tried to appeal to their rationality. "Look, be reasonable," he said. "I appreciate your courage, but this is— Look, you have wives and children. Sign. It's just a formality. Later, no one will notice what you did here."

"If we sign," André said, "we must keep our word; we must surrender our consciences to the marshal. No, we will not bind ourselves to obey immoral orders."

"So be it," the commandant told them. "You'll rot here indefinitely, if the Germans don't deport you first." Darcissac now begged to stay. The commandant refused, and the pastors convinced him to leave. André returned to the stunned prisoners in the barracks. "Refuse to sign a scrap of paper that will free you to resist the Fascists and defend the poor?" said a Communist. "This is idiocy."

The next morning, the commander told them they could sign a modified version and leave. He had received orders from the office of head of government Pierre Laval himself. Unbeknownst to them, Marc

Boegner, the president of the Reformed Church of France, and Albert Chaudier, the local Limoges pastor, had appealed to the secretary general of the police, René Bousquet, warning that the arrest could damage Vichy diplomatically.

André and Theis gathered their items, and the prisoners surrounded them. Together, they all sang "Ce n'est qu'un au revoir," to the tune of "Auld Lang Syne." Then they went to the station and boarded the train for home. When they stepped off, a crowd of villagers greeted them and silently parted to create a path for the pastors to walk through. At Sunday services, the three men told their story to a packed temple. At around the same time, the approximately five hundred prisoners they had left behind in Saint-Paul d'Eyjeaux were gathered up and deported to Poland and Silesia. They were never heard from again.

———

One of the projects André found most exciting was La Maison des Roches, a home for older boys that the European Student Relief Organization established at the Hôtel des Roches, a shuttered inn two kilometers from town. It opened in February 1942 and housed many Jews smuggled out of the internment camps. The American relief worker Tracy Strong recalled when the first refugees arrived from Rivesaltes: "It was a joyful scene that is so difficult to imagine during these times when the hopes of people have been totally destroyed." When the couple running the home asked to be replaced in March 1943, André, just back from his time in prison, asked his barely thirty-year-old cousin Daniel Trocmé to take over as director of its thirty residents. It would be Daniel's second responsibility at Le Chambon. André had already recruited him as director of Les Grillons (The Crickets), an old two-story stone boardinghouse for younger children ranging in age from four to nineteen two miles away, also funded mostly by the Quakers.

Before coming to Le Chambon, Daniel had been working at L'École des Roches, an elite private boarding school in Normandy where his father was dean and where he and his eight siblings had grown up. He was educated at the Sorbonne, spent time in Switzerland and Austria becoming fluent in German, studied at the American University in Beirut, and taught science in Rome.

Le Chambon was for Daniel "a place for a contribution to the reconstruction of our world, a vocation, an intimate calling, almost religious." At Les Grillons, he supervised eleven girls and nine boys, eight of them Jewish, of six nationalities. Thin, intense behind steel-rimmed glasses, and a bit ethereal, Daniel was, André wrote, "an intellectual given to rather vague ideas, and often rather absentminded, but totally free of selfishness, and possessed of a conscience without gaps." A serious heart condition made physical work in the high altitude of the plateau difficult, but Daniel threw himself into activity "like a madman," as Magda put it. He handled everything from false identity cards to math tutoring to food and clothing. He traveled the region in search of warm clothes, galoshes, and hot water bottles, and even visited the parents of his charges in Gurs. "I adore them," he wrote his parents of his Crickets, "and in return I can say they show me a lot of affection." He worried for the children who had been separated from their parents. He considered himself "the father, as I like to say, of twenty children who have no mother."

When he also became director of Les Roches on March 25, his workload increased exponentially. "It breaks my heart to be able to spend less time" with the Crickets, he wrote. But he was determined to balance his work in both houses without sacrificing his efforts in either. He worked tirelessly, resoling shoes with automobile tires by lamplight, patching clothes at all hours, and cooking a huge tureen of soup that he would cart up the steep hill to the Crickets on a wagon. Before bed, he would read the children stories. "Daniel Trocmé never thought of himself," recalled Jonathan Gali, a sixteen-year-old in the Crickets. "I am happy," Daniel wrote to his parents more than once.

The students in Les Roches came from fifteen different countries, but the biggest contingent was German Jews. Jewish students and those without papers were given false identities and trained to quickly flee to the homes of farmers and villagers in the event of a roundup, returning only if open shutters on a particular window signaled the all-clear. For some time, the students remained safe.

Then at around half past six o'clock in the morning in late June 1943, over a dozen armed plainclothes members of the Gestapo surrounded the three-story granite building and demanded the papers of everyone inside. The panicked students heard the shouting outside and rushed into the hallways. One young man tried to escape out the back window but ran immediately into a German machine gun. The Gestapo stormed in and forced all the boys into the refectory, most of them still in their pajamas, clutching blankets. According to one list, there were twenty-five boys, between twelve and eighteen. Even the non-Jews—the Spaniards and the Germans and Luxembourgers of military age who were considered deserters—were in danger.

The shutters were closed, so the boys could not see into the courtyard except through the kitchen door as the Gestapo ransacked the building. After several hours, the boys caught a glimpse of Daniel Trocmé being escorted inside to the director's office, his head lowered and leaning a bit to the side. When the Gestapo arrived, Daniel had been at Les Grillons, where he usually slept, and two officers went to get him. When they knocked on the front door, his students had begged him to run out the back to the nearby woods, but Daniel refused to abandon them. As he was escorted to Les Roches, a seventeen-year-old named Suzanne Heim rushed to the *presbytère*. The Trocmés were all on holiday in Pomeyrol except Jean-Pierre, who was finishing his semester, and Magda, who had returned early to help some of the École Nouvelle Cévenole students prepare for the baccalaureate. Suzanne told her that Daniel had been arrested.

Magda bicycled over to Les Roches, where three buses were

ominously parked outside. By then the Gestapo were refusing anyone entry, but somehow Magda walked right in. She was still wearing her apron and may have been taken for an employee. "In the large dining room, the Germans were armed with sub-machine guns and the students were lined up against the wall, on the other side of the room," she remembered. "The last man in the line was Daniel Trocmé." Magda casually moved in and out of the kitchen, bringing in water, and tried to get close to Daniel. One of the Gestapo men suddenly screamed at her, and she retreated into the kitchen for fear of giving away her cousin's identity.

Magda stayed in the kitchen with the cook, and even helped prepare eggs and toast when the Gestapo agents demanded it. Midmorning, one of the Gestapo walked through the kitchen to a small storage room on the far side, carrying a large notebook that contained a list of those in the house. Each of the young people was slowly checked off the list and interrogated. Some returned with bruised faces or black eyes. As they passed Magda, several whispered requests to her. One asked her to send money to his mother, another to send his watch to his family, another to write to his girlfriend. Daniel translated and negotiated with the Gestapo. The Gestapo thought his German too fluent for a Frenchman, and when he could not help himself from defending the Jews, they suspected that he was himself a refugee.

After the interrogations were complete at around ten, the Germans decided to eat and to give the prisoners bread and water. As Magda helped distribute the food and calm the teenagers, she managed a word with Daniel. He told her that one of his boys, Luis Gausachs, a refugee from Spain nicknamed Pepito, had saved a German soldier from drowning in the Lignon a few weeks earlier. Perhaps, he suggested, she could go to the German commanders staying at the Hôtel du Lignon to ask for their release, since the village had helped a German soldier.

"What a beautiful day it was!" she recalled. "The scotch broom was in flower; the sun was gentle and warm. It was extraordinary to see all this beauty, calm, and peace, to know there were such horrors going on at the Maison des Roches nearby." Magda furiously bicycled to the Hôtel du Lignon, talked her way in German past the guards, and found two senior officers, one of whom knew of the rescue.

She told them the Gestapo had arrived at Les Roches and appealed to him to come and tell them the story of the soldier's rescue.

"We have nothing to do with the Gestapo," one of them said.

Using her best charm, she begged them to serve as witnesses out of their sense of honor as officers. They finally agreed, and she commandeered two bicycles from girls passing by, who she knew. The three of them rode back to Les Roches. In the end, she managed to get Pepito released. Then she asked to speak to her cousin. The Gestapo told her to come back at noon. She rushed briefly to the *presbytère*, and Jean-Pierre insisted on accompanying her back. "By the time we got to the Maison des Roches, everything had changed," Magda remembered. "The atmosphere was horrifying." They saw a Gestapo agent standing on the outside staircase, one hand on the black iron railing and the other whipping a crouching blond, blue-eyed Dutch Jewish boy on the steps with his tefillin and shouting "Schweinejude!" It was all she could do to restrain her son from intervening.

Magda found Daniel at the head of a line of students under a little balcony, waiting to board a large truck covered with a tarpaulin, next to two gray Citroëns. "Do not worry. Tell my parents that I was very happy here," he told her. "It was the best time of my life. Tell them that I like travelling, that I go with my friends." As he watched his cousin board the bus, Jean-Pierre was crying with rage.

Daniel and eighteen students, fourteen of them foreign, were brought to the jail in Le Puy. These included several Jews, a few Spaniards, and an Iranian. A handful were subsequently released, but the majority were deported. At Moulins, they were imprisoned on the top floor of a fourteenth-century tower known as Mal-Coiffée. "He made a lot of effort to break the monotony of our days," one student recalled of Daniel, "and to make us forget the miserable situation that we found ourselves in." Daniel was called before the German police three times and beaten, barely able to remove his glasses in time before being struck. When accused of protecting a sixteen-year-old Jew, he said he was only helping the downtrodden. "Morale is quite good," he wrote his parents. "I hope to see you quite soon."

He was then sent to the Royallieu-Compiègne camp in a former French army barracks in the north of France. Although not a pious Protestant, he attended services, and the pastor there tried to protect him. He managed to write his parents twelve times, often scrawling requests for food and supplies on toilet paper and reassuring them about his situation. They sent him cakes and books, and he occupied himself reading Balzac, Shakespeare, Cervantes, Dante, and Flaubert, among others, and found some of his old school friends imprisoned with him. "My thoughts are constantly with each of the Crickets," he wrote his parents, asking for news of them and his other students and family. On September 12, he wrote to the Crickets, "I believe this separation will actually bring us closer, because now I will know a little better the adventures through which so many of your parents have passed." He could not wait to see them. "One of the most beautiful joys that I promise myself is that of seeing you again. It will be magnificent. . . . I will not leave you as long as it is my own will." He urged them to be courageous and kind. "Stay united among yourselves," he implored. "Our family is fragile and is so young."

Initially he hoped his physical weakness might free him, but he was found fit for camp. His heart condition flared, and he spent several months in the infirmary. By the time he arrived in the Dora-Mittelbau slave labor camp at Buchenwald in December, he was in precarious health, thin and sick, with problems breathing. One of the boys was shocked to see him, recalling, "He was just a shadow of a human and had very little physical strength." He was soon deported with many of the other sick inmates to Majdanek, an extermination camp in Poland.

Five of his charges died in Auschwitz, six disappeared, and seven survived. One of those who lived returned a year later to Le Chambon and reported that Daniel had been interrogated all the way to eastern Poland and continued to reiterate his compassion for the Jews.

A package sent to Buchenwald for him was ominously returned to sender, and when one of his brothers tried to get him freed, the Germans reported that he had died in the first days of April after a short illness. It was a few weeks before his thirty-second birthday. His students were devastated. When she heard the news of Daniel's passing, Madame Ermine Orsi, who cooked and cleaned at the Crickets, gathered the children, and they all cried together. "They love him with this innocent love, instinctive love, without limits and without barriers," she wrote his parents. Daniel was, she said, "a beloved and beautiful soul."

André could not help blaming himself for the tragedy. "It is not fair that he was struck," he wrote to Daniel's parents. "The weight of Daniel's death weighs upon me." In his view, Daniel was a true martyr who had been killed by the forces of evil. "He gave his life and thus found what he was searching for," they replied. André was touched. "These are people to be admired," he wrote. "They really love their son." A few months later, the Allied landings brought fighting to Verneuil in Normandy, where Daniel grew up. His mother Eve was killed by shrapnel as she hid under a bridge at their school, also a haven for refugees, surrounded by sacks of sand. Shortly thereafter, Daniel's father, Henri Trocmé, was struck and killed by an American jeep as he walked along the highway. "Oh, the somber, somber night of war," André wrote.

In July 1943, not long after the roundup at Les Roches, a maquisard (as the members of the informal rural resistance were known) claiming to be a German double agent warned André that he and Theis were on a

Nazi hit list. Initially suspicious that perhaps the Resistance wanted him to leave to have a freer hand with violence, he became convinced that the story was true when Theis received the same warning from a very reliable source. André's first reaction was to stay put, but Magda begged him to go, insisting that both the parish and his family needed him alive. Boegner sent Maurice Rohr, his vice president and André's distant cousin, to convince him to do so as well. The tragedy at Les Roches was enough, Rohr told him. "We have lived through many disasters. What would be the purpose of adding another martyr to a list that is already very long."

Reluctantly, André finally agreed. He bicycled with his family a few kilometers out of town for an alleged picnic and was picked up on the road to Saint-Agrève by a M. Lespet, who drove him down to Lamastre, a town in Ardèche. André had shaved his mustache and now wore thick dark frames for his glasses and a Basque beret, an image that appeared on the false papers Magda and Roger Darcissac had made for him under the name Béguet. A friend of his was covering for a vacationing pastor and had a room prepared for him in the parsonage. But it was not long before several factory workers recognized him through a window. When the regular pastor returned, he angrily insisted that André leave at once. He left just in time: the Gestapo soon arrived but had now lost the trail.

André next spent several weeks on a farm outside town in a freezing barn overlooking the valley, peeling chestnuts to pass the time at night, before Lespet brought him to another house toward Vernoux. His host was a businessman who poured concrete for German bunkers in Normandy but also stored weapons for the maquis. Although André was paying for his room, the man's Parisian wife forced him to make cheese and tend to their goats, with only a short respite at night to read. He managed to smuggle a letter to Magda inside someone else's correspondence, and she sprang into action, bicycling fifty kilometers down the winding roads to move him to a farmhouse on the east bank of the

Rhône. In the morning M. Brunet, a garage owner in Die, escorted André fifty kilometers through the hills of the Drôme, where he was housed in the Château de Perdyer, the comfortable country house of an old pacifist friend, Jacques Martin. The rooms were much larger, with high-beamed ceilings, and a cook managed to provide excellent meals despite local food shortages.

Magda soon got word to André that their son Jacques missed him so terribly that he was not able to do his schoolwork. They decided to send the boy to stay with André, which greatly relieved the father's melancholy. Together with a Jewish intellectual, André educated Jacquot, as his family called him, who sat at a small desk next to him as they both worked. André drafted a theological book entitled *Oser croire* ("Dare to Believe"), which he never published. Father and son played cowboys and Indians, raised a litter of mice, and even indulged in snowball fights. Other than one time when André was nearly arrested in the Perrache train station in Lyon with Jacquot, as his biographer wrote, it "was one of the happiest times in Trocmé's life."

Shortly after D-Day, André and Jacquot returned to Le Chambon. Theis had joined the Cimade and remained with them for a while, helping conduct refugees over the Swiss border. "It was not reasonable," he admitted. "But you know, I had to do it anyways." The end of the war felt not far in the distance. With André and Theis absent, however, the strict adherence to nonviolence had disappeared. Le Chambon, André noted, "had changed a great deal in ten months. The underground was no longer hidden. Young people parade in the streets, dressed in odd pieces of uniforms, with machine guns in their hands . . . There were more refugees than ever." Several hundred had joined the Resistance, including students of the École Nouvelle Cévenole and young French men on the run from the hugely unpopular mandatory corvée, the Service du Travail Obligatoire. As one young woman put it, "Le Chambon was a hot, hot center for the underground."

One day a woman with a prosthetic leg came to visit Bohny through a contact in Switzerland, claiming to be a journalist for the *New York Post*. She was Virginia Hall, an American secret agent who the Germans considered to be among the most dangerous. She set up headquarters in a barn nearby, which would be visited by Resistance fighters from as far away as Belgium, and coordinated the parachuting of small arms and materiel from the British.

Hall was not the only legendary member of the Resistance nearby. By the time André had returned, the great writer Albert Camus had left for Paris to edit the newspaper *Combat* after spending over a year two miles from Le Chambon in Panelier, a hamlet near the village of Le Mazet-Saint-Voy. He had come in July 1942 from Algeria after a tuberculosis diagnosis but then was trapped there, "like a rat," when the Nazis occupied southern France in November. Over the next year he completed the bulk of his novel *The Plague*. He and André had several friends in common. One, the Algerian Jewish scholar and OSE member André Chouraqui, later recalled Camus's interest in Trocmé and Theis and the hidden children on the plateau. "I studied the theory of nonviolence," Camus later wrote, "and I'm not far from concluding that it represents a truth worthy of being taught by example, but to do so one would need a greatness that I don't have." André, of course, did, and the war had brought it out in him. As Camus wrote, "What's true of all the evils of the world is true of plague as well. It helps men to rise above themselves."

André never wavered in his revulsion to violence. "The teaching about the less evil is wrong," he declared later. But while André maintained his strict nonviolent stance, he developed good relations with leaders of the Resistance, including Pierre Fayol, Léon Eyraud, Simone

Maitresse, and Joseph Bass, as long as they did not engage in assassination. "I felt it was insane to attack German units because it always resulted in bloody reprisals," he said. Fayol, a Jew from Marseille who had organized the dozens of groups in the area into one cohesive Resistance force, was of like mind. "He agreed with me and this probably protected Le Chambon from a destiny similar to that of Vassieux-en-Vercors," where the Nazis murdered many of the villagers.

The violence reached a fever pitch in the waning days of the war. The Resistance took retribution on collaborators, and the Germans committed atrocities, massacring opposition villagers all over the area. One of the most adored figures in Le Chambon was caught in the bloodshed at that time. Roger Le Forestier had come as a twenty-seven-year-old doctor to the plateau in early 1936, having worked for Albert Schweitzer at his hospital in Gabon. He had initially lived for a year in the *presbytère*, where he became something of a fourth son to Magda, whom he surprised by painting the walls of the dining room yellow and orange. Kind, gregarious, handsome, and funny, he became a beloved figure in Le Chambon, devoted to his patients. Soon after the fall of France, he married a girl from Cannes named Danielle, and brought back from his honeymoon a small monkey named Fifi who also moved into the *presbytère*, where the doctor would often imitate its movements to the delight of the Trocmé children. Le Forestier abhorred violence, refusing to carry a gun, but he did not ascribe to the strict doctrine of pacifism. Instead, during the war he tended to everyone—townspeople, maquisards, refugees, and even German soldiers.

In early August 1944 there was a rumor that two young men that Le Forestier knew, who were held in the prison in Le Puy, would be executed. Le Forestier was determined to argue for their release. André strongly urged him not to go, warning that the Germans would fire on a civilian car. When Le Forestier demurred that he had draped a large Red Cross banner over his car, making it an ambulance, André advised him not to trust the Nazis to obey the rules of war. His wife also begged him not to go, but the doctor was determined to. Bohny knew Le Forestier well: "He was something of an optimist and was perhaps not always careful enough." It was not without reason that André had called Le Forestier affectionately in his notes, "a *puro folle*, a purehearted fool." A brave but naively idealistic man, Le Forestier believed, the pastor André Bettex reflected, that all he had to do was speak a little bit loudly, and the Germans would leave France.

On the way to Le Puy, Le Forestier offered a lift to two hitchhiking maquisards. Before they entered the car, they did not tell him they had guns, as carrying weapons in an ambulance was forbidden. When they arrived in the main square in Le Puy, the two men went to a café while Le Forestier headed to the prefect to argue for the prisoners' release. A few minutes earlier, by pure coincidence, the maquis had robbed a local bank, and German police quickly poured into the square. When Le Forestier returned to his car, the Gestapo were searching it. Unfortunately, the maquisards had left two loaded revolvers under the seat cushion, where they were discovered by the Germans.

Le Forestier was beaten and hurled to the ground, losing two teeth, and placed into custody. Hauled before a tribunal, he was sentenced to death. He gave a spirited defense, which André summarized as "We in Le Chambon resist unjust laws, we hide Jews, and we disobey your orders, but we do this in the name of the Gospel of Jesus Christ." André, Danielle, and Bohny went to meet with Major Julius Schmähling, a senior military officer, former schoolteacher, and devout Catholic who was head of the Wehrmacht in Le Puy. The conversation was "quite humane," Bohny recalled, and Schmähling brokered a deal with the SS to spare Le Forestier if he volunteered to go to Germany to care for civilians wounded by bombings. "At his trial I had heard the words of Dr. Le Forestier, who was a Christian and who had explained to me very clearly why you were all disobeying our orders in Le Chambon,"

Schmähling told Trocmé later. "I believed that your doctor was sincere." Le Forestier's wife and two children saw him before he left, hopeful he would return soon.

He was instead sent to the Montluc prison in Lyon, the notorious Gestapo interrogation center run by Klaus Barbie, the "butcher of Lyon." Le Forestier could have escaped en route, but he felt bound to honor his promise. He kept the spirits up of his fellow prisoners, singing hymns, reading the Bible, and urging courage. On August 20, 120 people, Le Forestier among them, were taken from Montluc to Saint-Genis-Laval, a village outside the city, packed into a run-down house, and systematically machine-gunned by drunken Gestapo police. The house was then set on fire with gasoline and phosphorus. Four days later, Montluc was liberated by the Resistance. Le Forestier was identified by his wife by a button from his suit and a piece of fabric with his tailor's name.

———

On August 15 the Allies landed in Provence. On September 3 the forces of General Jean de Lattre de Tassigny liberated the area. As they moved from Saint-Agrève to Tence, they passed through Le Chambon. The villagers rushed out to see them, cheering and crying, throwing kisses and flowers. "The soldiers tossed out little gifts as the trucks drove through: boxes of Nescafé, candies, caramels, chocolates, little jars of jam. The children rushed into the streets to pick them up. It was the beginning of the end of the war," Magda remembered.

André did his best to prevent reprisals. "André had to stand up for non-violence amidst threats of revenge," Magda remembered. "In the Chambon area, there were no executions, but in Le Puy, and in the Ardèche Valley, it was terrible." André even felt obligated to preach to the German soldiers held in an old small château at Pont de Mars within his parish. "It was not easy for me," André acknowledged. "These hundred and twenty Germans were accused of abominable crimes." He preached reconciliation there, and at the Temple, but his message seemed not to resonate in a time when people wanted retribution. André could not do otherwise. "My father was always criticized," Nelly Trocmé recalled, "but he and my mother never changed their opinions and worked for their ideas of humanity, of generosity, and of rescue."

Soon after the liberation, most of the refugees left, and things quieted down. The children's houses and the sponsored houses closed, and the École Nouvelle Cévenole saw its student population cut in half. The maquis too left, joining the regular French army in pursuing the Germans across the Rhine. There was relief and exhilaration, but also exhaustion, after years of living at a profoundly intense level. Trocmé, just forty-three, believed he had lived the most important years of his life and felt "like a fighter, exhausted by battle." Autumn was soon upon the village, and two-thirds of the houses were vacant. André threw his energy into the École Nouvelle Cévenole, and traveled to the United States to raise money and recruit faculty. The school indeed made Le Chambon a viable and active community all year round, just as the Trocmés had envisioned before the war.

Then it was time for Magda and André to move on, after more than a decade and a half on the plateau. Their vistas were international, and they became co-European secretaries for the International Fellowship of Reconciliation (IFOR) for ten years, founding La Maison de la Réconciliation, an international meeting center in Versailles. André also worked with German Mennonites to create the group Eirene, which provided alternative service options in Morocco for conscientious objectors. The Trocmés became involved in a number of peace movements, speaking out against colonialism, atomic weapons, and the war in Vietnam and meeting with figures like Martin Luther King Jr., Rosa Parks, and Elie Wiesel. André published two books and in 1960 became pastor at Saint-Gervais, one of the oldest parishes in Geneva, where his sermons were broadcast over the Swiss radio.

André had received the Rosette de la Résistance, one of the highest honors given by the Resistance shortly after the war and was made a Righteous Among the Nations—a title which he believed should have been given to Theis, Magda, and the others involved as well—a few months before he died in June 1971. Magda received the medal in his name during his funeral at the temple in Le Chambon, and it went on display in the village town hall. She moved to Paris, where she lived until her death in 1996. She too was named a Righteous Among the Nations, as were Mildred and Édouard Theis, Daniel Trocmé, Roger Darcissac, August Bohny, and nearly thirty other of the Chambonnais.

The villagers in Le Chambon "genuinely don't feel that they were heroes," noted the filmmaker Pierre Sauvage, who was born there while his parents were in hiding and later returned to make a documentary on the plateau. "They think they simply did what was natural, what came naturally." As to why they had acted as they did when others did not, Bohny mused, "That remains a mystery." Perhaps it was a combination of the Huguenot spirit, the isolation, and the terrain. For Theis, it was the profound message at the root of his religion, as he summarized it: "You shall love the Lord your God with all your heart, your soul, your mind and your neighbor as yourself." While André and Magda were certainly the spark, as were other pastors and lay leaders on the plateau, the villagers all knew they were in something together, and they acted both as individuals and as a whole. "It was a very special atmosphere and it was beautiful," Bohny recalled. For his part, André was adamant that the spirit of nonviolence was at the heart of the effort's success. As he said in an educational film in 1955, "We are always going to save more people by non-violent methods than violent methods."

The French deported some 76,000 Jews, representing around a quarter of the total in France. Of these, around 25,000 were French citizens and 11,600 were children, many under the age of six. Just 10 percent of all those deported are estimated to have survived and only three hundred children in total. But on the plateau, there was not a single recorded instance of anyone betraying a refugee. It is estimated that as many as five thousand people found shelter there at some point. Of these around thirty-five hundred were Jewish, the majority of them children.

Le Chambon was an ordinary community like any other, reflected Lesley Maber, an English teacher who worked there during the war. Its people too had flaws and failings. "And I think that means that any community anywhere has the choice to make and can choose right. And that people who seem very ordinary people can do great things if they are given the opportunity." Perhaps it was the spirit of Le Chambon that inspired their sometime neighbor Albert Camus to write at the time, "There are more things to admire in human beings than to despise."

10

Ten POWs

WILLY FISHER WAS ONE OF A HUNDRED THOUSAND BRITISH PRISONERS OF WAR. Each day he and the nine others imprisoned at the Stalag 20B camp near Danzig were sent out to the village of Groß Golemkau and its surrounding farms on work detail. One morning in January 1945, a line of women stumbled down the road. Willy described the scene: "They came straggling through the bitter cold, about 300 of them, limping, dragging footsteps, slipping and falling, to rise and stagger under the blows of the guards—SS swine. Crying loudly for bread, screaming for food, 300 matted haired, filthy objects that had once been—Jewesses." One woman rushed into a nearby house to try to find bread, only to be smashed with a rifle butt by an SS soldier, still desperately shoving a loaf into her blouse as she fell.

Willy was struck with rage. "God punish Germany," he wrote. "Never again will I help a German, never again will I speak well or defend them in speech! I have seen today the filthiest, foulest and most cruel sight of my life. God damn Germany with everlasting punishment."

The women were part of the death marches then happening all over central and eastern Europe as the Nazis forced concentration camp inmates to travel hundreds of miles in the bitter cold toward Germany in front of the advancing Allied forces. While some of the marchers had clogs and coats, many were dressed in sacks, with a bit of straw for warmth if they were fortunate. Willy suddenly ran to the workshop where he worked, grabbed his boots, and gave them to a girl walking barefoot. An SS guard rushed over with rifle raised to club Willy, and the Englishman snapped and moved to attack the Nazi. Two German soldiers Willy worked with grabbed him as the SS officer reversed his gun to shoot him. Another guard shouted at the Nazi, warning that Willy was a British POW. The two soldiers pushed him into the crowd, whispering, "Come away quickly, Willy." Much later Willy would write, "Had I known then the extent of the horror of the concentration camps, I should have gone even more berserk. As it was, I was fortunate that the German soldiers who were working at the blacksmiths where I was, took my part, and prevented me from harm."

That night, Willy reflected on what he had seen. He had noticed a few bystanders throw bread over walls to the women, overhearing one say, "Poor Germany—what have we come to?" Another prisoner told him he had seen a soldier handing out bread and bacon from a car: an SS officer had threatened to kill the soldier, who drew his own revolver in defense. Blessed with naïveté, Willy assumed that the scenes had disturbed many of the Germans watching, but that they were too afraid to say anything.

The next day the death marches continued to pass through. Villagers gathered to watch the spectacle with fascination. Sixteen-year-old Sara Matuson, her mother, and her older sister were among the three hundred marchers still left of the thousand that had started the trek. The SS announced that they were twenty-six miles from their final destination. The three women were repeatedly beaten by the guards when they failed to keep up. Sara was convinced that both her mother and her sister were on the point of starvation, and she was herself crazed with hunger. "To be really hungry is a state that only other survivors can understand and feel; normal everyday people cannot fathom it," she later wrote. Desperate, she asked her mother for their last valuable possession, her father's diamond pinkie ring, so she could try to trade it for bread.

"Child if you must, then do so," Sara's mother, Gita, said, giving her the ring. "May God be with you, and guide you, in any other time I would not let you go." Her sister Hannah said nothing.

Sara suddenly dropped out of line. If she were seen, she would be shot. Hoping to quickly swap the ring and return, she did not even think about how she would get back or find her mother. "It wasn't a well thought out plan," she admitted, "but an act of courage by a daughter who knew her mother and sister would die without food."

She ran into a barn. A young German man entered, and she pushed the ring toward him, saying, "Here's a diamond ring. Bring me bread."

The man took the ring and agreed, but returned not with bread but with the police, who demanded to know what she was doing in the barn.

"I came for bread," Sara said.

"Don't you know that you are dirtying our *Judenrein* [Jew-free] town?" they shouted in German. A posse began to form, armed with pitchforks and guns, and Sara ran back out toward the spectators still lining the streets. With the group in hot pursuit, her only thought was that if they killed her, she did not want it to happen in front of her mother.

"I ran so fast and my feet were frozen!" she recalled in amazement. "I outran a whole town." Several soldiers in long brown coats were standing together watching, and she pushed between two of them and ran behind them in a panic. She found another barn and scrambled into it, climbing into a trough for cows. For what seemed an eternity, she cowered, waiting for her pursuers to burst in.

Eventually a man came into the barn. He noticed that the cow was frightened, and then he saw Sara crying.

Sara assumed he was Polish. "I'm hiding here," she stammered, and told him to either help her or kill her.

The man was Stan Wells, and he was a British prisoner of war like Willy. He and Sara spoke in German, which he had learned since his capture when he was serving with the Royal Norfolk Regiment in France in 1940. He too had seen the death marches, and he told her that the mob had stopped looking for her. That she was, for the moment, seemingly out of danger did not immediately sink in. Seeing that Sara was literally starving, Stan brought her bread and soup, which she instantly devoured. He later wrote that when he first found her, he was surprised that a bundle of rags was moving.

Stan told Sara that he would figure out how to save her. "We will think what to do about it," he assured her. A Russian girl named Zoya, who was in a forced labor camp nearby, also worked in the barn and had by now joined them.

"Listen, I am here with nine other men," Stan said. "We will discuss it, what we can do to save you. And in the meantime Zoya will go to the Russian camp and see; maybe the Russians are willing to hide a Jewish girl. The only thing is," he said, "you have to live through the night."

Stan came back with more food. There were horses and three cows in the barn, he told her. The widow who owned the farm, an ardent Nazi, regularly checked to make sure that Stan had fed the cows. "She comes every night," Stan warned, "so just know that she's coming." He then took the kerosene lamps away and hid them so that the widow would not see Sara.

"May God watch over you," he told her, and then she was alone.

Sara would remember that night for the rest of her life in minute detail. She sat in the trough, freezing, and leaned against the wall as a couple of chickens ran around. Silently she prayed to God.

She missed her mother and sister and the warmth of sleeping together with them. "I even welcomed the cows nibbling at my hair," she wrote. "I was grateful for the warmth of a living creature." Eventually she fell asleep.

She was awakened a few hours later. The widow who owned the farm was shaking her leg.

"Who's there?" the woman yelled, cursing in German. "Who's there?"

Sara froze, holding her breath. "I don't know how I didn't move. I really think my father was watching over me," she wrote later.

"Where is the lamp?" the woman shouted several times, looking for the missing light, and then left the barn in frustration. Sara was terrified the widow would return with another lamp, but she never did.

The next morning, Stan returned as he had promised. The widow had told him she suspected that a soldier had been in the barn overnight, and she wanted to know if the man was still hiding there. Stan had told her that there was only livestock, and he assured Sara that the widow would not return. He also told Sara that Zoya had reported that the Russians were not willing to take her. However, he and the nine other English POWs had unanimously agreed to hide her in a hayloft next to the room where they were locked in each night. One of his comrades would come for her after dark and bring her there, he told her, and then he left her again with food.

The wait felt like forever. Sick, devoured by lice, cold, and overcome with guilt over the fate of her mother and sister, Sara became terrified that no one would come.

Eventually another British soldier arrived with Stan. It was Willy, who was to escort her to the POWs' barn. He gave her his greatcoat and told her to put it on, while Stan kept a lookout for the widow. Willy told Sara to walk on the other side of the road, five paces away from him, and speak to no one. Weak and too terrified to understand anything, she grabbed his arm for support. His own heart was racing; as a prisoner, he was forbidden to speak or walk with a woman.

Willy crossed the street and went directly to the sentry at the camp who was standing there. Willy had been asked to fix a wireless set for a soldier but had avoided doing it. Now it was the perfect excuse. The sentry pointed him toward a farm where the radio was kept. Willy gestured to Sara and said that she was a Russian refugee who had lost her way, and he was returning her to her camp. The ruse worked and they headed off and then quickly slipped inside the building where Willy lived.

The men imprisoned in Stalag 20B worked a couple of miles away on surrounding farms and in factories. Every night they were locked in a room with grated windows. They had secretly cut three of the bars so they could get out whenever they wanted, but although they were only twenty-five or so miles from the Russian border, there was really nowhere to escape to and the police station was directly opposite the building.

The hayloft was in a functioning barn that housed nine police horses. The men had made a hole in the straw where Sara would hide. One of the POWs had made sure a fire was going all day so that the brick chimney next to the hayloft would be warm. The men planned to bring Sara food when they retrieved their laundry each morning and evening, so as not to arouse suspicion.

Sara was rushed up into the hayloft while one of the men kept watch for anyone who might wander in. Hot water, soap, towels, old clothes, and food immediately appeared. George Hammond, a twenty-six-year-old private in the Queen's Own Royal West Kent Regiment who had been captured in Belgium, was shocked at Sara's condition. She looked "like a rabbit—all skin and bone, no flesh on her, covered in cuts and bruises and very frightened of us. You couldn't recognize her as a girl." Because George was married, he was elected to remove Sara's clothes, bathe her, and re-dress her. He used paraffin to delouse her hair. Bert Hambling, a medic, arrived to tend to her. She had a gaping wound on her knee and on her foot, and her extremities were frostbitten. He treated her with a red ointment and, she remembered, made her "feel human again." Still ravenous, she devoured the food they gave her and became sick, taking refuge with the horses to relieve herself.

As Willy moved to leave her for the night, she grabbed his hand and kissed it and tried to thank him, calling him "Herr."

"Drop it," he said. "We are comrades, only doing what we can."

As he left, he realized he had not had a good look at her, but he judged her to be around twenty-five, nine years older than she actually was.

The next day the men came with bread, peas, duck, hen, and pork. Sara ate three loaves of bread and five bowls of soup, what Willy judged to be twenty-two pounds of food. She became quite sick again that evening, and the men suggested a diet of only milk for a few days.

In the morning, a Saturday, Sara began to feel better. That evening the men decided to bring her into their quarters, removing the bars of a window in the wall between their room and the hayloft. They were stunned to learn that she was just sixteen years old. She stood a statuesque five-foot-seven. "We had a good look at her. Her eyes are large as is usual with starvation, sunken cheeks, no breasts," Willy wrote. "Hair has not been cut, body badly marked with sores caused by scratching lice bites. Head still a bit matted and lice still obviously in. I got my forefinger and thumb round the upper part of her arm easily. . . . Feet blue raw with frostbite, the right heel is eaten away by frost and constant rubbing of badly fitting clog." She told them her name was Sonia, not wanting to use her Jewish-sounding name. She also told them that when Stan had entered the barn and said to her, "Don't move, I am English—don't be afraid," she had thought: "English! I knew I was saved!"

———

Sara Matuson had grown up in an affluent, religious home in Shavel,* then the third largest city in Lithuania. Its population was thirty thousand, a third of which was Jewish, and it had several synagogues. Her

———
* Schaulen in German.

father, Samuel Matuson, was a businessman from a wealthy family; her mother, Gita Kutasow, was a college graduate with a degree in languages and literature from the university in St. Petersburg. After their marriage in 1923, the young couple had honeymooned around the world for two years and then, with a streak of adventurousness, settled in a large house in Tel Aviv, where their first daughter, Hannah, was born. They soon returned to Lithuania at Gita's mother's insistence, moving into the luxurious six-room home on Dariaus ir Gireno Street where Sara was born in November 1928.

Sara's early years were filled with candy, ice cream, and French pastries, movies on Friday evenings, Romani music broadcasts, and tea from a brass samovar in the corner of the dining room. There was a big garden where she would grow vegetables and flowers; a picture shows her happily holding an enormous sunflower. Each week Gita would bake a challah for the family with help from their cook and maid and carefully unwrap the candlesticks from their navy-blue velvet coverings for Shabbat dinner. Sara's most precious memories were summer vacations to Polangen, a seaside resort on the Baltic.

Sara was especially close to her father. He had started as a jobber in the cigarette business, selling to kiosks, then opened a successful store selling boots and galoshes. In 1936, at Gita's request, he went into business with her brother Meyer in a leather factory called Promise, a much more difficult business. (Sara did get beautiful blue leather boots, lined in red, and a navy-blue leather coat she cherished.) In synagogue, Sara sat with her father in the men's section. They would play mathematical games afterward, and he would tell her stories about his childhood and explain how leather was made. At age four she began kindergarten at the local Hebrew school, taking great pride in her uniform. She excelled as a student, and every day after school she ran to the factory on her way home to show her father her good marks.

Samuel Matuson was a profoundly anxious man, traumatized in

childhood by the Russian occupation of Lithuania. Jews had not been allowed to move about, and once when he hid in a wagon of hay to get to another town, Russians had speared it with a pitchfork, leaving a large scar on his finger. The Russian pogroms arrived as well. One day a Cossack shot at him. His father jumped in front, taking the bullet to protect him. To his horror, Samuel watched him die before his eyes. He would live in terror of the Russians for his entire life, so much so that if he had to stay behind alone when his family went to the seashore, he paid a man to guard him.

In June 1940 the Russians again invaded Lithuania, marking the end of Sara's idyllic childhood at the age of eleven. Within a few weeks they had nationalized Samuel's business and taken control of the town. All the best food was sent to the motherland. Sara was no longer allowed to learn Hebrew, considered a bourgeois language; Yiddish was deemed a more suitable people's tongue. And although she was the top student in the class, her teacher came to her house to break the news that the honor of being first would go to a member of the Komsomol, the Communist youth organization. The Matusons were also forced to house a Russian pilot, Alexey Alexeyevich, and his pregnant wife Zoya, later joined by her mother when the baby was born. All privacy was gone. The pilot himself, Sara remembered, was a kind man. Sara gave him German lessons and her mother provided a tutor, a German Jewish immigrant across the street who needed work.

The Russians accused Sara's father and uncle of stealing a large amount of leather from their factory and arrested them. The charges were trumped up with evidence from a crooked bookkeeper: indeed, the quantities alleged were so fantastically large that they would have required an entire train to transport. "Suddenly," Sara recalled, "I lost the anchor of my life as my whole world collapsed." Hannah and her classmates attended the trial, in the hope that the sight of devastated young schoolgirls might sway the judge. It didn't. Sara's father and uncle were both sentenced to two years in prison. "It was as if his worst fears had come to pass," Sara wrote, "in that the Russians he dreaded imprisoned him."

The Russians had removed the cots from the cells of the jail where Samuel was incarcerated and boarded up the windows, forcing the prisoners to sleep on the floor in darkness. Sara and her family regularly brought food to the jail and waited outside all night. Gita eventually found a Communist lawyer who was able to get her husband and brother out of jail after six months. Samuel was forced to sign a paper saying that if he said anything about his experience, he would face reincarceration. Although he was only forty-five, Samuel looked old and weak. "I could not understand," Sara wrote, "how my strong father, whom I loved dearly, had become a shadow of his former self."

The Russians began to deport people to Siberia, especially the wealthy. Gita's brother Meyer and his entire family were sent east one day. The Matusons had their bags packed, but they were never taken. Workers at the factory had signed a petition saying that her father was a good boss, which saved the family from deportation. Unfortunately, this apparent salvation proved dubious; most of those deported, including Sara's aunt and uncle and cousins, survived the war far from the Nazis.

On Sunday, June 22, 1941, planes appeared in the air. War between the Soviet Union and Germany had broken out. The pilot living with them was leaving immediately for Russia, and offered to take Sara and her family with him. Her father had been out of jail for two weeks, and his terror of the Russians kept him in place. "At least Germans are an educated lot," he said. "These Russians are barbarians. . . . We are not budging. We're staying here and we're waiting for the Germans." It was, Sara wrote, "another fateful miscalculation that would ultimately lead to disaster and death."

As early as 1939, Jewish refugees from Poland had come bearing tales of horrendous atrocities inflicted by the Germans on the Jews.

Yet Samuel Matuson could not comprehend the peril he faced. He even traveled to Hamburg that same year to buy an expensive machine for the leather factory. "As wonderful as my father was, he was not realistic about the future," Sara wrote. "Even today, it is still amazing to me that my parents did not have a sense of what was happening."

On a Thursday, the Germans arrived. The next day, all Jews were ordered to wear the yellow Star of David and forbidden to walk on the sidewalk. On Sunday Sara went with her aunt's sister to look for food. When she returned home, her father was gone. The superintendent of their apartment building had told the Germans where all the Jews lived. The Nazis had arrested Samuel, along with two rabbis and her aunt's brother, Lazar Penn, a six-foot-six-inch giant with blond hair and blue eyes who could have passed as Aryan. A German who bore a striking resemblance to Adolf Hitler took over the family's living room. He promised to get their father out of prison, but there was no chance of that. Samuel Matuson, along with the others, was taken to a field in the town of Kuzai. There the men were forced to undress in a barn and dig a large pit, their own grave. Then they were shot.

The Matuson women were unaware of what had happened. Meanwhile, the Nazis organized two ghettos in the Traku and Kaukazas neighborhoods, poor areas of town whose residents were offered the chance to swap their small abodes, which often had no running water or bathroom facilities, for the homes, property, and household goods of displaced Jews. Without Samuel, the Matusons were at a huge disadvantage as the ghettos began to fill up. Those unable to secure places were rounded up in the synagogue and then sent to Zagar, a killing field north of the town. At the last minute the family found refuge with one of Hannah's friends, Sonia Berelowitz, who was able to offer one narrow cot in a two-room house. Unable to fit next to her mother and sister, Sara slept on a friend's couch.

Sara remembered little of her experience in the Kavkaz ghetto. Her most searing memory was of exceeding horror. One day, the ghetto

Jews were gathered to watch the hanging of a man arrested for smuggling in bread for his child. Despite the pleading of many, the Germans were unmoved, and even forced children to watch the execution. In a final act of defiance, the man kicked the chair out from underneath himself on the gallows. "Everybody just let out a big cry," Sara remembered. "It was terrible."

In the fall of 1943 Kavkaz was closed, and the inhabitants moved into the Traku ghetto. The Matusons were given two beds in a kitchen near the gate. By coincidence, the man who Sara's mother had arranged to tutor the Russian pilot was the head of the ghetto. Remembering that kindness, he arranged for Gita and Hannah to work in a brush factory, and for Sara to clean the house of the head SS officer, Herr Shleff, both jobs outside the ghetto. Shleff would pick Sara up in the morning to take her to his house, a five-minute walk away, and return her at night. After she cleaned, he would take a white cloth to the furniture to see how well she had done. "After the war you're going to thank me," he told her, "because I taught you how to clean."

One day in November 1943 Sara arrived at work, and Shleff locked her in the attic. "You're going to see something very beautiful today," he told her, instructing her to look out the window overlooking the ghetto. Outside, just two blocks away, she saw crowds of children and the elderly. Trucks covered with black tarpaulins pulled up, and the Germans threw shrieking children in like bags of garbage. Old people were pushed up ladders into the back of the trucks. Sara saw the father of a friend, a young man who had been blinded in an accident and was thus unable to work, also taken. She could hear the screams from the attic. "I was transfixed," Sara wrote. "I didn't want to see what was going on in front of my eyes, but I felt I had an obligation to be a witness to this horror." She was numb when she returned to the ghetto. There were no children anywhere. There were no elderly. Mothers were wailing in the streets, desperately searching for their missing children.

By the middle of 1944, the Russians were bombing near the ghetto.

The Germans issued an order to the Jews: prepare to be relocated. Gita packed what possessions they still had. In July 1944 the ghetto was evacuated. The Matuson women wore their clothing in layers, just two or three dresses. Sara took her blue leather boots and coat, the gifts from her father, and they carried their bedding and bundles on their backs. "I missed my father terribly," Sara remembered, "but optimistically still expected he would find us and everything would once again be all right." Her mother, however, was becoming alarmingly passive and had even stopped complaining. "What will happen to all the Jews will happen to us, too," she told her daughters, "and there is no use fighting." Her sister too had taken on a deep sadness. "Somehow," Sara wrote, "I knew that I would be the one to try to help us survive." Three weeks after their departure, the Russians liberated the area they had left.

The heat was unbearable as they set out. Three thousand people gathered in a line. There was no way to escape. Lithuanians killed Jews who tried to make it to the surrounding forests, while villagers looked on. The thirst was unbearable; some people tried to lap up the few puddles on the ground. Eventually they came to a holding point, where they leaned on their bundles overnight. Here Gita fainted. Sara rushed to find water for her mother but feared she would not make it through whatever lay ahead.

The next morning, the Nazis pushed the Jews into cattle cars ("a clear signal we were no longer people"), sixty to each, whipping them and prodding them with guns. The metal doors of the train car were sealed, and there was almost no room to move. Slivers of sunlight that shone through tiny windows during the day provided the only light. There was just one bucket for the entire train to use as a toilet, and many became sick on the floors. People had nowhere to lie down, so they stood all night, propping each other up. "When I think of my fastidious mother, who would check out of hotels for their [lack of] cleanliness, I realized the immensity of this trauma to her, both emotionally and physically," Sara wrote.

After several days they came to a station, Tiegenhof, where they were transferred to open trucks and taken to Stutthof, a death camp with a gas chamber and crematoria. The first such camp outside Germany, it was notorious for providing raw material for Dr. Rudolf Spanner's project to make soap out of human fat. SS officers in black uniforms attacked the arriving Jews with guns and whips, shrieking in German. They were instructed to leave their belongings on the train and assured they would be brought to them. It was pitch-dark as they stepped off the cattle cars. Men and women were separated. People began screaming the names of their relatives, trying to stay together. Searchlights roved back and forth, dogs were barking, people were running and screaming in panic. "It was a nightmare," Sara recalled, "but a reality."

The three women were frozen with terror. "I had no more tears to shed—everything was gone, except my mother and sister and I knew I had to cling to them," Sara said. Gita had managed to save her diamond watch, an engagement present from Samuel. It had a small face surrounded by diamonds and cobalt, and a band with more precious gems. In happier times, the girls had argued over who would get the Russian antique. Now Gita buried it in the sand in an attempt to save it, putting string around it so she could retrieve it later.

In the morning, the Jews were lined up for cold showers. When Sara undressed, she left her cherished leather coat and boots behind, her last links to her father, never to see them again. She was examined and given flannel underwear, wooden clogs, and a summer-weight dress, white with red, pink, and green stripes and a large red Star of David painted on the back. A number—54,384—was also attached to her clothes. At Stutthof they did not bother to tattoo: as it was exclusively a death camp, such an exercise was viewed as a waste of time and ink. Sara, her mother, and her sister now barely recognized each other. Sara saw a mountain of shoes in the distance, including thousands of children's. "I knew if there was a hell," she later wrote, "we were there!"

One day she found a note in one of the shoes with a message—"I am the Jew R.S. from Wilno, I am today to be gassed."

Jews were usually murdered on arrival. By a stroke of fortune, the Red Cross was scheduled to inspect imminently, so the new prisoners were kept alive so the Germans could claim that people actually lived in the camp. Inmates were fed red metal bowls of watery soup and cabbage leaves taken from a large cauldron, one for every three people. The guards would hurl them back at the prisoners when they returned them. The Matusons were given one blanket to share. There was no work at Stutthof, so the Jews were made to stand for many hours during roll call, the infamous *Appell.* "This was torture," Sara recalled. "We were no longer human."

A few weeks later they were sent in small boats to Baumgarten, a work camp, and assigned to dig ditches for the German army. Hannah and Sara used pickaxes to make a foxhole six feet deep and they gave their mother the lighter task of shoveling away the earth. They were kept slightly above starvation, subsisting on watery soup and coffee and a small piece of bread at night, when they were jammed into a small tent with seven other women, covered only by thin blankets. "Hannah and I would snuggle up to our mother, who always slept between us," she remembered. "That was our comfort—the three of us together."

When they had finished digging ditches at Baumgarten, they were transferred to another camp. They ended up working at four additional camps, the last of which was called Torn. When they were not digging, they were now crammed into wooden barracks with fifty other women. The rations got worse. There was still the soup, but now a loaf of bread had to be divided among ten people. There was no toilet, only a large pit with railings to sit on. "The smell was truly the stench of hell," Sara wrote. Lice were another torment. They could not get rid of the vermin, which constantly gnawed at their flesh.

In December it was bitter cold, and the Red Army was rapidly advancing toward them. The Nazis told the prisoners they needed to be moved further into Germany to "save" them from the Russians. Over a thousand women began the trek. Sara focused entirely on her mother and sister, talking to no one, trying desperately to "get through each day with the numbing cold, the ceaseless hunger and the all-consuming fear. But I also had hope for an end to this nightmare." Soon all hope seemed to disappear. They were not allowed to wash, and their hair was matted and crawling with lice. The SS men delighted in beating them with whips and guns. Hannah shivered and stared vacantly. Sara would later find out she had been brutally raped in the ghetto. Sara was terrified for her mother, who looked like a hunched-over old woman, though she was only forty-four years old.

Anyone who tried to flee was killed on the spot. "We were walking skeletons," Sara wrote, "trying to eat snow and to find a frozen turnip by digging in frozen soil. Our hunger was so severe that some were willing to risk being shot if they left the line to find anything on the frozen ground." Death was everywhere. The Germans gave Sara a piece of bread to remove a body from the road. It was one of her friends, the daughter of the assistant principal at the Hebrew school.

One day, as they passed a village, a German guard offered to save Sara by hiding her with his family nearby. "He had kind eyes when the other Germans had only bestiality lurking in their features," Sara recalled. "Little girl, I can save you," he told her. "My family lives right here, and I can take you to my family." She told him she had a mother and sister, but the man sadly said they did not have room for all three of them, and Sara would not leave her family behind. The man felt so sorry for her that he gave her a loaf of bread. The three women ate part of the bread, and her mother slept on the rest of it that night. When they woke, they discovered someone had stolen it. Sara became enraged and hit her mother in anger, not thinking what she was doing. "Starvation makes people senseless," she wrote. Gita was now deteriorating rapidly. Sara thought she was on the brink of death.

It was then that Sara had dropped out of the line to get bread for her mother and sister.

———

As Sara hid in the hayloft, the Russian front was approaching Groß Golemkau. People fled, leaving behind wagons of belongings, including clothing. One of the prisoners of war, Alan Edwards, purloined a maroon coat and a sweater to cover Sara's dress with the big red Jewish star on its back. He also brought her shoes and stockings. Grateful, Sara sat down in the men's quarters and worked until midnight, sewing a new hat from material they had procured.

As she worked, she recounted her story. The men were worried about her morale. "She will keep harping on her mother and sister and the concentration camp," Willy wrote with concern, "but we forbid her to mention them."

Sara remained in the hayloft for over three weeks. In constant fear of discovery, she tried to structure her time to keep herself sane. Moving the straw was a complex undertaking: in the morning, she made sure it was near the edge of the loft, so that the stable boy could easily reach it and not inadvertently discover her, while later in the day she covered herself with it when children wandered into the barn to play hide and seek, sometimes even jumping over her. In the late afternoon, as she waited for supper, her mind drifted back to the puzzles she used to do with her father. "During the time I spent alone, I tried to play mathematical games with myself and planned ways to find my mother, father and sister when this nightmare would finally end," she wrote.

The men arranged to pop in and out when they could. From the second night on, Alan became her primary companion and caregiver. He was twenty-five years old and had been captured in France in 1940 serving with the Royal Engineers. He was, Sara remembered, "their *bon vivant*," but extremely gentle and highly sympathetic to her plight. Every day he brought her food. Before Sara's arrival, Alan had been sneaking out to see various girlfriends. But after she told him about her fears, he kept her company each night. "I thought I was in love with him," Sara recalled years later with a laugh. "He was even better looking than Gregory Peck. And he was very kind." He also went to look for her mother and sister in the Praust subcamp at Stutthof, but was unable to gain entrance because of a typhus quarantine.

One night, to break up the monotony, the men brought Sara into their quarters for a talk. Alan led her down the ladder, and another of the POWs brushed away the footsteps she left in the snow. The large room was filled with beds and smiling British soldiers. In addition to Stan, Willy, Bert, George, and Alan were another five men: Bill Scruton, Jack Buckley, Roger Letchford, Bill Keable, and Tommy Noble, who had all taken turns at the risky job of climbing the ladder to bring her food. They each gave her a little present. They also apprised her of their contingency plan if the horses and straw were moved from the barn as people fled the Russians. They would build a double wall in their room and hide her behind it during the day while they worked, and then let her out when they returned.

As it turned out, events overtook them. One evening Alan told her that the British were being evacuated that night. He gave her two choices. They could shave her head and dress her as a man, bringing her along in place of Stan Wells, who was staying behind. Or alternatively, he had made arrangements with a Polish boy to take care of her, telling the teenager that she was his Lithuanian girlfriend who needed protection. The boy would come in the middle of the night to get her and let her stay on the extra bed in the attic where he lived. "So, you can sleep there, and he'll bring you food every day because the war can't last longer than two weeks, three weeks tops. What do you want to do?" Alan asked.

Afraid that the disguise would not work, and that she would wind up getting the nine men killed along with her, Sara decided to wait for the Polish boy. After her rescuers had left, though, she was terrified again. "They left, my surrogate family; I was so terribly lonesome and I remembered my mother's words, 'Whatever happens to all of the Jews will happen to us.'"

She tried to fall asleep while she waited for the Polish boy. "I was in agony that night." She knew that when the light came, the Germans would come for the horses and straw, and she would likely be discovered. When at dawn the boy had not shown up, she finally left the barn. Carrying herself with authority, she walked out past the police station without incident. When someone approached her, she told them she was rushing to work and disappeared.

She somehow managed to find her way back to the barn where Stan had discovered her. Once again, she felt her father was watching over her, guiding her steps. She ran into Zoya, the Russian girl she had met the first night with Stan.

"Zoya," she told her, "this is me, Sonia."

"Oh, my God," the girl said, "you look normal." The British had succeeded in nursing Sara back to good health in just three weeks.

"Zoya, will you take me tonight to your compound?"

"Sure," Zoya said, "but you will have to wait for me to finish work, and I'll take you with me. I'll tell them I have a friend."

While Sara waited, she wandered around the town. Most of the homes were quite modest, but there was one large, impressive redbrick house. Having second thoughts about the Russian camp, she decided to see if she could get work. She knocked on the door, and a very tall man answered. His name was Heinrich Binder. Sara told him that she was a Lithuanian refugee looking for work, and he asked if she could milk cows and feed pigs. "I thought how strange it would be to feed the pigs, this girl from Shavel whose mother had inspected all the food to make sure it was kosher," she wrote in her memoirs. But she told him she could do it, and he hired her on the spot. There was an extra empty bed in the attic where she could sleep.

Binder sent her into his small cellar and asked her to sort out the potatoes that had rotted during the winter. After a while, he came downstairs.

"Sonia," he said, "you're not Lithuanian."

"What do you mean, I'm not Lithuanian?" she said. "Of course, I'm Lithuanian."

"The Lithuanians don't speak such a German," he told her. "Your German is so perfect. You must be the Jewish girl we lost in town three weeks ago."

"My heart was racing, my mind was assessing the situation," Sara recalled. "I wondered what would he do if I told him the truth—kill me? No one would know or miss me."

"You know, Mr. Binder," she said finally, "you're right. I am the Jewish girl." She told him that if he told anyone, it would be a death sentence for her.

Binder was the highest-ranking local SS officer. Under any other circumstances, he told her, he would have turned her in. But now they could save each other. His wife was in Cologne, and he wanted to get there quickly, as it was about to be liberated by the British. Like most Germans, he was desperate to get to the Anglo-American zone before the war ended.

"I'm not going to stay here to wait for the Russians," he said. "I want you to write me a note in Yiddish that I saved your life, and that will save my life." She did so, and he was good to his word. "It is strange, indeed, that you should have found shelter with Heinrich Binder," Alan, who had worked on the same farm, later told her. "Binder was an old bastard, a typical German, but no doubt he became scared as the Russians approached."

She worked on the farm alongside a German girl named Annie who said, "You know, Sonia, we lost the war, but we did win the war against the Jews. We killed them all!" She also found herself at Binder's table, serving high-ranking Germans who made conversation with her, telling her that she had beautiful eyes. Sara was still wearing the dress with the red Star of David on it under her sweater, and she was terrified of being discovered and shot. Most dangerously, the local chief of police told Binder he was suspicious that Sara was Jewish. After that, Binder kept her out of sight until he departed for Cologne. When he left, he gave her Annie's German passport and left the farm in her hands.

The Russians were almost upon them and the Germans were fleeing in terror, taking many Polish and Lithuanian forced laborers with them. Sara convinced a group of other teenagers to hide in a cellar at the edge of town and wait for liberation. They ended up in the middle of fierce fighting once the Russians arrived. Sara could not tell which of the soldiers—the ones in the green uniforms or the ones in the white—were the Russians, and which the Germans. Russian artillery, pulled by horses, pounded German positions, and the teenagers cowered in the basement for several days.

And then it was over. The Russians arrived and were in control. "The Russians are [here]," she thought, "I have nothing to worry about."

Fluent in Russian, she sought out the commander of the liberators and told him she was a Jewish girl who had escaped from the concentration camps. The commander then took Sara to a storage room in the basement and began to chase her. She told him to keep away, and he suddenly stopped. "Perhaps," she noted later, "he finally recognized that I was a young girl and he had second thoughts."

"Ask me anything," he said, with some remorse.

"Don't touch me," Sara told him.

The commander wrote three notes, one to his mother in Moscow, one to his sister in Leningrad, and one "to whom it may concern," stating that Sara was his wife and should be given safe passage. Perhaps he secretly believed that they might one day indeed be married. He sent his attaché to escort her, but the man was cut down by a bullet.

A harrowing journey over three months followed. First, Sara was arrested and interrogated as a German spy by the Russians because of her fluency. Eventually they realized that she was just a young Jewish girl. As she made her way home, Russian men repeatedly tried to take advantage of her, but several strangers protected her. Eventually she traveled with another Jewish girl, Sonia, and a Polish girl, Anna, to Bialystok, a gathering place for Jewish refugees.

————

In his diary, Willy recounted his own journey back. About a week after leaving Sara, he escaped from the German march with Alan Edwards, Roger Letchford, and Jack Buckley. They had been taken to a British POW camp at Danzig and then force-marched with two thousand others toward Germany. Ten kilometers from the border, the four men slipped out of the column into the woods. They hid with a Polish family, who sheltered them for nearly a month as the SS searched for escaped prisoners. When the Russians arrived, the four POWs spent much of their time protecting Polish women from sexual assault. Willy's diary is filled with the horrors of brutal and repeated rapes by the Red Army, estimated in the millions across Europe.

The four were arrested and accused of being Germans. At one point, Alan was whipped in the face by a Russian. They were constantly hauled into the police station. After one such episode in July 1945, Alan refused to answer any more questions, got on his bicycle, and started to pedal off. He was shot by the Russian police, breaking his left leg in two places, and hospitalized for almost two months. The Polish family who had been sheltering the men nursed him when he was released. He married Wanda, the family's youngest daughter, taking her back to England in November.

During those few months, the full gravity of German atrocities began to become apparent. Willy saw "thousands of emaciated, stripe-clad figures, many suffering not only from malnutrition, but typhoid and other fearsome diseases." The scene was horrifying. "I have never been sure in my own mind," Willy wrote later, "whether or not the German people, on the whole, knew of the camps or what went on in them. I rather think they either did, or suspected, but did nothing to stop it." As they watched the Germans being rounded up and loaded for the journey west into the same cattle cars they had used to transport Jews to their death, the British had little sympathy.

———

In Bialystok, Sara found work and tried to decide what to do. She still held out hope that her mother and sister would return, and that they could return to Lithuania and find her father, until a girl from Shavel who had been on the death march with Gita and Hannah broke the news that Sara's mother had died of starvation and Hannah had succumbed to typhus on the very day of liberation. "I broke down," Sara wrote. "Much of my reason for going on had been to find my mother and sister. I began to feel that there was no reason to live and I felt guilt at leaving them. . . . I also wanted to die for now I felt truly alone in the world. . . . In the end, I clung to the hope that my father had made it through the war. I also wanted to stay alive to maintain the memory and legacy of my family." Only 3 percent of Lithuanian Jews survived. Most had been killed by their neighbors. Deep down, Sara suspected her father had not made it.

Sara joined a group of a few hundred young people who were planning to go to Palestine to train to work on kibbutzim. Organizers from the Holy Land prepared them for the journey. She had no papers and had to pretend she was Belgian or Dutch. The only documents she did have were precious to her: photographs of the British POWs she thought of as her adoptive family and Alan's address. The leader of her group took the papers and pictures—and lost them. It was another sharp loss in its own way, Sara noted, "another jarring shock to my bruised heart."

Eventually Sara arrived at St. Ottilien, a former monastery near Munich being used as a hospital. Most of the doctors and patients were Jewish, but the nurses were German, and they revived terrifying memories among the convalescents. Sara and a number of others were asked to train as nurses for six months, which delayed her voyage to Palestine. She lived with ten others on the third floor of the building in a single room, which came to feel like a dorm as the girls stayed up late, playing cards and chatting. Sara passed her nursing course and found an affinity and talent for the profession.

Luck intervened. One of her patients, Osia Magun, wrote to his mother in the United States and mentioned Sara. His mother put an advertisement in the New York papers, looking for members of the Kutay family as Sara's American relatives were known. Four of her mother's brothers had emigrated to America; indeed, Gita had almost gone to visit them in 1939, but her niece had convinced her not to. Now Sara's uncles urged her to come to America. But visas for Lithuanians at that time took years. A friend of her father's was working in Frankfurt for Vaad Hatzalah, an Orthodox rescue organization, and he offered to arrange a "marriage of convenience" with a rabbinic student, who would then divorce her on arrival. The cost was $500. Her uncle Joe did not hesitate: "Just come!" he wrote her. It was half his yearly income.

Sara arrived in New York on August 3, 1947. Although her aunts and uncles were helpful, the adjustment was difficult. She had to learn English and go to school with children much younger than her. On her nineteenth birthday she wrote a letter to her dead mother in broken English, pouring out her loneliness. "Today is my birthday," she wrote. "I'm already 19 years old as to the years I'm already a big girl but really I'm a child and need a mother and your caring. Mother that is already three years that nobody gave me a real mother kiss and look at me with so much loveness as you. O mother I need you I'm unhappy please hear me and take me to you with you I'll be happy elsewhere. O mother don't forget me."

Eventually Sara finished school, went to work as a nurse, and then married Bill Rigler, a young lawyer who was later appointed as a judge. She became a community advocate and local official and had a son and a daughter. Later she became involved in the campaign to free Soviet Jewry. And, in a tribute to her sister, she changed her name from Sara to Hannah so that, in some small way, the girl who did not survive the Holocaust might live on.

Almost immediately after her marriage, Sara had tried to find a way to get in touch with the British POWs. She wrote to every Edwards in the London phone book, but to no avail. Then one day she met a woman from London at her husband's Masonic lodge, who offered to use her contacts in the police department to help. In 1963 Sara received a postcard from the British War Department, asking what her claim was against Alan Edwards. She wrote back that she was trying to find the ten prisoners of war who had saved her life.

A year later a letter arrived from Alan, dated September 1, 1964. When he had received Sara's inquiry, he wrote, "I could not believe my own eyes. It seemed impossible, after all these years, that you would try to locate me." He told her that he and three of the other POWs remained in touch and often talked of her. He was profoundly relieved that she was safe. "I only tried to be kind to you and cheer you a little, please don't give *me* the credit for saving your life," he wrote, "although I must admit I prayed for you that night we left, so maybe it helped a little."

Sara followed up immediately and sent photographs. "Looking at your latest photo," Alan wrote back, "I note that you have become a very beautiful woman. . . . (The details and story of your survival are fantastic, almost unbelievable.) That same night we were marched from the camp at Golemkau, I did not have much time to make a decision, but I must confess to you that I often criticized myself for not staying behind with you, and wondered whether I had done the right thing." He reported that he had already told Bill Scruton that he had heard from her, and promised to get contacts for the others.

Sara kept up a correspondence with Alan for the next three years. In 1967, on the way to Israel with her husband, she stopped over in London to change planes, and Alan drove out to the airport to meet her. They had not seen each other in twenty-two years. The meeting was emotional and lasted but ten minutes. Alan gave her a toy soldier as a token. After the meeting, he shared the story with a reporter from the *People's Paper*, a Sunday newspaper, which ran an article with pictures of them both. It reminded a reader of a story told to her by a friend about his wartime experience. She sent it to him. Her friend was Willy Fisher.

Willy immediately wrote to Sara, telling her that reading the article made a "miserable cold day into perhaps . . . the sunniest and certainly one of the happiest of my life. I am by nature pretty hard and insensitive, but I must confess I do know now what [are] 'tears of happiness.' " His reaction echoed Alan's. "My joy at your being alive and well, and being transformed from that tragic waif I once met, into what your photograph shows, a very beautiful and obviously happy woman, in some measure made up for all the guilt I felt at being unable (or perhaps too cowardly) to do or risk more for you than we did, for I have never got over the feeling that we, perhaps, should have taken you with us." He enclosed the diary he had kept of the time of her rescue and of his subsequent escape.

Willy had a difficult time after the war. A Communist, he decided to go live in Russia after hostilities ended, and in late May 1945 he traveled with recently freed Russian forced laborers. On the train he assembled his diary from notes he had taken on scraps of paper and on the backs of photographs. The Russian laborers told him they would all be liquidated when they arrived back in the Soviet Union as bad citizens, because they had not been able to escape from Germany. Some killed themselves on the way to avoid that fate. Willy could not imagine that Britain would ally with such a nation. "I do not believe my country would bind itself to such criminals," he told them. He was sadly wrong. All of the laborers were in fact murdered upon arrival in Odessa.

Shaken, Willy made his way to England, his belief in communism destroyed. His diary had been confiscated, so he rewrote it on the boat. He had spent five years as a prisoner of war and now returned home to find his house bombed, his wife living with another man, and two of his brothers killed in action. On the night he arrived home, his father died in his sleep from excitement at his son's safe return. But now, he told Sara, he had fallen in love with a very religious woman named Margaret. They were devoted to each other, but she would not marry him because he had been divorced. Willy worked for Philips Radio and Rolls-Royce. At age fifty-nine, he would develop vertigo at the very time England entered a deep recession, resulting in his layoff. Through it all, he maintained a brisk correspondence with Sara and an upbeat, jolly attitude, and even proudly hosted her son in London.

In February 1972 Sara reunited with her rescuers at the Portman Hotel in Marble Arch, London. She was now forty-three years old. The previous year, Stan Wells had come to see her for tea when he was in New York to visit his daughter. She decided to throw a reunion to thank her rescuers. All of the men came. Bert Hambling, the medic who had nursed her back to health the first night, had written to her over the years, but now they met for the first time since he left the prison camp. "It was such a moving moment to see her," he told a newspaper. "We all had tears in our eyes." George Hammond, now a furniture maker, was also overjoyed. "I never dreamed that we would ever meet again," he told a reporter. "And when I saw the story in the paper, I just burst into tears." They all posed for a photograph, with Sara in the middle. She was overwhelmed to see them again. "My ten angels came with their wives to see a woman who was no longer a bag of bones but had a productive and satisfying life. They toasted their little sister who had found a special place in their hearts—and the stoic British cried."

The men continued to reunite periodically, always toasting Sara when they did. In 1988 the BBC aired a special about the story. Five of the men were told they were being honored as former prisoners of war and were shocked when Sara appeared. As a surprise, she and the BBC had petitioned Yad Vashem to announce them as Righteous Among the Nations on the air.

"These men risked their lives for me—not just 1 life but 11 lives," Sara had written to officials in Israel. "They had nothing to gain from hiding me—they took many great risks. They have received no recognition for saving my life." Every one of them had an equal part. "If one of the ten had been against hiding me, I would not be alive today," she wrote. "Had I been discovered, I would certainly have been shot together with the ten prisoners of war, all of whom had families and homes in England. I had nobody, and no one would have known had I been killed. I would just have been another of the Six Million but they had much more to risk and it was close to going home. They could touch freedom."

The next year, the ten men were honored in Israel. Five of the six then still alive made the journey to Jerusalem, including Stan and Alan. Sadly, Willy had died eleven years earlier of a heart attack. On his deathbed, he had mentioned two people: his mother and Sara.

Alan spoke on behalf of the group, and a tree was planted in the Garden of the Righteous Among the Nations. Alan had returned several times to Poland, and a few years earlier he had revisited the barn where the ten soldiers had hidden Sara. She would remain in touch with him until he died in 1998, but never saw him again.

The men of Stalag 20B were ordinary men from humble backgrounds. But they all rose to extraordinary heights. "There is a tree firmly planted at Yad Vashem and its branches reach out to shelter a young girl from Shavel and the ten English soldiers who cared enough to save a child," Sara wrote. "Often when people speak about the Holocaust they are overwhelmed by the evil that almost succeeded in extinguishing the human spirit. And then ten ordinary men appeared, whose humanity was so natural and real that they helped to restore faith in the ultimate triumph of life and love."

Conclusion

FOR MANY, THE MOST STRIKING THING ABOUT THE RESCUERS IS THEIR NEAR UNI-
versal modesty about their actions. Over and over, we hear the same
responses. They did not believe they had done anything special. They
had only done what was normal, what was natural, what any person
would have done in their shoes. Their words are often identical. "I am
not a hero," declared Miep Gies, who helped shelter Anne Frank, for
example. They did not brag about or often even mention what they
had done.* This commonality suggests that perhaps there was something—a belief system, a moral code, a personality type—that differ-
entiated those who acted from those who did not.

It is not only because of their modesty that so few rescuers were
celebrated or even acknowledged after the war. Many of them were
scarred by what we would now identify as post-traumatic stress. The
burden of keeping a profound secret was hard. As one psychologist has
noted, "secrecy about wartime rescue activities was an old habit not easily broken." Some lost faith in the world. Many suffered economically
or socially. And many, as we have seen, were punished for their actions.
The great Raoul Wallenberg disappeared into a Soviet prison with
barely a notice, never to emerge. Oskar Schindler had rocks thrown at

---

* Interestingly, the Jewish tradition of the thirty-six righteous people—the Lamed-Vav
Tzadikim—who are said to be necessary to save the world states that they are never identified, are not aware that they are righteous, and will never claim to be among them.

him on the streets of Frankfurt. When he punched a factory worker who called him a "Jew-kisser," he was lectured by a judge and ordered to pay damages.

Part of the animus was certainly driven by strong and embedded anti-Semitism in many communities, where many were more than pleased to see the Jews persecuted and to profit from it. Many of their neighbors were outraged that the rescuers had put them at risk through their actions, however noble. "It was considered a very unpatriotic, very anti-social, and a very stupid thing" to have rescued Jews, Mordecai Paldiel, longtime director of Yad Vashem's Department of the Righteous, explained. Governments and organizations, too, were angered by those who valued compassion over obedience and refused to follow orders. Behind the Iron Curtain, rescuers were threatened, harassed, imprisoned, or even killed.

But above all, for those many who claimed to have sympathized with the victims, to have been secretly opposed to the Nazis but powerless to act, the existence of the righteous was an inconvenient fact. As one historian said, it is perhaps "more comforting to believe that all were guilty than that the honor of the nation was saved by a tiny minority." By their actions and their courage, the rescuers showed what others might have done to help prevent the Holocaust. Hitler's secretary Traudl Junge came upon a plaque in honor of Sophie Scholl after the war. "I could see that she had been born the same year as I, and that she had been executed the same year I entered into Hitler's service," she admitted. "And, at that moment, I really realized that it was no excuse that I had been so young."

Could the Holocaust happen again? We have work to do to make sure it does not. Since the Second World War, there have been an estimated forty genocides. Two million people were murdered in the killing fields of Cambodia by the Khmer Rouge, and another two million in the Bangladeshi civil war. Since the end of the Cold War, we have seen atrocities that many would not have believed could occur. Once again concentration camps and ethnic cleansing were found in Europe during the Yugoslavian conflicts, culminating in the massacre at Srebrenica in Bosnia in 1995. And as the combined military might of the world declined to intervene, the Hutus slaughtered almost one million Tutsis in Rwanda and Burundi, often with rudimentary weapons. In recent years we have seen at least five hundred thousand die in the Syrian civil war; Christians, Yazidis, and other minorities massacred by the Islamic State; and atrocities against the Rohingya in Myanmar. As of this writing, one million Uighur Muslims are in concentration camps in the western province of Xinjiang in China. And Russian forces have leveled cities in Ukraine, much as they did in Aleppo and Grozny and as the Nazis' Condor Legion did in Guernica. "As long as there is hatred, intolerance and hunger for power in the world, there will be heroes," Varian Fry's young gopher Justus Rosenberg wrote in his memoirs as he neared his hundredth birthday. "We should dream of the day when they will no longer be needed." Sadly, the world is still very much in need of rescuers. It is even more in need of repair.

The rescuers of the Holocaust can perhaps offer hope. If we try to understand what made them act as they did, we can work to inculcate these values so that more might follow their example in the future, or, just possibly, create communities that will not permit violent hatred in their midst. There were very few systematic psychological studies of the righteous conducted after the Second World War. "It is only natural and expected that those who studied these tragic events focused first on the typical experience rather than the rare exception," wrote Nechama Tec, one such researcher of rescue and herself a Holocaust survivor. Most famously, the psychologists Pearl and Samuel Oliner, also survivors, interviewed and analyzed nearly seven hundred survivors, rescuers, and bystanders in a landmark study of the "altruistic personality." Among the traits to which they found no correlation among rescuers were gender, age, nationality, family size, religion, birth order, or race. The only identifiable pattern was that those whose parents disciplined them in a loving, consistent, and rational way—as opposed to an authoritarian, violent, and random manner—were far more likely to become rescuers.

Eva Fogelman, a psychologist whose father was hidden during the Holocaust, interviewed three hundred rescuers over ten years. As personality types, she concluded, rescuers tended to be resourceful, independent thinkers, confident in their abilities and convinced that what an individual does matters. They believed that all people were human beings with certain basic rights regardless of their differences, and they did not focus on how others viewed their actions. They were the people who see a common humanity and adhere to John Donne's famous line: "No man is an island, entire of itself; every man is a piece of the continent, a part of the main." They believed it was important to stand up for the needy and the marginalized, even those outside their family or community. Importantly, despite the significant risks, they believed that they could succeed. Rescuers were not suicidal.

Fogelman divided rescuers' motivations into five categories. The largest were those driven by a moral code that gave them a strong sense of what was right and just. Some were driven by religious beliefs, others by ideology or ethics, some by compassion, and many by some combination of all of these. Another group were those who had a favorable feeling toward Jews, often because they grew up with Jewish friends, believed they were of Jewish ancestry, had positive interactions with Jews, or—like the Calvinist and other fundamentalist Protestants—felt a kinship with the Jews and a connection to the Old Testament. There were those whose professions called on them to help others, such as doctors, nurses, and social workers, who would not refuse aid to those in need. There were also those who were part of networks, often in the context of broader anti-Nazi and antifascist activity, many of whom tended to be young, educated, and affluent. And in the last category were children, who helped their parents and siblings in rescue efforts, some with a sense of adventure, some with a sense of terror.

Like the Oliners, Fogelman found that the "innermost core" of rescuers' values and beliefs was formed during their childhoods. One or more factors were almost always present: "a nurturing, loving home; an altruistic or beloved caretaker who served as a role model for altruistic behavior; a tolerance for people who were different; a childhood disease or personal loss that tested their resilience and exposed them to special care; and an upbringing that emphasized independence, competence, discipline with explanations (rather than physical punishment or withdrawal of love), and caring." Rescuers were loved, their interests encouraged, their accomplishments praised. Above all else, the most important criterion was that their families accepted people who were different.

Shakespeare wrote: "Some are born great, some achieve greatness, and some have greatness thrust upon them." While rescuers come in all three categories, the vast majority fall into the last—ordinary people who met an extraordinary moment and rose to the occasion. Most had not been figures like Mother Teresa or Albert Schweitzer who devoted their lives to helping the unfortunate. To the rescuers, what they did was simply the decent thing to do, and entirely normal; only the circumstances they faced were extraordinary. Yet Yukiko Sugihara believed that what was actually extraordinary was her family's opportunity to help others. She believed their life was much better for that opportunity and was grateful for it.

Rescue was hard work. In addition to the terrifying risk of exposure, it was a drain on time, resources, and emotion. "It is amazing how much noble, unselfish work these people are doing," Anne Frank wrote of those sheltering her family in Amsterdam. "Never had we heard one word of the burden which we certainly must be to them, never had one of them complained of all the trouble we give." Most rescues began with an informal request for help, according to Mordecai Paldiel, who reviewed thousands of cases during his twenty-four years as head of the department of the Righteous at Yad Vashem. He has concluded that the personal connection between survivor and rescuer—whether stranger, acquaintance, or friend—was key. "Most of the stories began with a face-to-face encounter of close proximity between a Jew on the run and a would-be rescuer," Paldiel reflected. " 'Can I stay over at your house for just one night?' And then that one night can turn to two nights, then three nights. When the rescuer looked into the eyes of those people and saw the misery, he couldn't help himself, he had to do something." While some rescues followed deep contemplation, it was more often a spontaneous reaction at the start. As one rescuer, Otto Springer, said, "The hand of compassion was faster than the calculus of reason."

———

There is no one formula for rescue, but we can try to look for repeated patterns in the mosaic of stories. One of the strongest correlations seems to be having a lifelong religious conviction, particularly if it was intrinsic and internal rather than based on social and hierarchical desires. Such rescuers believed that they were answerable to a higher authority. In some cases they defied their own church or committed minor ethical lapses, such as lying, in the service of saving lives. The teachings of kindness, of helping one's neighbor, and of the importance of universal brotherhood inspired them to great courage and virtue. The Parable of the Good Samaritan alone saved many lives. A belief in God's unfiltered teachings also reinforced the three criterion that seemed most important in creating a rescuer: a belief in a higher spiritual authority than the government, a respect for the humanity of all people, and a thought system that encouraged noble action and caring for others, even if it meant thinking and acting on one's own.

The belief in something greater allowed individuals to see the moral failings of the totalitarian system. Cultural codes—a deep tradition of hospitality, a history of experiencing persecution, a society marked by tolerance and welcoming, a creed of nonviolence—could also be critical. A belief in human rights, in liberal democracy, and in international law were often motivating factors. Even the military code of honor, whether followed by prisoners of war or ordinary officers, trumped the politics of individual nations.

Those who were in professions such as diplomacy that caused them to travel, to interact with foreigners, and to work collaboratively were more likely to be found among the rescuers. People in jobs focused on helping—doctors, nurses, social workers, and the like—were likewise more likely to intervene. Educational background does not seem to have played a role. Many highly educated academics, lawyers, judges, and intellectuals were among the most ardent Nazis. But those in international communities—like businessmen, spies, and professional athletes—seemed disproportionately disposed to adopt a more tolerant approach to others. Similarly, those involved in creative endeavors where the individual's unique output is valued, from circus performers to chefs to amateur artists, seemed more likely to be rescuers.

Some rescues were based on personal loyalty, prior relationships, or kindnesses previously received. Some rescuers were driven to help Jews because they were also enemies of fascism or Nazism. The partisans saw the obsession of the Nazis with the Jews as another pathology to combat. Also, one did not need to like Jews to believe that they should not be killed. As Paldiel explains, it was sufficient to reject the premise that someone did not have a right to live simply because he had been born.

The terrible behavior of groups is critical to how the Holocaust happened. John Stuart Mill declared, "Bad men need nothing more to compass their ends, than that good men should look on and do nothing." Most striking is when this concept is turned upside down. The positive behavior of a group such as a whole community was often extremely powerful. When a group of people made a decision to all stand together, they were often able to thwart the Nazis. Edmund Burke once said, "When bad men combine, the good must associate; else they will fall one by one." As we have seen in Le Chambon, several small villages could work together to save thousands of refugees. Similar events happened in towns like Secchiano in Italy and Nieuwlande in the Netherlands. The island of Zakynthos in the Ionian Sea refused to turn over its two hundred Jews to the Nazis. And even more dramatically, almost the entire country of Denmark successfully prevented the roundup of their fellow Jewish citizens, and did not give up their efforts until the end of the war. Nor was Denmark an entirely unique example. The Bulgarian Jews were also almost entirely saved, as was the small Jewish community in Finland. And when the Nazis made up their infamous country-by-country list at the Wannsee Conference that decided the Final Solution, it included not only the 2.6 million in Poland, but also the 200 in Albania. Yet the Muslim country of Albania, adhering to *besa*, its iron-clad code of hospitality, hid not only most of its own Jews but many refugees who had fled to its mountains and hills. It is believed that every Jew in Albania survived the war.

When people take a stand together, even anonymously, it can make a difference. This is why those who went along with the initial boycotts of Jewish businesses in Germany in 1933, just months after Hitler assumed the chancellorship, emboldened the Nazis to take far more drastic steps. Even quiet but determined passive support for rescue and resistance can be critical. "For three years our neighbors put up a protective shield around us by acting as if they did not notice anything," one Dutch rescuer recalled. "We [the rescuers] were only the tip of the iceberg." In addition, when a community had a generally tolerant culture, as in the Netherlands, rescuers were often people of the mainstream, making their actions somewhat easier, whereas in places like Poland, where anti-Semitism was rampant, they tended to be outsiders, from the margins of society. A community's values dictate behavior across the board.

It is hard to generalize about rescuers, in the end, but that too is part of their power. "Try as we might," writes Patrick Henry, "they always elude our grasp whenever we attempt to seize them collectively. This mystery of goodness is uplifting. The rescuers embody the moral potential that makes us proud to be human beings. But when we look at the people of Europe as a whole from 1933 to 1945, the mystery of why and how so few cared about the fate of so many darkens the horizon."

———

What can we do to make a world more like the one the rescuers believed in, to help us combat hatred and make our society a better place? We may never have an inoculation against prejudice, but we can do our best to create a community that will resist the pathogen. The most important thing we can do is to educate and raise our children with the values of tolerance, openness, and universal respect, and with a strong moral compass. We can value them and love them and treat them fairly, and instill in them a belief that an individual can make a difference. We do this most impactfully through our own actions if we are to believe Albert Schweitzer, who said, "Example is not the main thing in influencing others. It is the only thing." Indeed, 89 percent of Fogelman's subjects had a parent or other adult who acted as an altruistic role model. We can further encourage creativity and kindness, exposure to other peoples and cultures, and reinforce the importance of something beyond ourselves and our selfish interests, including spirituality, a free society, and a common international law.

Who and what we value says a great deal about our society. We seem to live in decadent times, when we too often value people who have accumulated money, fame, or power regardless of how they have done so. In a talk about rescue, Abe Foxman once asked a group of high-school girls how they would wish to value their lives: "What is most important at the end of the day? How much money you have in the bank, how many titles you are given, how many likes on your social media post you received? Or how much you have made a positive impact on other people's lives?" But one way we can change this is to focus on stories of those like the Righteous Among the Nations, who risked their lives to save others and who abided by an inner morality when the rest of society fell apart around them, giving itself up to its basest instincts.

There are, every day, people who selflessly rise to the occasion as heroes. There are so many stories that have not been told, not just from the Holocaust or other genocides, but whenever humanity is confronted with evil or devastation. We should seek them out, celebrate them, reward them, and hold them up as exemplars. "If now we find such gems, we dare not let them lie in the dust of ages," the humanitarian Henrietta Szold said. They are the best of us, and the more we aspire to be like them as a group and as individuals, the better will be the world we live in.

Small gestures make a difference. They improve the world and make others' lives better. We are not all given the opportunity to make epochal change, but we can all contribute to the project of improving the world. "It is not your obligation to finish the work," says the Talmud, "but neither are you free to refrain from it." Even at the worst of times, as we know from Holocaust survivor testimonies, a friendly word or moral support can mean everything. Not everyone, thankfully, is presented with life-and-death situations, but we can all speak out against injustice and stand in solidarity with the persecuted to let them know they are not alone. In our everyday lives, we can all stick up for someone being bullied, help the poor and the sick and the indigent and the frightened, provide encouragement where there is none, or even show kindness to a friend going through a difficult time. Everything matters, and some seemingly insignificant effort may have positive reverberations we cannot even imagine.

Hannah Senesh was a Hungarian-born poet who moved to Israel. In her early twenties, she volunteered as an agent for the British military and parachuted into the land of her birth to fight the Nazis and to try to save other Jews. Like the White Rose, she was captured and executed. She once wrote about those who risked their lives to save others: "There are stars whose radiance is visible on earth though they have long been extinct. There are people whose brilliance continues to light the world though they are no longer among the living. These lights are particularly bright when the night is dark. They light the way for Mankind."

If you take your inspiration from the rescuers and bring kindness and compassion and courage with you, you will make the world a better place.

And then you, too, will walk in the footsteps of the righteous.

Acknowledgments

THIS BOOK IS, IN LARGE PART, ABOUT GRATITUDE. AND I AM PROFOUNDLY GRATE-ful to the many people who have generously offered their help, time, and energy and whose contributions have been critical to this project. They often say that books are solitary endeavors but the best part of this one has, in fact, been meeting, working, and collaborating with so many wonderful people who have shared my passion for telling the stories of the rescuers.

First, my profound thanks to my amazing agent, Jennifer Joel, of ICM Partners, who has been a tireless advocate for this book from the beginning and whose advice—literary, personal, and commercial—has been invaluable. Jenn is a dynamo and I feel very lucky to have her as both a friend and adviser.

My wonderful editor Gail Winston at Harper is nothing short of spectacular, and I am so fortunate that she wanted to work on this book and with me. Gail worked magic on the manuscript, offering suggestions to story, prose, and structure that were invariably both wise and correct, as well as unflagging encouragement and support. She has been an exceptional coach, partner, and guide, and I am grateful to her for pushing me, with exceptional tact and diplomacy, to make the sometimes painful cuts that were necessary in the service of you, dear reader, and that have made this book much better.

My fabulous copyeditor, Miranda Ottewell, offered terrific suggestions on prose and grammar, protected me from errors, and offered encyclopedic knowledge of all things from horse riding to botany to Portuguese geography. Thank you also to Rebecca Holland and Hayley Salmon for all their hard work on the myriad things necessary to prepare this book for publication and making sure it is as good as it could possibly be. I am very proud to have Harper as my publisher and would like to thank the entire team there, including Tina Andreadis, Jonathan Burnham, Rachel Elinsky, Jocelyn Larnick, Jared Oriel, Elina Cohen, Becca Putman, and Brian Murray. Thank you also to Norman Courtright, who did exceptional work obtaining the photographic images that illustrate this volume.

I would like to thank those kind editors who initially published the articles that were the foundation of this book, including Jim Dao at the *New York Times*, Susan Brenneman at the *Los Angeles Times*, Paul Gigot and Mark Lasswell at the *Wall Street Journal*, and my Yale classmate John Avlon at the *Daily Beast*, who also encouraged me to turn the idea into a broader project. Claire Wachtel brought a keen editorial eye, provided critical suggestions and insights to early chapters of the manuscript, and helped inform the structure of the book.

The research behind these stories has been a significant effort and I am fortunate to have had support from several talented and brilliant researchers who proved themselves wizards in locating documents and information, no matter how obscure, in archives, in libraries, and in cyberspace, including Luke Cregan, Britt O'Daly, John Bennett, and Lesley Keene. As the project neared completion, Caroline Parker was truly incredible at proofreading, formatting citations, and fact-checking everything, from what films played in Bordeaux in June 1940 to the proper name of Elsinore castle to what time of night the invasion of Italy took place. This book could not have been done without them. Any errors, however, are entirely mine.

This book involved primary research in nearly a dozen languages, and I am grateful to the amazing translators who parsed through illegible eighty-year-old documents and largely inaudible interviews, including Anna Quarta, Maria Persinos, Helena Salarini, and Ewa Stoch. I am particularly indebted to the incredible Sim Smiley, who expertly navigated archives around the world, flawlessly translated materials in French, Italian, and occasionally Spanish, served as interpreter for a number of interviews, and has for some years dealt with innumerable impossible requests from the author, all with great professionalism, intelligence, and aplomb.

A number of Holocaust survivors generously shared their stories and reflections with me, including Peter Feigl; Hanne and Max Liebman; Ann Wallersteiner Dorzback, who spoke to me about her childhood best friend, Sophie Scholl; Fred Einstein; Justus Rosenberg; and Elie Wiesel. A number of children and grandchildren of rescuers also kindly offered their thoughts and memories of their relatives, which were truly priceless in telling these stories. Thank you to Gioia Bartali; Abigail Endicott Bingham, Robert Kim Bingham, William Bingham, and Tiffany Bingham; Nobuki Sugihara; Rob Zwartendijk; James Fry; Nelly Trocmé Hewitt; and Marie-Rose de Sousa Mendes, Gérald Mendes, and Aristides Sousa Mendes. Thank you as well to Nardo Bonomi Braverman, who graciously provided information about his cousins Giorgio Goldenberg and Aurelio Klein.

Many experts and scholars generously shared their knowledge, contacts, and insights. Abraham Foxman has been an ally, cheerleader, supporter, and advocate of this book from the beginning, and has spent many hours talking to me about the Righteous, their stories, and their importance. I cannot thank him enough. Mordecai Paldiel, the longtime director of the Department of the Righteous at Yad Vashem and among the world's leading experts on rescue, graciously reviewed the manuscript and offered his well-considered views on rescuer motivation. I am also grateful to Olivia Mattis, president of the Sousa Mendes Foundation, who provided unfettered access to the foundation's remarkable archives and many crucial introductions; Stuart Eizenstat, America's foremost diplomat on Holocaust issues and a strong advocate of this project; and Pierre Sauvage, director of the definitive Le Chambon documentary *Weapons of the Spirit* and head of the Le Chambon Foundation and the Varian Fry Institute, who generously shared his insights and knowledge on both Le Chambon and the ERC.

Other scholars who took the time to speak with me and provide critical assistance and who I am profoundly grateful to include: the cyclist and scholar Paolo Alberati, Natalia Indrimi of the Primo Levi Center, and the director Oren Jacoby on the Gino Bartali story; Eric Saul of the Institute for the Study of Rescue and Altruism in the Holocaust, an exceptional expert on rescue in general and diplomatic rescuers in particular and who also kindly provided some of the photographs for the book; Jack Mayer, whose book on Irena Sendler was the first to tell her story in the United States; and Le Chambon scholars Patrick Henry and Paul Kutner who shared their extensive knowledge of the plateau. Without librarians and archivists there is no scholarship, and numerous archivists, museum officials, and librarians throughout the world offered critical access and assistance, even as we navigated the coronavirus pandemic. These include, in particular, Eillene Leistner and Joel Zisenwine of Yad Vashem; Susan Gibbons, chief librarian of Yale, and Bill Landis, Michael Frost, and Kevin Glick of Manuscripts and Archives at Yale; and Patricia Heberer-Rice and Rebecca Erbelding of the United States Holocaust Memorial Museum.

Many others have provided advice, input, help, introductions, moral support, friendship, and encouragement. Among those who have my deepest thanks for kindnesses large and small (but all important), and in no particular order other than alphabetical are: Michael Abramowitz, Elliot Ackerman, Matteo Bologna, Tina Brown, Paul Burke, Leslie Cahmi, Jennifer Chaitman, Thierry Colin, Thomas Demand, Faye DeWitt, Irene Dorzback, Monica Dugot, Marc Faber, James Grant, Mark Greenberg, Emily Hamilton, Steven Hurowitz, Tia

Ikemoto, Thomas Kaplan, Yaakov Kermaier, Igor Kirman, Bernard-Henri Lévy, Lawrence Levy, Keith Lieberthal, Aaron Lobel, David Meyers, David Millstone, Sam Munson, David Nasaw, Jud Newborn, H.R.H. Prince Pavlos of Greece, Matthew Pearl, Margarida Ramalho, Maurice Samuels, Stacy Schiff, Danny Schwartz, Shaheen Shah, James Shapiro, Daniel Shuchman, Alexander Steinberg, Caroline Steinberg, Stephanie and Marc Steinberg, Michael Steinhardt, Katia Trocmé, Sindhu Vegesana, Peter Wand, Shelley Wanger, and Lucas Wittman. I would also like to thank my late mother, Susie Hurowitz, and my father, Monte Hurowitz, for their love and support and for everything they have given me. I truly have had wonderful parents.

Most of all, I would like to thank my incredible family. My children's interest in this book has been beyond gratifying and gave me added inspiration to write it. Both have been enthusiastic supporters of the project in every way. My son, Asher, gave me wonderful stories and ideas on rescue wherever he found them, many of which made their way into this book, offered insights from his wide breadth of knowledge and interests, and is a passionate supporter of my creative endeavors. My daughter, Sasha, shares a strong passion for twentieth-century history, for current events and the world around us, and for understanding the moral choices in the Holocaust, about which she offered many valuable insights, and she is a fierce advocate for her father's writing. I cherish my special dialogue with both, which has enriched my own understanding of the themes of this book and of life in general. Above all, I am so grateful for the joy both of you have given me and for your kindness, creativity, and love. I could not have asked for two more wonderful children, and I thank God every day for the blessing of being your parent. And thank you, of course, to my amazing, talented, beautiful, and brilliant wife, Sharon. I am so fortunate to have her as my partner in everything. She is a wonder and her style, flair, sense of humor, passion, and insights added greatly to this book and, in fact, to everything we do together. Our marriage and our family are the best things that ever happened to me. I love all three of you more than words can say.

August 2022

Notes

NOTE ON SOURCES

THIS BOOK IS BASED ON SIGNIFICANT RESEARCH IN PRIMARY AND SECONDARY
materials. I have consulted archival materials on multiple continents
in many languages, including English, French, Portuguese, Italian,
German, Greek, Polish, Hebrew, Yiddish, and Dutch. This includes
the files kept at the Department of the Righteous at Yad Vashem in
Jerusalem for each rescuer who has received that award. I have spoken,
where possible, to eyewitnesses and those who knew the individuals in
this volume personally, including their families. I have also consulted
many of the world's leading experts on rescue in general, and on the
particular countries and cases that are contained in the stories herein. I
have included detailed citations of sources in the endnotes and a bibliography of works consulted.

Any work of history is at best an honest attempt to report what
actually happened. In any such attempt, a historian encounters on a
constant basis inconsistencies. People's recollections of the same events
differ, certainly with time but even in the immediate aftermath of
events. Certain details can also simply be lost to time if they were not
recorded. I have done my best in this volume to refer only to details of

which I have confirmation. Where there are conflicting narratives of the same events, I have chosen the one that I believe is the most likely and tried to cite references to alternatives. And for information that is questionable, I have erred on the side of not including it. There are some stories, including from survivors, that I am actually convinced are accurate, but for which I could not find corroboration, and so I have not included them. For others, I have included the questions raised in the endnotes. The extensive bibliography also provides the reader with the opportunity to go much deeper into any of these stories and weigh the evidence for themselves.

This book is intended for a general audience. However, as I have become immersed in these stories, I am aware of certain historical and historiographical debates regarding specific rescuers. For those audiences that are deeply involved in these questions, I would like to note a few things. There has arisen in recent years questions about the extent of Gino Bartali's rescue activities. I have spoken to some of those who have questioned the story, who generally have a belief that eyewitness testimony can never be reliable. But for a story of a clandestine network during wartime, there will by definition never be much more than eyewitness testimony available. In the Bartali case, I have examined almost all documents and sources available, including Bartali's own unpublished will and the property records of Florence. Testimony regarding Bartali's activities dates back decades, and to question it, one would have to believe that many people who never met each other—including nuns, children, and soldiers—coordinated a grand conspiracy to fabricate the story. Some of those who question the story also question the incontrovertible evidence that Italians as a group did much to save Jews in their territories.

Certain details of the story of Chiune Sugihara are murky, and I have done my best to reconstruct what occurred. The timeline of his correspondence with Tokyo is particularly complicated. Questions about his attendance at a Hanukkah party in Kovno have been raised, and I have included the version of that story which I believe, based on consultation with many authorities, to be historically accurate. Similarly, the exact timeline of Aristides de Sousa Mendes's actions on the ground in June 1940 and certain of Irena Sendler's actions in Warsaw are also somewhat conflicting. I have done my best to reconstruct them from multiple sources.

While there is no question that Hiram Bingham was a critical part of Varian Fry's rescue efforts, some have pointed to anti-Semitic and conspiracy-theory ramblings he made very late in his life. I agree with a survivor who said that what mattered was what he did in Marseille, not what he may have believed as an elderly person. In Le Chambon, the role of Major Julius Schmähling in preventing round-ups on the plateau has been the subject of a great deal of controversy among survivors, which I believe detracts from the broader story, so I have included only that information which is largely beyond doubt. However, I do believe that Schmähling was at a minimum a moderating influence. Some have also criticized scholars of Le Chambon for not giving sufficient credit to other pastors and overemphasizing the Trocmés, but it is in my view hard to dispute their central role.

Any anecdotes or stories that I believed were suspicious—and there were some—I have not included. It is important that all historical evidence be carefully studied, weighed, and analyzed without any prior agenda. I have tried to do so here as best I can, as a trained historian and lawyer. I have also tried to include as much evidence as possible in the endnotes, but they can never be comprehensive, and to have included all the information I have reviewed would have required a volume far too long. I welcome feedback from readers and from any of the scholars who have devoted themselves to the stories of the Holocaust and of rescue I have told in this book.

Introduction

xii "What I want most of all": Scholl, *White Rose*, 12.

xiii "Finally, a man has the courage": Scholl, 20.

xiii "Every honest German today": Scholl, 79.

xiii "in the most bestial way": Scholl, 78.

xiii They pulled no punches: Scholl, 85.

xiii Sprinkled with erudite references: Scholl, 88.

xiv "There are half starved children": Dupas and Harper, "Bad Conscience."

xiv "We will have to let the truth ring out": Scholl, *White Rose*, 36.

xiv "Are we forever to be a nation": Scholl, 89.

xv "There is a higher court": Scholl, 59.

xv "Long live freedom": Scholl, 62.

xv "What we wrote and said": Sophie Scholl, statement to court, February 21, 1943, in Richard F. Hanser, *A Noble Treason: The Story of Sophie Scholl and the White Rose Revolt Against Hitler* (New York: G. P. Putnam, 1979), 38.

xvi "to vindicate the righteous": 2 Chron. 6:23.

xvi As of 2021, over twenty-seven thousand: Yad Vashem, "Names of Righteous by Country," https://www.yadvashem.org/righteous/statistics.html.

xvii "Why did the Polish farmer": Paldiel, interview.

xviii "Which code of ethics": Fogelman, *Conscience and Courage*, 12.

xviii "Darkness cannot drive out darkness": Martin Luther King Jr., *Strength to Love* (New York: Harper & Row, 1963), 37.

xviii "We must know": Rittner and Meyers, *The Courage to Care*, 2.

xviii "In the darkness": Hausner, *Justice in Jerusalem*, quoted in Fogelman, *Conscience and Courage*, 301.

xviii "saved hope and faith in the human spirit": "The Dedication of the Avenue of the Righteous Among the Nations," in *I Am My Brother's Keeper*, Yad Vashem, https://www.yadvashem.org/yv/en/exhibitions/righteous/milestone05.asp.

xix "The existence of rescuers": Bauer, *Rethinking the Holocaust*, xi.

xix "For the first fifty years": Henry, *We Only Know Men*, 144.

xix The filmmaker Pierre Sauvage: "Bill Moyers Interviews Filmmaker Pierre Sauvage," PBS, aired August 9, 1990.

xxii "We must carry his spirit": Mináč, *Nicky's Family*.

xxiii "There are no Jews in Morocco": Hurowitz, "You Must Remember This."

xxiii It is what the philosopher: Lévy, *The Will to See.*

xxiv "I believe that it was really": Henry, *We Only Know Men*, 170.

xxv "Pharaoh's daughter did not": Sacks, "Light at the Heart of Darkness"; see also Jonathan Sacks, "Women as Leaders," Rabbi Sacks Legacy Trust, Covenant and Conversation, https://www.rabbisacks.org/covenant-conversation/shemot/women-as-leaders/.

xxv According to Jewish tradition: Sacks, "Light at the Heart of Darkness"; Derekh Eretz Zuta 1.

xxv "Although Moses had many names": Shemot Rabbah 1:26.

xxvi "We cannot raise the question": Boethius, *Consolation of Philosophy*, book 1, sec. 4.

xxvi The acts of the rescuers: Henry, *We Only Know Men*, 140.

1. We Are All Refugees

3 They brought it back: Borden, *Journey That Saved Curious George.*

3 more than seventy-five million: Judith Rosen, "Curious George Turns 75," *Publishers Weekly*, August 12, 2016.

6 Whenever they were home: Aristides de Sousa Mendes, file M.31 /264, Yad Vashem Archives, Jerusalem (henceforth Yad Vashem Archives).

7 Sousa Mendes was constantly expanding: Sousa Mendes, Yad Vashem Archives.

9 "behind that cold exterior": Gallagher, "Life and Afterlife of Salazar."

10 "Take Versailles": Victor Hugo, *En voyage*, vol. 1, *Le Rhin: Lettres à un ami* (Paris: Librarie Ollendorf, 1906).

11 "The fear of Hitler": Sousa Mendes, Yad Vashem Archives.

13 On November 11, 1939: Minister Luis Teixeira de Sampaio, Circular 14, in English and Portuguese, Sousa Mendes Foundation Archives, Greenlawn, New York (henceforth Sousa Mendes Foundation Archives).

13 "I considered that it was a duty": Aristides de Sousa Mendes, statement of defense in the disciplinary proceedings brought against him, August 10, 1940, Sousa Mendes Foundation Archives.

13 "A university professor": Franco, *Spared Lives.*

13 He defended himself: Sousa Mendes, statement of defense.

14 "Any new fault": Franco, *Spared Lives.*

14 Aristides wrote to his brother: Sousa Mendes, Yad Vashem Archives.

14   "Visas to clean people": Sousa Mendes; Franco, *Spared Lives*.

14   "check thoroughly if those": Sousa Mendes, Yad Vashem Archives.

15   Sousa Mendes met Chaim Kruger: "Aristides de Sousa Mendes: The Courage to Defy; Themes, a Tribute to the Righteous Among the Nations," Yad Vashem, https://www.yadvashem.org/yv/en/exhibitions/righteous/mendes.asp.

16   "Why, in the street": Sousa Mendes, Yad Vashem Archives; Harry Ezratty, "The Portuguese Consul and the 10,000 Jews," *Jewish Life*, September-October 1964, Sousa Mendes Foundation Archives.

16   Sousa Mendes confided: Sousa Mendes, Yad Vashem Archives. The name Mendes means "New Christian," and Beira Alta, where Sousa Mendes was from, was one of two northern areas once known as the Jewish Provinces.

16   "No Jew is safe": Sousa Mendes.

16   "It's not just me that needs help": Fralon, *Good Man*, 57.

16   "All of a sudden": Fralon, 59.

17   "The situation here": Aristides de Sousa Mendes to his brother-in-law Silvério de Sousa Mendes, June 13, 1940, De Winter family collection, Sousa Mendes Foundation Archives.

17   "There were lots of old and sick people": Sousa Mendes, Yad Vashem Archives.

17   "I am sure there will be": Pedro Nuno Sousa Mendes, "Que o meu pai sirva de exemplo."

17   "shipwrecked": Sousa Mendes, Yad Vashem Archives.

18   "My father got up": Fralon, *Good Man*, 57.

18   "Look, Gigi," he told her: Pedro Nuno Sousa Mendes, "Que o meu pai sirva de exemplo"; Sousa Mendes, Yad Vashem Archives.

18   "I cannot allow": Sousa Mendes, Yad Vashem Archives; Paldiel, *Diplomat Heroes*.

18   "I have it all in my hands now": d'Avranches, *Flight through Hell*, 56.

18   "I am going to issue": Sousa Mendes, Yad Vashem Archives; Sousa Mendes Foundation website, sousamendesfoundation.org; d'Avranches, *Flight through Hell*, 56; Pedro Nuno Sousa Mendes, interview by Marta Vitorino.

18   "I know that Mrs. de Sousa Mendes": Sousa Mendes, Yad Vashem Archives; d'Avranches, *Flight through Hell*, 56.

18   "I would rather stand": d'Avranches, *Flight through Hell*, 56.

19   He set up a veritable: Ezratty, "Portuguese Consul and the 10,000 Jews," 17–20.

19 "For the sake of your wife": Fralon, *Good Man*, 62.

19 The American consulate: Sousa Mendes, Yad Vashem Archives.

19 "It is a fantastic commentary": Thompson, *Refugees*, 28.

19 One of their sons played: Sousa Mendes, Yad Vashem Archives.

19 His signature morphed: Images of Sousa Mendes's signature, artifact boxes 1–6, Sousa Mendes Foundation Archives.

19 "Come back when the dictator": Fralon, *Good Man*, 62.

19 "Visas have been issued outside": Fralon, 62.

20 "He did not eat": Sousa Mendes, Yad Vashem Archives.

20 "My attitude was motivated": Sousa Mendes, statement of defense.

20 His son recalled one eight-year-old girl: Fralon, *Good Man*, 63.

20 "My uncle turned the offer": Sousa Mendes, Yad Vashem Archives.

20 "filled with pity": Dr. Charles Oulmont to Mrs. Joana Mendes, February 7, 1968, Sousa Mendes Foundation Archives.

20 A French ambassador: Sousa Mendes, Yad Vashem Archives.

21 Many other prominent leaders: Register of Sousa Mendes visa recipients, Sousa Mendes Foundation Archives.

21 "There was something": Sousa Mendes, statement of defense.

22 *Adventures of Sherlock Holmes*: "Les Spectacles," *La Petite Gironde*, June 18, 1940, https://www.retronews.fr/journal/la-petite-gironde/18-jun-1940/241/1383189/1.

22 "The Ministry is concerned": Sousa Mendes, Yad Vashem Archives.

23 Sousa Mendes confronted the local consul: d'Avranches, *Flight through Hell*, 59.

24 "The Portuguese government requests": Sousa Mendes, Yad Vashem Archives.

25 "We wanted to keep out": Armando Lopo Simeão, report on special mission to Bayonne, July 1, 1940, Sousa Mendes Foundation Archives.

25 The pro-Axis Teotónio Pereira: Madrid Embassy to Foreign Ministry of Portugal, June 25, 1940, Sousa Mendes Foundation; Franco, *Spared Lives*; Sousa Mendes, Yad Vashem Archives.

25 Simeão telegrammed: Armando Lopo Simeão to Foreign Ministry, June 23, 1940, Sousa Mendes Foundation Archives.

25 He was there on June 23: Sousa Mendes, Yad Vashem Archives.

25 "out of his mind": Madrid Embassy to Foreign Ministry, June 25, 1940; Teotónio Pereira, statement to Salazar, Sousa Mendes Foundation Archives.

25 "All visas issued in Bordeaux": Sousa Mendes, Yad Vashem Archives.

26 "I'm the Portuguese consul": Sousa Mendes, Yad Vashem Archives; Fralon, *Good Man*, 95.

26 Permission was immediately: Sousa Mendes.

26 "To refuse a visa": Francisco de Paula Brito, "Nota de Culpa: Examination of Guilt," August 1, 1940, Sousa Mendes Foundation Archives.

26 a local newspaper in San Sebastian: Sousa Mendes, Yad Vashem Archives.

26 "lucid and determined": Pedro Teotónio Pereira, deposition, July 26, 1940, Sousa Mendes Foundation Archives.

26 Other eyewitnesses begged to differ: Fralon, *Good Man*, 83–84.

27 A Viennese Jewish: Marguerite Rollin to David Alcalay, March 4, 1966, Sousa Mendes Foundation Archives.

27 "By day Lisbon": Erich Maria Remarque, *The Night in Lisbon: A Novel*, trans. Ralph Manheim (1964; repr., New York: Random House, 2014), 111–12.

28 Simeão testified that: Simeão, report.

28 "slime": Simeão, report.

28 "allowed himself to be overcome": Francisco de Calheiros e Menezes, statement in defense of Aristides de Sousa Mendes, Sousa Mendes Foundation Archives.

29 "My aim was first and foremost": Sousa Mendes, statement of defense.

29 Sousa Mendes strongly disputed: Franco, *Spared Lives*.

29 "You are the best advertisement": Sousa Mendes, Yad Vashem Archives.

30 "It may be that I made mistakes": Sousa Mendes.

30 "caused a situation": Count Tovar, report on the disciplinary proceedings of Aristides de Sousa Mendes, October 19, 1940, Sousa Mendes Foundation Archives.

30 But it was Salazar's friend: Franco, *Spared Lives*; Tovar, report.

30 "One cannot find any remorse": Tovar, report.

30 Salazar personally sealed: Statement of Ministry of Foreign Affairs, Secretariat General, October 30, 1940, Sousa Mendes Foundation Archives.

31 "the powerful imperatives": Fralon, *Good Man*, 118.

31 "one of the largest in Portugal": Sousa Mendes, Yad Vashem Archives; Aristides de Sousa Mendes, appeal to Salazar, 1940s, Sousa Mendes Foundation Archives; Fralon, *Good Man*, 118.

31 "a civil servant is not competent": Tovar, report.

31 At one point: Sousa Mendes, Yad Vashem Archives; Abranches, interview.

31 Sousa Mendes was sanguine: Sousa Mendes.

31 "If thousands of Jews": Chaim Kruger, "Der Portugeser Konsul" (interview), *Yiddish Daily* [*Der Tog*], August 8, 1941, Sousa Mendes Foundation Archives.

31 To its credit: Sousa Mendes, Yad Vashem Archives.

32 It provided him with a monthly stipend: The stipend was 3,000 escudos. Sousa Mendes would not, however, take anything from any refugee he saved, many of whom were unaware of the consequences he had suffered. He maintained, his son noted, an "absolute refusal to receive any monetary compensation from the refugees seeking asylum in Portugal." Sousa Mendes, Yad Vashem Archives.

32 "Impressed by his presence": Sousa Mendes; Isaac Bitton to Mrs. Diana Adringa, January 15, 1992, and Isaac Bitton to John Paul Abranches, September 14, 1986, Sousa Mendes Foundation Archives.

32 "As long as Salazar": Goebbels, *Diaries*, March 6, 1943.

32 "Mr. Sousa Mendes never": Sousa Mendes, Yad Vashem Archives.

33 "As regards the refugees": Fralon, *Good Man*, 122. A different translation, giving a date of May 18, is at https://holocaustremembrance.blog /2017/12/14/aristides-de-sousa-mendes-resisting-refugee-policy-in-port ugal/, citing publication of Salazar's papers in 1951 in Portuguese.

33 He wrote again: Aristides de Sousa Mendes, protest, December 10, 1945, Sousa Mendes Foundation Archives.

33 "praise of the administration": Sousa Mendes, Yad Vashem Archives.

33 "Papa always showed": Luís Filipe de Sousa Mendes, "Memories of Luís Filipe de Sousa Mendes," 1987, private collection of Gérald Mendes.

33 Sousa Mendes wrote to every member: Sousa Mendes, protest.

34 How horrible could the dictator be: In 1970, one of Mendes's daughters felt compelled to write strongly to Yad Vashem in response to rumors that either Franco or Salazar might be made a Righteous Among the Nations following the appearance of many articles about their offering refuge to those fleeing Nazism. "I know it is easy for them to get these articles published because they have great influence over the press but one thing is sure: They never rescued nor helped the Jews in their time of terror and despair. . . . Now because they have a guilty conscience they are taking advantage of their high positions to mislead the world with their fallacies and to make people believe they were saviors of the Jews." She further wrote, "What the Government [of Portugal] wants is to take away the glory from my father to have the whole world believe that Salazar was the savior of the Jews in 1939 and 1940, he who had no scruples in forbidding my father to issue visas to Jews and then later

to punish him severely for having disobeyed his orders. If only my father's humanitarian action could be known around the world it would have a decisive impact and the Portuguese [sic] Government would be forced to reject his unjust desire to enjoy the fame he does not deserve." Correspondence between Joana Mendes and Moshe Landau, President, Commission for the Righteous, Yad Vashem. An article titled "How Salazar Aided Jews to Escape," with no byline, is annotated "This is completely untrue," "He never did!" and "This is the influx of refugees my father saved against the orders of Salazar." Sousa Mendes, Yad Vashem Archives. See also John Abranches, letter to the editor, *San Francisco Examiner*, December 25, 1968.

34 "Your Excellency no doubt": Fralon, *Good Man*, 124.

35 "had disobeyed an order": Sousa Mendes, Yad Vashem Archives.

35 "We had a lot of misery": Sousa Mendes.

35 When Sousa Mendes could no longer: Sousa Mendes.

35 The older children failed: Two of his sons fought for the United States, one landing in the Normandy invasion. Another fought in the Korean War.

35 The American Jewish Joint Distribution Committee: Sousa Mendes, Yad Vashem Archives.

35 "Anxiety and despair": Luís Filipe de Sousa Mendes, "Memories of Luís Filipe de Sousa Mendes," 1987, private collection of Gérald Mendes. "Both Father and Mother suffered in solitude as they witnessed the dispersion of their family," said their son Luís Filipe.

36 "He seemed at peace": Sousa Mendes, Yad Vashem Archives.

36 write the king of Belgium: Fralon, *Good Man*, 132. Members of the Belgian cabinet had been hosted in Sousa Mendes's home after their escape before moving on to the government-in-exile.

36 a local newspaper in the Belgian Congo: "A Great Friend of Belgium Is Dead," *Pourquoi Poi?*, April 26, 1954, Sousa Mendes Foundation Archives; Sousa Mendes, Yad Vashem Archives.

36 Salazar sent Cesar: Fralon, *Good Man*, 144.

36 "he had never regretted": Sousa Mendes, Yad Vashem Archives.

37 "I disobeyed": Sousa Mendes to his lawyer, January 1941, Sousa Mendes Foundation, https://sousamendesfoundation.org/the-timeline/.

37 "To his last days": Luís Filipe de Sousa Mendes, "Memories of Luís Filipe de Sousa Mendes," 1987, private collection of Gérald Mendes. "I am filled with emotion when I talk about him to my children, young adults of to-day. May this sacrifice of a true Portuguese fidalgo [sic] remain a source of inspiration for them as it is for myself."

37 "I shall tell the whole world": Sousa Mendes.

37   "Was he mad in showing": Fralon, *Good Man*, 146–47; Sousa Mendes, Yad Vashem Archives.

37   "extraordinary acts of mercy": Sousa Mendes.

37   A European stamp: Sousa Mendes.

37   "I believe that my father": Abranches, interview.

37   1,575 official visas: Sousa Mendes, Yad Vashem Archives.

38   "the largest rescue action": Bauer, *History of the Holocaust*, 249.

38   "I wanted to say to you": Otto von Habsburg to the grandson of Aristides de Sousa Mendes, António Pedro Moncada de Sousa Mendes, September 16, 1984, Sousa Mendes Foundation Archives.

2. Life in the Circus

39   an exquisite beauty: Prior, "Die Reiterin," 38–42.

40   "The world may be Balkanised": Kober, *Star Turns*, xv.

40   "Wherever variety or circus artists": Kober, 12.

41   Jeanette Meyer: Saltarino, *Artisten-Lexikon*, 129.

41   "A circus man": Kober, *Star Turns*, 45.

44   a circus journalist recalled: Kober, 53.

45   "one of the most technically proficient": D. Nevill, "Obituary: Adolf Althoff," *Independent*, October 21, 1998.

48   Her teacher personally led: Prior, "Die Reiterin."

49   afraid to go in the ring: Prior.

49   At fifteen, Irene was forbidden: Adolf and Maria Althoff, file M.31/6433, Yad Vashem Archives.

49   the Carolis received a letter: Prior, "Die Reiterin."

49   went to Italy: Althoff, Yad Vashem Archives. Peter Storms says Julius was in Belgium.

50   seven Ovitz siblings of Romania: Yehuda Koren and Eilat Negev, "The Dwarves of Auschwitz," *Guardian*, March 23, 2013.

50   an act with three elephants: *Rescue in the Circus: Righteous Among the Nations Adolf and Maria Althoff*, video, July 11, 2010, Yad Vashem, Jerusalem.

50   "The Three Bentos": Althoff, Yad Vashem Archives.

50   a poorly kept secret among her coworkers: Prior, "Die Reiterin."

50   both joined Adolf Althoff: "Peter Bento Storms," *Times* (London), June 17, 2013.

51 Irene and Peter fell in love: Althoff, Yad Vashem Archives.

51 Irene almost died: Althoff.

51 "What pig committed this crime?": Prior, "Die Reiterin."

51 "Without Dr. Grobe": Althoff, Yad Vashem Archives.

52 "You and your bastard": Althoff.

52 The great family house: Althoff.

52 Irene again prevailed upon: Althoff.

52 "There was no question": Rescue in a Circus, Yad Vashem.

52 he went underground: Althoff, Yad Vashem Archives.

52 "He was good to everybody": Prior, "Die Reiterin."

53 minor wartime luxuries: Prior.

53 "The years in the circus": Althoff, Yad Vashem Archives.

53 A subtle knock: Prior, "Die Reiterin."

53 Sometimes they would hide: Althoff, Yad Vashem Archives.

53 When there was no time: Prior, "Die Reiterin."

53 "developed a great skill": Althoff, Yad Vashem Archives.

53 as Adolf entertained the Gestapo: Prior, "Die Reiterin."

53 Althoff would turn on the charm: Prior.

54 "I kept telling them": Prior.

54 "One had to improvise": Prior.

54 "They admired our circus": Prior.

54 "saving our lives": Althoff, Yad Vashem Archives.

54 "People in the circus knew my opinion": Rescue in a Circus, Yad Vashem.

54 "Why are there Jews in this circus?": Rescue in a Circus.

55 When their children grew up: Prior, "Die Reiterin."

56 "Whoever once sniffs the ring air": Prior.

56 "His operation was regarded": Pace, "Adolf Althoff."

56 "It was only natural": Althoff, Yad Vashem Archives.

56 "What have I done that is so special?": Prior, "Die Reiterin."

56 "We circus people": Althoff, Yad Vashem Archives.

56 "Without their help": Althoff.

3. On the Glory of Athens

57   "If you wish to hang me": "Special Issue: The Jews of Greece," *Hellenic News of America*, January 29, 2017.

57   "our prelates are hung and not shot": "The Holocaust in Greece: Athens," United States Holocaust Memorial Museum, https://www.ushmm.org /information/exhibitions/online-exhibitions/special-focus/holocaust-in -greece/athens.

58   "Berobed in the black garb": "Greece: If We Hold Fast," *Time*, October 1, 1945.

59   "a Jewish labor city": Naar, *Jewish Salonica*, 20

59   "Jerusalem of Turkey": Naar, 2.

61   "These books matter": Stein, *Family Papers*, 163.

62   "Salonika is filled": Stein, 167.

64   "We all decided to protest": Matsas, *Illusion of Safety*, 56.

64   "a protest by the totality": Matsas, 56.

65   "Let no one forget": "Protest by Archbishop Damaskinos and Greek Intellectuals against the Persecution of Greek Jewry," Shoah Resource Center, International School for Holocaust Studies, Yad Vashem, Jerusalem, https:// www.yadvashem.org/odot_pdf/Microsoft%20Word%20-%205114.pdf.

65   "no Jewish issues exist": Archbishop Damaskinos Papandreou, file M.31 /547, Yad Vashem Archives.

65   "those admirable and terrible Jews": Levi, *Survival in Auschwitz*, 71.

65   "their aversion to gratuitous brutality": Levi, 79.

66   "The Italians are extremely lax": Goebbels, *Diaries*, December 12, 1942.

66   "I have made my cross": Papandreou, Yad Vashem Archives.

67   Evert was joined: Papandreou.

68   "to the great chagrin": Angelos Evert, file M.31/553, Yad Vashem Archives.

68   "I followed this advice": Evert.

68   "provided counsel to Jews": Evert.

69   "the order that the priests should assist": Papandreou, Yad Vashem Archives.

69   at least 250 Jewish children: "Introduction to Rescue in Greece," Institute for the Study of Rescue and Altruism in the Holocaust, https://www.holo caustrescue.org/introduction-to-rescue-in-greece,

70   "Here is the list": Loukas Yiorgios Karrer, file M.31/1257, and Dimitrios Chrysostomos, file M.31/1257a, Yad Vashem Archives.

70 "the island of the just": Eptakili, "Greek Island That Hid Its Jews."

72 "As far as the Cohens": Princess Alice Battenberg, file M.31/5643, Yad Vashem Archives.

72 "very small, thin & dark": Queen Victoria, journal, February 25, 1885, queenvictoriasjournals.org.

73 "God will punish us severely": Ю.В. Клотц, "Great Russian Saint, Born in Germany," Язык. Культура. Образование 2 (2017): 83–87.

74 "Virtue with the crown on it": Shelley, *The Speckled Domes*, 220.

76 "moved deeply": "Greek Jews Mourn Metaxas, Foe of Anti-Semitism," *Jewish Telegraphic Agency*, Daily Bulletin, January 30, 1941.

78 Alice tried her best: Battenberg, Yad Vashem Archives.

80 "relentless in his devotion": Battenberg.

80 The Princess regularly visited: Battenberg.

81 "You can take your troops": Battenberg.

81 "She thus saved": Battenberg.

81 "living in humble": Macmillan, *War Diaries*, 558–59.

82 "They tell me that": Vickers, *Alice*, 311.

82 "We were very privileged": Battenberg, Yad Vashem Archives.

82 "She showed her courage": Battenberg.

83 "I expressed to her my sincerest thankfulness": Battenberg.

84 "In retrospect, this reticence": Battenberg.

4. Some Medals Are Pinned to Your Soul

85 "The ovations": McConnon and McConnon, *Road to Valor*, 85.

86 "They always tried to": Jacoby, *My Italian Secret*.

86 "Not a cat": McConnon and McConnon, *Road to Valor*, 86–87.

86 The Ufficio Stampa: McConnon and McConnon, 87.

86 "The party has started": Jacoby, *My Italian Secret*.

87 "A lot of time": Lazzerini and Beghelli, *La leggenda di Bartali*, 14, quoted in McConnon and McConnon, *Road to Valor*, 13.

88 "From that pile": Bartali and Pancera, *La mia storia*, 13–15, quoted in McConnon and McConnon, *Road to Valor*, 16.

88 "You can imagine": Bartali and Pancera, *La mia storia*, 16.

88   "When I descended into Florence": McConnon and McConnon, *Road to Valor*, 17.

88   "Despite their perfect bicycles": Bartali and Ricci, *Tutto sbagliato*, 16, quoted in McConnon and McConnon, *Road to Valor*, 23.

88   "I didn't want to disrespect him": Lazzerini and Beghelli, *La leggenda di Bartali*, 16.

89   "They took a bicycle": McConnon and McConnon, *Road to Valor*, 25.

89   "enchanted": Bartali and Pancera, *La mia storia*, 17.

89   When a friend attached: Bartali and Pancera, 19.

89   "One day you will bring": McConnon and McConnon, *Road to Valor*, 30.

89   "My heart leapt": Bartali and Pancera, *La mia storia*, 19.

89   "capacity for suffering": McConnon and McConnon, *Road to Valor*, 33.

89   "like the olive trees": McConnon and McConnon, 71.

90   "he looked like he was being electrocuted": McConnon and McConnon, 34.

90   "He was so embarrassed": Alberati, *Gino Bartali*, 48–49.

91   "The deepest sadness fell": Bartali and Ricci, *Tutto sbagliato*, 33.

91   "Politics is a trap": McConnon and McConnon, *Road to Valor*, 20.

92   "to understand that at the Tour": McConnon and McConnon, 52.

92   "A soldier who defends": McConnon and McConnon, 52.

93   "I had such great dreams": Bartali and Pancera, *La mia storia*, 46.

93   "When the doctor": Bartali and Ricci, *Tutto sbagliato*, 37–38.

93   "the greatest injustice": Lazzerini and Beghelli, *La leggenda di Bartali*, 73.

93   "There was nothing else to say": Bartali and Pancera, *La mia storia*, 47.

94   "now no force": Count Galeazzo Ciano, entry for May 9, 1938, *Diary, 1937–1943*, 89.

94   Forty-seven thousand Italian Jews: "L'Olocausto in Italia," Presidency of the Council of Minister, Italy, https://www.governo.it/sites/governo.it/files /olocausto_italia.pdf.

95   During Hitler's visit to Florence: McConnon and McConnon, *Road to Valor*, 64.

95   After his 1938 win at the Tour: Ministry of the Interior, Informant Report, October 11, 1938, quoted in Alberati, *Gino Bartali*, 174–75.

95   "The pedestal of fame": Bartali and Pancera, *La mia storia*, 51.

95 "reed-thin": McConnon and McConnon, *Road to Valor*, 95.

95 "A great tragedy": Lazzerini and Beghelli, *La leggenda di Bartali*, 109.

96 In the late 1920s: Nardo Bonomi Braverman, interview by author, February 2, 2022.

96 "I started to cry": Jacoby, *My Italian Secret*.

96 In June 1940: Gino Bartali, file M.31/12663, Yad Vashem Archives. Testimony here says this occurred on January 31, 1944, but the timing doesn't make sense.

97 Giorgio would keep: Bartali, Yad Vashem Archives.

97 "Bartali was a kind of demigod": McConnon and McConnon, *Road to Valor*, 100.

98 "Better a widow": Lazzerini and Beghelli, *La leggenda di Bartali*, 110.

99 the forty-three thousand Jews: "Italy," Holocaust Encyclopedia, United States Holocaust Memorial Museum, Washington, DC.

100 Bartali offered shelter: The provenance of the apartment is worth discussing. In Jacoby, *My Italian Secret*, Giorgio Goldenberg says his family was originally in the apartment, then moved to the basement. In the statement of Goldenberg's cousin Nardo Bonomi Braverman at Yad Vashem, Giorgio recalls the address as Via del Bandino, 45, but that the cellar was in a building next door. According to Yad Vashem, Braverman, with whom I also spoke directly, inspected the real estate registry of Florence, which confirmed Bartali as the owner of a property in Via del Bandino corresponding to 81 and 83, renamed Piazza Cardinale Elia dalla Costa, 7. Bartali owned individual apartments on the ground floor, floors 1–3, and the *sottosuolo*, or basement. When Goldenberg returned to Florence on June 2, 2011, and with Braverman visited Andrea and Adriana Bartali, he immediately recognized the courtyard that the cellar where he had been hidden faced. According to Gioia Bartali, Goldenberg also identified the street by its wartime name.

According to Bartali's will of May 21, 2000, which the author has inspected, the property at Via del Bandino, 81 (now Piazza Cardinale Elia dalla Costa, 7) was still in Bartali's possession when he died, property, Bartali says, "which had been my residence and that of my parents." More specifically, Bartali owned floors 2 and 3 at that time; he left them to his wife and subsequently, following her death, to their three children. According to Gioia Bartali, who subsequently inherited the property and its original plans, it had been built by Torello Bartali. She believes the basement was likely in an apartment two doors down from where her grandparents and father lived, also owned by Bartali, that faced the garden in the courtyard Goldenberg recognized. The author undertook an independent investigation of the Real Estate Registry of Florence in November 2021 and confirmed that Bartali had purchased a plot of land in Via del Bandino in the 1930s, where a building was built. The original land deed was destroyed in the flood of 1966. Other documents confirm the house number was 81 with an attached garage at 25/R, as per email from Dr. Andrea Venturini to author, November 24, 2021. The Yad Vashem file for Bartali also gives the address for Adriana Bartali as Piazza Cardinale Elia dalla Costa, 7 (the previous Via del Bandino), both during the war and at the time, with five other addresses after the war (it is unclear if these are other places where the Bartalis lived). Paolo Alberati's dissertation "La guerra di Gino Bartali" puts Bartali's home at 23. See also Jacoby, *My Italian Secret*, 2014; Bartali, Yad Vashem Archives; Nardo Bonomi Braverman, interview and correspondence with author, February 2022; Gioia Bartali, interview with author May 15, 2022; Alberati, "La guerra di Gino Bartali."

100   "The Germans were killing": Jacoby, *My Italian Secret*.

100   He was allowed to stay: Bartali, Yad Vashem Archives.

100   "I spent most of my time": Bartali.

100   "With quick reflexes": Bartali, *Gino Bartali*, 75.

101   young chief rabbi: Bartali, Yad Vashem Archives.

102   As archbishop: Cardinal Elia Angelo Dalla Costa, file M.31/12282, Yad Vashem Archives; Yad Vashem, "Cardinal Elia Angelo Dalla Costa, Archbishop of Florence, Recognized as Righteous Among the Nations," press release, November 26, 2021, Yad Vashem Archives, https://www.yadvashem.org/press-release/26-november-2012-14–13.html.

102   Meetings of the underground: Bartali, Yad Vashem Archives.

102   Bishop Nicolini was really: Oren, My Italian Secret.

103   It is reported: Other members of Bartali's network included Luigi Gedda, the president of Catholic Action, and the Rome-based Prince Marte Lòsego. Bartali, Yad Vashem Archives.

103   Although he wasn't the only courier: Ramati, *Assisi Underground*. Ramati claims Giorgio La Pira, the future mayor of Florence, was also a courier.

103   "I put myself to work": Jacoby, *My Italian Secret*.

103   "He would leave the home": Bartali, Yad Vashem Archives.

104   "As a child": Jacoby, *My Italian Secret*; Bartali, Yad Vashem Archives.

104   "In case they catch me": Jacoby, *My Italian Secret*.

104   "He would arrive": "Cosi Bartali salvo' gli ebrei, 1943–44," *La Nazione*, July 2, 2003; Paolo Alberati, interview by author, November 30, 2021; Alberati, "La guerra di Gino Bartali," in which Alberati interviewed both Sister Alfonsina and Sister Eleonora; "Firenze-Assisi per ricordare Gino Bartali."

105   Sometimes he would leave: Alberati, interview.

105   Other times he had barley coffee: Alberati, "La guerra di Gino Bartali."

105   Mother Giuseppina: Garibaldi, "Così Bartali." Andrea Bartali and others read the diaries, "where Bartali's visits were recorded."

105   "We just acted spontaneously": Jacoby, *My Italian Secret*.

105   "More than once": Alberati, "La guerra di Gino Bartali."

105   When there was acute: Jacoby, *My Italian Secret*.

106   "I fought for three years": Andrea Biavardi, "La straordinaria storia di uno stampatore di Assisi: Quest'uomo ha salvato cinquemila ebrei," *Gente*, June 15, 1989.

106   "While several of my friends": Biavardi.

106   "What a scare": Biavardi.

107   "pretend to be evacuees": Biavardi.

107   "I put three- or four-year-old tags": Enrico Maionica, interview, April 30, 1998, Trieste, Visual History Archive, USC Shoah Foundation.

107   The documents would then: Maionica.

107   After the first batch: Biavardi, "La straordinaria storia."

107   "a gift from Assisi": Biavardi.

107   "Instead, as soon as I arrived": Biavardi.

108   "I saw him get on": Biavardi.

108   A stunned Trento: Biavardi.

108   "escaped by pure miracle": Bartali, *Gino Bartali*, 75; Bartali, Yad Vashem Archives.

109   "I was the only one": Bartali, *Gino Bartali*, 75.

109   "My father would play": Jacoby, *My Italian Secret*.

109   "It was easier for the Jews": Bartali, *Gino Bartali*, 75.

110   "it's not logical": Segment on Giorgio Goldenberg, *La Vita in Diretta*.

110   The sons of the chief rabbi: Jacoby, *My Italian Secret*; "Under the Wings of the Church: Florence Network," in *I Am My Brother's Keeper*, https://www.yadvashem.org/yv/en/exhibitions/righteous/florence_network.asp.

110   It was barely ten by ten feet: Braverman, interview. Braverman accompanied Giorgio Goldenberg in Florence when he visited the apartment on June 2, 2011, and definitively recognized the courtyard.

111   "What can you do": McConnon and McConnon, *Road to Valor*, 147.

111   "These are terrible times": Jacoby, *My Italian Secret*.

112   Carità accused him: Alberati, "La guerra di Gino Bartali."

112 "It's not true": Lazzerini and Beghelli, *La leggenda di Bartali*, 123–25.

112 "I hope I never": Lazzerini and Beghelli, 124.

112 "I think that was one": Bartali, *Gino Bartali*, 75.

113 "A bleak spectacle": Lazzerini and Beghelli, *La leggenda di Bartali*, 124.

114 "For me, that was the end": McConnon and McConnon, *Road to Valor*, 159.

114 "You feel like you have gotten": Bartali and Ricci, *Tutto sbagliato*, 76.

114 "This is not the Italy": Turrini, *L'uomo che salvo l'Italia*, quoted in McConnon and McConnon, *Road to Valor*, 161.

114 "like clowns": Alberati, *Gino Bartali*, 48–49.

114 "It seemed like they": Bartali and Ricci, *Tutto sbagliato*, 77.

115 "I ended up completely demoralized": Bartali and Ricci, 77

116 "Bartali, the old king of the mountains": McConnon and McConnon, *Road to Valor*, 200.

116 "The good Lord": McConnon and McConnon, 224.

117 "What happened at the Tour?": McConnon and McConnon, 227.

117 "I feel like a lion": Bartali and Ricci, *Tutto sbagliato*, 147.

117 "Bartali wrote in these last": McConnon and McConnon, *Road to Valor*, 231.

117 "I have won": McConnon and McConnon, 340.

117 "Everyone in their life": McConnon and McConnon, 239.

117 "I don't know if I saved": McConnon and McConnon, 247.

117 "For a quarter of a century": McConnon and McConnon, 256.

118 "I want to be remembered": Andrea Bartali, "Mio padre aveva ragione," introduction to Alberati, *Gino Bartali*, Kindle ed., loc. 36.

118 "These are things": "Bartali suo pensiero ebrei," Courtesy of Gioia Bartali, c. July 1994, video, MP4 file, 1:17. He elaborated: "You can't do something nice for someone and then rub it in his face."

118 When a film starring: Bartali, "Mio padre aveva ragione," loc. 4.

118 "I don't want to talk about it": Bartali, *Coppi e Bartali*.

119 "Life is like a Giro d'Italia": McConnon and McConnon, *Road to Valor*, 256.

119 "Heaven should be a happy place": Jacoby, *My Italian Secret*; McConnon and McConnon, *Road to Valor*, 256.

119 "great sportsman": McConnon and McConnon, 257.

119 "When we were poor": McConnon and McConnon, 247.

119 "When the time comes": Bartali, Yad Vashem Archives.

120   Over 7,600 Italian Jews: "Italy During the Holocaust: Historical Background," Yad Vashem, yadvashem.org/righteous/stories/italy-background-history.html.

120   "The Jews of Italy have Italian blood": Ramati, *Assisi Underground*, 171.

120   "Gino Bartali saved my life": Jacoby, *My Italian Secret*.

120   "You had a great father": Bartali, *Gino Bartali*, 75.

120   "These are medals": Bartali, "Mio padre aveva ragione," loc. 4.

5. Samurai Spirit

122   "new eyes in Lithuania": Chiune Sugihara, file M.31/2861, Yad Vashem Archives.

122   "My main task": Pałasz-Rutkowska and Romer, "Polish-Japanese Co-Operation," 285–316.

123   "Chiune, come back to us": Sugihara, Yad Vashem Archives.

123   "The cosmopolitan nature of Harbin": Sugihara, *Visas for Life*, 36.

124   "He was very influenced": Nobuki Sugihara, interview by author, February 17, 2021.

124   Chinese Eastern Railway: Sugihara House, Kaunas, Lithuania, www.sugiharahouse.com. Sugihara House refers to the "Northern Manchurian Railroad Acquisition Office."

124   "I resigned from my post": Sugihara, Yad Vashem Archives.

126   Sugihara provided diplomatic cover: Pałasz-Rutkowska and Romer, "Polish-Japanese Co-Operation," 285–316. Yukiko Sugihara noted they had hardly any contact with other diplomats.

126   "The people there": Sugihara, Yad Vashem Archives.

126   The family continued to grow: "Historical Discovery: Chiune Sugihara's Third Child Was Born in Kaunas, January 4, 2018," Vytautas Magnus University, January 4, 2018, https://www.vdu.lt/en/historical-discovery-Chiune-sugiharas-third-child-was-born-in-kaunas/.

126   "We would go to out-of-the-way places": Sugihara, *Visas for Life*, 15.

126   Jewish population of 32,000: "Kovno," Holocaust Encyclopedia, United States Holocaust Memorial Museum, Washington, DC.

126   At least ten thousand additional Jews: "Zwartendijk—His Activities."

127   "an eerie atmosphere": Sugihara, *Visas for Life*, xiv.

127   "between the jaws of two lions:" Levine, *In Search of Sugihara*, 185.

127   "you are crazy to stay here": Ganor, *Light One Candle*, 37.

127 "if I were you": Ganor, 37.

127 "Tell him," Sugihara said: Ganor, 41. Sadly, the Ganors did not take Sugi-hara's advice, and they remained trapped in Lithuania and eventually were deported. Remarkably, Solly was liberated from Dachau by the Japanese-American 522nd Field Army Battalion. It is worth noting that the veracity of the Hanukkah party story has been challenged, mostly by unreliable sources but also by Nobuki Sugihara. Almost every scholar of Sugihara I consulted, however, believes it to be true and Ganor to be a reliable narrator. The story was also confirmed more than once by Yukiko Sugihara. I have tried to only include details of the story that are based on eyewitness testimony.

129 "commercially we are finished": Jan Zwartendijk, file M.31/7793, Yad Vashem Archives.

129 "a veritable pall": Brokken, The Just, 81.

130 "Send me your passport": "Zwartendijk—His Activities."

130 "The admission of aliens": Zwartendijk, Yad Vashem Archives.

130 Eleven days later: "Zwartendijk—His Activities"; Zwartendijk, Yad Vashem Archives.

130 "We were more afraid": Levine, In Search of Sugihara, 230; Zwartendijk, Yad Vashem Archives.

130 Gutwirth did not need the visa: Zwartendijk, Yad Vashem Archives.

130 "My office carpet": Zwartendijk.

131 he implored Gutwirth: "Zwartendijk—His Activities."

131 De Dekker had by now left: Zwartendijk, Yad Vashem Archives.

131 Issued another thousand: "Zwartendijk—His Activities." Accounts range from 900 to 1,050; Zwartendijk puts the figure at 1,050.

131 visa number 2,345: "Zwartendijk—His Activities"; Zwartendijk, Yad Vashem Archives. Yad Vashem states that 2,193 visas were issued and that the last one was to Herssz Praskier. Elsewhere, Jan Zwartendijk Jr. gives an estimate of 1,200–1,400.

131 "allowed the workers": "Zwartendijk—His Activities."

131 "he knew he was in a position": Zwartendijk, Yad Vashem Archives.

131 "enraged him from the start": Zwartendijk.

132 "humming noise": Pałasz-Rutkowska and Romer, "Polish-Japanese Co-Operation," 285–316. The timelines in various sources are often inconsistent.

132 "This was indeed an extraordinary sight": Sugihara, Visas for Life, 2.

132 "for many days": Gold, A Special Fate, 59; Sugihara, Visas for Life, 3.

132 "It was an upsetting sight": Sugihara, *Visas for Life*, 5.

133 They clung to their parents: Sugihara, Yad Vashem Archives.

133 Sugihara told his children: Mochizuki, *Passage to Freedom*.

133 "Those five men": Sugihara, *Visas for Life*, 9.

133 "With tears in their eyes": Levine, *In Search of Sugihara*, 202–3.

134 "That night was one": Sugihara, *Visas for Life*, 10.

134 he composed a cable: Sugihara to Foreign Minister, cable no. 50, July 28, 1940, quoted in Levine, *In Search of Sugihara*, 236.

134 "More and more requests": Levine, *In Search of Sugihara*, 249.

134 The telegram put consulates: Matsuoka to the Berlin Consulate, cable, July 23, 1940, Sugihara House.

135 Exceptions could be made: Sakamoto, *Japanese Diplomats*, 56.

135 Outside the crowd continued to grow: Sugihara, Yad Vashem Archives. According to Yukiko, the crowd the first day was around 100 and continued growing.

135 "They came to my office": Sugihara.

135 "Even the hunter cannot": Sugihara, *Visas for Life*, 13. Gold, *A Special Fate*, 62, states that Sugihara said this after first meeting the refugees.

135 Sugihara wondered: Gold, *A Special Fate*, 84.

135 "Chiune really wanted": Sugihara, Yad Vashem Archives.

135 "Tokyo stubbornly refused": Sugihara.

135 "I cannot allow": Levine, *In Search of Sugihara*, 259; Sugihara, Yad Vashem Archives.

135 "I will issue visas": Mochizuki, *Passage to Freedom*; Sugihara, *Visas for Life*, 20–21.

135 "The magic of the moment": Sugihara, *Visas for Life*, 21.

136 Sugihara personally interviewed: Sugihara, interview.

136 July 26: "Zwartendijk—His Activities"; Brokken, *The Just*, 95.

136 August 6: Sugihara's list is available at Sugihara House, http://www.sugi harahouse.com/en/the-rescued/the-list-of-the-rescued.

136 "I had to look up": Sugihara, Yad Vashem Archives; Sugihara House.

136 Sugihara wondered: Gold, *A Special Fate*, 94.

136 The Japanese government: Sugihara House.

136 "I had to do something": Sugihara, Yad Vashem Archives.

136   "I decided to halt": Sugihara.

137   "It was very dangerous": Pałasz-Rutkowska and Romer, "Polish-Japanese Co-Operation," 293.

137   including Stalin himself: Brokken, *The Just*, 171; confirmed in Sugihara, interview, and Robert Zwartendijk, interview by author, February 9, 2021. Sakamoto, *Japanese Diplomats*, states that Warhaftig claimed he spoke to the Soviet deputy prime minister of Lithuania, Pius Glovacki, who then got permission from Moscow.

137   "Chiune was very persuasive": Sugihara, *Visas for Life*, 19.

138   "The consul will never allow this": Levine, *In Search of Sugihara*, 245–47.

138   "All right," he finally said: Levine, 245–47.

138   When Zupnik entered: Levine, 245–47.

138   In the hallway: Zwartendijk, Yad Vashem Archives.

138   Zupnik offered to help: Zwartendijk.

138   "He simply handed over": Levine, *In Search of Sugihara*, 245–47.

138   "Whatever came in, I stamped": Zwartendijk, Yad Vashem Archives.

139   "a tzaddik": Levine, *In Search of Sugihara*, 195.

139   Sugihara kept a log: Sugihara, Yad Vashem Archives.

139   the official stamp: According to Nobuki Sugihara there were three stamps: a round stamp for Sugihara, a square consulate stamp, and then a third stamp that was used to expedite the handwriting. Only the latter would have been used by Zupnik. Sugihara, interview.

139   Sugihara worked methodically: Sugihara, *Visas for Life*, 22.

139   "He was in a hurry": Pałasz-Rutkowska and Romer, "Polish-Japanese Co-Operation," 293.

139   Eventually, he even halted: Sugihara, *Visas for Life*, 24.

139   Sugihara quickly realized: Zwartendijk, Yad Vashem Archives.

140   None of the refugees actually went to Curaçao: Zwartendijk.

140   "I'd say more than half": Sugihara, Yad Vashem Archives.

140   Conditions were difficult: Sugihara.

140   "They were in a panic": Levine, *In Search of Sugihara*, 136–37.

140   "The world says that": Levine, 242.

141   "He looked very sympathetic": Sugihara, Yad Vashem Archives.

141   As he wrote: "Lucille Szepsenwol Camhi Describes Obtaining Japanese Transit Visas from Chiune Sugihara in Kovno," oral history interview with Lucille Cahmi, June 8, 1999, United States Holocaust Memorial Museum,

Washington, DC, https://encyclopedia.ushmm.org/content/en/oral-history /lucille-szepsenwol-camhi-describes-obtaining-japanese-transit-visas-from -Chiune-sugihara-in-kovno; Levine, *In Search of Sugihara*, 255.

141   He did this for women: Sugihara, interview.

141   "I thought that he was a real gentleman": Sugihara, *Visas for Life*, 131.

141   "We cannot permit them": Sakamoto, *Japanese Diplomats*, 111.

141   "to deny transit visas": Sugihara House.

141   Sugihara composed a telegram: Levine, *In Search of Sugihara*, 248.

142   a cable on August 24: The cable is actually dated August 1, but it seems likely it was sent September 1, as it refers to cable 22. The response to this cable was sent from Tokyo on September 3. See also Sakamoto, *Japanese Diplomats*, which notes that things were so busy with such large issues that it is unlikely the foreign minister even saw the cables.

142   "Close the Consulate": Sugihara, Yad Vashem Archives; Sugihara, *Visas for Life*, 24. The first telegram from the Foreign Ministry was on August 2, instructing him to close the consulate.

142   "Handling Refugees": Sugihara House.

142   "From now on please": Levine, *In Search of Sugihara*, 258.

142   Zupnik bade farewell: Levine, 245–47. According to Nobuki Sugihara, Gudze was sadly shot and killed during the war. Sugihara, interview.

142   "Those were the best two weeks": Levine, *In Search of Sugihara*, 248.

143   "I will never forget": Sugihara, *Visas for Life*, 26.

143   "permission papers": Sugihara, 27.

143   He wrote visas: Hiroki Sugihara says his father wrote for two days. Sugihara, Yad Vashem Archives; Sugihara, *Visas for Life*, 27.

143   "They stood frozen": Sugihara, *Visas for Life*, 27.

143   "I didn't know what to do": Sugihara, Yad Vashem Archives.

143   "Don't go, please!": Sugihara, *Visas for Life*, 27. The Sugiharas later heard that some of the stationery was actually used successfully.

144   "I was sad for the people": Sugihara, 27.

144   "Father, are we going to Berlin?": Mochizuki, *Passage to Freedom*; Sugihara, *Visas for Life*, 27; Sugihara, Yad Vashem Archives.

144   "They were tearful and terrified": Zwartendijk, Yad Vashem Archives.

144   "There wasn't a tree": Brokken, *The Just*, 78; Zwartendijk, Yad Vashem Archives.

145   two officers showed up: Zwartendijk, interview; "Zwartendijk—His Activities."

145 "It is the more astonishing": Zwartendijk, Yad Vashem Archives.

146 On February 4: Levine, *In Search of Sugihara*, 273; cable to Matsuoka, February 28, 1941, Sugihara House.

146 he had issued 2,132 visas: Sugihara Museum, Yaotsu-cho, Japan, http://www.sugihara-museum.jp/shared/pdf/about/issued_list.pdf. The precise number is not entirely certain. Sugihara's initial telegram said 2,132, but the actual list is different at 2,139. The original "Sugihara's list" is in the Gaimusho (Foreign Ministry) archives and consists of 31 pages of people saved in Lithuania, and some additional rescuees in Prague and Konigsberg. It is contained in a black loose-leaf binder labeled "consular activities." Levine, *In Search of Sugihara*, 5.

146 Sugihara was now being viewed: Levine, *In Search of Sugihara*, 272. Nobuki Sugihara said he was "persona non grata" to the Germans in Kovno. Sugihara, "Evening with Nobuki Sugihara."

146 "I feel good today": Sugihara, *Visas for Life*, 58.

147 "gorgeous life": Levine, *In Search of Sugihara*, 275.

147 "I'm not a spy": Sugihara, Yad Vashem Archives.

148 "The excitement I felt": Sugihara, *Visas for Life*, 105.

148 Two days later: Sugihara, 106.

148 "We have come back to Japan": Sugihara, 106.

149 "Thank you, Mr. Sugihara": Sugihara, 108–9.

149 "If I admit your way": Sugihara, Yad Vashem Archives.

149 "start a new life": Sugihara. The Japanese government has disputed that Sugihara was dismissed for insubordination, asserting that he was let go as part as a wide-scale postwar downsizing at the Foreign Ministry.

149 "In the days after the war": Sugihara, *Visas for Life*, 110.

149 "helpless and vacant-eyed": Sugihara, 111.

149 They blamed the war: Sugihara, Yad Vashem Archives.

150 "He never used money": Sugihara.

151 The Foreign Ministry had records: Sugihara, *Visas for Life*, 124.

151 "very old and worn out piece of paper": Sugihara, 123.

151 "emissary of G-d": Sugihara, 125.

151 "I am proud to have issued visas to the Jews": Sugihara, Yad Vashem Archives.

151 "In 1963 an article": Schreig, "Inside Report."

152 "He did not wish": "Zwartendijk—His Activities."

152 "He just wanted to do good": Zwartendijk, interview.

152 And he did not like being called: Zwartendijk, Yad Vashem Archives; "Zwartendijk—His Activities." The *Jerusalem Post* also called Zwartendijk "the man who saved Judaism because of his rescue of so many Torah scholars."

152 a cedar grove was planted: It was originally intended to be of cherry trees, but cedars are better suited to the desert climate. *Sugihara* means "cedar grove" in Japanese.

153 "symbolize the ripple effect": Sugihara, *Visas for Life*, 144.

153 "courageous and humanitarian act": Chinue Sugihara Memorial Hall, Yao-tsu, Japan, http://www.sugihara-museum.jp/about/honor_en.html.

153 "He took us out from hell": Goldberg, "Honors Come Late."

153 "I think he was a man sent by God": Sugihara, Yad Vashem Archives.

153 "There's a choice to be made": Zwartendijk, interview.

153 "I didn't do anything special": Sugihara, Yad Vashem Archives.

154 "What I did as a diplomat": Sugihara, *Visas for Life*, 128.

154 "I felt pity for the people": Sugihara, interview.

154 "My father told me that a samurai": Sugihara, Yad Vashem Archives.

6. Miracle on the Øresund

156 From the outset, Germany announced: Werner, *Conspiracy of Decency*, 9.

156 "under protest": "Denmark Protests but Yields to Nazis," *New York Times*, April 9, 1940.

156 The oldest members: Flender, *Rescue in Denmark*, 28.

156 "I considered our own Jews": Lidegaard, *Countrymen*, 19.

157 "Hitler's canary": Werner, *Conspiracy of Decency*, 13.

157 "the cloven hoof of Nazism": Lidegaard, *Countrymen*, 12

157 "an absolute correct and dignified behavior": Werner, *Conspiracy of Decency*, 9; "Denmark Protests."

158 "My utmost thanks": Werner, *Conspiracy of Decency*, 21.

159 "would ruin the government's": Werner, 24.

159 Best blamed the press: Werner, 13.

160 "It has finally happened": Werner, 27.

160 "It is my opinion": Werner, 29–30.

160 "In order to arrest": Werner, 30.

160 "a very heated discussion": Werner, 31.

161 "She was my best moral support": Werner, 31.

161 "Deep down he's decent": Lidegaard, *Countrymen*, 48.

161 "all that can be done": Werner, *Conspiracy of Decency*, 32. "Vorbereitet sein, ist alles, was getan werden kann."

162 "Now I know what I have to do": Werner, 33.

162 "If we were to stay silent": Werner, 84.

163 "Everything I do": Lidegaard, *Countrymen*, 67.

163 Three hundred "specialists": Werner, *Conspiracy of Decency*, 35.

163 "No power in the world": Werner, 35.

163 The next day, Duckwitz went: Werner, 35.

163 "for the duration": Werner, 35.

163 "as if he had just said": Werner, 36.

164 "the operation will place": Werner, 35–36.

164 "Disturbances requiring use": Werner, 36.

165 "He took great personal risk": Werner, 37.

165 "It is good that Annemarie": Werner, 36.

166 in their innermost hearts": Hans Hedtoft, introduction to Bertelsen, *October '43*.

166 "cabin of trust": Lidegaard, *Countrymen*, 71.

166 "white with indignation": Hedtoft, introduction.

166 "Now the disaster is about to occur": Georg Duckwitz, file M.31/679, Yad Vashem Archives.

166 "Henriques, a great disaster": Hedtoft, introduction.

167 "You must immediately": Hedtoft, introduction.

167 Henriques was in shock: Hedtoft, introduction.

167 "Everything is dark and hopeless": Werner, *Conspiracy of Decency*, 41.

167 "I have very important news": Werner, 41.

167 The seventy-two-hour head start: Duckwitz, Yad Vashem Archives.

168 "to emphasize to you": Lidegaard, *Countrymen*, 132.

168 "We understand by freedom": Werner, *Conspiracy of Decency*, 48.

169 "horrible brutalization": Dolgin, "Danish Hero."

170 "I called my colleagues": Mark, "Splitting of the Sea."

170 Knud immediately went: Karen and Knud Marstrand Christiansen, file M.31/10633, Yad Vashem Archives.

171 "It was faster": Christiansen.

172   "The thoughts flew": Christiansen.

172   His host came: Christiansen.

173   "I knew from Germany": Christiansen.

173   "First we have to get": Christiansen.

173   "It was as if": Christiansen.

173   "You will not leave": Christiansen.

174   "I had to eat": Christiansen.

174   "Are we going to Sweden": Christiansen.

175   "You are cold": Christiansen.

175   "I was saved": Christiansen.

176   "have a good trip": Werner, *Conspiracy of Decency*, 72.

176   In the end: "Rescue in Denmark," Holocaust Encyclopedia, United States Holocaust Memorial Museum, Washington, DC, https://encyclopedia.ushmm.org/content/en/article/rescue-in-denmark.

176   "Sweden is open to all": Lidegaard, *Countrymen*, 96.

176   many soldiers were not interested: Dolgin, "Danish Hero."

178   "redeemed as a human being": Werner, *Conspiracy of Decency*, 114.

178   "The gate was opened": Werner, 120.

178   "One does not think": "German Who Saved Danish Jews Here," *Jerusalem Post*, 1971; Duckwitz, Yad Vashem Archives.

178   "When I heard the news": Werner, *Conspiracy of Decency*, 144.

179   "In most cases": Werner, 154.

179   "How could you risk all": Christiansen, Yad Vashem Archives.

180   "I had noticed:" Lidegaard, *Countrymen*, 19.

180   "Denmark created greater difficulties": Lidegaard, 198.

180   "put one's faith in a new Germany": Duckwitz, Yad Vashem Archives.

7. Beneath the Apple Tree

182   "I grew up": Sendler, "O pomocy Żydom."

182   "Don't spoil her": Mazzeo, *Irena's Children*, 11.

183   "My father was a doctor": Mazzeo, 18.

183   "I was beaten": Mazzeo, 23.

183   "Everyone here was dedicated": Mazzeo, 21.

185   "creative social work": Mayer, *Life in a Jar*, 79.

185 "Our streets were flooded": Skinner, *Irena Sendler.*

186 "There were families": Mazzeo, *Irena's Children*, 43–44.

186 "The basis of receiving": Mazzeo, 47.

187 "With the creation": Sendler, "O pomocy Żydom."

187 "We made contact": Sendler.

187 gave the two Irenas: Sources universally state that the two Irenas received passes. Elsewhere, Irena indicates there were five people who received passes, growing to ten. Interview with Irena Sendler, "Irena Sendlerowa (1): Trudno się nie przejąć, jak do dzieci strzelano," www.wilnoteka.it, May 16, 2013, https://www.youtube.com/watch?v=g5kAQrqIWkM&t =13s.

187 "At first, I was": Sendler, "The Valor of the Young," 21.

187 "The first time": Lefkovits, "Heroism in the Warsaw Ghetto."

187 "I'd go out": Skinner, *Irena Sendler.*

188 "One thing is certain": Interview with Irena Sendler, "Irena Sendlerowa (1): Trudno się nie przejąć, jak do dzieci strzelano," www.wilnoteka.it, May 16, 2013, https://www.youtube.com/watch?v=g5kAQrqIWkM&t=13s.

188 "By order of Hitler": Irena Sendler, file M.31/153, Yad Vashem Archives.

188 "It was hard not to be": Interview with Irena Sendler, "Irena Sendlerowa (1): Trudno się nie przejąć, jak do dzieci strzelano," www.wilnoteka.it, May 16, 2013, https://www.youtube.com/watch?v=g5kAQrqIWkM&t=13s.

188 "who knowingly provides": Mayer, *Life in a Jar*, 134–35.

190 "like a ray of sun": Skinner, *Irena Sendler.*

190 "Why are you doing this": Mayer, *Life in a Jar*, 142.

190 "an important friend": Mayer, 142.

190 "Pani Sendler": Mayer, 143.

191 "God bless you": Mayer, 146

193 "I was teaching them": Skinner, *Irena Sendler.*

193 "doubled by the tragedies": Sendler, Yad Vashem Archives.

193 "How many mothers": Sendler.

193 "Jan Dobraczyński came to an understanding": Mazzeo, *Irena's Children*, 110.

194 "There had to be some record": Skinner, *Irena Sendler.*

194 They also needed the addresses: Mazzeo, *Irena's Children*, 111.

195 Sometimes, she would add: Sendler, "O pomocy Żydom."

195 In May, Irena tried: Mazzeo, *Irena's Children*, 106–7.

195 One of Irena's teenage: Mazzeo, 107, says it was rather Ala Golab-Grynberg,

who as chief nurse had rare permission to travel into the Jewish ghetto after curfew.

196 "Very quickly": Mazzeo, 132.

197 "We witnessed Dantesque": Sendler, Yad Vashem Archives.

198 One day Irena took: Mayer, *Life in a Jar*, 176.

198 Irena walked with Guta: Mazzeo, *Irena's Children*, 149, in great detail has this a boy saved by Jaga Piotrowska and not Irena. Jack Mayer told the author that he heard this story directly from Irena, but surmised that perhaps similar incidents had occurred throughout the ghetto.

198 "At last they would be able": Szpilman, *The Pianist*, 96.

198 "Though the storm": Mayer, *Life in a Jar*, 182.

198 "Good riddance": Mayer, 193.

199 Dr. Korczak "kept walking": Irena Sendler, "Irena Sendler Tells the Story of Janusz Korczak," *Gariwo Network*, July 23, 2013, https://en.gariwo.net/multimedia/documentaries/irena-sendler-tells-the-story-of-janusz-korczak-9114.html; Skinner, *Irena Sendler*.

199 "I will stay with the children": Mayer, *Life in a Jar*, 184.

199 "It was not a simple": Mazzeo, *Irena's Children*, 124.

199 "Remembering that tragic procession": Mazzeo, 124–25.

199 Eighty-five percent: Mazzeo, 155.

200 "Poland is silent": Mayer, *Life in a Jar*, 197.

201 "to lead as many Jews as possible": Sendler, "O pomocy Żydom."

201 Irena was taken: Sendler, "Those Who Helped the Jews," 45–46.

201 "a man with a big heart": Sendler, "O pomocy Żydom."

202 "You know the people": Lefkovits, "Heroism in the Warsaw Ghetto."

202 In the fall of 1942: Sendler, "The Valor of the Young," 21.

202 "Vast sums passed": Mazzeo, *Irena's Children*, 166.

202 "I'm a good organizer": Skinner, *Irena Sendler*.

202 The penalty: Sendler, "Those Who Helped the Jews," 45–46.

203 "I'll come for Mirjam": Mayer, *Life in a Jar*, 208.

204 "What you're doing": Mayer, 206.

204 One night at three: Sendler, "Those Who Helped the Jews," 45–46.

205 Janina responded that Irena: Mazzeo, *Irena's Children*, 183; Mayer, *Life in a Jar*, 213.

205 "I felt sorry for you": Irena Sendlerowa, "Ci Którzy Pomagali Żydom

(Wspomnienia z czasów okupacji hitlerowskiej)," *Biuletyn Żydowskiego Instytutu Historycznego* (Warsaw: Żydowski Instytut Historyczny, 1963), 233–47.

206   "The ghetto was on fire!": Sendler, "Those Who Helped the Jews," 45–46.

206   "Every day, every hour": Sendler, "The Valor of the Young," 21.

206   "There was no air": Mazzeo, *Irena's Children*, 200.

207   "The former Jewish Quarter": "Warsaw Ghetto Uprising," Holocaust Encyclopedia, United States Holocaust Memorial Museum, Washington, DC, https://encyclopedia.ushmm.org/content/en/article/warsaw-ghetto-uprising.

207   They stayed up late: Sendler, Yad Vashem Archives.

207   "During the occupation": Sendler.

208   "They came to your house": Mayer, *Life in a Jar*, 221.

208   "It went on for two hours": Sendler, Yad Vashem Archives.

209   "As they arrested me": Skinner, *Irena Sendler*; Sendler, Yad Vashem Archives.

209   "The owner was arrested": Sendler, "O pomocy Żydom."

210   "I'll tell you everything": Mayer, *Life in a Jar*, 225.

212   One day: Sendler, "O pomocy Żydom."

212   "Don't worry": Mayer, *Life in a Jar*, 231.

212   "They valued my work": Sendler, Yad Vashem Archives.

212   Then, on January 20: Sendler, "O pomocy Żydom."

212   "Be careful": Mayer, *Life in a Jar*, 297.

213   "I remember feeling": Sendler, "O pomocy Żydom."

213   "I was confused": Mayer, *Life in a Jar*, 298.

213   In shock, Irena: Mayer, 298; Sendler, "O pomocy Żydom."

214   "It was," she said: Mayer, *Life in a Jar*, 298.

214   "Luckily I found a seat": Mayer, 299.

214   "I was so naïve": Mazzeo, *Irena's Children*, 231; Sendler, "O pomocy Żydom."

215   "I was so exhausted": Mayer, *Life in a Jar*, 299.

215   "One of the burdens": Mayer, 319.

215   "You are not even allowed": Sendler, "O pomocy Żydom."

215   "They'll be looking for you": Mayer, *Life in a Jar*, 329.

215   "There were no more children to rescue": Mayer, 321.

216 One night, after Jaga's daughter: This seems to have happened during the Warsaw Uprising in August 1944 according to Irena Sendler's statement in Sendler, Yad Vashem Archives; Irena Sendler, "How I Rescued Children in the Warsaw Ghetto," *Stowarzyszenis "Dzieci Holocaustu" W Polesce* [Association of Children of the Holocaust in Poland], https://dzieciholocaustu.org.pl/szab3.php?s=en_sendlerowa.php.

216 They decided they would dig: Mayer, *Life in a Jar*; Sendler, Yad Vashem Archives, implies during Warsaw Uprising.

216 "In case of my death": Sendler, Yad Vashem Archives.

216 "Almost all Warsaw is a sea of flames": Hans Frank, *Diary of Hans Frank, vol. 37: Tagebuch 1944*, 1944, United States National Archives, https://www.archives.gov/files/research/captured-german-records/microfilm/t992.pdf.

217 "I had promised": Mayer, *Life in a Jar*, 311.

217 The two women went out: Mayer, 311.

217 "We now began to realize": Mayer, 312.

218 "It is hard to be": Rojek, "To była maka całego świata."

218 "You and your family": Mayer, *Life in a Jar*, 277.

219 estimate that 2,500 children: Sendler, Yad Vashem Archives.

219 "We think that there are many more": Sendler.

219 "it was a need of my heart": Mayer, *Life in a Jar*, 219.

219 "when someone is drowning": Skinner, *Irena Sendler*.

219 "I only did what any decent person": Mayer, *Life in a Jar*, 336.

220 "I am a veteran of war": Skinner, *Irena Sendler*.

220 "I still hear mothers": Sendler, Yad Vashem Archives.

220 She died peacefully: Mayer, *Life in a Jar*, 351.

220 "I could not have achieved": Skinner, *Irena Sendler*.

220 "Every child saved": "Heroic Sendlerowa Dies at 98," *Jewish News*, May 15, 2008; Quetteville, " 'Female Schindler' Irene Sendler"; Schislowska, "Polish Holocaust Hero"; Sendler, Yad Vashem Archives.

8. The Ivy Leaguers

222 "like a sage old owl": Bingham, "Hiram Bingham IV."

222 married shortly after: "Hiram Bingham, Jr. Marries Miss Rose Morrison at Waycross, Georgia," *Honolulu Star-Bulletin*, September 29, 1934.

223 A nineteen-year-old Viennese Jew: Lawrence Bodner to Robert Kim Bingham, June 29, 2008, www.hirambinghamrescuer.com.

224 "We can delay": Breckinridge Long, memo to assistant secretary of state Adolf Berle, June 26, 1940, National Archives and Records Administration, College Park, MD, RG 59 Central Decimal Files 811.111 W.R/107.

224 "The Germans are going to win": Hiram Bingham IV, interview by Tiffany Bingham, c. 1980.

224 "Visas were granted": Isenberg, *A Hero of Our Own*, Kindle ed., loc. 794.

224 "getting as many visas": Hiram Bingham IV, interview.

224 "Fullerton took the bad way": Danny Bénédite, June 25, 1985, Exiles Film Project, ms. 1734, ser. 2.

224 "The French Government": Marino, *Quiet American*, 43.

225 a large crowd pulled Jews: "Editor Holds Riots Inspired by Nazis," *New York Times*, July 26, 1935.

225 Plate-glass windows: "Editor Describes Rioting in Berlin," *New York Times*, July 15, 1935.

225 In a nearby café: "Editor Describes Rioting."

225 "We mustn't forget": Marino, *Quiet American*, 44.

226 "it was a complete mess": Bénédite, Exiles Film Project.

228 "I had my books": Feuchtwanger, *Devil in France*, 5.

228 "We had been celebrated": Feuchtwanger, 21.

228 "There was never a case": Feuchtwanger, 85.

229 "It lay in the sunshine": Feuchtwanger, 163.

229 "Plato places courage": Feuchtwanger, 175.

229 Feuchtwanger decided to walk: Feuchtwanger, 184.

230 "going to town": Feuchtwanger, 184.

230 "What wore a man down": Feuchtwanger, 232.

230 "It was a July night": Feuchtwanger, 245.

230 "I wanted to make sure": Feuchtwanger, 248.

231 Bingham's deputy Myles Standish: Both Varian Fry and Mary Jayne Gold identify Bingham as the rescuer, but most accounts refer to Myles Standish as the actual driver of the car.

232 "They told me that you had gone bathing": Feuchtwanger, *Devil in France*, 260.

232 "The good-natured, embarrassed Bingham": Lion Feuchtwanger, diary, July 21, 1940, Lion Feuchtwanger Papers.

232 "Our house was pretty isolated": Hiram Bingham, August 4, 1987, Exiles Film Project, ms. 1734, ser. 2.

232 "a very, very heavy heart": Golo Mann, July 23, 1985, Exiles Film Project, ms. 1734, ser. 2.

233 Marta and Lion exhaled: Marta Feuchtwanger, afterword to Feuchtwanger, *Devil in France*, 266.

233 The vice consul told his neighbors: William Bingham, interview by author, July 19, 2020.

233 "The servants are bad": Feuchtwanger, diary, July 22, 1940.

233 "Bingham is an awkward": Feuchtwanger.

233 "I miss you so much": Hiram and Rose Bingham Papers, 1991.240.15, United States Holocaust Memorial Museum.

233 "The whole world": Hiram Bingham IV to Rose Bingham, Institute for the Study of Rescue and Altruism in the Holocaust, https://www.holocaust rescue.org/bingham-bibliography-and-quotes.

234 "affidavits in lieu of passport": Fry, *Surrender on Demand*, 57.

234 "Bingham had a great idea": Feuchtwanger, afterword, 271; Feuchtwanger, diary, August 17, 1940.

234 Bohn had told Fry: Fry, *Surrender on Demand*, 10.

235 "Her name alone": Gold, *Crossroads Marseilles*, 122.

235 "sensuous lips": Marino, *Quiet American*, 62.

235 "Werfel looked exactly": Fry, *Surrender on Demand*, 5–6.

236 "The prospect of escape": Feuchtwanger, diary, August 12, 1940.

236 "Half the refugees in Marseille": Fry, *Surrender on Demand*, 54.

237 "All through dinner": Fry, 56.

237 "If you will come": Fry, 57.

237 "I am in a good mood": Feuchtwanger, diary, August 29, 1940.

237 "never went around the block": Fry, *Surrender on Demand*, 57.

237 Fry also invited Heinrich: Karel Sternberg claimed that Fry told him that also in the group were the film publicity director Egon Adler and his wife, Bertha Maria Adler, but they were cut out of Fry's memoir because they were not famous. They carried US emergency visas. Other descriptions of the event by third parties do not mention this, however. Isenberg, *A Hero of Our Own*, Kindle ed., loc. 2788.

237 Heinrich Mann was extremely concerned: Hiram Bingham, Exiles Film Project.

238 Mahler's unfinished symphony: Mary Jayne Gold claims the Mahler

manuscripts stayed in the luggage, although she was not present. Gold, *Crossroads Marseilles*, 137.

238   "the most sensible walking gear": Gold, 132.

238   "on and off the train": Rosenberg, *Art of Resistance*, 109.

239   "Panic seized us": Fry, *Surrender on Demand*, 62.

240   "It's an unlucky day": Fry, 64.

240   "We are obliged": Fry, 65.

240   Ball and Golo had to carry him: This is according to Fry, who did not mention Rosenberg's presence. In *Art of Resistance*, Rosenberg says he and Nelly helped Heinrich Mann and Alma Mahler, and Ball helped Werfel.

240   "It was sheer, slippery terrain": Marino, *Quiet American*, 169.

241   "So you are the son": Fry, *Surrender on Demand*, 68–69.

243   "Once again, Bingham proved his worth": Feuchtwanger, afterword, 273.

243   "Shut up": Harold von Hofe, "About Lion and Marta Feuchtwanger," Feuchtwanger Memorial Library, USC Libraries, Los Angeles, https://libguides.usc.edu/c.php?g=234957&p=1559413.

244   "The author spoke repeatedly": "Flight Described by Feuchtwanger," *New York Times*, October 6, 1940, 38.

244   "have repeatedly spoken": Bingham, *Courageous Dissent*, 28.

244   "It was a great chance": Bingham, 20–21.

244   he made a tour: Hiram Bingham IV, "Concentration Camps for Foreigners in the Marseille Consular district," memorandum, December 20, 1940, Institute for the Study of Rescue and Altruism in the Holocaust, https://www.holocaustrescue.org/bingham-letters-and-testimonies.

245   Hans Schlesinger was interned: Schlesinger, "Saved by the U.S. Consul."

245   "God, it was such a relief": "Rescue in the Holocaust by Diplomats—Hiram Bingham, IV," Institute for the Study of Rescue and Altruism in the Holocaust, https://www.holocaustrescue.org/hiram-bingham.

245   "I could write a treatise": "Hiram Bingham, IV."

246   "When he reaches paradise": "Hiram Bingham, IV."

246   "a bit of an innocent abroad": Albert Hirschman, October 22, 1985, Exiles Film Project, ms. 1734, ser. 2.

246   "knew how to do": Davenport Ebel, "Unsentimental Education."

247   "Joseph Goebbels is personally": Gold, *Crossroads Marseilles*, 104.

247   He also married: Marino, *Quiet American*, 239–40; William Bingham, interview.

248　The mood in Marseille: Albert Hirschman and Wolfgang Roth, October 25, 1985, Exiles Film Project, ms. 1734, ser. 2.

248　"There were very often terrible decisions": Albert Hirschman, circa 1980s, Exiles Film Project, ms. 1734, ser. 2.

248　"It was terribly sad": Charles Fawcett, oral history interview, June 24, 1993, RG-50.428.0006, United States Holocaust Memorial Museum, Washington, DC.

248　"I saw myself": Justus Rosenberg, oral history interview, RG-50.428.0004 United States Holocaust Memorial Museum, Washington, DC.

248　"a great man": Francis Zamponi, Nelly Bouveret, and Daniel Allary, *Jean Moulin: mémoires d'un homme sans voix* (Paris: Editions du Chêne, 1998), 98.

249　While Fry was away: Fry, *Surrender on Demand*, 80.

249　the State Department's return cable: Cordell Hull to the American embassy, telegram, September 18, 1941, in Fry, *Surrender on Demand*, 81.

249　"in danger of becoming": Matthews to Hull, cable, September 14, 1940, in Varian Fry, file M.31/6150, Yad Vashem Archives.

249　"the refugees were really trapped": Fry, *Surrender on Demand*, 85.

250　"The atmosphere is the atmosphere": Fry to his mother, February 3, 1941, in Fry, Yad Vashem Archives.

251　The poet waited nervously: Fry, *Surrender on Demand*, 173–74; Marino, *Quiet American*, 263; Walter Mehring to Varian Fry, December 22, 1947, Box 7, Varian Fry Papers, Rare Book and Manuscript Library, Columbia University Library, New York.

252　"I have never before": Varian Fry to Danny Bénédite, October 31, 1941, Box 2, Varian Fry Papers.

252　"one of those magnificent views": Varian Fry to Arthur Fry, May 14, 1941, Box 3, Varian Fry Papers.

253　"a splendid, private hotel": Davenport Ebel, "Unsentimental Education."

253　Bingham had suspected: William Bingham, interview.

253　"In my experience": Albert Hirschman, Exiles Film Project.

254　"It will only be a short time": Fry, *Surrender on Demand*, 141.

254　"I have to admit": Fry, 143.

255　"I am sorry you should": Fry, 146.

255　"one of the most surprising": Varian Fry to Eileen Fry, December 8, 1940, Box 3, Varian Fry Papers.

255　"He'll find me": Miriam Davenport Ebel Papers, 1991.158.88, United States Holocaust Memorial Museum, Washington, DC.

255 "redouble our efforts": Davenport Ebel Papers.

256 "He was just comfortable": Hiram Bingham, Exiles Film Project.

256 "green, purple and red": Wullschlager, *Chagall*, 375.

257 "Are there cows in America?": Fry, *Surrender on Demand*, 130.

257 "Beautiful beyond belief": Varian Fry, "Surrender on Demand" (draft manuscript), March 10, 1931, Box 13, Varian Fry Papers; Marino, *Quiet American*, 272.

257 Bingham brought along his movie: William Bingham, interview.

258 "Thank you with all our hearts": Bingham, *Courageous Dissent*, 26–27.

258 "If, by any chance": Fry, *Surrender on Demand*, 106–7.

258 "Through sheer audacity": Robert Kim Bingham, "Hiram ('Harry') Bingham IV, Diplomat Rescuer in France," Simon Wiesenthal Center Tribute Video to Hiram Bingham IV, June 2, 2011, https://www.youtube.com /watch?v=N6MfzibYZFU

258 "all the reluctance": Marino, *Quiet American*, 279.

258 On May 7: Rosenberg, *Art of Resistance*, 134–35. Rosenberg recalled, "The American vice consul, Hiram Bingham, an admirer of Chagall's, had him and his wife driven in a diplomatic limousine (providing a cover of diplomatic immunity) all the way to Lisbon—with only a US visa."

258 Many of the paintings: William Bingham, interview.

259 "When you are ready": Isenberg, *A Hero of Our Own*, Kindle ed., loc. 8024.

259 "In some ways I owe": Jacques Lipchitz, Remarks at the Memorial Service for Varian Fry, November 8, 1967, quoted in Isenberg, *A Hero of Our Own*, Kindle ed., loc. 8055; Fry, Yad Vashem Archives.

259 "Lipchitz is the best": Varian Fry to Eileen Fry, July 16, 1941, Box 13, Varian Fry Papers.

260 "if all the talented people": "The Fight against Loose Talk Spreads," *Newsweek*, March 2, 1942.

260 "With all his genius": Fry, *Surrender on Demand*, 157.

260 He would never betray France: Fry, 159.

260 "has worked very hard": Fry, Journal, May 7, 1941, Box 13.

261 On April 26: Secretary of State Cordell Hull to Marseille consul general, telegram, April 26, 1941, NARA, RG 59, Entry (A-1)205E General Records of the Department of State, Central Decimal Files, 1940–41, File 123 BINGHAM, HIRAM/196.

261 "His going will be": Fry, "Surrender on Demand," May 7, 1941.

261 "He was also very weak": Fry, *Surrender on Demand*, 215.

261 "It doesn't make any difference": Fry, 215–16.

261 "Why do you have so many Jews": Marino, *Quiet American*, 298.

262 "The situation here is bad": Miriam Davenport Ebel Papers.

262 One State Department memorandum: Fry, Yad Vashem Archives.

262 More than seventy-six thousand: "The deportation of the Jews from France," Yad Vashem, Jerusalem, https://www.yadvashem.org/holocaust/france /deportation-from-france.html.

263 "Péron and his whole gang": Bingham, *Courageous Dissent*, 43–46.

263 "blasted": Robert Kim Bingham, interview in Lopes, *America's Diplomats*, March 1, 2016, https://americasdiplomats.com/actors/robert-bingham/.

263 "PROMOTIONS!": Bingham, *Courageous Dissent*, 46.

263 Instead, he was offered: William Bingham, interview.

264 In one last petty slight: William Bingham.

264 "a spark of divinity": Abigail Bingham Endicott, interview by author, February 10, 2021.

265 "Your father broke every rule": William Bingham, interview.

265 "I do not think": Fry, *Surrender on Demand*, 254; Fry, Yad Vashem Archives.

265 "I felt as though": Varian Fry to Bruce Bliven, March 30, 1945, quoted in Isenberg, *A Hero of Our Own*, loc. 8852n1505.

266 "like the stones left": Varian Fry to Eileen Fry, September 7, 1941, Box 3, Varian Fry Papers; Fry, Yad Vashem Archives.

266 "Maybe I can become": Fry, *Surrender on Demand*, 326.

266 "Though it is probably not the thing": Russell Maloney, "Scarlet Pimpernel, Streamlined," *New York Times*, April 22, 1945.

266 "He'd complain a little": Hiram Bingham, Exiles Film Project.

266 Over time, the two comrades: William Bingham, interview.

267 "a legendary hero": Isenberg, *A Hero of Our Own*, loc. 9426.

267 "the more famous they were": Rosenberg, *Art of Resistance*, 132–33.

267 When he asked Breton: Breton's daughter Aube, who was five when they were rescued, later said, "My father always said . . . that we owe so much to Varian Fry. . . . He had very, very big admiration and esteem for [him]." Isenberg, *A Hero of Our Own*, Kindle ed., loc. 6456.

267 "I think he was always": James Fry, interview by author, February 14, 2021.

267 "severe case of psychoneurosis": Fry, Yad Vashem Archives.

267 "I think that today": Rosenberg, *Art of Resistance*, 137

268 He was proud: *America's Diplomats*, 2016.

268   "There is no question": Bingham, *Courageous Dissent*, 28.

268   "My father was all about": Bingham.

268   "He believed you": Bettijane Levine, "A Tie That Binds Jews and a Special Family," *Los Angeles Times*, September 27, 2001.

268   he had visions: William Bingham, interview.

269   "Look at what he gave": Fawcett, interview.

269   "He will always be the hero": Fry, Yad Vashem Archives.

269   "like a racehorse": Lipchitz, remarks at memorial service, recalled by Lucy Burchard, in Isenberg, *A Hero of Our Own*, loc. 8055.

270   "loyal faithful friend": Davenport Ebel, "Unsentimental Education."

270   "the man for the moment": Harold Oram, August 1987, Exiles Film Project, ms. 1734, ser. 2.

270   "He was so proud": Endicott, interview.

270   "my partner in the crime": Bingham, *Courageous Dissent*, 9.

9. The City of Refuge

271   "Dreary granite facades": Boismorand, *Resistance Figures*, 63; Trocmé Papers.

271   "Le Chambon was": Boismorand, *Resistance Figures*, 64.

272   "When I was still a young child": Boismorand, 80–81.

272   "The one in the middle": Unsworth, *Portrait of Pacifists*, 31–32; Memoirs of André Trocmé, 94–95, Trocmé Papers.

272   "The experience was like a purifying bath": Unsworth, *Portrait of Pacifists*, 38; Memoirs of André Trocmé, 106–9, Trocmé Papers.

273   "If every one of us": Memoirs of André Trocmé, 86–87, Trocmé Papers; Unsworth, *A Portrait of Pacifists*, 90.

274   "Her face was harmonious": Memoirs of André Trocmé, 233; Unsworth, *A Portrait of Pacifists*, 111.

274   "And that was it!": Boismorand, *Resistance Figures*, 35.

275   "In the case that war": Boismorand, *Resistance Figures*, 69.

276   "Here, you can see forever": Boismorand, *Resistance Figures*, 77.

277   the population of just under: Henry, *We Only Know Men*, 16, citing François Boulet, "Quelques éléments statistiques," [in] *Le Plateau Vivarais-Lignon: Accueil et Résistance 1939–1944*, ed. Pierre Bolle et al. (Le Chambon-sur-Lignon: Société d'Histoire de la Montagne, 1992), 287, in which it is reported that the total Protestant population of the Plateau is 38 percent

but both Le Chambon and Le Mazet-Saint-Voy are 95 and 94 percent, respectively; see also, Grose, *A Good Place to Hide*, 265–68, for a discussion of the population on the Plateau and the number of refugees saved.

277 "He is an absolutely striking": Unsworth, *A Portrait of Pacifists*, 148.

277 "eyes clouded with tears": Boismorand, *Resistance Figures*, 77.

278 "I had long dreamed": Boismorand, 72.

278 "He has all the qualities": Boismorand, 64.

279 "a demonstration of the same spirit": Boismorand, 78–79.

279 "Once more, atrocious persecution": Boismorand, 79–80.

279 "No government can force": Unsworth, *A Portrait of Pacifists*, 147.

279 "diabolical forces of Nazism": Hallie, *Lest Innocent Blood Be Shed*, 83.

279 "Today, I am still": Boismorand, *Resistance Figures*, 84.

280 "Let us humble ourselves": Boismorand, 90–95.

280 "In the church": Grose, *A Good Place to Hide*, 43.

280 "The peace that was concluded": Bohny-Reiter, oral history interview. Gril-Mariotte, *The Plateau*, quotes André Philip as saying "It's armistice with dishonor" (37).

280 "For the Pétain regime": Sauvage, *Weapons of the Spirit*.

280 "The bells don't belong": Boismorand, *Resistance Figures*, 106; Hallie, *Lest Innocent Blood Be Shed*, 96–97.

280 "Although we were supposedly": Boismorand, *Resistance Figures*, 101. According to Paul Kutner, this did not actually happen in France until 1942.

281 recalled Gurs as "a horror": Unsworth, *A Portrait of Pacifists*, 170.

281 While the refugees starved: Boismorand, *Resistance Figures*, 101.

282 Chalmers had heard: Hallie, *Lest Innocent Blood Be Shed*, 132–33.

282 they developed an inspired idea: Hallie, *Lest Innocent Blood Be Shed*, 135.

282 "Do you wish to be that community?": Hallie, 135; Boismorand, *Resistance Figures*, 101–2.

282 If André could provide: Boismorand, *Resistance Figures*, 101–2; Hallie, *Lest Innocent Blood Be Shed*, 136.

282 biblical "cities of refuge": Num. 35:9–31; Josh. 20:1–9; Deut. 19:1–13; Deut. 19:7–10.

283 "Keep your spare rooms free": Paul J. Kutner, "The Rescue of Jews in Le Chambon-sur-Lignon and the Surrounding Villages of the Plateau Vivarais-Lignon, France," unpublished dissertation, Yeshiva University, New York, December 2021, 10.

283   "gradually persuaded": Boismorand, *Resistance Figures*, 105.

283   In May 1941: Desaix and Ruelle, *Hidden on the Mountain*, 15.

284   "Fear was our companion": Desaix and Ruelle, 121.

284   "there was enough love": Daniel Trocmé, file M.31/1037, Yad Vashem Archives.

284   Magda would take children: Hanne Liebman, interview by author, February 28, 2020; Nelly Trocmé, interview by author, April 24, 2022.

285   "It may sound stupid": Peter Feigl, oral history interview, August 23, 1995, RG-50.999.0676, United States Holocaust Memorial Museum, Washington, DC.

285   "It was a very pleasant": Peter Feigl, interview with author, April 30, 2022.

285   "they kept our noses": Feigl, oral history interview.

286   Two Jewish girls: Hallie, *Lest Innocent Blood Be Shed*, 141; Nelly Trocmé, interview.

288   Refugees also were hidden: Gril-Mariotte, *The Plateau;* Tracy Strong quote is in Browning, "From Humanitarian Relief to Holocaust Rescue."

287   "There are no refugees in here!": Hallie, *Lest Innocent Blood Be Shed*, 182.

287   "The people of Le Chambon": Kutner, "The Rescue of Jews," 1. As André Trocmé put it, "So these people who do not read the papers but the scriptures do not stand on the moving soil of opinion but on the rock of the word of God." Sauvage, "A Most Persistent Haven: Le Chambon-sur-Lignon," 32.

287   "We have in our house": Hallie, *Lest Innocent Blood Be Shed*, 183; Sauvage, *Weapons of the Spirit.*

287   "It was there that we received from God": Hallie, *Lest Innocent Blood Be Shed*, 173.

288   "doing something of consequence": Hallie, 199.

288   "If it had been an organization": Hallie, 199.

289   "I am sending you five": Unsworth, *A Portrait of Pacifists*, 168.

289   "They were justified lies": Boismorand, *Resistance Figures*, 96.

289   the seventeen-year-old daughter: Desaix and Ruelle, *Hidden on the Mountain*, 33.

290   "In the few months": Desaix and Ruelle, 37.

290   "the whole rhythm": Elizabeth Kaufmann Koenig, oral history interview with Elizabeth Kaufmann Koenig, January 29, 1990, RG-50.030*0111, United States Holocaust Memorial Museum, Washington, DC.

290   She almost cried: Desaix and Ruelle, *Hidden on the Mountain*, 34.

290   "They did not understand": Elizabeth Kaufmann Koenig, oral history interview.

292   After the service: Unsworth, *A Portrait of Pacifists*, 183.

292   "Pastor Trocmé, this day": Hallie, *Lest Innocent Blood Be Shed*, 103; Boismorand, *Resistance Figures*, 110–11; Memoirs of André Trocmé, 361, Trocmé Papers, Collection: DG 107, Swarthmore College Peace Collection, Swarthmore College, Swarthmore, PA; Unsworth, *A Portrait of Pacifists*, 183. Nelly Trocmé believes the second part of this conversation happened two weeks later, but André Trocmé's memoirs place it here.

292   "To the good listener, warning": Boismorand, *Resistance Figures*, 111.

293   Their first stop: Bohny-Reiter, interview.

293   "But even if I had such a list": Hallie, *Lest Innocent Blood Be Shed*, 107–8.

293   "Do the will of God": "Under the Wings of the Church," in *I Am My Brother's Keeper*, Yad Vashem, https://www.yadvashem.org/yv/en/exhibitions/righteous/trocme.asp.

294   "They searched first the houses": Hallie, *Lest Innocent Blood Be Shed*, 111–12.

294   "The entire village": Bohny-Reiter, interview.

294   "I think we felt safe": Hanne Liebman, interview.

294   Rank-and-file officers: Hallie, *Lest Innocent Blood Be Shed*, 114.

295   "They didn't tell us": Feigl, oral history interview. Sometimes someone showed up in the classroom and the children were sent for mushrooms even when they weren't in season; Feigl, author interview.

295   Rudi Appel remembered: Desaix and Ruelle, *Hidden on the Mountain*, 54.

295   "Those in hiding": Bohny-Reiter, interview.

295   "This place is full of Jews": Sauvage, *Weapons of the Spirit*.

295   "These soldiers had gone through hell": Feigl, oral history interview.

295   "the head of the escape route": Unsworth, *A Portrait of Pacifists*, 186.

297   In a letter to his half-brother: Boismorand, *Resistance Figures*, 115–16.

297   From Nice to Toulouse: Boismorand, 116; Hallie, *Lest Innocent Blood Be Shed*, 147–48; Henry, *We Only Know Men*, 22.

297   "a very personal matter": Boismorand, *Resistance Figures*, 119.

298   "Magda," he told her: Hallie, *Lest Innocent Blood Be Shed*, 19; Boismorand, *Resistance Figures*, 119.

298   "I didn't do it out of generosity": Boismorand, *Resistance Figures*, 120.

298   "I don't know": Hallie, *Lest Innocent Blood Be Shed*, 21.

298   They brought gifts: Hallie, 32; Boismorand, *Resistance Figures*, 120–21.

298   "Things will change": Hallie, *Lest Innocent Blood Be Shed*, 29.

299   "What? Jews?": Hallie, 30.

299   The encounter changed André: Hallie, 30.

299   On March 15: Boismorand, *Resistance Figures*, 122; Unsworth, *Portrait of Pacifists*, 192.

300   "We cannot sign": Hallie, *Lest Innocent Blood Be Shed*, 39; Boismorand, *Resistance Figures*, 122.

300   "On at least one point": Hallie, *Lest Innocent Blood Be Shed*, 39.

300   The commandant exploded: Hallie, 39; Unsworth, *Portrait of Pacifists*, 192.

300   "If we sign": Hallie, *Lest Innocent Blood Be Shed*, 39.

300   "So be it": Hallie, 42.

300   The next morning: Boismorand, *Resistance Figures*, 123; Kutner says compromise language was found: Gril-Mariotte, *The Plateau*, 81.

301   "It was a joyful scene": Gril-Mariotte, 61.

302   "a place for a contribution": Daniel Trocmé, Yad Vashem Archives.

302   "an intellectual given to": Hallie, *Lest Innocent Blood Be Shed*, 206.

302   "like a madman": Hallie, 206.

302   "I adore them": Henry, *We Only Know Men*, 9.

302   "the father, as I like to say": Henry, 10.

302   "Daniel Trocmé never thought of himself": Daniel Trocmé, Yad Vashem Archives.

303   came from fifteen different countries: Desaix and Ruelle, *Hidden on the Mountain*, 206: Germany, Poland, Austria, Russia, Hungary, Lithuania, Romania, Netherlands, Spain, Czechoslovakia, Iran, Belgium, Luxembourg, France, and Tonkin (Vietnam).

303   over a dozen armed plainclothes members: Boismorand, *Resistance Figures*, 124, says June 23; Unsworth, *A Portrait of Pacifists*, 199, says June 29. According to Peter Kutner, Dr. Jean Wallet claimed it was Vichy police, not the Gestapo, although all other accounts refer to the Gestapo.

304   "In the large dining room": Trocmé Papers; Unsworth, *A Portrait of Pacifists*, 200.

305   "What a beautiful day": Boismorand, *Resistance Figures*, 128.

305   "The Gestapo is at": Boismorand, 129; Hallie, *Lest Innocent Blood Be Shed*, 212.

305   "By the time we got": Boismorand, *Resistance Figures*, 130–31.

305   "They saw a Gestapo agent": Boismorand, *Resistance Figures*, 131, says there were two or three agents.

305   "Schweinejude!": Boismorand, 131; Hallie, *Lest Innocent Blood Be Shed*, 215. *Schweinejude* means "Pig-Jew."

305   "Do not worry": Daniel Trocmé, Yad Vashem Archives; Boismorand, *Resistance Figures*, 131.

306   "He made a lot": Trocmé, Yad Vashem Archives.

306   "Morale is quite good": Trocmé; Henry, *We Only Know Men*, 58.

306   "My thoughts are constantly": Trocmé, Yad Vashem Archives.

306   "I believe this separation": Trocmé.

306   "One of the most beautiful": Trocmé.

306   "He was just a shadow": Trocmé.

307   A package sent to Buchenwald: Trocmé. He was likely gassed.

307   "They love him": Trocmé.

307   "It is not fair": Trocmé.

307   "He gave his life": Unsworth, *A Portrait of Pacifists*, 201; Trocmé, Yad Vashem Archives.

307   "These are people to be admired": Trocmé.

307   "Oh, the somber, somber night": Trocmé. Daniel was made a Righteous Among the Nations on March 18, 1976, and a carob tree was planted along the Avenue of the Righteous.

308   "We have lived through many": Unsworth, *Portrait of Pacifists*, 5.

309   "was one of the happiest times": Hallie, *Lest Innocent Blood Be Shed*, 224.

309   "It was not reasonable": Hallie, 233.

309   "had changed a great deal": Boismorand, *Resistance Figures*, 125.

310   "Le Chambon was a hot": Grose, *A Good Place to Hide*, 156.

310   the great writer Albert Camus: Patrick Henry, "Albert Camus and the Secret of Le Chambon," *Tablet Magazine*, June 22, 2020; André Chouraqui to Patrick Henry, October 10, 1999, in Henry, *We Only Know Men*, 113. Some have speculated that the character of Dr. Rieux in *The Plague* is named after Dr. Paul Riou of Le Chambon. Pierre Sauvage believes Roger Le Forestier is a more likely candidate given the probability that Camus likely consulted with him and his age is closer to Dr. Rieux's. Email from Pierre Sauvage to author, June 5, 2022.

310   "I studied the theory": Farrell, "Albert Camus' 'The Plague,'" *City of Refuge*.

310   "What's true of all the evils": Albert Camus, *The Plague*, trans. Stuart Gilbert, 1948 (New York: Vintage, 1991), 125.

310   "The teaching about": Farrell, "We Will Do Our Best to Hide Them," *City of Refuge*.

311   "He agreed with me": Memoirs of André Trocmé, Papers of André and Magda Trocmé, 323; Unsworth, *A Portrait of Pacifists*, 205.

312   "he was something of an optimist": Bohny-Reiter, interview.

312   "a purehearted fool": Hallie, *Lest Innocent Blood Be Shed*, 246–47.

312   believed, the pastor André Bettex reflected: Nelly Trocmé, interview.

312   "We in Le Chambon resist": Hallie, *Lest Innocent Blood Be Shed*, 243.

313   "At his trial": Hallie, 246.

313   "The soldiers tossed out": Boismorand, *Resistance Figures*, 147.

313   "André had to stand up": Boismorand, 147.

314   "My father was always criticized": Nelly Trocmé, interview.

314   "like a fighter": Hallie, *Lest Innocent Blood Be Shed*, 262.

315   "genuinely don't feel": "Bill Moyers Interviews Filmmaker Pierre Sauvage."

315   "That remains a mystery": Bohny-Reiter, interview.

315   "You shall love the Lord": Sauvage, *Weapons of the Spirit*.

315   "It was a very special atmosphere": Bohny-Reiter, interview.

315   "We are always going to save": Sauvage, *Weapons of the Spirit*.

316   The French deported: Desaix and Ruelle, *Hidden on the Mountain*; Henry, *We Only Know Men*, 138.

316   "And I think that": Sauvage, *Weapons of the Spirit*.

10. Ten POWs

317   "They came straggling": Willy Fisher, diary, in Rigler and Blumfield, *10 British P.O.W.s*, 139.

317   "God punish Germany": Fisher, diary, 139.

318   "Come away quickly, Willy": Rigler and Blumfield, *10 British P.O.W.s*, 207.

318   "Poor Germany—what have we come to?": Rigler and Blumfield, 139.

318   "To be really hungry": Rescuers of Sara Hannah Rigler, file M.31/4042a-i, Yad Vashem Archives, Jerusalem.

319   "Child, if you must": "Willy Fisher's Diary Transcribed," Rigler and Blumfield, *10 British P.O.W.s*, 141.

319   "May God be with you": Rescuers of Sara Hannah Rigler, Yad Vashem Archives.

319   "It wasn't a well thought out plan": Rigler and Blumfield, *10 British P.O.W.s*, 54.

320   "I'm hiding here": Rigler and Blumfield, 57.

320   "I even welcomed the cows": Rigler and Blumfield, 57.

321   "Who's there?": Rescuers of Sara Hannah Rigler, Yad Vashem Archives.

322   "like a rabbit": Rescuers of Sara Hannah Rigler.

323   "We had a good look": Rigler and Blumfield, *10 British P.O.W.s*, 141.

326   this apparent salvation: Sara Hannah Rigler, oral history interview by Lyn E. Smith, September 21, 2010, Imperial War Museum, London, 11.

326   "At least Germans": Rigler, interview, 12–13.

326   "another fateful miscalculation": Rigler and Blumfield, *10 British P.O.W.s*, 21.

327   "As wonderful as my father": Rigler, interview, 10.

328   "Everybody just let out": Rigler, 15.

328   "After the war": Rigler, 16.

328   "You're going to see": Rigler, 17.

329   "I missed my father terribly": Rescuers of Sara Hannah Rigler, Yad Vashem Archives.

331   "I am the Jew R.S.": "Willy Fisher's Diary Transcribed," Rigler and Blumfield, *10 British P.O.W.s*, 141.

331   "Hannah and I would snuggle": Rigler and Blumfield, *10 British P.O.W.s*, 49.

331   "The smell was truly": Rigler and Blumfield, 50.

332   "get through each day": Rigler and Blumfield, 51.

332   "We were walking skeletons": Rigler and Blumfield, 51.

332   "He had kind eyes": Rigler and Blumfield, 53.

332   "Little girl, I can save you": Rigler, interview, 22.

332   "Starvation makes people senseless": Rigler and Blumfield, *10 British P.O.W.s*, 54.

333   "She will keep harping": "Willy Fisher's Diary Transcribed," 147.

334   "their *bon vivant*": Rigler, interview.

334   "I thought I was in love": Rigler.

334   One evening Alan told her: Rigler.

334   "So, you can sleep here": Rigler.

335   "They left, my surrogate family": Rigler.

335   "I was in agony": Rigler and Blumfield, *10 British P.O.W.s*, 61.

335   Once again, she felt her father: Rigler and Blumfield, 62.

335   She ran into Zoya: Rigler, interview.

335   "I thought how strange": Rigler and Blumfield, *110 British P.O.W.s*, 62.

336　"Sonia," he said, "you're not Lithuanian": Rigler, interview.

336　"My heart was racing: Rigler and Blumfield, *10 British P.O.W.s*, 62–63.

336　"You know, Mr. Binder": Rigler, interview.

336　"I'm not going to stay": Rigler.

336　"It is strange, indeed": Rigler and Blumfield, *10 British P.O.W.s*, 167.

337　"You know, Sonia": Rigler and Blumfield, 63.

337　"The Russians are [here]": Rigler, interview.

337　"Perhaps," she noted later, "he finally recognized": Rigler and Blumfield, *10 British P.O.W.s*, 65.

339　"thousands of emaciated": Rigler and Blumfield, 207.

339　"I broke down": Rigler and Blumfield, 72.

340　"another jarring shock": Rigler and Blumfield, 74.

340　Four of her mother's brothers: Rigler, interview.

341　"Today is my birthday": Rigler and Blumfield, *10 British P.O.W.s*, 82.

341　"I could not believe my own eyes": Rigler and Blumfield, 62–63.

342　"Looking at your latest photo": Rigler and Blumfield, 62–63.

342　ran an article: "Woman's 20-year Search for Rescuers," May 26, 1968, *Johannesburg Sunday Times*; Rigler and Blumfield, *110 British P.O.W.s*, 130.

342　"My joy at your being alive": Rigler and Blumfield, *10 British P.O.W.s*, 173.

343　"I do not believe my country": Rigler and Blumfield, *10 British P.O.W.s*, 142.

343　"It was such a moving moment": Rescuers of Sara Hannah Rigler, Yad Vashem Archives.

344　"My ten angels": Rigler and Blumfield, *10 British P.O.W.s*, 121.

344　"These men risked their lives for me": Rescuers of Sara Hannah Rigler, Yad Vashem Archives.

344　"If one of the ten": Rescuers of Sara Hannah Rigler.

345　"There is a tree firmly": Rigler and Blumfield, *10 British P.O.W.s*, 122.

Conclusion

346　"I am not a hero": Gies and Gold, *Anne Frank Remembered*, prologue.

346　"secrecy about wartime rescue": Fogelman, *Conscience and Courage*, xvi.

347　"It was considered": Paldiel, interview.

347　"more comforting to believe": Henry, *We Only Know Men*, 138.

347   "I could see that": Hirschbiegel, *Downfall*.

348   "We should dream of the day": Rosenberg, *Art of Resistance*, 273.

348   "It is only natural": Henry, *We Only Know Men*, 138.

348   nearly seven hundred: Oliner and Oliner, *The Altruistic Personality*, 261.

349   interviewed three hundred: Fogelman, *Conscience and Courage*.

349   "No man is an island": John Donne, *Devotions upon Emergent Occasions*, Meditation 17, 1624. Or, in the original beautiful early modern English: "No man is an *Iland*, intire of it selfe; every man is a peece of the *Continent*, a part of the *maine*."

349   five categories: Fogelman, *Conscience and Courage*.

350   One or more factors: Fogelman, 254.

350   "Some are born great": William Shakespeare, *Twelfth Night*, ed. Barbara A. Mowat and Paul Werstine (New York: Simon & Schuster, 2019), 2.5.149–150.

350   Yet Yukiko Sugihara: Yukiko Sugihara, oral history interview, October 27, 1999, RG-50.494.0020, United States Holocaust Memorial Museum, Washington, DC.

350   "It is amazing": Frank, *Diary of a Young Girl*, January 28, 1944, 178.

351   "Most of the stories": Paldiel, interview.

351   "The hand of compassion": Fogelman, *Conscience and Courage*, 57.

352   "it was sufficient to reject": Paldiel, interview.

352   "Bad men need nothing": John Stuart Mill, *Inaugural Address at St. Andrews*, 1867.

353   "When bad men combine": Edmund Burke, *Thoughts on the Cause of the Present Discontents*, April 23, 1770.

353   "tip of the iceberg": Fogelman, *Conscience and Courage*, 149.

354   "Try as we might": Henry, *We Only Know Men*, 157.

354   "Example is not the main thing": Schweitzer and Mellon, *Brothers in Spirit*, xviii.

355   Abe Foxman once asked: Abraham Foxman, Address to the Nightingale-Bamford School, April 8, 2019, New York.

355   "If now we find such gems": "Introduction to Rescue in Poland," Institute for the Study of Rescue and Altruism in the Holocaust, https://www.holocaustrescue.org/introduction-to-rescue-in-poland.

355   "It is not your obligation": Pirkei Avot, 2:16.

356   "There are stars": Senesh, *Life and Diary*, 1.

Selected Bibliography

ARCHIVES

Exiles Film Project Records. Manuscripts and Archives Repository. Yale
    University Libraries, New Haven, CT.
Feuchtwanger, Lion and·Marta. Papers. Feuchtwanger Memorial Library.
    Special Collections. University of Southern California Libraries, Los
    Angeles.
Fry, Varian. Papers. Rare Book and Manuscript Library. Columbia University,
    New York.
German Exile Archive, 1933–1945. Deutsche National Biobliotek, Leipzig and
    Frankfurt.
Holocaust and Genocide Studies Collections. University of Southern Florida,
    Tampa, St. Petersburg, and Sarasota, FL.
Imperial War Museums, London.
International Committee of the Red Cross Archives, Geneva.
JDC Archives, New York and Jerusalem.
Jewish Museum, Berlin.
Jewish Telegraphic Agency Archives. https://www.jta.org/archive.
Mann, Heinrich. Papers. Feuchtwanger Memorial Library. Special Collections.
    University of Southern California Libraries, Los Angeles.
Museum of Jewish Heritage, New York.
Rey, H. A. and Margaret. Papers. University of Southern Mississippi, Long
    Beach.
Sousa Mendes Foundation, Greenlawn, NY.
Trocmé, André and Magda. Papers. Swarthmore College Peace Collection.
    Swarthmore College, Swarthmore, PA.
United States Holocaust Memorial Museum, Washington, DC.

United States National Archives and Records Administration, College Park, MD.
Visual History Archive. USC Shoah Foundation, Los Angeles.
Yad Vashem Archives, Jerusalem.

AUTHOR INTERVIEWS

Alberati, Paolo. November 30, 2021.
Bartali, Gioia. May 15, 2022.
Bingham, Robert. Email interview. June 15, 2020.
Bingham William. June and July 2020.
Braverman, Nardo Bonomi. February 2, 2022.
Dorzback, Ann Wallersteiner. April 12, 2018.
Einstein, Fred. April 12, 2018.
Endicott, Abigail Bingham. February 10, 2021.
Feigl, Peter. April 30, 2022.
Fry, James. February 14, 2021.
Hewitt, Nelly Trocmé. April 24, 2022.
Indrimi, Natalia. November 7, 2021.
Levine, Hillel. May 1, 2022.
Liebman, Hanne and Max. February 28, 2020.
Mayer, Jack. January 11, 2022.
Mendes, Gérald. June 7, 2022.
Morgenthau III, Henry. June 3, 2014.
Morgenthau, Robert. January 23, 2017.
Paldiel, Mordecai. November 10, 2021.
Saul, Eric. February 6, 2021.
Sauvage, Pierre. February 28, 2020.
Sugihara, Nobuki. February 17, 2021.
Wiesel, Elie. February 15, 2015.
Zwartendijk, Robert. February 9, 2021.

BOOKS AND ARTICLES

Ackerman, Diane. *The Zookeeper's Wife: A War Story*. New York: W. W.
   Norton, 2008.

Alberati, Paolo. *Gino Bartali: Mille diavoli in corpo.* Florence: Giunti, 2006.

———. "La guerra di Gino Bartali: Ebrei e cattolici in Toscana e Umbria, 1943–1944." PhD diss., Universita degli Studi di Perugia, 2003–4.

Arendt, Hannah. *Eichmann in Jerusalem: A Report on the Banality of Evil.* New York: Viking, 1963.

Avranches, Michael d'. *Flight through Hell.* New York: Exposition, 1951.

Bartali, Andrea. *Gino Bartali, mio papà.* Milano: TEA, 2018.

Bartali, Gino, and Mario Pancera. *La mia storia.* Milan: Soc. Editrice Stampa Sportiva–La Gazzetta Dello Sport, 1958.

Bartali, Gino, and Pino Ricci. *Tutto sbagliato, tutto da rifare.* Milan: Mondadori, 1979.

Bauer, Yehuda. *A History of the Holocaust.* New York: Franklin Watts, 2002.

———. *Rethinking the Holocaust.* New Haven: Yale University Press, 2002.

Bertelsen, Aage. *October '43.* Translated by Molly Lindholm and Willy Agtby. With foreword by Sholem Asch and an introduction by Hans Hedtoft. New York: G. P. Putnam and Sons, 1954.

Bingham, Hiram, IV. Interview by Tiffany Bingham. Circa 1980.

Bingham, Robert Kim. *Courageous Dissent: How Harry Bingham Defied His Government to Save Lives.* Salem, CT: Triune, 2009.

Boismorand, Pierre. *Magda and André Trocmé: Resistance Figures.* Montreal: McGill-Queen's University Press, 2014.

Bohny-Reiter, August. Oral history interview by Raye L. Farr, May 27, 1994, RG-50.030.0031 and RG-50.030.0032. United States Holocaust Memorial Museum, Washington, DC. https://collections.ushmm.org/search/catalog /irn504536 and https://collections.ushmm.org/search/catalog/irn504537.

Borden, Louise. *The Journey That Saved Curious George: The True Wartime Escape of Margret and H. A. Rey.* Illustrated by Allan Drummond. Boston: Houghton-Mifflin Harcourt, 2016.

Brokken, Jan. *The Just: How Six Unlikely Heroes Saved Thousands of Jews from the Holocaust.* Translated by David McKay. Minneapolis: Scribe, 2021.

Browning, Christopher R. "From Humanitarian Relief to Holocaust Rescue: Tracy Strong Jr., Vichy Internment Camps, and the Maison des Roches in Le Chambon." *Holocaust and Genocide Studies* 30, no. 2 (Fall 2016): 211–46. https://doi.org/10.1093/hgs/dcw031.

Bülow, Louis. "Irene Sendler." The Holocaust: Crimes, Heroes, and Villains. 2020–22. http://auschwitz.dk/sendler.htm.

Cavendish, Richard. "Hitler and Mussolini Meet in Rome." *History Today*, May 2008.

Ciano, Galeazzo. *Galeazzo Ciano: Diary, 1937–1943.* Preface by Sumner Welles. Translated by Robert L. Miller. New York: Enigma, 2002.

Cummins, Paul F. *Dachau Song: The Twentieth-Century Odyssey of Herbert Zipper.* New York: Peter Land, 2014.

Davenport Ebel, Miriam. "An Unsentimental Education: A Memoir by Miriam Davenport Ebel." Varian Fry Institute, 1999. http://www.varianfry.org/ebel _memoir_en.htm.

Dolgin, Robyn. "Danish Hero: One Rosh Hashanah Burns Bright in Holocaust." *Jewish Post.* www.jewishpost.com.

Dumbach, Annette, and Jud Newborn. *Sophie Scholl and the White Rose.* 3rd ed. London: Oneworld, 2018.

Durland Desaix, Deborah, and Karen Gray Ruelle. *Hidden on the Mountain: Stories of Children Sheltered from the Nazis in Le Chambon.* New York: Holiday House, 2006.

Eisner, Peter. "Saving the Jews of Nazi France." *Smithsonian*, March 2009.

Ephraim, Frank. "The Mindanao Plan: Political Obstacles to Jewish Refugee Settlement." *Holocaust and Genocide Studies* 20, no. 3 (2006): 410–36.

Ephraim, Frank, and Stanley Karnow. *Escape to Manila: From Nazi Tyranny to Japanese Terror.* 2003. Reprint, Urbana: University of Illinois Press, 2008.

Eptakili, Tassoula. "The Greek Island That Hid Its Jews from the Nazis." *Kathimerini*, July 6, 2014.

Ezratty, Harry. "The Portuguese Consul and the 10,000 Jews." *Jewish Life*, September–October 1964.

Feuchtwanger, Lion. *The Devil in France: My Encounter with Him in the Summer of 1940.* Translated by Elisabeth Abbott. New York: Viking, 1941.

Flender, Harold. *Rescue in Denmark.* New York: MacFadden-Bartell, 1968.

Fogelman, Eva. *Conscience and Courage: Rescuers of Jews during the Holocaust.* New York: Anchor, 1995.

Fralon, Jose-Alain. *A Good Man in Evil Times: The Story of Aristedes de Sousa Mendes—the Unknown Hero Who Saved Countless Lives in World War II.* Translated by Peter Graham. New York: Carroll & Graf, 2001.

Franco, Manuela. *Spared Lives: The Actions of Three Portuguese Diplomats in World War II.* Exhibition catalog. Edited by Jaime Gama. Lisbon:

Diplomatic Institute, Portugal Ministry of Foreign Affairs, 2000. http://vidaspoupadas.idiplomatico.pt/en/.

Frank, Anne. *The Diary of a Young Girl: The Definitive Edition*. Edited by Otto H. Frank and Mirjam Pressler. Translated by Susan Massotty. 1944. Reprint, New York: Doubleday, 2001.

Fry, Varian. "The Massacre of the Jews." *New Republic*, December 21, 1942.

———. *Surrender on Demand*. 1945. Reprint, Boulder: Johnson, 1997.

Galchen, Rivka. "The Unexpected Profundity of Curious George." *New Yorker*, June 3, 2019.

Gallagher, Tom. "The Life and Afterlife of Salazar." *History Today*, September 2018.

Ganor, Solly. *Light One Candle: A Survivor's Tale from Lithuania to Jerusalem*. New York: Kodansha International, 2003.

Garibaldi, Andrea. "Così Bartali in bici portava ai conventi i documenti salva-ebrei." *Corriere della Sera*, January 28, 2009.

Gershman, Norman H. *Besa: Muslims Who Saved Jews in World War II*. Syracuse, NY: Syracuse University Press, 2008.

Gies, Miep, and Alison Leslie Gold. *Anne Frank Remembered: The Story of the Woman Who Helped to Hide the Frank Family*. London: Pocket, 2009.

Gilbert, Martin. *The Righteous: The Unsung Heroes of the Holocaust*. 2003. Reprint, New York: Henry Holt, 2004.

Goebbels, Joseph. *The Goebbels Diaries*. Translated by Louis P. Lochner. New York: Doubleday, 1948.

Goettel, Elinor. *Eagle of the Philippines: President Manuel Quezon*. New York: Julian Messner, 1970.

Gold, Alison Leslie. *A Special Fate: Chiune Sugihara: Hero of the Holocaust*. Providence, RI: TMI, 2014.

Gold, Mary Jayne. *Crossroads Marseilles, 1940*. 1980. Reprint, New York: Doubleday, 1998.

Goldberg, Carey. "The Honors Come Late for a Japanese Schindler; a Month of Tribute to a Savior of Thousands." *New York Times*, November 8, 1995.

Gril-Mariotte, Aziza, ed. *The Plateau: A Land of Welcome and Refuge*. Translated by Paul J. Kutner. Le-Chambon-Sur-Lignon, France: Éditions Dolmazon, 2017.

Grose, Peter. *A Good Place to Hide: How One French Community Saved Thousands of Lives during World War II*. New York: Pegasus, 2015.

Grünbaum, Irene. *Escape through the Balkans: The Autobiography of Irene Grünbaum*. Edited and translated by Katherine Morris. Lincoln: University of Nebraska Press, 1996.

Guggenheim, Peggy. *Confessions of an Art Addict*. Hopewell, NJ: Ecco Press, 1997.

Gutman, Dr. Israel. *The Encyclopedia of the Righteous Among the Nations: Rescuers of Jews during the Holocaust*. Associate Editors, Sara Bender and Pearl Weiss. 7 vols. 2003. Reprint, Jerusalem: Yad Vashem, 2007.

Hallie, Philip P. *Lest Innocent Blood Be Shed: The Story of the Village of Le Chambon and How Goodness Happened There*. New York: Harper Perennial, 1994.

Harris, Bonnie M. "Jewish Refugee Rescue in the Philippines, 1937–1941." *Journal of History* 62 (2016): 213–32.

Hausner, Gideon. *Justice in Jerusalem*. New York: Harper & Row, 1968.

Hellenic News. "Special Issue: The Jews of Greece." *Hellenic News of America*, January 29, 2017.

Henry, Patrick. *We Only Know Men: The Rescue of Jews in France during the Holocaust*. Washington, DC: Catholic University Press, 2007.

"Historical Discovery: Chiune Sugihara's Third Child Was Born in Kaunas." Vytautas Magnus University, January 4, 2018.

Horn, Dara. *People Love Dead Jews: Reports from a Haunted Present*. New York: W. W. Norton, 2021.

Hurowitz, Richard. "A Cycling Legend's Secret War Mission: Saving Italy's Jews." *Daily Beast*, November 19, 2017.

———. "How the Danes, and a German Turncoat, Pulled Off a World War II Miracle." *Los Angeles Times*, September 30, 2018.

———. "I May Have to Disobey My Government: Lessons from 'Japan's Schindler.'" *Daily Beast*, September 4, 2017.

———. "Remembering the White Rose." *New York Times*, February 22, 2018.

———. "The Ringmaster Who Helped Jewish Acrobats Escape the Nazis." *Daily Beast*, April 21, 2018.

———. "A Time to Remember Portugal's Schindler." *New York Times*, January 27, 2019.

———. "When Holocaust Refugees Almost Found a Caribbean Haven." *Wall Street Journal*, January 26, 2016.

———. "You Must Remember This: Sultan Mohammed V Protected the Jews of Casablanca." *Los Angeles Times*, April 25, 2017.

Isenberg, Sheila. *A Hero of Our Own: The Story of Varian Fry*. Kindle ed. Lexington, MA: Plunkett Lake, 2017.

Jones, Edgar, and Simon Wessely. "British Prisoners-of-War: From Resilience to Psychological Vulnerability: Reality or Perception." *Twentieth Century British History* 21, no. 2 (August 4, 2011): 163–83.

Kerem, Yitzchak. "The Survival of the Jews of Zakynthos in the Holocaust." *Proceedings of the World Congress of Jewish Studies* (1989): 394–87.

Kober, A. H. *Star Turns*. Translated by G. J. Renier. New York: Macmillan, 1929.

Koestler, Arthur. *Scum of the Earth*. 1941. Reprint, London: Eland, 2012.

Kotani, Apostal. *A History of Jews in Albania*. 3rd ed. Tirana, Albania: Albania-Israel Friendship Association, 2012.

Kotlowski, Dean J. "Breaching the Paper Walls: Paul v. McNutt and Jewish Refugees to the Philippines, 1938–1939." *Diplomatic History* 33, no. 5 (November 2009): 865–96.

———. *Paul V. McNutt and the Age of FDR*. Bloomington: Indiana University Press, 2015.

Kutner, Paul. "The Rescue of Jews in Le Chambon-Sur-Lignon and the Surrounding Villages of the Plateau Vivarais-Lignon, France." Paper, Yeshiva University, 2021.

Lazzerini, Marcello, and Romano Beghelli. *La leggenda di Bartali*. Florence: Ponte alle Grazie, 1992.

Lefkovits, Etgar. "Heroism in the Warsaw Ghetto." *Jerusalem Post*, June 8, 2004.

Levi, Primo. *Survival in Auschwitz*. 1947. Translated by Stuart J. Woolf. With a conversation between Primo Levi and Philip Roth. New York: Simon & Schuster, 1995.

Levine, Bettijane. "A Tie That Binds Jews and a Special Family." *Los Angeles Times*, September 27, 2001.

Levine, Hillel. *In Search of Sugihara: The Elusive Japanese Diplomat Who Risked His Life to Rescue 10,000 Jews from the Holocaust*. New York: Free Press, 1996.

Lévy, Bernard-Henri. *The Will to See: Dispatches from a World of Misery and Hope*. New Haven, CT: Yale University Press, 2021.

Lidegaard, Bo. *Countrymen: The Untold Story of How Denmark's Jews Escaped the Nazis, of the Courage of Their Fellow Danes—and of the Extraordinary Role of the SS.* New York: Alfred A. Knopf, 2013.

Lipstadt, Deborah E. *The Eichmann Trial.* New York: Nextbook/Schocken, 2011.

Lochery, Neill. *Lisbon: War in the Shadows of the City of Light, 1939–1945.* New York: Public Affairs, 2012.

Lowrie, Donald A. *The Hunted Children.* New York: W. W. Norton, 1963.

Macmillan, Harold. *War Diaries.* London: Macmillan, 1984.

Maloney, Russell. "Scarlet Pimpernel, Streamlined." *New York Times*, April 22, 1945.

Marino, Andy. *A Quiet American: The Secret War of Varian Fry.* New York: St. Martin's Griffin, 2000.

Mark, Jonathan. "The Splitting of the Sea, 1943." *NY Jewish Week*, April 18, 2011.

Matsas, Michael. *The Illusion of Safety: The Story of the Greek Jews during World War II.* New York: Pella, 1997.

Matuson Rigler, Sara Hannah. Oral history interview by Tori Lochler, April 8, 2010. Holocaust Survivors Oral History Project, Florida Studies Center, University of South Florida, Tampa.

Mayer, Jack. *Life in a Jar: The Irena Sendler Project.* Middlebury, VT: Long Trail, 2011.

Mazzeo, Tilar J. *Irena's Children: A True Story of Courage.* New York: Simon & Schuster, 2017.

McConnon, Aili, and Andres McConnon. *Road to Valor: A True Story of WWII Italy, the Nazis, and the Cyclist Who Inspired a Nation.* New York: Crown, 2012.

Meishar, Stav. "Past: Zoltán Hirsch." The Escape Act: A Holocaust Memoir. September 18, 2019. http://www.theescapeactshow.com/blog/past-zoltan -hirsch.

Milgram, Avraham. *Portugal, Salazar, and the Jews.* Translated by Natfali Greenwood. Jerusalem: International Institute for Holocaust Research, 2011.

Miliband, David. *Rescue: Refugees and the Political Crisis of Our Time.* New York: TED, 2018.

Mochizuki, Ken. *Passage to Freedom: The Sugihara Story.* New York: Lee & Low, 1997.

Musée du Désert. *Focus sur la complainte sur la mort de Monsieur Désubas.* Museum Catalogue. Translated by Paul Kutner. Musée du Désert, Mialet, France. http://www.museedudesert.com/article5994.html.

Naar, Devin E. *Jewish Salonica: Between the Ottoman Empire and Modern Greece.* Stanford, CA: Stanford University Press, 2016.

Neufeld, Jacob, and George M. Watson. "A Brief Survey of POWs in Twentieth Century Wars." *Air Power History* 60, no. 2 (2013): 34–45.

Neumann, Johanna Jutta, and Michael Schmidt-Neke. *Escape to Albania: Memoirs of a Jewish Girl from Hamburg.* Edited by Robert Elsie. Vol. 24. London: Center for Albanian Studies, 2015.

Okamoto Bunryō, Verkita. *Decido pro Amo: Humana Agado de Sugihara Tiune.* Loka Kongresa Komitato de la 91-Japana Esperanta Kongreso, 2004.

Oliner, Samuel P., and Pearl M. Oliner. *The Altruistic Personality: Rescuers of Jews in Nazi Europe.* New York: Free Press, 1992.

Pace, Eric. "Adolf Althoff, Circus Chief Who Hid People from the Nazis." *New York Times,* October 19, 1998.

Pałasz-Rutkowska, Ewa, and Andrzej T. Romer. "Polish-Japanese Co-Operation during World War II." *Japan Forum* 7, no. 2 (September 1995): 285–316.

Paldiel, Mordecai. *Diplomat Heroes of the Holocaust.* Jersey City, NJ: Ktav, 2007.

Pivato, Stefano. *Sia lodato Bartali: Il mito di un eroe del novecento.* Rome: Castelvecchi, 2019.

Pivato, Marco, and Stefano Pivato. *L'Ossessionedella memoria. Bartali e il salvataggio degli ebrei: una storia inventata.* Rome: Castelvecchi, 2021.

Polya-Somogyi, Gisèle. *Deported Children, Saved Children: The Young Jewish Refugees in Gers 1940–1944.* Translated by Peter Feigl. N.p.: Peter Feigl, 2021.

Preus, Margi. *Village of Scoundrels.* New York: Amulet, 2020.

Prior, Ingeborg. "Die Reiterin und ihr Retter." *Der Stern,* September 1995.

Quetteville, Harry de. " 'Female Schindler' Irene Sendler, Who Saved Thousands of Jewish Children, Dies." *Telegraph,* May 11, 2008.

Ramati, Alexander. *The Assisi Underground: Assisi and the Nazi Occupation as Told by Rufino Niccacci.* New York: Stein and Day, 1977.

Rigler, Hannah, and Hanita Blumfield. *10 British P.O.W.s Saved My Life: Sara/Hannah Rigler's Gift of Life.* New York: Jay Street, 2006.

Rittner, Carol, and Sandra Meyers. *The Courage to Care: Rescuers of Jews during the Holocaust*. New York: NYU Press, 1989.

Rojek, Iwona. "To była maka całego świata—córka Ireny Sendler opowiedziała nam o swojej mamie." December 9, 2012. Echodnia.eu. https://echodnia.eu /swietokrzyskie/to-byla-matka-calego-swiata-corka-ireny-sendler-opowied ziala-nam-o-swojej-mamie/ar/8561374.

Rosenberg, Justus. *The Art of Resistance: My Four Years in the French Underground, a Memoir*. New York: William Morrow, 2020.

Sacks, Jonathan. "The Light at the Heart of Darkness." December 23, 2018. Rabbi Sacks Legacy Trust, Covenant and Conversation. https://www.rabbi sacks.org/covenant-conversation/shemot/the-light-at-the-heart-of-darkness/.

Sakamoto, Pamela Rotner. *Japanese Diplomats and Jewish Refugees: A World War II Dilemma*. Westport, CT: Praeger, 1998.

Saltarino, Signor [Hermann Waldemar Otto]. *Artisten-Lexikon: Biographische Notizen Uber Kunstreiter, Dompteure, Gymnastiker, Clowns, Akrobaten, Specialitaten Etc. Aller Launder Und Zeiten*. Dusseldorf: Druck und Verlag von Ed. Lintz, 1895.

Sarfatti, Michele. "Did the Great Italian Cyclist Gino Bartali Actually Save Jews during the Holocaust? An Investigation." *Tablet Magazine*, July 18, 2017.

Sarner, Harvey. *Rescue in Albania: One Hundred Percent of Jews in Albania Rescued from Holocaust*. Cathedral City, CA: Brunswick, 1997.

Sauvage, Pierre. "A Most Persistent Haven: Le Chambon-sur-Lignon; The Story of 5,000 Who Would Not Be Bystanders—and of 5,000 More." *Moment*, October 1983.

Schislowska, Monika. "Polish Holocaust Hero Gets Highest Order." Associated Press, November 10, 2003.

Schlesinger, Hans L. "Saved by the U.S. Consul." *Valley News*, July 2, 2006.

Scholl, Inge Aicher. *The White Rose: Munich, 1942–1943*. Middletown, CT: Wesleyan University Press, 1983.

Schreig, Samuel. "Inside Report: The Angel of Curaçao." *B'nai B'rith Messenger*, January 25, 1963.

Schweitzer, Albert, and William Larimer Mellon Jr. *Brothers in Spirit: The Correspondence of Albert Schweitzer and William Larimer Mellon, Jr.* Translated by Jeannette Q. Byers. Syracuse, NY: Syracuse University Press, 1996.

Sendler, Irene. "How I Rescued Children from the Warsaw Ghetto." *Stowarzyszenie "Dzieci Holocaustu" W Polsce* [Association of Children of the Holocaust in Poland]. https://dzieciholocaustu.org.pl/szab3.php?s=en_send lerowa.php.

———. "O pomocy Żydom." In *Ten jest z Ojczyzny mojej: Polacy z Pomoca Zydom 1939–1942*, 2nd ed. Edited by Wladyslaw Bartoszewski and Zofia Lewinówna. Kraków: Znak, 1969. Online version at http://www.lewicowo .pl/o-pomocy-zydom/.

———. "Those Who Helped the Jews." In *Biuletyn Żydowskiego Instytutu Historycznego*, 45–46. Warsaw: Żydowski Instytut Historyczny, 1963.

———. "The Valor of the Young." *Dimensions* 7, no. 2 (1993).

———. "Youth Associations of Warsaw Ghetto." In *Biuletyn Żydowskiego Instytutu Historycznego*, 235–47. Warsaw: Żydowski Instytut Historyczny, 1981.

Senesh, Hannah. *Hannah Senesh: Her Life and Diary*. Woodstock, VT: Jewish Lights, 2007.

Shelley, Gerard. *The Speckled Domes. Episodes of an Englishman's Life in Russia*. New York: Charles Scribner's Sons, 1925.

Smith, Dinitia. "How Curious George Escaped the Nazis." *New York Times*, September 13, 2005.

Smulevich, Adam. "Sono vivo perché Bartali ci nascose in cantina." *Pagine ebraiche*, January 1, 2011.

Sousa Mendes, Aristides de. *Le Portugal: Pays de Rêve et de Poésie*. Antwerp: Association Belgo-Ibero-Américane, 1932.

Sousa Mendes, Luís Filipe de. "Memories of Louís Filipe de Sousa Mendes," 1987. Private Collection of Gérald Mendes.

Sousa Mendes, Pedro Nuno. "Que o meu pai sirva de exemplo." Interview by Marta Vitorino. *Aristidesdesousamendes.com*, January 23, 2005. https:// www.aristidesdesousamendes.com/zpedronuno.htm.

Stein, Sarah Abrevaya. *Family Papers: A Sephardic Journey through the Twentieth Century*. New York: Farrar, Strauss & Giroux, 2019.

Stella, Gian Antonio. "Gino Bartali fu un eroe, lo dicono gli ebrei che ha salvato." *Corriere della Sera*, January 11, 2021.

———. "L'enigma di Gino Bartali salvatore degli ebrei." *Corriere della Sera*, January 8, 2021.

Sugihara, Yukiko. *Visas for Life*. Edited by Lani Silver and Eric Saul.

Translated by Hiroki Sugihara with Anne Hoshiko Akabori. Privately published, 1993.

Szpilman, Wladyslaw. *The Pianist: The Extraordinary True Story of One Man's Survival in Warsaw, 1939–1941.* Translated by Anthea Bell. New York: Picador, 2019.

Thompson, Dorothy. *Refugees: Anarchy or Organization.* New York: Random House, 1938.

Tigay, Chanan. "The Untold Story of the Portuguese Diplomat Who Saved Thousands from the Nazis." *Smithsonian*, November 2021.

Tokayer, Marvin, and Mary Swartz. *Fugu Plan: The Untold Story of the Japanese & the Jews during World War II.* Jerusalem: Gefen, 2016.

Tomes, Jason. *King Zog of Albania: Europe's Self-Made Muslim Monarch.* New York: NYU Press, 2003.

Trocmé, Andre. *Angels and Donkeys: Tales for Christmas and Other Times.* Translated by Nelly Trocmé Hewitt. Intercourse, PA: Good Books, 1998.

Turrini, Leo. *L'uomo che salvó l'Italia pedalando.* Milan: Saggi, 2014.

Unsworth, Richard P. *A Portrait of Pacifists: Le Chambon, the Holocaust, and the Lives of André and Magda Trocmé.* Syracuse, NY: Syracuse University Press, 2012.

Vickers, Hugo. *Alice: Princess Andrew of Greece.* London: Hamish Hamilton, 2000.

Wallis, Russell. *British POWs and the Holocaust: Witnessing the Nazi Atrocities.* London: Bloomsbury Academic, 2017.

Weissman, Susan. *Victor Serge: The Course Is Set on Hope.* New York: Verso, 2001.

Werner, Emmy E. *A Conspiracy of Decency: The Rescue of the Danish Jews during World War II.* Boulder, CO: Westview, 2002.

Wiesel, Elie. *Night.* Translated by Stella Rodway. New York: Bantam, 1982.

Wiesenthal, Simon, Harry J. Cargas, and Betty V. Fetterman. *The Sunflower: On the Possibility and Limits of Forgiveness.* New York: Schocken, 1998.

Wullschlager, Jackie. *Chagall: A Biography.* New York: Knopf Doubleday, 2008.

Yad Vashem. "Cardinal Elia Angelo Della Costa, Archbishop of Florence, Recognized as Righteous Among the Nations." Press Release. November 26, 2012.

Zamponi, Francis, Nelly Bouveret, and Daniel Allary. *Jean Moulin: Mémoires d'un Homme sans Voix*. Paris: Du Chêne, 1998.

Zwartendijk, Jan, Jr. "Jan Zwartendijk—His Activities as Dutch Consul in Lithuania, 1940." Updated November 11, 2008. Privately published.

FILMS AND WEBSITES

Abranches, John Paul. Interview by Eric Saul. Sousa Mendes Foundation. September 10, 1996. https://vimeo.com/199415023.

Bartali, Gino. "Bartali suo pensiero ebrei." Courtesy of Gioia Bartali. Circa July 1994. Video, MP4 file, 1:17.

———. *Coppi e Bartali: gli eterni rivali*. Archival interview. DVD. De Agostini, Cinecitta Luce, 2009.

Bingham, Robert Kim. "Hiram Bingham IV: World War II Holocaust Rescuer." Stonington Free Library, Stonington, CT. June 26, 2017. YouTube video. https://www.youtube.com/watch?v=3AM7M6vvKFM.

———. "Hiram (Harry) Bingham IV, Diplomat Rescuer in France." Simon Wiesenthal Center. June 2, 2011. YouTube video. https://www.youtube.com/watch?v=N6MfzibYZFU.

Chambon Foundation. Los Angeles, CA. https://www.chambon.org/chambon_foundation_en.htm.

The Chiune Sugihara Memorial Hall. Yaotsu-cho, Japan. http://www.sugihara-museum.jp/index_en.html.

Davis, Zachary, and David Howell. "Bushido," November 12, 2020. In *Writ Large*, podcast, 30:46. https://www.writlarge.fm/episodes/bushido.

Dupas, Dr. Rebecca, and Erin Harper. "Bad Conscience." In *12 Years That Shook the World*, podcast, 22.32. https://www.ushmm.org/learn/podcasts-and-audio/12-years-that-shook-the-world/bad-conscience.

Facing History and Ourselves. Website. www.facinghistory.org.

Farrell, Bryan. *City of Refuge*, October 15–December 17, 2019. *Waging Nonviolence*. Podcast, ten episodes. https://wagingnonviolence.org/type/city-of-refuge/.

Felt, Megan. "The Irena Sendler Project | Megan Felt | TEDxOverlandPark." *TED Talks*, August 14, 2017. YouTube video. https://www.youtube.com/watch?v=TRFcrvVRb3o.

"Firenze-Assisi per ricordare Gino Bartali." May 22, 2009. YouTube video. https://www.youtube.com/watch?v=woGBAh38UzQ.

"German Camps—British & Commonwealth Prisoners of War 1939–45." Forces-war-records.co.uk. https://www.forces-war-records.co.uk/european -camps-british-commonwealth-prisoners-of-war-1939-45.

Gluck, Cellin, dir. *Persona Non Grata*. Film. Chiyoda, Japan: BS Nittere, 2015.

Graziani, Francesco. "Fuori dal Giro: quando la guerra non fermò Coppi e Bartali," October 1–2, 2020. Podcast. RAI Radio 1. https://www.raiplay sound.it/programmi/fuoridalgiro.

Grunberg, Slawomir, and Katka Reszke, dirs. *Shimon's Returns*. 2014. Poland: LogTV Ltd.

Guyot, Alain. "Villa Air-Bel 1940." November 28, 2013. YouTube video. https://www.youtube.com/watch?v=XAAlCMbQ_ds.

Hirschbiegel, Oliver, dir. *Downfall (Der Unterdang)*. Munich: Constantin Film, 2004.

"History Undercover. Diplomats for the Damned." *Undercover History*, History Channel, Aired 2000.

Hodge, Russell, and Cynthia Scott-Johnson, dirs. *Rescue in the Philippines: Refuge from the Holocaust*. Film. United States: 3 Roads Communications, 2013.

Holocaust Encyclopedia. United States Holocaust Memorial Museum, Washington, DC. https://encyclopedia.ushmm.org/.

I Am My Brother's Keeper: A Tribute to the Righteous Among the Nations. Yad Vashem, Jerusalem. https://www.yadvashem.org/yv/en/exhibitions /righteous/index.asp.

Jacoby, Oren, dir. *My Italian Secret: The Forgotten Heroes*. Film. New York: Storyville Films, 2014.

King, Michael, dir. *The Rescuers*. Film. La Quinta, CA: Michael King Productions, 2011.

Kirk, Robert, dir. *Sugihara: Conspiracy of Kindness*. DVD. Creative Production Group, 2000. Distributed by WGBH.

Lanzmann, Claude, dir. *The Karski Report*. Film. Strasbourg: ARTE, 2010.

"Life in a Jar: The Irene Sendler Project." The Life in a Jar Foundation. http:// www.irenasendler.org.

Lopes, Richardo, dir. *America's Diplomats*. Film. New York: Foreign Policy Association, 2016.

Mináč, Matej, dir. *Nicky's Family*. Slovakia: Mazl, 2011.

Museo del Ciclismo Gino Bartali. Associazione Amici del Museo Gino Bartali. https://www.ciclomuseo-bartali.it/.

Oren, Etain, dir. *I Want to Remember, He Wants to Forget. The Story of the Adizes Family of Macedonia*. Film. Bingham Films, 2011.

Rescue in a Circus: Righteous Among the Nations Adolf and Maria Althoff. July 11, 2010. YouTube video. https://www.youtube.com/watch?v=wgO8jnNQKwI.

"Rescue in the Holocaust." Institute for the Study of Rescue and Altruism in the Holocaust (ISRAH). www.holocaustrescue.org.

Sanders, Terry, dir. *Never Give Up: The 20th Century Odyssey of Herbert Zipper*. Film. Santa Monica, CA: American Film Foundation, 1995.

Santoni, Joël, dir. *Disobedience: The Sousa Mendes Story* [Original Title: *Désobéir*]. Film. Panama Productions, 2008.

Sauvage, Pierre, dir. *Not Idly By: Peter Bergson, America and the Holocaust*. Film. Santa Monica, CA: Varian Fry Institute, 2012.

———. *Weapons of the Spirit*. Film. France: Chambon Foundation, Pierre Sauvage Productions, 1989.

Segment on Giorgio Goldenberg. *La vita in diretta*. Aired January 27, 2011. RAI Uno, Italy.

Sendler, Irena. "Irena Sendler: The Apple Tree." January 14, 2009. YouTube video. https://www.youtube.com/watch?v=oR0WE3hASC4.

———. "Irena Sendler Tells the Story of Janusz Korczak." *Gariwo Network*, July 23, 2013. https://en.gariwo.net/multimedia/documentaries/irena-sendler-tells-the-story-of-janusz-korczak-9114.html.

———. "Irena Sendlerowa (1): Trudno się nie przejąć, jak do dzieci strzelano," www.wilnoteka.lt." May 16, 2013. YouTube video. https://www.youtube.com/watch?v=g5kAQrqIWkM&t=13s.

Skinner, Mary, dir. *Irena Sendler: In the Name of Their Mothers*. Film. Bronxville, NY: 2B, 2011.

Sousa Mendes, Marie-Rose de. "Marie-Rose de Sousa Mendes. Filha de Aristides recorda memórias que guarda do pai." RTP Noticias, October 19, 2021. Video, 5:31. https://www.rtp.pt/noticias/mundo/marie-rose-de-sousa-mendes-filha-de-aristides-recorda-memorias-que-guarda-do-pai_v1356801.

Spielberg, Steven, dir. *Schindler's List*. Film. Universal City, CA: Universal Pictures. 1993.

Sugihara: Conspiracy of Kindness. Film. United States and Japan: Creative Production Group, DENTSU Music and Entertainment, Digital Ranch, WGBH, Film Transits Intl., 2000.

The Sugihara House. Kaunas, Lithuania. www.sugiharahouse.com.

Sugihara, Nobuki. "An Evening with Nobuki Sugihara in Conversation with Ann Curry." Museum of Jewish Heritage. YouTube video. May 22, 2019. https://www.youtube.com/watch?v=z6Iwf-i80LU.

Varian Fry Institute. Los Angeles, CA. http://varianfry.org.

White Rose Foundation. Weiße Rose Stiftung e.V. https://www.weisse-rose -stiftung.de/white-rose-foundation/.

"White Rose History: January 1933–October 1943." https://whiterosehistory .com/.

The White Rose Project. http://whiteroseproject.seh.ox.ac.uk/index.php/the -white-rose/.

Yad Vashem. "Names of Righteous by Country." yadvashem.org. https://www .yadvashem.org/righteous/statistics.html.

Index

About the Author

RICHARD HUROWITZ is a writer and the founder and publisher of the *Octavian Report*. His writing has appeared in the *New York Times*, *Financial Times*, *Wall Street Journal*, *Times* (UK), *Los Angeles Times*, *Time*, *History Today*, and *Jerusalem Post*, among other publications. He is a graduate of Yale University, where he received his bachelor's degree in history, and of Columbia Law School. He lives in New York City with his family.